Praise for

The Timbuktu School for Nomads

'A passionate paean to the Sahara.'
New York Times, Season's Best Travel Books

'The risk-taking Mr Jubber enters the desert-scape of North Africa. An education.'
Scotland on Sunday, Travel Books of the Year

'Insightful, warm and humorous.'
Publishers Weekly, starred review

'Sedentary civilization has been telling itself that nomads are an anachronism for many centuries. But nomadic cultures are still vibrantly alive, as the intrepid Nick Jubber shows us in North Africa. This book is both a wonderful travel adventure, and a defense of journeys without end.'
Richard Grant, author of Ghost Riders:
Travels with American Nomads

'An abundantly energetic gold-mine of a book. Heaped with history and background information, with ideas, adventures, and poignant postulations, it stares right in the face of current events. This is a book that will remind us all to look with care at what is happening on the great sandscape of North Africa now. A work of inspiration and scholarship, it deserves all the attention it gets.'
Tahir Shah, author of *The Caliph's House*

'A well-informed and readable book based on time spent in nomad camps and a thorough survey of the literature. The Sahara and Sahel are complex, dangerous, productive, compelling pla... ...mads captures the feel o... ...ads about their livelih... ...ught or an al Qaed...

...Sahara

'*The Timbuktu School for Nomads* takes us on an unforgettable journey through time and space, plenty of it, and gives voice to voiceless communities that inhabit one of the most problematic corners of the globe.'

Amir Taheri, author of *Holy Terror*

The Timbuktu
School for Nomads

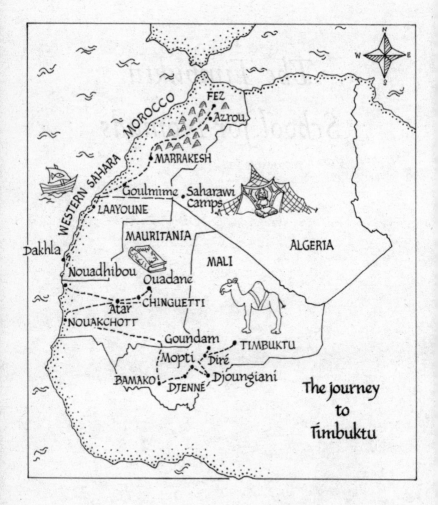

The journey to Timbuktu

The Timbuktu
School for Nomads

Nicholas Jubber

NICHOLAS BREALEY
PUBLISHING

London • Boston

First published in 2016 by
Nicholas Brealey Publishing
An imprint of John Murray Press

An Hachette company

The paperback edition published in 2017

1

British Library Cataloguing-in-Publication Data
A catalogue record for this book is available from the British Library.

ISBN 978-1-47365-544-7
eBook (UK) ISBN 978-1-85788-924-6
eBook (US) ISBN 978-1-47364-528-8

Map drawn by Sandra Oakin.
Printed and bound by Clays Ltd, St Ives plc

John Murray Press policy is to use papers that are natural, renewable and
recyclable products and made from wood grown in sustainable forests.
The logging and manufacturing processes are expected to conform to
the environmental regulations of the country of origin.

Nicholas Brealey Publishing
John Murray Press
Carmelite House
50 Victoria Embankment
London EC4Y 0DZ
Tel: 020 3122 6000

Nicholas Brealey Publishing
Hachette Book Group
Market Place Center
53 State St
Boston, MA 02109, USA
Tel: (617) 523 3801

www.nicholasbrealey.com
www.nickjubber.com

Contents

For Poppy

Africa, which country I have in all places travelled quite over: wherein whatsoever I saw worthy the observation, I presently committed to writing; and those which I saw not, I proved to be at large declared unto me by most credible and substantial persons, which were themselves eye-witnesses of the same.

Leo Africanus, *The Description of Africa and the Things Therein Contained*

Before the coming of the red sun,
we played upon the anthills,
like a breaking storm over the calm,
becoming death rattles in our turn,
a rainbow of arms and chanting
and thronging roads,
smashing the barriers, garrisons, and borders,
buried in vertigo's saddlebags
and in nausea's bile,
nostalgic,
voices of delirious trek.

Hawad (Tuareg poet), *Le coude grinçant de l'anarchie* ('Anarchy's Delirious Trek')

Prologue

THE CITIES WERE SCORCHING, SO THE DESERT WAS THE PLACE TO COOL OFF.

Banners were shaking on the grand public squares. People who had been gagged for decades were shouting themselves hoarse. The whole of North Africa was palsied with protest. But it was an urban phenomenon, lit by flashbulbs and LED, marshalled by social media. The people in the countryside were out of the frame.

I was looking south. I wanted to scale the mountains and ride the dunes, float along the rivers, camp under doum palms. I wanted adventure. I wanted to cross the desert, browse between the great bookends of Fez and Timbuktu. I wanted, specifically, to follow the journey of Leo Africanus, a sixteenth-century explorer who travelled with his uncle to the Kingdom of the Songhay in circa 1510.

Actually, it wasn't so much 'crossing the desert' that spurred me. It was the prospect of travelling *in* the desert. I wasn't hung up on mapping some unknown route or breaking a record – I just wanted to meet the people who lived there. I had been dreaming of something along these lines, I suppose, since I was 6 years old. That's when I saw the Sahara for the first time – like so many of my generation – although it was framed in teak and transmitted by cathode ray tube and I was safe on the saddle of my father's knees.

Ever since that first viewing of *Star Wars*, when the dunes of Tatooine floated thrillingly in my family's living room, I always associated the desert with the alien and faraway – the ultimate adventure. Reading under my duvet at night, I turned to the stories of Ali Baba and Sindbad, rather than the Kon-Tiki Expedition or Kipling's jungle tales. Rainforests and arctic poles never had the same impact. It was always the desert – the landscape of *Mad Max* and *Dune* as much as of TE Lawrence and Wilfred Thesiger – that offered the gateway to a world completely different from my own.

Science fiction had lit my early interest in the desert, but it was Leo Africanus's mealy book that lured me on this particular journey. First published in Venice as *Della descrittione dell'Africa et delle cose notabili che iui sono* ('The Description of Africa and the Notable Things Therein

Contained'), it has few peers among the travelogues of its age. Fizzing with observations on trade and traditions, history and hearsay, plenty of sixteenth-century prejudice, and the occasional racy anecdote,[1] it conjures up an Africa at once elusive and eerily familiar.

At first, I thought it was Leo himself I was following. But during the course of my journey, I realised I was responding less to the parallels with his journey than to the people he describes – and their descendants. Travelling often stokes its own goals: the more I dug into North Africa, the more I was drawn to the nomadic communities I met along the way. I would make their world the climax of my trip, I decided. I would join a camel caravan in Timbuktu, a company of nomads heading to the salt mines of Northern Mali. It would be a sumptuous end to my adventure.

Down in the dunes of South Morocco, I camped with a Berber cameleer called Salim under the jagged crest of the Black Mountain. I rode a camel that seemed to be practising the Harlem Shake, fell off twice and, after eating the salted goat that Salim hung off his saddle (a sort of desert jerky), I supplied a feast for the local insect population. One of my abiding memories of that experience was stumbling out of the tent to be sick, sliding past the hardened pizza of my earlier vomit, gazing in horror at the hundreds of pinprick eyes glowing in my torch beam. My desert learning curve would have to be as steep as the dune that sent me on my first tumble.

'Desert'. Our English word tells us so little. It derives from the Latin verb *deserere*, 'to forsake'. Arabic is much richer, as you would expect from a language born in the desert (quite literally: the root of 'Arab' is an ancient Semitic word for an arid tract). Just as Inuit languages cater for different grades of snow, so the textures of the desert are expressed in Arabic, from *baadiya* or the wild steppes, to the *tih* or trackless waste, to the *sahel* or 'shore', the semi-arid belt that runs under the belly of the Sahara. But it is 'Sahara' that receives the widest usage: *as-Sahra*, with its allusions to colour, specifically the mixing of yellow and red.

---

1 He tells, for example, of a Sufi sect 'addicted to feasting and lascivious song', who stripped off their garments in the heat of their dancing and 'lasciviously kissed' each other; and of lesbian fortune tellers who 'burn in lust' towards their customers, 'and will in the devil's behalf demand for a reward, that they may lie with them'.

Long before I rolled out of Morocco, the cities of North Africa were whipping up a storm. Strong Man politics was being chopped down for lumber, fuelling the flames of white-hot sectarianism. Egypt was undergoing the labour pains of revolution; Libya was being strangled in civil war. A few weeks earlier, Libyan rebels had dragged Colonel Gaddafi out of a drainage pipe to his death. His weapons hoard spilled into various hands, among whom were Tuareg fighters who had front-lined his 'Army of Islam'.

I was roaming in the same direction as the militants – and blissfully unaware of it. I travelled by bus, boat and occasionally donkey cart, carrying a backpack that weighed little more than my boots. The militants rode in Hilux jeeps loaded with rocket launchers, mortars and machine guns. By the time I reached Timbuktu the desert storm was already brewing, although I could see no more than a misty horizon.

Theoretically my timing could have been worse, but it didn't feel like it. A week before the salt caravan was due to set off, armed jihadists drove into Timbuktu while the town was at Friday prayers. Four tourists were seized in their hotel, and one of them was shot dead for trying to resist. Travelling in the desert was now inconceivable – if only for the fact there were no guides willing to take me. So I returned home, my plans foiled.

A month later, the desert of Northern Mali replaced Eastern Libya as the most violent place in Africa. One military post after another was knocked out. Whole swathes of the Sahara were seized. In the Malian capital Bamako, frustration boiled over; people were growing restless at the army's inability to stamp down the rebellion. In March 2012, a coup spun out of a military barracks and President Amadou Toumani Touré was ousted. Like a stray goat too close to drag itself clear, Mali was sucked into the quicksand. The militants exploited the chaos in the capital and pushed their advantage, declaring the independence of 'Azawad', the Northern Malian desert. Well-trained jihadists joined and later overwhelmed them, armed with lavish funds gleaned from Al-Qaeda in the Maghreb,[2] shady donors in the Middle East and naive

---

2 Although it shares its branding with the 'mother' organisation, AQIM has a complex par-
   entage, having grown out of the Algerian Salafist Group for Preaching and Combat, which
   emerged in the Algerian Civil War of the early 1990s. In 2006, its name was changed to
   align with international jihadist currents, linking its goal of an African caliphate with similar aspirations in the Middle East.

European governments dishing out ransom payments. Mali, for so long the most affable country on the Saharan belt, had disintegrated into a no-go zone as inhospitable as Syria or Iraq.

For a year, the black flag of the jihadists sagged in the breezeless air of Timbuktu. The people sagged as well, under prohibitions against music, visible female hair and fraternising between men and women. Those who could manage it voted with their feet; over the course of the occupation, the bulk of the population left. But in February 2013, there was another twist in the tale. The French army launched Operation Serval, swooping into the Sahara at the head of a pan-African alliance. The jihadists were driven out of Timbuktu and other strongholds; as the initial celebrations died down, the French army was sucked into the murky bog of long-term conflict – the phenomenon known to war reporters as 'mission creep'. Mali remained a teeth-jangling destination, but for the first time since my previous visit, it was possible to conceive of a return.

While the conflict had smothered the salt caravans for the time being, there were other reasons to travel back. I had already visited several nomadic communities in North Africa. I wanted to revisit them and meet some of the others, to fit the different pieces of the jigsaw together and form a picture of nomadic life in the twenty-first century. I wanted to learn from the nomads; to develop my raggedy skills at water drawing, camel riding and camp building; to deepen some of the lessons from my earlier trip.

It was time to go to school.

Imagine... you could still meet the Hun, ranging their horses between the Rhine and the Danube. Or if the felt tents of Scythians continued to pimple the shores of the Black Sea. Or if Goths still wrapped themselves in sheepskins on the Baltic Coast. In North Africa, there are Berbers, Fulani and Tuareg (and other equally ancient communities) who carry on traditions and ways of life that stretch back millennia. I am not suggesting we should celebrate them simply for their hoariness, but surely any lifestyle that has endured for so long has something to teach us. 'Pastoral peoples of Africa, who have lived in the closest relations to their lands for millennia,' write ecologists Aggrey Ayuen

Majok and Calvin W Schwabe, 'must be given some benefit of the doubt and it must be considered seriously that they know a lot about what they are doing and are not hell-bent on their own destruction.'

The more I learned about North Africa, the more its nomads resonated with me, herding a greater range of livestock, across a greater range of landscapes, than anywhere else I had travelled. Nomadic heritage permeates our modern, sedentary cultures. But in the last few centuries, itinerant lifestyles have been hacked down in Europe, felled by a mighty army of antagonists (led by enclosures, industrialisation and privatisation). Apart from a few rare pockets, the practice survives primarily in the vocabulary we have inherited from our pastoralist ancestors – words like 'capital' (which shares a root with cattle and a linked meaning of portable property), 'fee' (derived from the Old English *feoh*, 'livestock') and 'aggregate' (which evokes the Latin root *gregare*, 'to herd'). Nomadism may no longer play a significant role in our economies, but it has certainly left a legacy.

In Africa, very different circumstances are at play, enabling an archipelago of nomadic islands to survive in the sea of urbanisation. The contributing factors are many and complicated, key among them the prevalence of tribal systems, the comparatively slow rate of industrialisation and geographical practicalities. From the sixteenth century onwards, as the Sahara region succumbed to 'progressive dessication', the reins of power increasingly fell to the people best equipped to navigate the desert. Nomads lorded over their sedentary neighbours, establishing slave castes and systems of tribute that are still being untangled. Far from being in retreat, for large periods of the last millennium nomadism was flourishing. For many of North Africa's nomadic groups, it is only recent times that have found them on the back foot.

You can hack a trail through North African history by focusing solely on its itinerant tribes. The classical era gives us the cattle-breeding Gaetulians, who raided their Roman vassals and refused to pay them tribute; along with the shadowy Mauri, ancestors of the Moors, who traded with Carthage and supplied many of Rome's most distinguished cavaliers. The medieval period is dominated by the arrival of the Bani Hillal ('Sons of the Crescent Moon'), an Arabian tribe who led their flocks into Egypt and spurred them on to Morocco, looting, burning and deforesting the eleventh-century Maghrib. According to the great Maghrebi historian Ibn Khaldun they 'attached themselves to the country, and the flat territory was completely ruined'. For many medieval observers they typified all that was wrong with nomads. Yet they also sealed Arabic as the region's lingua franca and Islam as its faith, smashing their sedentary opponents in a wave of victories that are still narrated by bards across the region.

The most dynamic medieval dynasties sprang from nomadic stock, such as the drum-beating Almoravids, scourge of El Cid and the Spanish Reconquista; or the Merinids, who ruled late medieval Morocco. When Sultan Abdelhafid signed off Morocco's independence to the French in 1912, it was Berber tribesmen from the Middle Atlas who protested most actively against foreign rule, although it was the urban elites who reaped the benefits of independence. More recently, the drive for Tuareg separatism hovers over Saharan politics like a planing sparrowhawk, while traditionally nomadic Saharawis continue to campaign for independence against Morocco in Africa's last colony. Contrary to the assumptions of many armchair anthropologists, the story of Africa's nomads is far from over.

'Nomad' derives from the Greek *nomas*, 'roaming', and its cognate *nomos*, 'pasture' or 'grazing'. For this reason, anthropologists (who often have to work within stricter parameters than travel writers) tend to define nomads as pastoralists, moving about with their herds in search of grazing. But the Arabic word has a broader, more interesting derivation. *Bedawi* (anglicised as 'Bedouin') comes from the noun *badw*, which means both 'desert' and 'beginning'. For desert-dwelling Arabians, living in a landscape unsuited to hunter-gathering, pastoral nomadism was the original, and the only viable, lifestyle. It is scorned by urban Arabs for this very reason – why do something so old-fashioned when you can pile up the moolah in the oil trade? – and at the same time revered.

This ambiguous attitude, this switch between scorn and awe, is the double-edged sword on which the nomadic reputation has been impaled for most of recorded history. Whether or not Cain killed Abel, it is pretty likely some farmer knocked some herder over the head at some very early point (I would hear of many such incidents among the Fulani of Central Mali) and it has been hammer and tongs ever since.

Nobody captures this cognitive dissonance better than the historian Ibn Khaldun. 'It is their nature to plunder whatever other people possess,' he wrote in the fourteenth century. 'Their sustenance lies wherever the shadow of their lance falls.' *But, but, but...* in another passage, this nimble thinker expresses the never-ending schizophrenia: 'Bedawi [nomads] are closer to the first natural state and more remote from the evil habits that have been impressed upon the souls [of sedentary people].'

Centuries later, the same inconsistency prevails. Nomads are accused of denuding hills, deforesting woods and desertifying plains (the 'Tragedy of the Commons', cited by William Forster Lloyd in the nineteenth century and popularised in the 1960s by the ecologist Garrett Hardin[3]) and failing to pay taxes – but are co-opted by politicians eager to show their environmental consciousness or cultural sensitivity. Just how useful they are for political gain was underlined by Colonel Gaddafi, who spent four decades parading himself in a tent, trading on nomadic stereotypes.

Is nomadism really the 'death in life' that TE Lawrence called it? It still has millions of practitioners in North Africa, and in Mali it accounts for an estimated tenth of the population. Not every nomad wants to call it a day; at least, not today. Travelling among various nomadic communities, I hoped to understand why so many still toil at such a challenging lifestyle: how they relate to their complicated past, what obstacles preoccupy their present, what future they envisage. Not just how they lived in Leo Africanus's time, but how they live now.

So I set off for North Africa once again, to continue my education in another world. It was a training that had begun at the back end of the Sahara, in a town so notoriously off the beaten track that its own inhabitants hail you with the greeting: 'Welcome to the middle of nowhere.'

---

3 This concept has been used to impose restrictions on grazing rights and even to justify forced settlements, despite the safeguards historically deployed by nomadic communities. Ecologist Katherine Homewood observes: 'the Tragedy of the Commons has underpinned powerful national and international policy pressure to privatise rangelands, with drastic implications... This drive for privatisation has interacted with twentieth-century colonial and post-independence trajectories of boundary formation, which have themselves left most pastoral populations marginalised on the geographical and political periphery of African nation states, fragmented between adjacent and often hostile nations, under intense pressure to sedentarise and often drawn into violent and destructive geopolitical confrontations.'

Part One

The Middle of Nowhere

Wide Afric, doth thy sun
Lighten, thy hills enfold a city as fair
As those which starred the night o' the elder world?
Or is the rumour of thy Timbuctoo
A dream as frail as those of ancient time?

Alfred Lord Tennyson, *Timbuctoo*

I

City of Gold

Howbeit there is a most stately temple to be seen, the walls whereof are made of stone and lime; and a princely palace also built by a most excellent workman of Granada.[4] The rich king of Tombuto hath many plates and scepters of gold, some whereof weigh 1300 pounds, and he keeps a magnificent and well-furnished court.

THAT WAS THE ASSESSMENT OF LEO AFRICANUS, ARRIVING IN TIMBUKTU circa 1510 after a 1200-mile journey across the Sahara. I arrived by boat five centuries later, and here is what I scribbled in my diary:

You come out of the desert anticipating a town, and you're already in the middle of it before you realise you're here. The Grand Mosque is the most impressive building and next to the Mosque of Djenné, it looks like a termite mound (plus I couldn't bribe anyone to let me look inside). The streets are so dusty, I'm constantly rubbing the grit out of my eyes, and I'm sweating so much I feel like those slabs of meat the flies are buzzing around outside the butcher shops.

But but but. It's Timbuktu! Tim-buk-bloody-tu! I'm walking in the streets of TIMBUKTU!!!

Anywhere else, it would matter. Any iconic historical city – Fez, Venice, Jerusalem – the name is insufficient. The city has to match its reputation or you feel short-changed. But being a shadow of its former self is no shame for Timbuktu – it only makes the place *all the more* Timbuktu. It is the Miss Havisham of famous metropolises – a fading relic whose character is drawn not from its rose-tinted prime but from the long decline that slumbered in its wake.

---

4   His name was Abu Ishaq as-Sahili (although his friends knew him as 'the Little Casserole') and he was paid the handsome sum of 440 pounds of gold for his trouble.

After several months on the road, *I've made it to Timbuktu at last!* The thought bounced me around town, and my eye was on the lookout for anything to fit my mood: women with giant spatulas spooning wheat bread out of street-corner ovens; a girl in a yellow dress plaiting her sister's cornrows on a bench outside a *dépôt de boissons*; a cavalier on a winged horse, mounted on a concrete arch – the Al-Farook monument – towering over a couple of blue-veiled Tuaregs as if he were eavesdropping on their conversation.

It was my first visit, and I was as high as a rocket. I had dreamed of this day ever since, aged 8, I watched the Disney classic *The Aristocats*. At the end of the movie, the dastardly butler was bundled into a trunk with the mysterious label: 'To Timbuktu'. *Where was this strange-sounding place? Did it even exist?* We hear the name 'Timbuktu' so often, a byword for the back of beyond, a metaphor uprooted from geography, 'a mythical city in a Never-Never land', as Bruce Chatwin put it. Now I was here, discovering that some metaphors can be stepped on and walked around and slept in... and now the travelling could really begin.

When the Sultan of Fez dispatched Leo Africanus's uncle on an embassy to the King of the Songhay, Timbuktu was the lodestar of a great empire. This was no backwater, but a thriving city at the heart of the international gold trade. For Europeans, the New World was still news and its treasures were yet to saturate their markets. West Africa remained Eldorado. It was this region that drove the currencies of Europe, from the Venetian ducat (with its 99.47 per cent fine gold quotient) to the British guinea (named for the West African lands where much of the gold originated). With hard cash, city states could be built, soldiers salaried, merchant voyages commissioned.

Was it 'Dark Continent' gold that burned out the Dark Ages in Europe?[5] For Timbuktu, however, the sun was already setting. It was about to enter its own dark age – an age still awaiting its climax. So it is no wonder that when I visited a local historian, he was weighed down by a chronicle from the seventeenth century.

---

5 As late as the seventeenth century, Samuel Purchas could write that 'the richest Mynes of Gold in the World are in Africa'. Scholarship supports this position: 'until the discovery of America,' writes Nehemiah Levtzion, 'the Sudan was the principal source of gold both for the Muslim world and for Europe.'

Salim Ould Elhadje is an author, retired teacher and civil servant whose two-volume *Tombuctou* is the first history of the town written by an inhabitant in situ. A Chevalier de l'Ordre National du Mali, he has appeared on West African television and spoken at conferences in the USA, and his name was the one I heard most often when I asked who could tell me the tale of Timbuktu's rise and fall.

He was sitting in a parapeted limestone house near the central market. Lemony strings of light peeled through a fretted window like rind through a grater, oozing around his silvery hair, which quivered in the air spun by the ceiling fan. The book on his lap was the *Tarikh as-Sudan* ('History of the Blacks'), written by a notary and imam called Abdarrahman As-Sadi. The creases on its cover were as tight as the laughter lines around Elhadje's eyes. 'Have a look,' he said, thumbing through this comprehensive tome, which swung from brutal massacres to fabulous accounts of Timbuktu's glory days.

'The story of Timbuktu,' said Elhadje, 'begins a thousand years ago with the Tuareg nomads. They were gathering at the river. But they saw there were mosquitoes and insects, the water was bad, there was a smell of fish, everyone was getting sick from the humidity. So they decided to move into the desert to a place without insects, where the water was good. A lady was living there called Bouctou, and she was known as a kind, trustworthy woman. So, when they travelled, people left their luggage with her and when they came back they said, "we're going to the place of Bouctou's well" – "Tin Bouctou" in the language of the Tuareg.'

It was under Mansa Musa, the 'Lion of Mali', that Timbuktu's legend started marching. He was a 24-carat bling king, greased in the fat of the West African gold mines. He trumpeted his wealth when he set off on the *hajj*, the pilgrimage to Mecca, caravanning with 60,000 soldiers, 500 slaves, and 100 camels loaded with gold. Largesse was sprinkled along the way, most notably in Cairo, where Mansa Musa distributed so much gold that he stripped a quarter off its value; and rumours percolated across the Mediterranean, where the first European reference to Timbuktu appeared on a Catalan map in 1375 (as Tenbuch), hieroglyphed by a king with a sceptre and a nugget of gold.[6] Forget

---

6   The description reads: 'This negro lord is called Musa Malli, lord of the negroes of Guinea. So abundant is the gold which is found in his country that he is the richest and most noble

Bill Gates, the Rothschilds or even Croesus: according to a 2012 survey by the financial data website Celebrity Networth, Mansa Musa's inflation-adjusted $400 billion fortune makes him the richest man who ever lived.

But for the common folk there were smaller fish to try. Literally, in the case of the river dwellers who came to Timbuktu to trade with the nomads from the dunes.

'Timbuktu is the city of the pirogue and the camel,' Elhadje explained. 'People from the dunes brought milk and skins and salt. And people came from the river with rice and karité butter, fish and gold. The town became a big gathering place for people looking for knowledge, for trade, for everything.'

Here is the whole Saharan region encapsulated: a swap-shop for nomads and sedentarists, an entrepôt for their goods. Tribesmen wander out of the desert, bringing salt and fattened livestock; they carry back the rice and sugar and tea they need on the long caravan trails. This interdependence has endured for nearly a millennium, and for good reason. In a desiccated region where grass is mostly confined to dreams, only the nomadic life can sustain the vast herds necessary to supply the meat and dairy required by town dwellers. Timbuktu is more than just a metaphor – it is the lynchpin of this relationship. It was the heart of my journey; the port from which I hoped to sail the nomad sea.

When Leo Africanus made it here, the gold trade through the desert had a rival on the coast: Portuguese caravels were starting to prove as lucrative as camel caravans. Still, Timbuktu was in fine fettle. Leo marvelled at the markets, the trade in books, the high-spirited music. Under the Songhay dynasty – and especially Mohammed Askiya, 'the usurper'[7] – Timbuktu was the engine room of a grand regional power. An effective administration had been established, along with a

---

king in all the land.' According to the historian John Hunwick, West African gold at this time accounted for two-thirds of the global supply.

7   His predecessor, Sunni Ali, had been 'a tyrant, a miscreant, an aggressor, a despot, and a butcher,' according to As-Sadi, who 'killed so many human beings that only God most high could count them'. Mohammed was his military commander. Figuring that Sunni Ali's son would carry on the vicious family tradition, Mohammed decided to take matters into his own hands and toppled Sunni Ali in a coup.

standing army, and Songhay rule stretched from the Atlantic coast to Lake Chad. This magnificence was still visible to Leo, but the moral cohesion of the Askiya's empire was already starting to melt. Timbuktu was turning into a cesspit of vice, records As-Sadi, 'such as drinking fermented liquors, sodomy and fornication – indeed, they were so given over to this latter vice that it appeared to be nothing forbidden'. The city was ripe for plucking. And for the Sultan of Morocco, it was high time to seize this gateway to the land of gold.

In 1591, a Moroccan army of 5000 men (including Christian slaves, mercenaries from Eastern Europe and 1000 musketeers from Andalusia) marched across the desert, supplied by more than 10,000 camels and led by a Castilian eunuch called Jawdar. Their blunderbusses and English cannons terrified the Malian cattle, and their technological superiority was so emphatic that the Songhay troops dropped to the ground, lying in the dust with their legs crossed over their shields. 'Jawdar's troops', declared As-Sadi, 'broke the army of the *askiya* in the twinkling of an eye.'

'It was', said Elhadje, 'the biggest catastrophe for our city.' Steepling his hands under his beard, he shook his head, as if the invasion had just taken place: 'Because they took away all the intellectuals. Before this, if you came from Cairo, from Al-Azhar University itself, to teach at our University of Sankoré, you would be turned away. Nowhere else had such a high level. And then, in one black night, all was lost.'

It was an event collapse. Over the next few generations, everything went wrong for Timbuktu. Droughts and famine wiped the land of vegetation and killed off herds, forcing the inhabitants to eat the corpses of animals and even their fellow citizens; the rise of shipping directed merchant traffic towards the coast; and the influx of precious metal from the Americas deflated the value of African gold. At the very moment that Europe was emerging into its brightest epoch – the Renaissance, the Age of Discovery, the Scientific Revolution – the region around Timbuktu disintegrated. Other caravan towns fell away altogether, such as Sijilmasa in southern Morocco; or snoozed even more deeply, like Ouadane and Walata in Mauritania. Yet none became more iconic, more synonymous with occlusion and inaccessibility. Slowly, Timbuktu earned for itself the soubriquet with which it is promoted on tourist posters all along the Niger river: *Timbuktu la Mystérieuse*.

2

Dinner with the Blue Men

THE BLAST WHIPPED THE AIR AND GLUED ME TO THE SPOT. IT WAS UNMISTAKABLY gunshot. I stood rigid beside the fourteenth-century Sankoré mosque, the university extolled by Salim Ould Elhadje: a crumbly mud pyramid spiked with rodier palms, built in the fourteenth century at the behest of a Tuareg benefactress. It looked like a rocket that has landed on a desert planet, gathering dust long after its passengers have run out of air.

'Don't be scared,' said a blue-robed figure, stepping out from under a goatskin awning. 'It's only a party for someone's circumcision.'

His face was mummified. His turban left only a slit for the eyes, like a woman's *niqab*, but those eyes were sparkling with welcome. A dust-smeared hand beckoned and I followed the man to the awning, where he invited me to sit down. Scattered underneath were the tools of his trade – scraper, crucible, sewing awl, a hardwood bellows with a clay nozzle. He patted down the sand and dug a pit of earth to boil his teapot.

His name was Ousmane. He was working on an earring, with circles to denote the wells of a caravan route and silver dots for the stars. Beside him was a knife, the handle scored by chevrons to signify the caravan trail. Cusped edges suggested camel saddles; there were crescent shapes for the moon. A goatskin toggle bag hugged the sand next to him, scarred with enough motifs to satisfy a semiologist. A triple-dotted triangle connoted a fawn; a spoked circle conjured the tracks of a jackal. Code is intrinsic to Tuareg culture, expressed in a fondness for word play, riddles and secret languages, and this cryptic atmosphere extends to the people's clothing. Ousmane's *tamelgoust* (the Tuareg veil) had to be worn over the nose in front of his elders, but when he was hanging out with friends he let it drop.

'Maybe you only see a veil,' he said, 'but there are more than a hundred ways to wear it.'

Tugging a couple of glasses out of the toggle bag, he shook a few pellets of gunpowder tea into the pot, initiating the elasticated process of Tuareg refreshment.

When it comes to making tea, the Tuareg have no rivals. There are so many pourings out and pourings back, so much fiddling about, so many longueurs of tantalising inaction, that you start to wonder if you're witnessing some obscure exercise in alchemy. I tried to count how many times Ousmane reintroduced the water to the pot, but after the fifth outpouring, all my concentration was focused on restraining myself from snatching the glass in thirst. Ousmane – thin, expressionless, delicate as a figure in a miniature painting – raised his arm for a frothy cascade and finally presented me with a thimble of delicious, amber-coloured tea.

'Welcome', he said, 'to the middle of nowhere.'

Leo Africanus describes 'a dry and barren tract ... [which] extends to the south as far as the land of the blacks; that is to say, to the kingdom of Gualata and Tombutto.' Here, in the 'desert of Arouane', his party encountered the camel-riding chief of 'the Zanaga tribe', who demanded substantial custom from the travellers, but also invited them to stay in his camp. Camels were slaughtered, ostrich meat roasted, mutton cooked. 'And thus we remained with him for the space of two days,' reports Leo, 'all which time, what wonderful and magnificent cheer he had made us, would seem incredible to report.' The cost to the chief he estimated at ten times the value of the custom they paid.

Leo's account represents a vivid, early encounter with the Tuareg, the 'Zanaga' or Sanhaja Berbers, who he terms elsewhere the 'people of ... Terga' and tells us 'they live after all one manner, that is to say, without all law and civility'. Of all the nomadic groups I would meet on my travels, none is more iconic.[8] More independent, more restive,

---

8   A few words on the origin of 'Tuareg'. Etymologists trace it to the Fezzan region of Libya, but it is traditionally believed to derive from the Arabic root 't-r-q', meaning 'abandoned (by God)', a reference to the people's late adoption of Islam. The French writer Jacques Hureiki traces it to the word 'taqaqa', meaning to knock, referring to genies who knock on doors and tents at night: 'the true meaning of Touareg', he writes, 'is that of genies, recognised by the imouchar and by Touaregs in general, because that is appropriate to their culture.' The broader endonym used by Tuareg across the Sahara is *imuhaghan* or *imashaghan*, which is conventionally translated as 'the free people', although according to anthropologist Jeremy Keenan it may derive from the verb 'to raid' or 'to plunder'. Malian

more mysterious, they are the über-nomads. They loom over the history of Northern Mali like aliens in a pulp sci-fi tale: descending on the natives in a storm of pillage and blood, plugging the bloody gaps between periods of settled rule. Leo's account of Tuareg hospitality is rare: they are remembered mostly for what As-Sadi calls their 'many acts of gross injustice and tyranny'. Describing events in fourteenth-century Timbuktu, he tells us the citizens appealed to Mansa Musa to take over their town: 'They began to roam about the city, committing acts of depravity, dragging people from their homes by force, and violating their women.' In the fifteenth century, Tuareg raids drove the townsfolk to invite the first Songhay ruler, Sunni Ali, to invade. When the grip of the Moroccans weakened, the Tuareg took control again. And when central rule was collapsing in the nineteenth century, they were once more in the ascendancy. Observing their 'most cruel depredations and exactions' in 1828, the French explorer René Caillié noted: 'The people exposed to their attacks stand in such awe of them, that the appearance of three or four Tooariks is sufficient to strike terror into five or six villages.'

Later that century, when the French army was spreading the net of *Soudan Français*, none resisted more defiantly than the Tuareg. In 1894, Tuareg tribesmen charged a French camp, killing the French military chief, 12 officers and 68 African troops – the worst French reverse in the whole of their Saharan campaign. Punitive expeditions were launched, unarmed Tuareg were massacred, crops raised by Tuareg slaves were destroyed, thousands of livestock were confiscated and the severed heads of Tuareg combatants were displayed in village marketplaces.

Summing up the mood in the French camp, colonial officer Louis Frèrejean wrote in his journal of 'one of those sinister pirates of the desert', who was tied up and left to burn in the sun, despite his protestations of innocence: 'Before the column set out, a soldier received the order to kill the captured Tuareg with a rifle shot; and in the abandoned camp, his dead body remained stretched out near the stake to which he was still attached.' As far as the colonial officers were concerned,

---

Tuaregs generally call themselves *Kel Tamasheq* – the people of Tamasheq, referring to their language.

it was war. 'Considering that we will never succeed in making friends with these tribes because of their religious and racial hatred towards us,' wrote the Governor of the French Soudan in September 1898, 'and because we have deprived them of their only resource, namely plunder and theft, we have to eliminate them if we can.' Yet many of the intellectuals who accompanied the *colons* were more ambivalent.

'They are barbarians,' wrote the anthropologist Émile Masqueray in 1890, 'but barbarians from our race with all the instincts, all the passions, and all the intelligence of our ancestors. Their nomadic customs are those of the Gauls who took Rome.' To some of the more romantically minded French officers, the Tuareg were the 'knights of the desert', as Lieutenant de Vaisseau Hourst wrote in 1898: 'When I imagine their wandering life, free of any hindrance, their world in which courage is the first among virtues, in which the people are nearly equal, I ask myself if they are not happier than us.'

In the rosy sheen of evening, Ousmane took me to the edge of town to meet his family. Behind the neighbourhood midden and the concrete pile of the Libya Hotel (built by the largesse of the recently deceased Colonel Gaddafi), a ragged canvas tent was pitched on the far side of a dune. Ousmane's father and a couple of brothers were sitting in the lee of the tent, gorgeted in blue. Slumped across a frayed rug, on a plateau of buff-coloured sand speckled with goat droppings, they were sipping glasses of tea and smoking through a pipe made from antelope horn.

Talking to traditionally veiled Tuareg can be a forensic activity. You're trying to gauge everything from the tiniest clues: inflections in their voices, the slightest blink or dilation of an eye. I spent a couple of afternoons with Ousmane's family and was invited to join them for a meal. On this occasion, his brother Haka lowered his veil and ate with us, outside the tent, while his father and several other veiled relatives moved inside. We sat over a metal tray, cross-legged, with our elbows on our knees, rolling the buttery rice into gummy balls in our palms. The menu may not have been as lavish as the one enjoyed by Leo Africanus in the desert, but at least there was no toll, and I was able to enjoy the meal all the more, knowing I was as free as my hosts.

I was thrilled to be dining with the 'blue men'. As *enadan* (artisans or smiths), Ousmane and his family are members of a hereditary caste that is credited with access to the spirit world and called on to recite epic poems during feasts and celebrations. Scorned by the noble caste (the *imajeren*), still they have a huge breadth of utility in Tuareg culture, acting as cattle branders, dentists, matchmakers and apothecaries, among numerous other functions.

The caste system is one of many features of Tuareg culture that has bewildered visitors, along with the vestigial traditions of raiding, slavery and the *adanay* ritual (by which girls had to drink huge quantities of milk to fatten them up for marriage). What fascinates many Western observers is the tension between the far-out and the familiar. Alongside these more exotic elements are parallels with our own culture, such as the crosses that recur in Tuareg decorative imagery and the relative freedom of their unveiled women (although the traditions of matrilinealism are as alien to European observers as to Arab Muslims). Seeking Tuareg origins in the ambiguous surfaces of their culture, scholars have traced them to the Iberian Peninsula, Crusader armies, 'cultures babylonienne, chrétienne, mandéenne, biblique, arabe pré-islamique, perse, grecque et égyptienne' (to cite Jaques Hureiki's exhaustive list), without pegging any theory down with sufficient proof. The Tuareg became a tabula rasa onto which the most romantic theories could be projected; a nexus of the imagination, linking 'civilised' Europe to the 'savages' of Africa.

There is, however, one point on which Tuareg at large are in agreement with their Western observers. As a captured rebel declared in 1963, they are 'nomads of the white race, [who] can neither conceive nor accept to be commanded by blacks whom we always had as servants and slaves'. Behind the *enadan*'s veils, I noticed flatter noses and darker complexions than among other Tuareg, suggesting closer links to their black neighbours than they wish to admit. But the feeling of separateness was keenly felt, and Ousmane's relatives expressed it that evening as we worked through the platter of rice.

'My father is telling Haka he must eat more.'

Ousmane had been talking for a while in Tamasheq with his brother. Now he turned to me.

'Oh, has he been ill?' I asked.

'No, but he was in jail so he is not accustomed to big meals.'

Haka picked up a few grains of sand and held them, pinched between thumb and forefinger. Spinning his head underneath them, he rolled his eyes in mock wonder, before drawing the grains towards his mouth as if he were about to taste some exquisite delicacy. He reminded me of Charlie Chaplin's improvident tramp, making noodles out of boot laces in *The Gold Rush*.

'When they gave us something to eat, those were the lucky days,' explained Haka, through Ousmane's translation. 'And even if they gave you bread you had to eat it straightaway, or someone would take it from you. A Tamasheq in the Malian jail is a rat in the nest of a snake.'

It was hard to establish what crime he had committed. Haka insisted he had been stitched up by his employer, a Koro-Boro (a member of the town's majority Songhay ethnicity), who had taken on a construction job without the correct licences.

'The government thinks Tamasheq people don't need to eat.' Haka dipped his fist and patted the rice into a ball. 'Maybe they are confused by the *tamelgoust*. They think we only need the sand. We can eat the grains and we can sleep on the dunes.'

A born satirist, Haka bristled with dark humour. When the uprisings began a few months later, I kept thinking of him rubbing the sand between his fingers in angry pantomime, and wondered if he had taken up arms.

As the historical accounts testify, the Tuareg were never on easy terms with their settled neighbours, so joining them together was always going to be a challenge. 'Know that the Tuareg race was entirely self-reliant and self-governing until the coming of the French,' wrote a Tuareg chief to Charles de Gaulle in 1959, '... it should not disperse them between different peoples with whom the Tuareg people [do not share the same] race, religion, or language.' Speaking in 1962, just two years after Mali's independence, the governor of the Niger Bend region communicated this awkward union, declaring that 'nomad society, as it is left to us by the colonial regime, undoubtedly poses us problems in light of the objectives of our socio-political program'. Marginalising pastoralists, the new regime pursued a policy of aggressive agricultural development, asserting ownership of all Malian land, leasing out pasture and planting rice paddies in place of nutrient-rich *bourgou* (*echinochloa stagnina*, or 'hippo-grass') that had sustained flocks along the Niger river for centuries. It was only a matter of time before the first insurrection would flare.

That was launched the same year, by a renegade called Alladi Ag Allal, who attacked a pair of camel-mounted policemen near the northern stronghold of Kidal. But Ag Allal and his comrades were armed only with a few Mauser rifles and some curved swords; their campaign was crushed by the Malian army's superior firepower and the ruthless tactics of its commander, Captain Diby Diarra, known as the 'Butcher of Kidal'. Wells were poisoned, cattle slaughtered, women raped and civilians executed without trial. President Modibo Keita might have been a fierce critic of the *colons*, but his regime had certainly been paying attention to them.

Decades would pass before the launch of another full-scale rebellion. By then, the Tuareg had been driven to desperation by a wave of catastrophic droughts and the government's failure to engage with the issues that had been raised: notably the lack of development and the independence of a culture that refuses to be shackled to regulations invented by, and for, its sedentary neighbours. And another factor had emerged, overshadowing the Tuareg movement into the present calamities: Colonel Gaddafi's Libya.

As the only African leader to engage with the Tuareg – however dodgy his motivations – Gaddafi earned the goodwill of a people who were treated by other African leaders as parasites. They provided manpower for his army, and in return he supplied training and munitions (later, he would also offer regular salaries and amnesties for those who found themselves on the Malian government's 'Wanted' list). In 1990, a group of Tuareg soldiers recently returned from Libya attacked a police post at the desert outpost of Menaka. Although their impact was deflated by infighting, they excited enough concern to draw concessions from Bamako, including a pledge for limited self-rule in

Kidal. This 'National Pact' was marked by a spectacular ceremony, known as the 'Flame of Peace', in which 3000 guns were incinerated in the sand north of Timbuktu, a short walk from the house where I was staying.

Yet many of the terms were left unfulfilled, and resentment continued to simmer. During the 1990s anti-Tuareg paramilitary groups were formed with names like Ganda Koy ('Masters of the Land'), who distributed pamphlets exhorting their followers: 'Let us drive the nomads back into the sands of the Azawad.' Inevitably, the pressure cooker exploded once again, with a new uprising in 2006.

Armed with machine guns from Libya (where, under Gaddafi's eccentric tutelage, they mixed with IRA paramilitants, Basque Separatists and Germans from the Baader-Meinhof group), the Tuareg insurrectionists now represented a more substantial challenge. Between periodic ambushes they were able to disappear in the desert, hiding out in the hills around Kidal. The Malian government conceded to peace discussions, in which various rights were stipulated, including recognition of the Tamasheq language, investment in the north and the formation of security units consisting of local Tuareg. But again, there was little evidence of the promised investment.

Mohammed Ag Ossade, director of a Tuareg cultural NGO called Tumast, outlined Tuareg grievances to me when we met beside a ceremonial tent in Bamako.

'What people want', he said, 'is not independence. What they want is an improvement of their life and conditions. A minister will say there is money being invested, then he divides the money with the project director and there is nothing left to put it into effect, and another big villa appears in Bamako, while the rest of the population remains poor.'

So many villas sprouted in one suspicious neighbourhood in Bamako that it was known as Quartier de la Sécheresse, 'Drought Quarter', after the embezzlement on which it had been built. No wonder frustration was growing. That gentle afternoon, it was hovering on the horizon, ready to unleash the next bloody chapter in Timbuktu's history.

3

White Man's Grave

TIMBUKTU IS NOT A BOASTFUL CITY. IT DOESN'T THRUST UP PROUD TOWERS, or bristle behind defensive parapets and bastions. Instead it sprawls, low lying and shy, hunkering down against the sandy bed that eats away its edges. Few cities are so evidently of the desert: in Timbuktu, you can never get away from the sand.

This environmental cohesion expresses itself in the architecture. Tents and huts made from woven reeds are just as common as houses in some quarters, especially those where the recently sedentarised have bivouacked, their possessions stored in saddlebags rather than trunks. Even the grander establishments betray elements of nomadic life. Delicate pargetting and fretwork echo the patterns on Tuareg jewellery and nomadic carpets, while the layout matches the functions of a tent. Occupants loll about in sprawling yards, like they would on their dunes; but high walls and gates protect their privacy, performing the same role as the vast distances of the desert.

Some of the finest architecture of Timbuktu appears in the homes of the explorers. Next to a loitering donkey and a pair of palm-reed tents belonging to Bella (former slaves of the Tuareg), a plaque commemorates Major Alexander Gordon Laing, one of many ill-fated pioneers of the search for Timbuktu. Keyhole shapes draw shadows over benippled grids in the pretty wooden shutters, above a heavily bossed door with a rusty swollen knocker. Now inhabited by a calligrapher, the house is an elegant contrast to Laing's torrid experience.

Travelling in the twilight of the Georgian era (that golden age for daredevil explorers), Laing was determined to 'rescue my name from oblivion' by becoming the first modern European to record his impressions of Timbuktu. The myths had swollen over the centuries,[9] while a

---

9   In 1620, the sailor Richard Jobson told of a city in West Africa, 'the houses whereof are covered only with gold'; and in the early nineteenth century, a Moroccan traveller called Abd Salam Shabeeny informed his listeners in London that 'Timbuctoo is the great emporium for all the country of the blacks, and even for Marocco and Alexandria'.

religious prohibition made the city all the more enticing for cravers of fame, like trying to break into Raqqa in 2016.

On 14 July 1825, Laing married the daughter of the Consul of Tripoli. Two days later, he kissed his wife goodbye and set out in full military uniform for Timbuktu. Robbed at every turn, attacked by bandits, living off desiccated fish moistened in camel's milk, he carried on despite losing his luggage and his money, not to mention all the wounds he received. 'I have five sabre cuts on the crown of my head,' he wrote after one ferocious attack by Tuareg bandits, 'and three on the left temple ... one on my left cheek which fractured the jaw bone and has divided the ear ... one over the right temple ... A musket ball in the hip ... Five sabre cuts on my right arm and hand ... Three cuts on the left arm ... One slight wound on the right leg ... to say nothing of a cut across the fingers of my left hand, now healed up. I am nevertheless, as I have already said, doing well, and hope yet to return to England with much important geographical information.' The sterility of the desert spared him infection and against all the odds he made it to Timbuktu – a bloody wreck strapped to his camel, as immobile as a slab of salt. He was the first known European to cross the Sahara from north to south. Nearly six weeks later, he hurried out of the city, his 'situation in Tinbuctu rendered exceedingly unsafe by the unfriendly disposition of the Foolahs of Massina ... whose Sultan has expressed his hostility towards me in no unequivocal terms'. But it was not the ruling Fulani who brought about Laing's demise; he was betrayed by a sheikh of the Berabish tribe, who, according to one of Laing's local hosts, 'ordered his negroes to seize the traveller in a cowardly manner, and to put him to a cruel death'.

Others, such as Laing's fellow Scot Mungo Park (drowned when his canoe capsized on the Niger river) and Major Daniel Houghton (who disappeared without trace near the village of Simbing), were equally unlucky. Jean Louis Burckhardt, who had been planning a trip for years, fell to dysentery in Cairo before he could launch his expedition. And Joseph Ritchie, dispatched from Tripoli, was a victim of insufficient funds and fever. But one success story (the term is pretty relative in this context) was Robert Adams, an American sailor shipwrecked off the African coast and sold into slavery in 1812. According to his account, Adams was dragged to Timbuktu, bartered to a group of tobacco merchants, hauled back across the Sahara and freed at last by the British Consul in Mogador. When his story made it to print in 1816, it was dismissed by sceptics, and for all its authenticity never caught on.

By the 1820s, Timbuktu had snacked on so many ambitious adventurers it had earned the nickname 'White Man's Grave'. Yet that did not stop René Caillié. This remarkable traveller had dreamed of visiting Timbuktu since childhood. Overcoming his lowly birth and the indifference of French officers in Senegal, he mastered Arabic and passed himself off as an Arab heading home from Christian captivity. Succeeding where so many others had failed, he stole into the forbidden city in 1828, scribbling notes whenever he had a moment to himself. His reward for being the first European to reach Timbuktu and report back on his findings was 10,000 francs from the French Geographical Society. Like Adams's account, Caillié's had its doubters. How, they asked, could such a landmark achievement possibly have fallen to the son of an assistant *boulangier*? That, surely, was a far greater enigma than any of the mysteries enclosed in Timbuktu itself.

The house where Caillié stayed is round the corner from Laing's. Delicately rendered, with pilasters projecting from the walls and a roofline threaded by copings, it looks like a pioneering work in mud-Palladian. Further away, past the Sidi Yahia mosque and the library of the Wangara family, is the house that hosted Heinrich Barth (unusual among Timbuktu explorers of the nineteenth century in that he travelled across the Sahara for primarily scholarly purposes) in 1853.

Wandering between these houses, I was struck by the different geometries of space and time. The travellers may never have met, but Timbuktu brings them together: its first three European visitors of modern times. Strolling down this 'Street of the Explorers', I could see them in my mind's eye – sharp-nosed Caillié, sidling past Laing's house en route to peruse some manuscripts; the groaning major cleaning his wounds on his stoop, or starting one of the hundred letters he tried to write to his wife, straining with his lesser-wounded left hand; Barth pottering by with a thermometer, performing one of his three daily temperature readings. Ghosts of the past, unexorcised from these streets that have changed so little since they visited.

I was staying on the brink of the desert, in a gated villa with solar panels on the roof and delicate star patterns incised on the walls. You could trace the daily movements of shadow by the indentations left by people's backsides, as residents sought the most durable shade. Towering over its neighbourhood, it was like a feudal keep, fringed by a motley band of tents and palm-reed huts. It was owned by a Berabish family – members of an Arabic-speaking tribe that has been pitching its tents in this patch of the Sahara since at least the fifteenth century. Originally Berbers, descended from the indigenous North African population, the Berabish mixed with Arabs, adopting their language and culture. Leo Africanus writes of Arabian tribes in North Africa who 'lead a most miserable and distressed life' and 'use commonly to exchange camels in the land of negros'.

As desiccation and drought made life harder for the townsfolk, it was these desert tribes who flourished. By the time the nineteenth-century explorers were stumbling to Timbuktu, the Berabish had an ambiguous, elastic reputation. They were blamed for the murder of Major Laing, among other fatalities, although one of my host's ancestors had protected Heinrich Barth in the 1850s. But they were well established as kings of commerce, running monopolies on salt and bulk goods that continue to this day. The most successful Saharan tribes were not always the mightiest warriors – they were also the ones who could adapt to market interests, exploiting loopholes, answering public demand. The Berabish, widely considered to be masters of *frud al-haram* (or 'forbidden fraud', the local term for the black market), are the exemplars of this principle.[10]

---

10 These days, Timbuktu's underground economy encompasses everything from flour to motor fuel to class A drugs. Cocaine, in particular, is a massively lucrative business. According to a report by the United Nations Overseas Development Commission, 'its wholesale value on arrival in Europe would exceed the national security budgets of many countries in West Africa'. The most notorious smuggling event to date was the 'Air Cocaine' incident in 2009, when a Boeing 727, believed to be transporting ten tons of South American powder, crashed in the

Lapping the desert, the broad gated house was an ideal meeting point for nomads from the dunes, most of them traders fresh off the caravan trails. I was intrigued by these people: caravaneers and agile border hoppers, some of them smugglers. They rubbed their hands over a brazier in the yard, discussing price differentials between Mali and Algeria, fuel dealers who filled your tank with sand, a government plan to build military posts all the way to the salt mines of Taoudenni (they had mixed feelings on this, because it might restrict the movement of goods) and other matters my Arabic lacked the subtlety to follow. Many a night I sat there, sharing a platter of noodles with them, trying to untangle the chatter.

'*Isma*, listen.'

One night, a trader lit a couple of cigarettes off the brazier and passed one over. 'You have a satellite phone?'

'I'm afraid not.'

'A memory card?'

'I... yes, but I kind of need it!'

He leaned closer, and I felt the strap of his digital watch on my arm. 'Listen, friend. I have Marlboro Red. Best price in Timbuktu. Come on, we can pick them up now.'

∞

'*Toubob*, white man, come and see!'

One morning while I was having my breakfast, there was a rattle at the gate. Standing there was a boy who lived in one of the nearby tents. He may not have been a fully operational merchant, but he had a super bargain for me. Because there, at the base of a dune, a short walk from the house, was a caravan of salt. It was a scene so timeless,

---

desert north of Gao. A dispute arose between the clan that was trafficking the drugs and a rival clan in whose territory the plane had landed. Violence ensued, with hostages taken on both sides. The dispute was resolved by the intercession of a government minister, who demanded a share of the profits in return for his mediation. More recently, drug smuggling across the Sahara has continued to rake in the big bucks, with Islamist groups reportedly profiting from their windfalls, sending drug mules across the desert in Totoya 4x4s, armed with Kalashnikovs and satellite phones, hiding their narcotics in spare tyres and in the gaps between their fuel tanks.

I half expected to turn around and see Jean-Léon Gérôme or Eugène Delacroix bending over an easel.

Light crackled on the slabs – eighty-pounders, as long and wide as tombstones. They hung from the sides of the camels, shackled to their saddles with braided ropes of grass, pronging the air with darts of incandescent light. The animals looked broken, scarred across their bellies and sides, their eyes teased by flies. Their legs buckled and their bellies slammed into the powder. They gave the impression they might never rise again. As for the men, they busied themselves with the grass ropes, untethering their salt slabs and carrying them like cut-glass chandeliers across a tiled floor. The slabs were gathered in pairs, forming trestles across the sand, as if the men had been appointed to erect a banqueting table for the chiefs of the desert.

That night, the house played host to the salt merchants, who gathered in the yard, smoking, pinching snuff from boxes of beaten tin, scooping spaghetti from the communal platter.

'It is too hard,' one of them muttered. 'Thirty-six days, walking all the time. It is too hot and Taoudenni is hell.'

'So why do you do it?' I asked. 'Does it make a lot of money?'

Another salt merchant laughed. 'I would thank God for that!' He picked up a twig and stirred the fire, gazing into the embers. 'Someone who doesn't travel, his head is like a watermelon.'

The men spent six months a year on the *azalai*, the seasonal salt caravan, and the other six resting, when the heat was too strong. They cut the salt themselves (and sometimes bought it from the miners), carrying as much as they and their camels could manage, on 10-hour night-time marches, all the way back to Timbuktu. It sounded magnificent and horrific in equal measure. But how could such an austere system endure? Surely these days it would be a lot easier – and faster – to go by truck?

'By God!' one of them snorted. 'Do you not understand the price of gasoline?'

'There are many trucks these days.'

His companion shook his head, pitying such foolishness. 'We pass them on the journey, and many are broken down or they run out of fuel. But camels can give themselves fuel in the desert, and if they are lame we kill them and thank God for the meat. We think one day no more cars will go to the salt mine because they lose too much money this way. Our way is the better one.'

For centuries, salt has been the 'white gold' of the Sahara. The precious metal came from the forests, the riverlands of Guinea and Ghana; but salt was a true product of the desert. As a result, the carava-neers who traded it became some of the richest nomads in the region. In Leo Africanus's time, a single camel's load of salt fetched as much as 80 ducats (a phenomenal sum when you consider that he bought a sword in Fez for half a ducat). Later, in the nineteenth century, Mungo Park saw slabs of salt for sale for 8000 cowrie shells. Like the cow-ries, salt could be used for currency (hence our word 'salary'), and it proved a more effective instrument of barter, since you could weigh it directly against gold. Historians judge the condition of the slave indus-try according to the amount of salt that was sold in exchange for a slave – a piece no bigger than a slave's foot in more wretched times, a whole bar at others.[11] Not until French colonisers introduced paper money in the 1880s did salt recede as a form of currency, although it never lost this role entirely.

'It is still really important today,' said Dr Habibulleye Hamda, an expert in the salt trade whom I met at Timbuktu's top academic cen-tre, the Ahmed Baba Institute.[12] 'It can be used for medicine, animals, human consumption.'

'But it can't be as big as in the past?' I asked.

'Well, of course it has problems. Young men don't want to go on the *azalai* any more. They find it easier to stay in the town and sell other products. And in the south you have sea salt, which erodes the activity here. But people still prefer the salt from the mines because it is sweet. It's the best salt. Sea salt is bitter, and the camels won't eat it, they prefer the salt from the north.'

---

11 This triangular relationship between salt, slaves and gold is expressed in an old saying, describing Timbuktu as the city of three kinds of gold: 'black gold', 'yellow gold' and 'white gold' (or slaves, gold and salt).

12 Named after a celebrated Timbuktu savant, who flourished in the late sixteenth century. Ahmed Baba wrote hundreds of works, from a biographical dictionary to treatises on slav-ery and tobacco, and spent most of his life in exile as one of the literati taken away in chains after the Moroccan invasion of 1591.

The salt traders were some of the first nomads I met, and these encounters had the feeling of First Contact. I might as well have been on an intergalactic space station, stretching my hand towards the bug-eyed ambassador from Alpha Centauri. But I craved something less corralled, more intimate.

On previous travels in the Middle East, I had experienced tantalising glimpses of nomadic life: Bedouin in scrappy tents among the terraced hills of the West Bank, Iranian Bakhtiaris on the summer trails of the Zagros. Yet I was always looking through a picture frame; my focus was elsewhere. Now I wanted to break through that frame. I wanted to sit around the evening fire with them, walk the trails with them, hold the bowl while they milked their camels.

Nomads are obsolete – or so our century decrees. When books and documentaries pay them attention, it is framed in doom-laden titles, like *The Last Nomad* or *The Last Caravan*. More often they are pushed to the side, a spam narrative that is easily deleted. Pasture trails are dismissed as 'marginal land' ripe for cultivation if only someone would take the effort to develop it; and the people making these observations rarely hang around long enough to witness the people using the trails.

Even travel writers tend to shun such communities these days, as if the nomadic world is being punished for Bruce Chatwin's inability to reconcile it with his own pathological restlessness.[13] The great British tradition of travel writing cut its teeth on adventures with nomads – from Richard Burton and CM Doughty in the nineteenth century to Wilfred Thesiger's peerless explorations of mid-twentieth-century Arabia. But Thesiger's fears came true and the 'abomination' of the motor car shovelled Arabia's nomads to the sidelines. In the late 1970s, Jonathan Raban reflected the tilt in perspective, arguing in *Arabia through the Looking Glass* that Bedouin culture was most dynamically expressed in the adaptation to urban life. For Raban, nomad

---

13   'I have a compulsion to wander and a compulsion to return – a homing instinct like a migrating bird,' wrote Chatwin. He travelled among many nomadic communities and felt great empathy for them. He echoed the words of Ibn Khaldun in writing 'they are closer to being good than settled people because they are closer to the first state'. But his attempt to write the definitive book on nomadism floundered on his inability to reconcile the personal and the anthropological. For all they have in common, travelling and nomadism are driven by very different motivations.

camps (and the desert itself) were sideshows to the energy of the cities. This pattern prevails to this day, when time and again the totems of travel writing ignore the nomads they pass, like social high-fliers looking over the shoulders of the shabbiest, least-connected people at parties.

I don't presume to change this pattern. I was looking for a subject, something other people weren't writing about so much. The nomads of North Africa are such a thing. I wasn't sure in those first days in Timbuktu what was drawing me to them. I was responding to a sensation in my heart and guts, more than my head. But I knew they weren't irrelevant; and I was pretty sure they weren't on their last legs, despite what anthropologist Anja Fischer calls 'the apocalyptic sentiment at the forefront of nomadism discourse in recent decades'. I had already been travelling for months, and at last I knew why. Quite simply, I wanted to learn what it is like to live as a nomad today.

Spurned by the rest of the world they may be, but it is this separation that is the nomads' greatest strength (arguably, it is their greatest weakness too). They are independent and largely self-sustaining. Sure, they have to pop into town occasionally, to pick up a sack of rice or sugar (and latterly, pay-as-you-go mobile phone scratch-cards on the '*nomadis*' roaming tariff). But they are still more independent than people in towns. If anyone is going to survive the eventual Apocalypse, it won't be the all-American action man of Hollywood movies. It will be nomads like the ones I met in North Africa.

❧

'Lamina? Yeah, he's a good man. He's really serious, he knows the desert as well as anyone.'

My friend Mahmoud, a spiky black Tamashek who swung me round town on his motorbike, gave a solid thumbs-up. Lamina was an *azalai* 'pilot', a caravan leader with a 'gift' for orientation in the desert, and he had a gap in his schedule. He couldn't take me on the caravan – I wasn't proven yet – but he agreed to show me the ropes. He would teach me some of the critical skills, such as saddling your camels and riding them, tracking, navigation, pitching camp, drawing water.

I hoped that if I spent long enough with him, I would learn what you need to be a nomad today.

'If you go with Lamina,' said Mahmoud, 'there's one thing you can be sure of. You won't get lost!'

I imagined a stately figure in long robes, throwing up his hands at all my errors, then breathing a sigh of relief when (if!) I managed to get the knack; slowly moulding me from unpromising raw material into something more substantial, someone who could sing, like the Tuareg rock band Tinariwen, 'I know how to go and walk/ Until the setting of the sun/ In the desert, flat and empty, where nothing is given.' When I think back to it, I realise there was something a little fable-like about it all. I thought I was learning for the *azalai*; but the lessons would have a different, wider application.

That evening, my last before my journey with Lamina, I climbed up to the roof and embedded myself between the solar panels. A hazy mass of dust was rising off the dunes, like smoke blown out of the mouth of the earth. In the falling light, the sand was turning a gentle shade of rose. Its kindest, most approachable colour. Somewhere out there was my teacher, and by tomorrow evening I would be alongside him.

I couldn't wait.

The School for Nomads

Lesson One: Baggage

MY TEACHER ARRIVES SHORTLY BEFORE DUSK. LAMINA LOOKS EVERY INCH A man of the desert, short and wiry with a high sagacious brow and hair like tangled thorns. He smells it too, with a natural aroma of dust and camel skin. I offer my hand, but his furtive expression is fixed on the sand. I try to speak to him: '*Ana bi'l haqiqa saeed li'lrihlah ma'ak*, I am by the truth happy for the travelling with you.' He offers no response; he mumbles something to my host, then bolts for the gate, eyes scouring the ground beyond the threshold, like a restless animal too wary to stay put.

So this is the man I am entrusting with my safety, the man who will protect me from the outlaws at large in the Sahara. By the time we leave the house, eye contact has yet to be made. We cross the dune without a single word being exchanged, joined only by the melding of our shadows. I think of Paul Bowles's short story 'A Distant Episode', in which a philologist ventures out to the desert to learn its dialects, only to be stripped of his clothes and his tongue, doubled up in a sack lashed to a camel and carted around the desert, tinkling with tin cans to entertain the local tribespeople.

My disguise, at least, should keep me from drawing too much undue attention. I am wearing black pantaloons, a light blue smock, black gloves, plastic slip-on sandals and four metres of indigo-blue cotton wound three times around my head. Only a strip of skin is exposed (a postbox slit above my nose) and a pair of sunglasses wipes it away. My skin is an instant giveaway – hence the gloves. But close-ups aren't really the point. This disguise is for the desert, a silhouette to ward off second glances. Although the context in which you feel compelled to conceal yourself is a little unsettling, it is at least tempered by the childlike fun of dressing up. It's an echo of travellers from the past, who really did have to disguise themselves for any chance of survival: Richard Burton, playing the part of a Pathan quack to steal into Mecca; TE Lawrence, wearing his friend Ali's headcloth and cloak, 'that I might present a proper silhouette in the dark upon the camel'. I am hoping my disguise will achieve something similar.

The dromedaries are couched in a hollow at the base of a dune. Two others are waiting for us: a child and a man, the latter a head taller than me. They are Lamina's 10-year-old son, Abdul-Hakim, and his brother Jadullah, who has the sinewy, intimidating look of a Dothraki chieftain from *Game of Thrones*. They exchange whispers with Lamina, and throw cautious glances at me, but nobody addresses me until my first lesson.

'*Shuf!*' they chime. 'Look!'

The camel's saddle is a pad of palm fibres wrapped in rawhide, rigged over a wooden vice. A wooden palanquin girths a folded coverlet, which hugs the camel's belly. At the back of the saddle, the rear pad forms a perch above the rump. Heavy *guerbas* (inside-out goat-skins turned into water containers) dangle from the pommels of the palanquin, slurping at the camel's shoulders, obscene and sweaty as the bladders of monsters. At Lamina's instruction, I set a foot on the camel's neck and lever myself up, grabbing a fistful of fur for balance. I am riding in front of the hump, in the North African tradition, making the most of the camel's powerful shoulder muscles. As Lamina explains later, it's the ideal position for 'control'. A skilled cameleer can manipulate his steed by digging his toes into the animal's neck, like a gamer working a joystick with his thumbs.

'*Nibda!*' calls Lamina, which translates as 'we begin' or 'we go into the desert', depending on the context. In this case, it means both.

At the last moment, Abdul-Hakim jumps on, resting on the back-piece of the palanquin, clinching the rump between his legs to reduce the impact on his bony perch. A child, I figure, should be more receptive to my attempts at social interaction, so I call out in desperate Arabic: '*Ya allah!* Hey, isn't this great! Beautiful camel!' But all I get in reply are a few puzzled exhalations.

'*La atakallam ajnabi,*' he replies primly. 'I don't speak foreignish.'

Our departure has been timed deliberately late in the day, to avoid attracting attention. This means we have travelled just a couple of miles when the sun abandons us, like a scout whose responsibility ends at the edge of town. Bending in the silvery wasteland, acacias and doum palms probe the sky on trunks as bowed as the necks of the camels. Burrs of cram-cram skitter over the bunchgrass, spiking our clothes and the skin of our fingers whenever we dismount. I am not trusted to ride yet. Lamina holds the head rope, orientating the animal in a mixture of stage-like whispers and sudden wordless commands: '*Oooooosshhh-ooooooshhh-ooooooshhh! Khirrrrr-khirrrr!*' The camel bunches to a scuttering halt, magically in thrall to Lamina's exhalations, or the occasional cry lassoed by Abdul-Hakim. Strange, elongated sounds, they hover somewhere between war cry and babytalk. Listening to these gnomic utterances, I realise that Arabic is not the only language I need to master.

A sweet breeze is skimming the earth. Along with the gentle gradient, it makes for a mellow lead-in. We have been enveloped in the smoky blue of dusk, a balm after the raging furnace of day; and latterly in night's tarry black, when you start to hear the howling of wild donkeys and other desert animals, and you wonder how deserted the desert really is. Four hours in, Lamina chooses a resting place, a shallow amphitheatre studded by wiry acacia bushes. No need to give the camels the go-ahead: they are onto dinner as soon as we dismount. Prehensile lips wrap around the thorny branches, loud munches and grunts wafting around them. They are like hungry strangers in a dead-end bar, each intent on his own meal and minding his own business.

The new moon is only a couple of days old, so I am leaning on sound for any sense of my whereabouts: the low *basso* chomping of the camels, the ghostly bray of wild donkeys, the soughing of the wind in the bushes. I am feeling utterly useless – I want to be allotted a task. I try helping Lamina with the baggage, but I don't happen to be a cat, so when he points out the ropes I have no chance of seeing their knots in the dark. He nudges me back to Jadullah, who has dug a pit in the sand and is stoking a fire.

'*Ya, hadha huwa an-nar!*' I exclaim (I'm piling on the decibels in my eagerness to ingratiate myself). 'Oh, this is the fire!'

Jadullah's grunted reply is less expressive than any of the sounds he has directed at the camels.

Crawling away, all-fouring through the sand, he digs around in the thorns and comes back with a handful of droppings the size of pecan nuts. The fire turns them dry and crozzled, like the tips of matchsticks. It is not until he jerks his head at the bush and grunts the first word I understand from him – *jamal*, camel – that I realise what they are: camel turds, adding fuel to the fire. With their high ammonia content, they make for excellent tinder.

The rice is scooped in calloused handfuls out of a painted goatskin bag. It cooks in a pot, lifted a few inches over the flame by a forked stick from the bushes, while Lamina separates the embers to form a second, smaller fire for the teapot. Waiting for the pot to boil, he unclasps a leather pouch and shakes out a few grains of snuff. His nostrils quiver and he presses the skin with the pads of his fingers, like a potter putting the last delicate touches to a rim. I watch him a little too closely (I'm not sure if there is a protocol about gawping when someone is taking snuff) and he looks up. For the first time, our eyes lock. The flames conjure shadows across his face and give him a potent, supernatural aura: a campfire king.

'What is your country?' he asks.

His voice is slower now, his expression relaxed – soothed, I suppose, by the snuff. I think of al-Idrisi's description of Britain in the *Book of Roger*, written for the King of Sicily in the twelfth century: 'This is a great island, shaped like the head of an ostrich ... the winter there is permanent.' But I've been away for nearly half a year. Here, among people I barely know, in a landscape I haven't the knowledge to interpret, I feel a cloying nostalgia. I talk of sheep on chalky hills the colour of mint... of mighty cities full of commerce... of fairgrounds and theatres and the rowing boats in Battersea Park...

'But it is very cold,' I add, remembering al-Idrisi. 'Sometimes the wind blows so hard and the air is so cold you can see the steam coming out of people's mouths.'

'At night?' asks Lamina.

'No, in the daytime too.'

Now I've got their attention. I tell them about ice and hail and snowball fights, floods in the West Country when people slide off their roofs into the rescue boats. I am laying it on pretty thick, but hey, they live in the Sahara. They are used to extremes.

'May God preserve us!' Lamina turns to Jadullah, explaining what I've told him, and they both wrap themselves in their arms. They're looking at me differently. In a strange way, I think they're impressed. If the *toubob* can survive such intemperate conditions, maybe he isn't a complete dolt. Even if he doesn't know how to saddle a camel.

After tea, Lamina points me to the spot where the fire has burned. This is the best place to lie, cosy as a mattress with a hot-water bottle. I stretch myself into the warmth, enjoying the mild ache in my thighs, the pleasure of fatigue. Dangling above me, the starfield is low and close, a barrage of light so intense it is hard to identify any of the constellations, like trying to pick out a friend in a bustling crowd. A meteorite flashes in a clot of stars, then winks out of existence, like an alien SOS from thousands of years ago. I immerse myself in the stars – an unworldly relief from the mental effort of conversation, and a distraction from all my anxieties. All those bandits I've heard about, smugglers and hostage takers, who haunt the sands like the *djinn* and ghosts that scared off travellers in earlier centuries, or the tribesmen who did for explorers like Major Laing. But when I turn my head to the sand, the worries trickle back, so I shift round to Lamina for reassurance.

He is sitting upright, his turban laid across his lap, tweezering burrs of cram-cram from its wrinkly folds. With his high bald forehead and his aquiline nose, he has a look of honesty about him, like a guide in a storybook: the White Rabbit or Mr Tumnus. Someone who can teach me all the lessons I need to absorb. Today, we've touched on saddling and baggage. But there are many more to learn; he has intimated that tomorrow we will focus on my riding. I have only known Lamina a few hours, and I still hardly know him at all, but there's something about him. For all the scary talk in Timbuktu, I feel sure he is one of the good guys.

Well... A voice prickles at the back of my mind, like the burrs of cram-cram snagging on our clothes. *Of course you trust him. You're out in the desert now – what choice have you got?*

Part Two

City

[T]he goal of civilization is sedentary culture and luxury. When civilization reaches that goal, it turns toward corruption and starts being senile, as happens in the natural life of living beings.

Ibn Khaldun, *The Muqaddimah*

4

The God-Blessed Lair of Pigeon Shit

A PIGEON WHEELED OVER MY HEAD, ITS PURPLE-TINGED FEATHERS SPARKING like metal in the late afternoon light. I was standing on a rooftop in Fez, 1200 miles north of my destination. Black smoke puffed out of chimneys fuelled by olive pits and a hinged line, like a V or an Arabic seven, resolved itself into a swoop of swallows. Sunlight gilded their wings and splintered against the sandstone walls, sinking behind the broad green hills that hugged the city on every side.

'Look!'

A saffron-stained finger arrowed towards the sky. Standing beside me was the *sahib dukkan* ('shop master' or boss), head of a tanning collective in whose factory I found myself an unlikely apprentice. Describing an arc with one arm, he took in the moon pearling over the hills, the oily light and the skins laid across the roof around us, fastened with saffron dye.

'You see? The moon is the colour of the skins when they come out of our vats, and the sun is the colour when we put the dye on them. You understand what this shows us? It shows we are doing God's work!'[14]

From the material point of view, it was hard to imagine a place less demonstrably blessed. Squatting at the back of a zig-zag of wood-scaffolded, flaking-plaster alleyways as organically decrepit as Hieronymous Bosch's hell, the Ain Azletoun tannery may well be the stinkiest place in the whole of Fez. To reach it, you tilt off the Tala'a Kabira (literally 'Big Street', the old city's principal thoroughfare) and delve into a matrix of alleys. Pressing yourself to the mud-brick walls, you breathe in to let the hide-laden mules pass. The thickening reek is your guide: a ureic stench so heavy it feels like something solid is foraging in your nostrils. No wonder visitors to the tanneries often carry sprigs of mint or rosemary under their septa.

---

14 The Arabic language supports this connection: *badr*, the word for a full moon, also denotes a bucket of lambskins.

The tannery itself squats, fortress-like, at the back of its maze. Goat hides pile against walls of crumbling brick, festering among disembodied heads and rancid offal, like the remains of slain adventurers outside a dragon's lair. Inside, dust-lagged cobwebs sag from wooden joists and gaps in the roof suck down the sky, spotlighting whoever is standing below, like an unwitting stage performer, before they crab up the ledges, levering onto the catwalk above.

Here you have the best view of this antique factory: a honeycomb of more than 40 concrete pits, filled with lime and dyes and speckled with goat hair. You keep back from the edge, watching for anyone tilting out of the tiny work cells around you – knowing the slightest stumble will knock you into the pits. And that is definitely something to avoid: the men have good reason to go about in knee-length waders.

The tanners were tough, thick in the shoulders and thighs, which were clearly visible under stained vests and crinkly leather shorts. They had the concentration of masculine energy I had witnessed among desert nomads like Jadullah and Lamina. But their posture was cramped and their movements jerky. During intervals of pipe smoking, they never settled into the graceful calm of my nomad companions.

Splashing the hides together, scraping off the last tangles of wool with pieces of tile, then gathering more hides out of the weaker vats, they were at it all day, from dawn till dusk. Once a batch of skins had been depilated, they carried it over to the *ghaseel* (washer), a wooden barrel that looked like a giant's beer keg. An electric pulley turned the barrel, while a pipe at the back filled it with water.

Loading the barrel was one of the simpler jobs on the site – judging by the fact it was allotted to me. I worked with Najib, a rap-dancing alley cat with hair the colour of a tabby, who always had a few balls of *keef* (marijuana) in his back pocket. I had been pestering him for weeks to bring me to the tannery, and slowly we thrashed out a deal: I funded his social excursions and paid for presents for his 'girlfriends', and in return he acted as my gateway. By the end, I think we were friends.

The tannery is run as a co-operative, with a couple of cells for Najib and his team. As soon as you burrow inside, the light is sucked out behind you. Cobwebs dangle overhead and you have to duck to avoid the pelts hanging from nails in the wooden beams. Sitting next to

Najib, I held a Supermax razor blade and pierced the pelts with slits. We pulled ourselves up from the greasy debris and brown scrapings to hang the hides from the nails, while Najib's colleagues 'broke' them with a knife, slicing rough edges, buffing them to creamy leather on a mushroom-shaped stool. It was tiring work, and you didn't slack unless you fancied a bollocking from the boss. But every so often, Najib would chuck me a smile and whisper: 'Only be patient! Soon is the sitting time!'

All being well, I was hoping to return to Timbuktu in a couple of months. It had been whipped by recent history, battered on the front line of a triangular war between Tuareg secessionists, Islamist militants and a French-led, pan-African army. Whenever I thought of my last days in Mali, my head bristled with martial imagery: tank tracks in the sand outside Timbuktu; hobnail boots poking out of rickety pick-ups; mounted guns shuddering over sun-bleached helmets. But it fluttered, too, with memories of the nomads I had travelled with – Lamina and Jadullah and little Abdul-Hakim, the adventure they had taken me on and the lessons they had taught me: not only saddling but the different skills they dealt out every day, from tracking and navigation to drawing water and pitching camp.

In the intervening two years, I had heard only rumour; I hoped now to find out what had happened to them. Timbuktu was free again, or so the authorities claimed. For several months I had been laying plans for my return. Fez was a good starting point. It was Leo Africanus's old hometown, a twin to my destination and his, a place that never stopped intriguing me. I felt I could live here for a hundred years and only ever scratch the surface.

Alongside Timbuktu, Fez is the most magical and mysterious of North African cities, an 'enchanted labyrinth sheltered from time', in Paul Bowles's phrase. It was founded in the early ninth century by Moulay Idriss, a *sharifi* (a descendant of the Prophet Mohammed) whose family had been massacred in a battle near Mecca. Hotfooting it across North Africa with his servant, swapping clothes to avoid detection, he set the breadth of the continent between himself and his enemies, and gathered a following among the local Berber tribes. In doing so, he grafted the ancestry of the Prophet to the early shoots from which the Moroccan nation would grow, rooting Islam in the fresh soil of the Maghrib – 'the land of the setting sun'.

This union was symbolised in the person of his son, Moulay Idriss II, whose mother was the daughter of a Berber chief. Building across the river from his father's original settlement, Idriss II established Fez as a city of many parts, a labyrinth whose structure is both an antidote to the desert and its mirror (in Arabic, the word for labyrinth, *mataha*, derives from the same root as *tih*, a desert waste). Migrants from Andalusia and Tunisia filled the different flanks of the *medina* (city), bringing their skills in craftsmanship and scholarship. Mosques and *zawiyas* (shrines) scythed the sky with crescents. Minarets shot up like trees, brambled in exquisite calligraphy, between green tiled domes as lush as the hills that frame them.

Scholarship – the great provision of the Tunisian refugees – flourished at Kairaouine University, which predates the first Oxford college by four centuries. Founded, like the Sankoré mosque in Timbuktu, by a woman (although as patriarchal as all the universities that followed), it hosted some of the greatest minds of the medieval era. It was here that Maimonides composed his commentary on the Mishnah (the collection of Jewish oral traditions), the Sufi philosopher Ibn Arabi experienced some of his most powerful revelations, and Pope Sylvester II learned about Arabic numerals.

Wandering around the old town, you can easily imagine you're in some pastiche of *The Thousand and One Nights*. A Berber herbalist stuffs your nostrils with a twisted ball of black anise, promising it will ease your mind and stop you snoring. You pass a door lintel smeared with blood to beseech the supernatural blessing of the *djinn* on the night before a circumcision. Crocodile scutes shadow a poky dispensary, where tortoises are pulled out of mesh-grilled cages, to be sold as ingredients in traditional medicine. Snapping open and shut like hungry mouths, or muzzled by heaped carts and sliding gates, passageways redirect you around the *medina* depending on the time of day. A crack in a wall yields an alley, flattening you between wooden scaffolds, ripping open to hurl you onto a sun-kissed square, then hoicking you between walls that are hell-bent on slicing off your elbows.

What all this bustle reinforces – in a physical, visceral and in the best sense medieval way – is that Fez is still a place where things get made. If my stinky mornings at the tannery taught me anything, they taught me that. It is a city of artisans, a giant workshop, where every turn reveals someone busy at craft. A cotton spinner hooks his yarn across the width of an alley, like vines on a trellis. A wood carver slices a panel, soaked in the perfume of fresh cedar. A silk weaver works his needle under shelves that glisten with freshly made gowns, while his friends sip tea at the edge of his cell.

This prodigious trade was all recorded by Leo Africanus, who grew up here around the turn of the sixteenth century, son of a landowner and nephew of a court favourite. 'A world it is to see,' he wrote, 'how large, how populous, how well-fortified and walled this city is.' Here, more than anywhere else – where the bath-houses still run on the system he described, brides continue to be carried about in 'a wooden cage or cabinet ... covered with silk', and the dealers in perfume and books (traditionally the most valuable merchandise) still operate close to the mosques – I was surrounded by the vestiges of his world.

People find different ways of approaching the past. Back in the 1920s, it was all about séances and spiritualism. This was how WB Yeats made acquaintance with Leo Africanus. Through an American medium and several sessions of automatic writing, the great Irish poet exchanged a series of bizarre communications with the long-dead traveller (among other matters, Leo apparently advised Yeats on the thorny subject of Irish nationalism). Leo became Yeats's 'daimon', drawn to him because 'in life he had been all undoubting impulse', whereas the poet himself was 'doubting, conscientious and timid'. Over the coming weeks, I would often find myself stricken by uncertainty, especially in the bandit-infested tracts of Northern Mali; I hoped Leo could be my daimon too, spurring me on and lifting me whenever my confidence flagged.

The place in Fez where I was able to channel him – my equivalent to a 1920s séance, I suppose – was the Henna souk. I enjoyed drifting among the stalls selling sandalwood incense, amber-coloured deer musk and black *hammam* soap made from the kernels of olive nuts, smelling my way to a calmer world than the acrid bustle of 'Big Street'.

'Perhaps you know about this place?'

A chatty stall owner lifted me out of my diary. Bushels of walnut bark (for cleaning your teeth or staining women's lips) brushed against his head, while rows of soap and aromatic stones clustered on the wooden counter in front of him.

'A little,' I said. 'I read a book by a man who used to work here.'

'Then you know about Hassan? Oh, the times have changed, for pity! When he lived, Islamic civilisation was the greatest in the world. Now look at us! All the young people take drugs, the civilisation is ruined.'

Hassan was my Leo. Born to a Muslim family who fled the fall of Granada in 1492, he grew up as al-Hassan Ibn Mohammed al-Wazzan, 'Hassan son of Mohammed the weight-master'. But a few years after his journey to Timbuktu, he was kidnapped off the Algerian coast, sold as an exotic gift to Christendom and baptised by Pope Leo X, whose name he took. In a revealing passage, he tells of a 'wily bird' who was 'so indued by nature, that she could live as well with the fishes of the sea, as with the fowls of the air'. Not only is this a modus operandi for Leo's own life, it is a fair objective for any traveller. After my turbanned disguise in Mali, it certainly felt like something to aim for.

It was during his Italian sojourn that Leo collected his travelling experiences together and wrote the book for which he is remembered. Describing his journeys across North, East and West Africa, the tribes he met on the way, their customs and trade, and sprinkling his account with enough legendary matter and titillation to ensure a healthy box office, he remained essential reading for anyone with aspirations in Africa well into the nineteenth century. He may not have been the first writer to describe the continent, but he was probably the most influential.[15]

---

15 In 1599, a year before the first English edition of Leo's *Description* was published, George Abbot was able to write (in *A Briefe Description of the Whole Worlde*): 'From beyond the hils Atlas maior, unto the South of Africa, is nothing almost in antiquity worthy the reading, and those things which are written, for the most part are fables.' But Leo provided a vivid account of precisely this region, on which, as EW Bovill put it (in his classic *The Golden Trade of the Moors*), 'geographers and cartographers remained dependent for almost all they

Behind us was a building that Leo knew intimately. With its rust-smeared window grilles and the warping on their hoods, the hospital of Sidi Frej doesn't exactly bask in historical glamour. Still, I was intrigued, imagining the 'frantic and distraught persons' who used to dwell here. Half a millennium earlier, Leo would have advised me not to step too close: the inmates were liable to 'call out to passersby, take hold of them and defile them with dung'. And he should know, for he moonlighted here, earning three ducats a month as a notary.

Time wasn't going to oblige me at the Sidi Frej. The building hasn't been a medical institution since 1944. When I stepped inside the keyhole-shaped gateway, instead of finding myself beside a sixteenth-century clerk I was rubbing shoulders with polyurethane mannequins in silk dressing-gowns. Leo's asylum is no more: it has morphed into a store for household goods and lingerie.

From the rooftop, however, something very different could be witnessed. I was in luck: today was the *moussem* (holy day) of Moulay Idriss, the city's founder, and the old town was clamouring with processions. Helped along by a cheery bra seller, I picked my way between freshly cleaned horse saddles, crossed a couple of wobbling sheets of corrugated iron, and stood on the rooftop, taking it all in.

Underneath us paraded members of the city's long-standing guilds, laden with gifts for Moulay Idriss's mausoleum. The bra seller pointed out the candlemakers, the blacksmiths, the shoemakers (although, he admitted with a grin, his own trade was unrepresented – 'maybe one day we will have something for the cheap goods from China!'). Barrel-sized poles of wax floated beneath us, striped with bright colours; banners stitched with Quranic verses; a black bull heading for sacrifice, skidding against the tiles. Most distinguished of all were the silk weavers. Gowned in red and white burnouses (the hooded cloak common in the Maghrib), heads bound in tight yellow turbans, they stood in an archway and beat the air with the rattling of their frame drums. The

knew of the interior of Africa for the next 300 years'. Other writers, from Herodotus to the Arab geographer Ibn Hawkal, had written about Africa, but none had penetrated so far, nor written in such depth; and 'nothing as fundamental or dramatic as Leo's *History* was to be added to Englishmen's knowledge of Africa', writes Eldred Jones, 'until the famous nineteenth-century telegram of Speke and Grant, "The Nile is settled".'

chant was winding and circular, matched to a comical degree by the wiggling of their leader's backside, which pointed rhythmically towards the crowd. Borne ahead of them, raised by men in pure white *djellabas* (the traditional Arabic male robe), was the centrepiece of the procession: a four-tiered catafalque, inscribed with gold Quranic verses over a red silk background, freshly woven to adorn Moulay Idriss's tomb for the coming year.

The parade was intricately coded, but I found it all rather cosy. The flickering candlelight, the gleam of metal under muffled cloth, the gnomic chanting: I spent my teens in a monastic boarding school, so it reminded me of Sunday mornings in the abbey. This kind of procession – give or take the Arabic lettering and the odd turban – used to take place all over the Mediterranean world. Europe's guilds have been replaced by unions, campaigns for wage increases and decent pension plans; there is less ballast in the Moroccan artisan's career. Yet the procession of the guilds illustrates how time in Fez wraps around itself. How history isn't something solid, to be locked away in storage, but fluid and adaptive; and if you can find the cracks, you might see it pouring through.

⁓

'Come on, Nicholas! If we do this fast we have longer for the sitting time!'

Najib was on a mission. He led me through the streets, bearing a pile of pelts on his head, the yellow pleats dangling over his shoulders like a lion's mane in a pantomime. I was never allowed to carry the hides myself. He knew people who had been picked up by the police for 'hassling' foreigners, so we moved in well-spaced single file. Najib shuttled forwards, hands up to steady the load, rushing to meet the *babouche* makers' deadlines. When we reached them, they exchanged only skeletal greetings. Monastically bowed in their work cells, they were grizzled, busy men, scissors flashing over dusty moustaches in acrid bubbles of solvents and glue.

All around me was the buzz of life – men cutting, dousing, spinning, scraping; as physical and hard-working as the nomadic society I had encountered in the Sahara. But it was different from that world – because it was urban. The tannery and its workshops were a factory, a stable environment, pulling men together to produce goods that could be sold in the streets around them. You saw it in shops lining the main streets and alleyways, from saffron-dyed *babouche* slippers (Najib's team's speciality) to rawhide belts dangling from the canopies; handbags and satchels piled at the front; sandals slotted in neat rows; purses, wallets, wide-brimmed hats, cushion covers, sequin-dotted camel toys, pencil cases, covered bellows, shagreen diaries and Qurans bound in classic 'morocco'.[16]

'Now', said Najib, 'we have the sitting time!'

Keen for a smoke without the boss breathing down his neck, he picked out one of the *medina*'s numberless arteries, weaving a path between the cages of battery chickens and carts of Barbary figs, simultaneously rolling a joint from a ball of *keef* the shape of a chickpea. By the time we reached his target – the shop of his friend Mansur – he was ready to light up.

'Nicholas! You never buy anything from me!'

Mansur was from the south, taller and darker than most Fassis. Usually to be found at the back of his store, he tucked himself into the shade like a napping cat, his turban dangling over his brow. The merchandise around him was a treasure trove of desert-ware. Silver bracelets inscribed in Tamasheq reflected light off gazelle-horn bracelets. *Keef* pipes made from alfaca alloy perched above walking canes with camel-bone hilts and saddlebags painted with the same vegetable dyes used at the tannery. Much of it was tourist tat (and it really plumbed the depths with the blue-veiled Tuareg fridge magnets), but I still loved Mansur's store for the headrush of the desert it gave me.

'I can't believe you've forgotten.' I pointed out a brass and camel-bone ashtray I'd picked up a fortnight ago. 'We haggled over it for at least half an hour!'

---

16 Leather goods were a major part of the economy back in Leo Africanus's day too. He wrote of shops 'that make sword-scabbards and caparisons for horses', shops for shoes and buskins, about 40 shops specialising in 'stirrups, spurs and bridles, so artificially [made] as I think the like are not to be seen in Europe', makers of leather tankards, tailors specialising in leather shields and a whole street of saddlers, 'which cover the saddles before mentioned threefold with most excellent leather'.

'Two weeks ago doesn't count!'

'Oh, don't bother Nicholas,' Najib called from the back. 'He's got no money, he's like us.'

He tugged on his joint so it glowed, the seeds popping and ash feathering down between the trinkets.

I knew I had to be careful. A whiff of fancy and we'd spend all afternoon spiralling round a price. Besides, I wanted to hear about Mansur's family.

He was full of stories about them – wealthy Bedouin uprooted from seventeenth-century Palestine, who had travelled the breadth of Africa with their camels. He was particularly proud of his grandfather, a notable caravan guide in the days of the French protectorate.

'My grandfather could never live away from the desert,' said Mansur. 'So when my father moved to the city, he was really mad. He said the Sahara purifies the soul, just as water purifies the body.'

One of his grandfather's greatest feats was to find water when his caravan had fallen off its track.

'It's the most important thing in the desert, you have to know where the wells are. But the caravan leader was a fool and they went more than three days without any new supplies. They were in a dangerous situation: if they didn't find water soon, they would run out. So my grandfather knelt down and prayed to God for help. While he was praying, he had his face to the ground, and he could sense something. The smell of the water! So he carried on, walking on his knees because he didn't want to lose the scent. He had to climb over many dunes, but he found the source, and saved all the people who were travelling with him.'

Mansur was like a watercourse when the sluice gate has lifted: sit back and watch him flow. I wondered if he envied his grandfather's more adventurous life. But when I asked him, he whisked the idea away like an irritating fly.

'Don't be stupid, how can I survive in the desert? I'm a son of the city. To be a true nomad you must live all your life in the desert. There's no other way.'

My reply was something like 'hmmmmm'. Mansur could certainly teach me a lot, but I wasn't sure he was going to do my morale any good. Sometimes, it's best to keep your travel plans under your turban.

One morning, when the sky was still cowling the city in an indigo veil, I drove out with Najib to collect skins for the boss. Rutted tracks braided the smooth roads out of Fez, past cornfields where olive trees shimmered above the hayricks. On the roadsides, goods were tied down under hessian sacks. Sitting on ledges of rubble and smoking on the hardstanding were men in greasy overalls and dusty shirts, waiting for transport into town. This is the best time to visit a market – when the produce is still as fresh as the air.

In the little town of Ein Nukbeh, rubbish banked the roads in slushy piles and stains splattered the sides of apartment blocks, like children's shirts after bowls of *bissara* soup. Behind a metal gate the colour of dried blood, tufts of wool drifted like tumbleweed and salt sparkled on the crusty earth. Pick-up trucks charged towards a steel overhang, where tarpaulin sheets battened down the piles of skins, held in place by bullhorns and stones.

'Come on, I know this man – he always does a good price,' said Najib's colleague Tamar, striding between the vendors.

There were skins everywhere, wrinkled and rubbery on the undersides, shaggy on top, spilling the grains of salt rubbed into the hair. Standing by a mound of lambskins, I counted more than 200 pelts – and that was just one pile! The wool was tough and dry, the undersides riddled with cracks as intricate as the writing on a palimpsest.

'We're the butchers.' One of the sellers turned round from a heap. 'We buy the animals in the nomad markets and carry them to the abattoir. We sell the meat to the big hotels, then we bring the skins here.'

He had nearly a thousand pelts to flog. The most valuable cattle hides fetched €44, while 'low-quality' goatskins only raised €3 or €4.

The traders were practical, bristly chinned men. They laughed at my questions and rattled out flinty answers while slinging the skins into their vans or emptying them out of plastic buckets. They reminded me of Najib's colleagues at the tannery: robust alpha males, who would welcome you warmly and offer a draw on their *keef* pipe, but wouldn't hold their punches if a quarrel broke out. They were the middlemen, the hinge that joins the nomadic herders to the industries of the towns.

'We're from Marrakesh,' one old-timer told me. He was standing on the tailgate of a jeep, working on a cliff of cowhides so precipitous the men had to swing the skins over their heads. 'We're taking five hundred. We'll sell them to the tanneries in Marrakesh. We get a good price there and it's not short of craftsmen.'

'You've got a lot of skins,' I said, to a round of laughter as dry and tough as some of the hides.

'This?' One of them threw back his head. 'This is nothing. You should come here around Eid (when sheep and goats are slaughtered all over the country). That's when you see the real trade!'

Pragmatism hung around the place, like the flies confabulating over the pools of animal blood. Najib was just as direct – by the time I made it back to the overhang, he was already calling for me.

'*Ya'la*, come on, I was afraid they'd turned you into a goat!'

Heaving a pile of skins onto his back, he shuffled towards the gate. Before I followed, I turned to the dealer, a twentysomething in a 'Fxxk Police' T-shirt. He was tipping more skins out of a bucket, fresh blood trickling over the crusty stains on his trainers.

'We've got four buckets to empty,' he said, 'it's about 50 skins altogether. We collect them from the markets round Taza, then bring them here to sell. In the past we went to the Guissa Gate in Fez, but now they've set up this place and it's the biggest market in the country.'

'I guess it's hard work?'

'Sure.' He flicked his brow, a ready smile on his lips. Blood spat around the falling skins, dribbling into a fly-misted puddle. 'We used to have our own animals, but my father sold them and bought the car. Machines are easier, aren't they? Now we only deal with the animals when they're dead.'

There was one last hide in the bucket, caught against the rim. The dealer shook the bucket but the skin wouldn't fall, so he thrust his hand inside and pulled it out. The blood smeared his fingers and sprinkled thick red gouts that gleamed in the sun like rubies.

5

Learning to Love the Glottal Stop

'OPEN YOUR THROAT, NICHOLAS! IT'S EASY! YOU ONLY HAVE TO OPEN YOUR throat and make the sound.'

'Ugh... nghh... aaaaaarghhh!'

'No, no, that is completely wrong! You're not opening your throat!'

Sitting in a tea-house near the Kairaouine mosque, Mansur was losing patience with me. I had asked him to help with my Arabic. As a speaker of Hassaniya (the dialect spoken in southern Morocco and Mauritania, and among the Berabish in Mali), he was an ideal tutor. But he didn't have the patience of his desert forefathers; and to be fair to him, his pupil was no model.

I was like a tanner trying out for a job at a perfume counter. When it came to the tricksier letters – the throat-scraping *khaaf*, the hard 'd' and worst of all that dreaded glottal stop, the *aieeeeen* (which 'should sound like the bleating of a sheep', as Peter Mayne's teacher advised him in 1940s Marrakesh), I was hopeless. I came from a language in which your epiglottis is out of the picture; a language in which moving your lips as little as possible is a sign of good breeding. Now I was showing my gums to the flies, gagging and spluttering and plugging my epiglottis to my posterior pharyngeal wall. And for what? So Mansur could tell me to 'try again, that was nearly right!' I did wonder sometimes if Arabic was really a language at all. Trying to learn it was like squirrelling away at a strategy for Snakes and Ladders. One mistimed glottal stop and it's back to square one.

'Maybe you are thinking too much.' Finally accepting defeat, Mansur retreated into his tea-glass. 'Maybe you need to... leave it a while.'

My synapses were experiencing the neural equivalent of a desert storm. How to get on top of it all, all those unfamiliar rules? The gendering of numbers, for example, which never agree with the associated noun; the ditching of plurals for the numbers eleven to a thousand (but not three to ten). I was confused by the distinction between the dual and the plural; by the way some plurals split open and stuffed themselves with unexpected new letters; by the way pronouns and prepositions attached themselves to the edges of words, like stowaways clinging to the back of a train.

Fans of Arabic extol its mathematical, musical order, likening it to a Bach motet or a Gödel metric. For myself, I could hardly imagine a more intractable system. Except... oh yes, there was a perfect fit... and it was right under my nose. Because if anything matched the inscrutability of Arabic, it was the city where I was trying to master it! There was the division of gender; the tendency for building compounds out of apparently disparate materials; the rootedness, which you find in Arabic's tendency to form groups of words around a cluster of base letters, echoed in the clusterings of Fez's neighbourhoods (each mini-community built around a mosque, bath-house and fountain). And there was another, even more striking parallel. In both cases, one careless mistake (whether mispronouncing a soft *seen* for a hard *saad*, or taking the first right at the Brass-Makers' Square when you meant to take the second) and you're screwed.

At dinner, in the sprawling house where I was staying, I would compliment my host mother on her cooking – 'The taste of honey is strong in this delicious meal!' 'More succulent is this tagine than a piece of fruit after a long journey in the desert!' I certainly made the family laugh: teenager Fathin sniggered into her hand, while her younger sister Sawsan (not yet house-trained for weird, Arabic-mangling foreigners) splattered her couscous across the table before running out to guffaw in the courtyard. At the tannery, Najib and his colleagues sometimes cracked up so violently that a single mispronunciation had potentially lethal consequences. I lived in constant fear they would fall off the walkway and crash into one of the limepits – all because I'd failed to harden my 'd'.

The sixteenth-century philologist Guillaume Postel (who studied an Arabic grammar written by Leo Africanus and probably knew the traveller) picked up Arabic so fast his teacher thought he might be a demon. In that respect, I was proving myself all too human. If I was going to lift my Arabic to the point where I could actually talk to people, I needed help. And sometimes, just sometimes, if you wish hard enough...

The beat was all around us – shaking the walls, quivering the stools, vibrating in the tiles under our feet. Najib had plugged his phone into a speaker to give us his dance moves.

'Nicholas! Tell me, tell me, what does it mean?'

It was amazing how much leverage he managed, considering that Mansur's walk-up was too small to swing any of Fez's innumerable cats. I was sitting under swags of electric wiring, watching Najib by the light of a candle, through the mist of a joint smouldering in an empty tea-glass.

He had worked out the dance steps to dozens of Busta Rhymes's tunes. Gliding across the floor with rapid switches between toes and heels, he popped out his elbows and chopped the air with his arms, whirling to the turnaround with spasmodic wrenches of the hips. I was doubling up with laughter, but it was laughter of wonder and awe, when you find out a friend has a talent you never imagined. The level of difficulty was clear enough when I tried to join in and had to pick myself off the floor before the end of the first verse.

'Your job is to tell me the words.' Najib wagged a finger and hooked it towards the rug. 'Please, Nicholas, sit down!'

I tried my best. I had enough vocabulary at this stage, and it's amazing how you can make yourself understood to somebody who really wants to know what you're saying. Although Busta wasn't the easiest subject for a first-time translator. How to convert 'def squad'? Or 'flip-mode'? Or 'camel-toe groupie'? Not knowing the Arabic for 'crib' (as in a rap star's home), I rendered it as *beit*, or house. I was similarly stuck on 'acid' and felt I needed something closer to Najib's experience, so I turned it to *keef*. But I feared I was doing injustice to Busta, failing to conjure the particular coding of his language. Eschewing the stodgy offerings of my dictionary, I sought out alternative translations on online forums and wrote down new words culled from friends in the *medina*. My translations were a long way from the slickness of the original, but they were slowly becoming more ingrained in the texture of the world Najib had asked me to evoke.

This was progress – of a sort. My Arabic was proving useful to someone, and if nothing else... well, at least I knew how to say '*al-hara' laysa*

*shi' gheir al-'ushb baad e dhaalik al- madagh/ wa tilka hiyyeh kurah as-sawdah
min mu'khrah al-baqarah'*, or in Busta's idiom 'Bullshit ain't nothin' but
chewed-up grass/ And that's a black ball that came out of a cow's arse'.

At Mansur's bedsit, we were in the right setting to conjure these
songs. Visitors often stopped by: sleepy-eyed wide boys wielding *keef*
pipes like sorcerers' wands, rattling out prices from the underworld
supermarket ('One fifty and she'll give you the massage of your life!'
'Give me a hundred and I'll fix you up: super-duper, zero zero, whatever you wanna smoke!'). Sometimes they unsealed herbal sachets
known as 'chocolate', which Leo Africanus also mentions, noting that
it causes people to 'fall laughing, disporting, and dallying, as if [they]
were half drunk'. It goes very well with baklava and a glass of mint tea.

On evenings in the Ville Nouvelle (the 'New Town' laid by the
French during the colonial era), Mansur took me to a bar that called
itself – wincingly – Le Progrès. A surly barkeeper handed out bottles of
Spéciale beer to sad-looking men who sat around the wood-panelled
bar. *Keef* smoke curled in the gleam of electric red, dancers lifting gar-
tered legs in cheap prints of the Folies Bergère. There were no dancers
tonight, but a whiff of feminine glamour was supplied by a couple
of women in the back corner, wearing the vampish uniform of the
Moroccan prostitute (black eye-shadow, black jacket, black heels, black
scowl). Mansur gave them smiles and small talk; they worked their
jaws on the sunflower seeds. Sometimes, when the going was slow and
we turned up late, they offered special rates. One of them occasionally gave us a smirk. I rallied with my politest phrases, explaining I
had someone back home, and they detonated the most contemptuous
laughs I have ever heard.

'This one speaks like a child,' rasped the smirker.

'Sedentary people', noted the great fourteenth-century historian Ibn
Khaldun, 'are much concerned with all kinds of pleasures. They are
accustomed to luxury and success in worldly occupations and to indul-
gence in worldly desires.' Nomadic people, on the other hand, are
interested in 'wordly things' where they 'touch only the necessities of

life and not luxuries or anything causing, or calling for, desires and pleasures.'

Leo Africanus's *Description of Africa* casts an intriguing light on the town/country dynamic – if only because there is no comparable account of North Africa at the time. Leo doesn't dispel the binary division. His Fez is lusty and vicious, as appetite driven as 1920s Berlin or twenty-first-century Las Vegas. Charm sellers con the public, dervishes force kisses out of unsuspecting wedding guests, fortune tellers 'commit unlawful veneries among themselves' and 'from the twentieth hour you shall see none at all in their shops, for then every man runs to the tavern to disport, to spend riotously, and to be drunken'.

But Leo is committed to impartiality, 'to describe things so plainly without glossing or dissimulation'. In the towns, he depicts gatherings of learned men and secret sects, hospitals, courtly pomp, the full range of merchandise. As for the countryside, he shows us idylls as well as dystopias: from a prince of the Drâa whose tribute to Fez includes 100 slaves, 12 camels, a giraffe, 16 civet cats and nearly 600 skins of addax antelope, to squalid villages where the 'houses are very loathsome, being annoyed with the stinking smell of their goats'. Yet occasionally Leo alights on something more complicated. In a camp north of the Atlas, he notes a 'greater quantity of cloth, brass, iron and copper, than a man shall oftentimes find in the most rich warehouses of some cities'.

These contrasts and parallels intrigued me, and I was keen to learn more. One opportunity arose during the *moussem* of Moulay Idriss, the holy day when the guilds processed down the streets of the old town. I persuaded Najib to take me along, to see a ritual that punctured the barrier between town and country, deflated it with a bloody knife, just as it bridged the gulf between Leo's time and my own.

6

Death of a Camel

HE WAS DRESSED FOR CELEBRATION, BUT HE WAS GOING TO HIS DEATH. HIS lips flung apart, swinging cords of spittle. Two turbaned stewards were struggling to keep him out of kicking range. They criss-crossed their hands in the air, trying to hold back the baying crowd, lest anyone be knocked down by the animal's jerking legs, which flickered across the prayer hall like fur-clad switchblades.

Some had climbed up the pillars: small boys balanced on their fathers' shoulders, clawing at spandrels to keep themselves steady. Others were pitched together, backing against the walls. A little girl in a pink tracksuit peered at the camel, her tiny nose aligned to the same diagonal plane as its enormous snout. There were old women gripping the edges of their robes between their teeth, businessmen in creased suits and teenage girls with fake eyelashes; although the largest number – and the most voluble – were the young men, mobile phones ready in their hands. They were all glued together, as if by some invisible resin, pressing forward as one insistent, unified mass.

'Hold the phone for me,' said Najib. 'Go on, Nicholas. You're taller! Press the red button. My mother's gonna be really happy when she sees this.'

I could hardly say no – after all, it was Najib who had slipped me in. He had also arranged my *djellaba*, after warning me that everyone would be wearing the traditional gown tonight. I chose a cream-coloured one with stripy grey banding on the cuffs; I was quite pleased with it. So far, apart from Najib and myself, I had counted just three *djellabas* in the entire prayer hall. I was starting to wonder if Najib had some kind of secret deal with the tailor.

'Go on, make sure you get this part – this is the best.'

The cameleer was dragging the beast into the heart of the prayer hall, guiding him by a harness rope around his jaw. Hind legs dug in. Front legs paddled at the air. An eerie, agonised noise – a moan, I think, long and weary but pitched with the urgency of panic – barrelled over our heads, only half-drowned by the murmuring of the crowd. If you had come here simply out of a detached interest in sound, you might have drawn a telling conclusion about which animal – camel or human – has a greater capacity to communicate through its voice.

As the crowd drew closer, the camel keeled. The 'ship of the desert' was sinking in the storm. His roars were drowned by the goading of the crowd and he collapsed, to a rolling cheer as loud as the cries of alarm. Several men jack-knifed back to avoid being crushed by his weight. At their head was a barrel-chested goliath. Blood trickled down his arm and a knife stuck out of his fist. His expression – cracked open by a toothy flash of pride – could have been the same kind worn by champion gladiators when the Romans were driving North Africa's animals to extinction in their *colossea*. A gang of tyros leaped around him, grabbing at the knife, as if it had become some kind of talisman – an Excalibur that would ennoble anyone bold enough to hold it.

Now the camel was felled, the atmosphere shifted: still frenzied, but trimmed of fear. Breaking the banks of the twitching stewards' arms, the crowd flooded the carcase, hands and feet sliding around in the blood. Boys pasted their faces and shirts in the fluid, strutting about in masculated packs, faces glowing with a sense of belonging, being part of some transcendent, unifying experience.

'It's so good!' Najib grabbed a fistful of my arm, his brow gleaming with a scintilla of blood.

I wanted him to tell me more. 'Good' in what way exactly? But this was no time for drawn-out analysis. The first ripple of excitement was dying. The crowd was losing its firmness, its glue was drying up. Others moved into the slack: small boys with Disney logos on their zip-ups, old women in tightly knotted headscarves, young men who stripped down to their vests and smeared the blood across their bare shoulders like sun cream. I had been to other communal gatherings in Fez, such as the bath-house and Friday prayers, but this was the first one that brought the sexes together: gender division overlooked for the sacred cause of dromodocide. It reminded me of hot days in Trafalgar Square, when you see people mucking about near the fountains, mindless of the spray as it varnishes their shoulders.

'You know why we do this?'

One of the men took my hand, thumb-printing it with camel ichor. His face was a rouged mask; his eyes were pools of afterworld certainty.

'It is the tradition for our city. The camel is the favourite animal of our prophet.'

'And that means you have to *kill* it?'

'Of course. But we distribute the meat to the poor. The camel comes from the Idrissi family. They are the first dynasty of Fez, so it is a blessing for God. We do this for God, not for us.'

There was no time for further explanation. I could hear rumblings behind me, too fast to untangle the Arabic. I didn't want to outstay my welcome, and the cloying smell of the blood was driving me outside, back to the surface, like a diver running out of oxygen.

It was later in the evening that I heard a more detailed analysis of the event. I was sitting with Najib and his friend, Yusuf the pastry seller. The air around us was thick and spicy, scented by pistachio and rosewater, hot bread and the marijuana leaves Najib was chopping on the terracotta tiles of a medieval street fountain.

'You are confused,' said Yusuf, using the technical term for a sacrificial camel. 'This is because of your Western mentality. You see things too literally. You have to remember, the camel is symbolic.'

'It didn't look very symbolic.' My voice hung in the air, more shrill than I intended. It was the first animal sacrifice I'd seen, and I was feeling a little stirred. 'It was bleeding all over the floor!'

'It represents the desert.' Yusuf had a customer, so he was wrapping a kilo of walnut-filled *kataif* while he talked, weighing each sugary pancake on the scales. 'It is a symbol of us as Arabs. We are nomadic people. We built cities like Fez, but we never left the desert.' He taped down the box and handed it over on a flurry of well-wishes. 'Our biggest families must show us their camels at important events, like the *moussem* and Eid. And God appreciates this. When we sacrifice a camel, it pleases Him and He gives us many blessings for the coming year.'

Later, in a tea-house, Mansur showed me a verse in the Quran that aligned with Yusuf's words: 'Their meat will not reach Allah, nor will their blood, but what reaches Him is piety from you' (*sura* 22, 37). This verse might illuminate the theology underpinning the sacrifice, but it doesn't necessarily explain the ritual itself. Like many features of Islam, camel sacrifice long predates the faith. Among the early witnesses was Saint Nilus in the fourth century. Observing Arab nomads in Sinai, he tells us the camel 'is bound upon a rude altar of stones piled together, and when the leader of the band has thrice led the worshippers round the altar in a solemn procession accompanied with chants, he inflicts the first wound ... and in all haste drinks of the blood that gushes forth. Forthwith the whole company fall on the victim with their swords, hacking off pieces of the quivering flesh and devouring them raw.' More brutal than the event I witnessed, still it felt an awful lot closer than a gap of nearly two millennia. As with so many Christian rituals, it is moments like this, when a religion wormholes back to the roots from which it sprang, that it becomes most engrossing for the outsider.

∽

Fez truly is a magical place. After a hard day at the tannery, I felt like I had been farted out of the arse of the giant from the third voyage of Sindbad. Cocooned in my pigeon-shit miasma, there was only one way to conjure myself back to a respectable condition: every few days, Najib and I purged our odours at the Qariwiyya *hammam*.

The building dates back to medieval times and the system isn't much different from the one described by Leo Africanus. Like Leo, we had to 'pass through a cold hall, where they use to temper hot water and cold together', followed by 'a room somewhat hotter' and finally 'a third hot-house, where they sweat as much as they think good'. The main differences were that instead of wearing 'a linen cloth' to cover our 'privities', we stripped down to Y-fronts and boxer shorts; the water was no longer heated by fires 'made of nought else but beasts' dung'; and in the absence of slaves we had to 'cleanse and wash' ourselves.

Today, we passed by Mansur's gimcrack store and towed him along.

'Yes, I'm coming, but you go ahead.' He pinched his nose, waving us forward. 'You guys have no idea how much you stink!'

While Mansur picked up some fruit from a street stall, Najib and I carried on to a marble tiled passage at the back of the market. Inside, we stripped off our clothes and entered a barrel-vaulted room where light funnelled through holes in the ceiling, spotlighting the washers passing through the fug of steam. The slurp of water muffled the chatter, splashing our bodies and hissing on the stones, carrying our sweat and the yellow slick of saffron dye down the runnels at the side of the hall.

One of the regulars was the *hammam*'s official masseur, a man as formidably built as my old nomad companion Jadullah. At a nod from Mansur, he came over and treated me like a rundown machine in serious need of maintenance. He yanked my legs like draw-pumps, kneed me in the stomach, nearly snapped my coccyx and smeared black soap across my skin like axle grease. At the end of the procedure he slapped his hands, as if to say 'and don't think I'll ever let you do that to *me*', and left me alone.

'You will sleep like a baby tonight,' said Mansur. He was right.

What most appealed about the *hammam* was the social side of it. People sat in groups, offering grapes and beakers of juice, rubbing each other's loosened flesh with soap. I'd bought my own bar at the henna market, beside the old asylum where Leo Africanus used to work. Nobody approached us directly, but there were flutters of chatter with the men upstream. I enjoyed those interactions, but mostly I enjoyed talking to Mansur and Najib, who were quite merciful with their Arabic constructions and kept their vocabulary to a level I could follow. Since translating hip-hop lyrics for Najib, my Arabic was starting to take off. At a book stall on Big Street, I had picked up a bilingual copy of *Gulliver's Travels* and was enjoying it hugely. Somehow, the experience of reading it in Arabic felt even more authentic than Swift's original: hammering away at all those complex verbal constructions was a sure way of empathising with Gulliver, lost in a world where his most basic assumptions no longer made sense.

'You like the *hammam*?' asked Najib.

We were sitting with our backs to the mould-stained wall, around a five-point star with soap scum frothing at the edges.

'Well, yes,' I said, 'it's kind of essential, isn't it? My host mother won't let me back in the house when I'm smelling of pigeon turd.'

'I come here at least twice a week,' said Najib. 'You know, in Fez every mosque has a *hammam* near it, and it is good to do these things with others. If you pray with others, God gives you a higher recompense.'

'So you go to the mosque to clean your soul and the *hammam* to clean your body?'

'Exactly. And God likes us to be clean. That is why we have the ablutions fountain in the mosque.'

'But it must be a challenge to keep clean when you work at the tannery?'

'Of course. But the tannery is part of God's work too.'

I remembered the boss pointing out the moon and the sun, linking them to the colours of the hides. For my friends in Fez, everything was linked through faith.

From *hammam* to *hamaameh* – or bath-house to bird-keeping. Later, we bought some millefeuille from Yusuf the pastry seller, and squeezed up a narrow stairwell near the Kairaouine mosque. On one side of the terrace was a wooden coop with a mesh grille, warbling with a dozen *hamaamat* – pigeons. Most were adults, but a few squabs were tucked under their mothers' purple-tinged feathers. Up here on the city's shoulders, the smell was less striking, and once Mansur lit his pipe our noses were otherwise occupied.

'This is for my free time,' Mansur explained, setting aside a couple of sticks tied with rags. 'I want to teach them to fly, but I have to take lessons from the old pigeon keepers. When I started this, I never thought it would be so hard!'[17]

Among the challenges were the frequent cleaning of the coop and the damage the pigeons wreaked around the terrace.

'My landlady gets angry,' said Mansur, 'because they put marks on the laundry and she finds their shit all over the roof.'

There was some consolation: the boss occasionally paid him a couple of dirhams for a kilo of dung, which was used in the hair-extraction process at the tannery.

Leading me over to the coop, Mansur pointed out the different colours of the wings. There was a couple, brown and grey, with tighter

---

17 For advice on dove-keeping, he could have turned to Leo Africanus, who writes about the 'keeping of doves, which are here in great plenty, of all colours. These doves they keep in certain cages or lockers on the tops of their houses, which lockers they set open twice a day, to wit, morning and evening, delighting greatly to see them fly.'

faces and more streamlined feathers, bred as *voyageurs* – descendants of the carrier pigeons who used to deliver the sultans' mail. Mansur was hoping to enter them one day in an intercity racing contest.

'You see how they beat their wings? But they cannot fly. A wing has great power but it cannot open a door.'

My smile was bittersweet. I could see where this was going. I had told my friends about my plans to move on. Najib, whose social life I had been funding for the last few weeks, had not taken it well. We sat down for glasses of tea, while Mansur produced a BIC lighter and a sachet from his back pocket, rolling a ball of *keef* on the table. For my friends, there was no contradiction between piety and pipe. Like many of the Muslims I know, they recognised and accepted the tension between reality and religious ideals. In this case, the *keef* was *burqadi*: the best shit in town. The BIC glowed and Mansur's fingers rubbed together at the head of his pipe, then a gasp of smoke and the stem hovered under my nose.

'I want to ask you something.' Mansur leaned back, resealing the bag with his lighter. 'Why do you travel?' His eyes flickered with curiosity. 'Don't you love your family? The people at home?'

'Of course I do.' The directness of his question threw me, and I could feel my voice cracking slightly. 'Yes, I do, very much, but... Well, I guess I love travelling too, and if I don't travel for a long time then I think I become a bit of a pain.'

He nodded, but his face flattened with incredulity. It was a good moment to change the subject, so I turned my attention back to the pigeons.

'If Nicholas was one of your pigeons,' said Najib, looking at me crossly, 'he would fly away as soon as you opened the cage.'

'But they come back,' Mansur pointed out. 'They always come back.'

'Only because you've trained them.'

'Exactly. All of us are trained, by our fathers, our mothers, our teachers. And that is why we always come back. Even you. You will travel a long time perhaps, and see many things, but you will come back.'

'To Fez?'

'No, no, of course not. To here.'

He was about to pour another glass of tea. But before he did, he showed me what he meant, by tapping his heart.

The School for Nomads

Lesson Two: Riding

OUR SECOND DAY'S TROT BRINGS US TO THE FEATHERY SHADE OF AN ACACIA tree. Thank God for their taproots, snaking down to reach water tables that other trees are too stubby to channel. My camel drops to his brisket pads so I can dismount, and Lamina passes me the halter rope to lead him to refreshment. We have been walking for most of the night, but now in some ways is the harder part: 12 hours of lounging around. Conserving our energy, like a miser protecting his gold.

When the baggage has been arranged, the camels watered and their fetlocks hobbled, we retreat under the acacia. There, we nap and pick the burrs of cram-cram from each other's trousers and feet. Lamina is particularly fastidious about this. He has a pair of tweezers, specially procured for the task. He runs a hand over my ankles and rubs my sides. When he finds a rogue burr, he plunges and holds up the offending thorn for inspection, shaking his head, like a schoolmaster who has found a mischievously placed pin just in time.

'Now,' he announces, 'we must see if you are studying well.'

The time has come for my first test. To be specific: I have been called on to make the tea.

I dig a rut of sand, pile some sticks on top and light a fire (helped by Abdul-Hakim to get it going). I scoop sugar and tea into the glasses, half fill the pot with water and wait for it to boil. The end result – aerated by enough outpourings to satisfy a Tuareg – is deemed a modest success. Although, Lamina points out, it could have done with more froth on the second glass.

Lessons now come thick and fast. In the laboratory brightness of daytime, there is no excuse to miss the details of saddling. I try my best to take it all in: the slinging of the ropes, the girthing of the saddle, the lay of the covers, the water skins balanced on either side. But there is so much to absorb, and red-hot vertical skewers of sunlight are jabbing my skin, so some of the lessons go straight through me like laser beams.

'Every camel must have water on the journey to Taoudenni,' explains Lamina, 'because the wells are not easy to find. It is important to know how much water is left in the *guerbas* (the goatskin water containers), and how far to the next well.'

To make the camels sit, he calls out a long, rasping 'ooooosh!' It has the effect of a sorcerer's incantation. Legs buckle, bellies plunge, heads remain steady on rickety necks. Lamina nooses the camel's neck, fitting the headrope over the snout, cinching it on the lower jaw, fastened with a small stick. He tells me my camel's name – 'Naksheh' – offering the word like a reward. I press a foot on the nape, trying to be gentle now we've been introduced, but also trying to be firm because I don't want to screw it up.

'Now,' says Lamina, dropping the headrope, 'you must ride him yourself.'

I feel like a rookie about to perform before a packed stadium. Tugging left or right to steer direction, I click my tongue between my teeth and flute my lips: 'oooshhhh-oosh-oosh-oosh!' To help spur Naksheh, Abdul-Hakim perches on the back of the cantle. His whispering voice is a magic wand. The camel bounces and shudders, his lumbering walk turns to a trot, growing steadily, alarmingly, into a gallop. Whenever I feel I am losing control, I grab the nape fur in a panicky hold and yank him to an awkward deceleration, like slamming the brakes in fifth gear.

Naksheh is not the only new name of the afternoon. 'Nicholas' sounds too outlandish on the Berabish tongue, so I am asked to choose something more suitable. My answer is instant: 'Yusuf!'

The dream interpreter and colourful coat wearer – Joseph in the Bible, whose story is as vivid in the Quran as in the Old Testament. While I was living in Fez, there was a mini-series about him on the telly, and I was hooked.

Lamina's eyes gleam between his kindly crow's feet: 'God protect you, this choice is a good one.'

I just hope my new name won't encourage my companions to throw me down a well. My cameleering isn't exactly a strong recommendation in my favour.

'You must speak to him more,' urges Lamina.

I am finding the sounds hard to master. They start low in the belly and come out as delicately as the notes from a flute, soft but tremulous. For Lamina they are second nature, so he doesn't drill me with technical tips and procedures. As for the riding, he is still cautious with me. On steep downhill stretches, he tells me to couch. When the ground is flat enough, he gestures for me to mount, advising a slow pace and a backward lean. The camel's legs are well designed for insertion and extraction, like surgical needles excavating pliable tissue, but on gradients they are vulnerable.

A flat plain spreads towards the well of Aketkod and blast debris rings under the camels' tread: shards of iron castings, splinters of shell. The patinated karst of the *hammada* (the crust where the sun has hardened the desert surface) vibrates through Naksheh's legs, shockwaving my diaphragm and echo-locating every major bone in my body. The surface fractures, sandy grains thicken, and for a few minutes I feel like I'm getting the hang of it. What a joy to be out here, out in the Sahara, the heat of a beast warming your thighs, wind dancing in the stubble-grass, dunes cresting in the distance, the earth and sky exchanging one another's light, melding in a pearly, lemony tapestry of graduating horizontal bands. *This is life... this is nature... this is IT!*

❧

Has any domesticated animal been more cruelly maligned? John Ruskin dismissed the camel as 'disobedient and ill-tempered'. Edmund Spenser made it his image of 'Avarice' in *The Faerie Queene*. More recently, in *Arabia through the Looking Glass*, Jonathan Raban declared that 'no animal is more stolid, stupid and utterly unresponsive'. But the most withering put-down is surely the Nobel laureate Elias Canetti's: 'They put me in mind of elderly English ladies taking tea together, dignified and apparently bored but unable entirely to conceal the malice with which they observe everything around them.'

I cannot disagree more passionately! Leo Africanus spent a fair amount of time on camels, and he called them 'gentle and domesticall beasts'. I don't always find them the easiest creatures to ride, but I am right behind René Caillié, who declared: 'What a masterpiece of nature's workmanship is the camel!' Ungainly they might look, as if a giraffe had mated with a put-you-up, but few animals are so perfectly designed for their environment.

Without camels, the desert would have remained as mysterious to nomads as it is to the town-dwellers on its rim. 'Once the North African nomads became acquainted with this highly useful animal,' writes Nehemiah Levtzion, 'they lost no time in adopting it. Mounted on camels, the nomad tribes, roaming beyond the *limes* which protected the agricultural population of Roman Africa, began to move southwards into the Sahara. They settled the oases in the middle of the desert, and reached its southern fringes.' They represent a watershed in the history of the Sahara, transforming the desert into what Labelle Prussin calls 'a habitable, controllable region that could support nomadic populations'.

Now, as we trek north, I am juddering on top of 900 pounds of muscular grace: the perfect desert vehicle, able to consume 120 litres at a single watering, to modulate his body temperature according to the heat, to reflect sunlight off his coat and pee backwards (which may not be so good in a caravan, but is certainly useful in small numbers); endowed with a third eyelid, a tripartite stomach and muscular nose flaps that keep out the sand. What a masterpiece indeed – René Caillié was right!

That said, I can't wait to get off the bloody thing. My thighs are absolutely killing me. The skin around the top of my legs is so tender I am pretty sure it will soon peel off. I can only ride a few more miles; the rest of the night I walk, a cumbersome weight lolloping through powder. Lamina is walking as well, and he advises me to watch him, because even leading a camel on foot can be fraught. We slow down on downhill stretches, stopping every few moments so the camels don't trip; I have to yank Naksheh away from the bunch-grass, because he over-ate at the last stop and now his breath is as odorous as a tannery at dusk. A few days ago, the smell would have made me want to gag. Now it is weirdly addictive: a new, camelesque sensation that binds me to my stinky steed. And hey, it's not like I'm smelling of Bleu de Chanel these days!

I look into the distance, where Jadullah is riding so tight to his beast they seem to be centaurised. Oh, if only if only if only I could ride like that! Right now, there is nothing I want more, nothing in the whole world, than to handle a camel as brilliantly as Jadullah. In the school of nomadism, to ride as one with your steed – that would be a sign of real distinction!

Part Three

Mountain

You shall find many among the Africans which live altogether a shepherd's or drover's life, inhabiting upon the beginning of Mount Atlas, and being dispersed here and there over the same mountain.

Leo Africanus, *The Description of Africa and the Things Therein Contained*

7

The Sultan's Road to Azrou

THE HEAVENS WERE WEEPING. WATER THREADED THE WINDOWS OF THE BUS, a liquid veil over the suburbs. By the time the rain cleared, we were in open country. The muscular roots of pines and cypresses entwined with moss-clad oaks whose wrinkly branches tickled the maize and barley stubble. The bus climbed higher up the Atlas and cloud enshrouded us, muffling the fields behind the pines like curtains at the back of peristyle courtyards. It felt like some transitional stage: the sterile whiteness of limbo, a process of cleansing before entering a new world.

I was on the slow road to Timbuktu, riding Route No. 24. More grandly known as the Sultan's Road, it was cut through the mountains in medieval times to link Fez to the trans-Saharan trade. Outcrops of shale threw back the light and volcanic cones shouldered between ranked cedar, nudging the boles of the holm oaks.

The Middle Atlas is Morocco's reservoir. Sinkholes and caves tunnel under the limestone plateaus, licked by some of the country's most important river systems. But natural irrigation is not enough. The soil is poor and the harsh climate is scribbled on the faces of the villagers you pass. The Middle Atlas is no bread basket – it has always worked best as grazing land. It was here, in the hills around Azrou, that I hoped for a meeting with mountain nomads.

A few miles south of the hill station of Ifrane, an arc of wooded slopes shielded a black volcanic outcrop, like bodyguards flanking their king. Flat-roofed houses rippled out from a green-tiled mosque. Texting teenagers darted between men in hooded gowns and shawled women with tribal spots on their chins. I had arrived in Azrou.

'This is very unfortunate.'

The owner of my hotel was sitting under a deep-pile rug and an embroidered burnous, tipping his head gently. I had asked where I might go in search of nomads. He clasped his hands together for the prognosis, like a doctor delivering bad news: 'It was better if you came some years earlier.'

This was not my first journey to the Moroccan highlands. A couple of years before, I had rambled in the Rif with friends from Fez, tramping through marijuana groves and swinging our legs from a rooftop while ceremonial horn blowers roused the dancers at a village wedding. The beat of timpani and the rhythms of Berber poetry chimed at a festival in the High Atlas. And the fierce winds of Mount Toubkal buffeted us on the ascent of Morocco's highest peak, before we plunged down-hill, bending our knees and following our guide's lessons in 'Berber skiing'.

The people I met on those trips were Berbers – Amazighen in their own language (a name meaning 'free' or 'noble', which is related to the Tuareg *imashaghan*). Crawling out of the lush swamp and forested highlands of Neolithic Africa, long of hair and pointed of beard, the original Amazighen mastered the horse and made a name for them-selves among the classical Mediterranean superpowers. They were chariot-riding Garamantes, unruly Gaetulians and wily Numidians, whose chiefs were decorated with ivory sceptres and purple cloaks when the Romans cast favour on them. They were also witty thinkers like Apuleius, author of *The Golden Ass* (the mad, bawdy tale of a man who slavers himself in a magic potion and metamorphoses into an ass – the only novel in Latin that has survived in its entirety), who also concocted a treatise on daemons that was criticised by his fellow Berber, Saint Augustine of Hippo.

Apuleius and Augustine, along with later luminaries such as the traveller Ibn Batutta and Saint Adrian of Canterbury, rip a big hole through the name foisted on their people. It was coined by the Romans from the Greek word for outsiders, *barbaroi*. Awkwardly enduring in English as 'barbarians', it was adopted by the Arabs, when they estab-lished the province of Ifriqiya in the late seventh century, because it tallied with their word for babbling. This, Leo Africanus tells us, is because 'the African tongue soundeth in the ears of the Arabians, no otherwise than the voice of beasts, which utter their sounds without any accents'. Not that the language gap mattered: Berbers weren't being rounded up for their conversation. Their women were sent to

Arabia as slave-girls, their men were enlisted. They were a boon for any army – the inclement mountains had bred them tough, muscular and barrel-chested. But this made them a pain in the butt when they refused to play ball.

Ibn Khaldun tells us they launched 12 different rebellions during the early years of Islam.[18] So indomitable were they that an Arab governor wrote to the Caliph: 'The conquest of Africa is impossible. Scarcely has a Berber tribe been exterminated than another comes to take its place.' The most iconic of all the rebels was the Kahina, a priestess with streaming hair and the gift of second sight, who drove the Arabs all the way back to Egypt in the 690s. 'The Arabs search for towns,' she proclaimed, 'for gold and for silver, but we only seek for pasturage.' She was a devoted nomad, but a terrible tactician. From Tangier to Tripoli, she promoted a policy of burning cities, smashing down walls and uprooting fruit trees. Town-dwelling Berbers were appalled, and when the Arab army returned the Kahina's under-motivated force was easily vanquished.

The history of the early Berbers attracted nobody's study more than Ibn Khaldun. It is to him that we owe so much of our knowledge about them. His familiarity with the tribes made him indispensable to the courts of the Maghrib, and Berber history was a major focus of his *Kitab al-'Ibar* ('Book of Lessons'), which expanded into a universal history. Its introduction, the *Muqaddimah*, is a seminal work in global historiography, pioneering the concept of history's cyclical nature.[19] Ibn

---

18 These were not only in Africa. A Berber commander called Munnuza, who was in charge of a crucial pass on the Pyrenees, conspired with the Duke of Aquitaine to overthrow the Arabs – as revenge for his people's treatment in North Africa. The revolt was suppressed, but it is a symptom of the tensions that derailed the Arabs' invasion of Europe and led to their defeat at Poitiers in 732 AD. Without the recalcitrance of the Berbers, the history of Western Europe might have been very different.

19 This theory can be applied to events like the French Revolution (where radicals turned to counter-revolutionaries and distributors of venal offices), Soviet Russia and the Ayatollahs' Iran, as much as to the North African kingdoms on which Ibn Khaldun focused. No wonder British historian Arnold J Toynbee wrote of the *Muqaddimah*: 'he has created and formulated a philosophy of history which is undoubtedly the greatest work of its kind that has ever yet been created by any mind in any time or place'. What makes Ibn Khaldun all the more remarkable is the abundance of groundbreaking economic, philosophical and sociological matter in which this theory is enmeshed. For example, his analysis of the negative impact of an overbearing state on a lively economy (and the parallel significance of judicious public works) anticipated John Maynard Keynes; and he identified coordinated specialisation as the primary source of economic surplus three centuries before Adam Smith.

Khaldun was a city boy, nomadic only in the sense that he saw service with seven different royal masters (from most of whom he was forced to leave in a hurry – he was a great scholar, but a hapless schemer). It was during one of his flights, holed up in the Algerian highlands under the protection of the Berber Kabyles, that he wrote the *Muqaddimah*. The Berbers, in his view, were the acme of rural toughness, yoked together by *asabiyyah* (which is usually translated as 'solidarity' or 'tribalism'). It was this solidarity that made them such a formidable force against the heterodox town-dwellers; and applying Ibn Khaldun's theory more broadly, it was *asabiyyah* that enabled so many of the region's nomadic tribes to defy the city governors who would enchain them and build powerful kingdoms of their own.

The Amazighen roar through the history of medieval North Africa – whether hillmen like the puritanical Almohads or desert Berbers, such as the drum-beating Almoravids who thwarted the Christian armies of eleventh-century Spain. But over the centuries, road building and centralised rule started to make their mark. By the time Leo Africanus travelled across the region, the mountain people were in the doldrums. Occasionally, Leo came across a chieftain wealthy enough to send slaves and exotic beasts as tribute; but more often they were like the 'base and witless people' he met in the High Atlas, who refused to let him go until he had judged 'all the quarrels and controversies of the inhabitants'. He was rewarded for his pains with a cockerel, some onions and garlic, a pile of nuts and a goat: a frugal reward, 'by reason that there was no money in all the said mountain', which underlines the indigence so many Berber communities were suffering at this time.

It was an afternoon for pastries and café-sitting. The hotel owner had lent me a regional map, and I unfolded it at a chrome table in a smoky café, grazing on a slab of millefeuille. A silver-framed photograph of King Mohammed, looking plump in a cream burnous, hung above me, squatting over the pastries like an advert – *eat these cakes and one day you too could be king* – rather than the state propaganda it actually was.

While I was poring over cartographic cross-hatchings and contours, I felt the sunbeam of other people's attention. Three men were eye-balling me from a neighbouring table. With their bronze faces and high cheekbones, they looked as if they had been hewn out of the nearby limestone. One of them spoke French, which was fortunate, because I couldn't understand a word of their Arabic. It was heavily aspirated, as if to save wasting too much breath on it. They only spoke it, they told me, when there was no alternative. Their mother tongue was Tamazight, the language of the Middle Atlas Berbers.

The Francophone was called Jagha. Lean and tight-coiled, with sharp cheekbones and sunken eye sockets, he had the haunted look of someone fresh out of prison. He told me he had been living in Casablanca, but had given up because it was impossible to find work.

'*Le chômage, quel dommage*! Unemployment, what a shame!'

We sat back, glancing at a football match on the overhead tele-vision, and I asked a few simple questions: how life had changed in the mountains over the decades, and whether there were laws against strip-ping the wood for firewood (there were – pastureland is still technically common, depending on intertribal agreements over grazing ranges, but the forests belong to the state). I struggled to make headway with my halting Arabic, but the others were keen to talk and advise me on my route over the next few days, and Jagha edged his chair closer to explain what they were saying.

'My friend Bushtu wants you to know that life is very hard if you are Amazigh.'

Drawing on a cigarette, Bushtu talked fast, his words and the smoke fusing with Jagha's translation.

'In the time of King Hassan,' he explained, 'it was really difficult. There was a big policy of Arabisation. It's because of the French. They used a policy of divide and rule to keep us apart from the Arabs. And they were very angry with us, because it was always the Amazighen who fought against them.'

Bushtu and his thick-browed friend, Jamal, both leaned forward. They weren't keen on Jagha monopolising the conversation, just because he happened to speak the tongue of the *colons*. Jamal probed the air with his bony middle finger, drawing the five-point star that is the symbol of the Moroccan monarchy. Then he snapped his fist and rubbed his fingers, crumbling the invisible image to dust.

'He wants to tell you something,' Jagha explained. 'When the French came to Morocco, it was the king who invited them. He betrayed the Moroccan people, because he was scared the Amazighen would seize the power. Because of this, there have been many tensions between us. We don't like to trust Arabs. They made a lot of promises but they never kept them. You know what we say? We say if you see an Arab, you always find a snake.'

'But now the king's married to an Amazigh,' I said. 'Haven't there been improvements?'

'Of course. In my father's time, you never even heard Tamazight on the radio and there were no newspapers in our language. King Hassan set up the Institute for Arabisation. They wanted to make sure we lost our identity. If people wanted to register their children they couldn't use Amazigh names. Now, there have been some concessions, but it isn't enough. Many people from the villages, they went to Fez or Meknès or Casablanca to find work, but the Arabs won't give them any work because they say we don't speak good Arabic. Our country has a lot of economic problems, and it is the Amazighen who suffer the most.'

'The past resembles the future more than one drop of water another,' declared Ibn Khaldun. Reading around the cycle of invasion and oppression endured by the Berbers, you get his point. 'After the preaching of Islam,' he relates, 'the Arab armies penetrated into the Maghrib and captured all the cities of the country; but they did not establish themselves there as tent-dwellers or as nomads, since their need to make sure of their dominion in the Maghrib compelled them to keep to the towns.' For a while, the going was good. But as the Middle Ages stumbled towards the modern era, the Berbers were driven higher into the mountains, and deeper into the Maghrib's least accessible corners. By the time the French started casting their net in North Africa, the nomads were shut away in their mountainholds, as isolated as desert monks – which made them perfect fodder for the colonialists.

Roaming the Atlas hills in the nineteenth century, map-carrying ethnologues engineered a revival of Berber self-awareness, translating poems and key texts like Ibn Khaldun's *Muqaddimah*, which Leo Africanus had introduced to the West. Sometimes, this was spurred by genuine scholarly curiosity. More often, monocled colonels were behind the work of the academics, keen to establish what the French sociologist Jacques Berque described as 'a Berber reserve, a sort of national park which was to be sheltered from the ideologies of the plain'. Political institutions emphasised the division: the urban population was administered by *shariah* (Islamic law), but the tribal *izref* code was maintained in the mountains.

A neat divide and rule was the plan, but the policy ricocheted against the *colons*. Pan-Islamic preachers accused them of evangelising. Protests were organised and prayers given for 'our Berber brothers' in the mosques; polemics were published in the nationalist press and included in a 'Plan de Reforme' submitted to the colonialists in 1934.

Meanwhile, the Berbers were rising – showing those faint-hearted town dwellers what insurrection is all about. And, had this still been the eighth century, they might have succeeded. But they were fighting a modern European army: chutzpah and solidarity were no match for state-of-the-art military equipment and heaps of cash. Whether buying off the Sultan's *caids* (local chiefs) in the High Atlas or strafing the Rif with aeroplane bombs, the French army did a textbook job. Even more disastrous, if less dramatic, were the restrictions on movement, which forced nomadic Berbers to spend all year in summer or winter pastures. 'The result', writes anthropologist John Shoup, 'was financial ruin as their livestock starved and died from the lack of grazing, forcing the tribes to submit to French control.'

Now triumphant, the protectorate followed the model of previous North African invaders. Berbers were conscripted into the *Armée d'Afrique*, as *goumiers* or native soldiers (they excelled at Monte Cassino but also committed mass rapes of thousands of Italian women). While this worked to the French advantage in the short term, it also increased contact between Berber and Arab. 'Berber-speaking areas

... became more and more integrated,' writes the historian Jonathan Wyrtzen, '... due to the increased ease of travel, the enlistment or conscription of much of the male population into the colonial army, and economic upheaval that encouraged, or forced, much of this population to migrate to the cities.' Like Apuleius's hero in *The Golden Ass*, the French had cast the wrong spell. Fusion instead of division was their legacy, doing more to spread orthodox Islam in the mountains than anyone else in the last millennium, inspiring alliances that would bounce them back across the Mediterranean.

The fire that burned out French rule in North Africa was lit by the assassination of a trade unionist in Tunisia (the same country in which the Arab Spring would spark, six decades later: another of Ibn Khaldun's timeless drops of water). Like those recent conflagrations, the 1950s revolts identified themselves as pan-Arabist – despite the heavy Berber involvement. This left the Berbers in an uncomfortable position when independence finally came. Fenced outside the triumphant national identity, they were vulnerable to accusations of anti-patriotism. Their language and culture were oppressed and the very act of listening to Tamazight radio was imprisonable until the 1990s.

In the later years of King Hassan's reign, and particularly during the era of Mohammed VI, there had been developments. These included the establishment of a Royal Institute of Amazigh Culture in 2001 (although critics accused it of 'folklorising' Berber culture and co-opting Amazigh activist groups). Yet it was the Arab Spring that did more than anything to thaw the glacier around Amazigh self-expression. King Mohammed had no wish to join the growing roster of fallen North African rulers, so he reached out to the people who represented around 40 per cent of his subjects. Since my first visit a couple of years before, there had been noticeable change: improvements in cultural rights, signs in the Tifinagh script appearing above schools and on buses, Tamazight accepted as an official language in the new constitution. Nevertheless, there were prevailing economic issues, as Jagha suggested, that would be harder to resolve.

8

Market Forces

EVERY TUESDAY, AZROU HOSTS A MARKET. ONE OF THE BIGGEST IN THE region, it draws farmers and herdsmen from all over the Atlas. It takes place on the outskirts of town: a patchwork camp pitched behind an arched gateway. Ripped-open rice sacks, canopies and parasols jostle together, shielding the stalls from the sun. A water carrier in a red leather hat chimes a bell, filling tin cups from a goatskin slung over his shoulder. Popcorn rattles out of a gas-powered bucket. A garlic seller balances a set of weighing scales on the handles of his trolley cart.

For Middle Atlas nomads, this place is Ikea, Tesco and Wickes all in one. Tent poles, rubber shoes, wide-brimmed straw hats, donkey saddles, sacks of flour, gas canisters, metal feed buckets, tin packing trunks, shepherds' crooks with dyed leather handles: the market has it all. The centrepiece is at the back: the chief ingredients of nomadic life, perfumed like any English county fair by the tang of truck fuel and the gassy odours of animal shit.

Lowing, bleating and howling, livestock strafe the air with laryngeal whines, semibreves of panic, deep *basso* moans. I tried to count how many there were, but gave up and asked one of the regulars – he estimated the day's intake at 4000 animals. Glossy, lanolin-smelling curls glistened on the backs of brown-faced Timahdite sheep. Fluked tails tapered behind polled ewes, while dandyish rams eyed them up, locks tendrilling and horns spiralling magnificently. There were whitefaces, blackfaces, pied panda-faces. There were black-haired goats, appreciated for their resistance to cold, with horns like spires of barley sugar; and a dozen breeds of cattle, including local tan and chestnut breeds and map-backed Holstein-Friesians, which fetched the best prices for their high dairy production (around 10,000 *dirhams* per head, equivalent to £7000); and there were calves with cut-off bottle ends strapped over their muzzles to stop them drinking their mothers' milk.

The owners stood beside the clustered herds, while potential customers came over to haggle, tweaking the cows' udders, pinching ears and tails, cupping the billy goats' balls and pressing down on the rumps of the ewes.

'This is the ancient method,' one customer told me. 'Anybody who wants to sell his animals can bring them here. There is no inspector to pay, but you have to make a contract saying the price and that it is in good health and hasn't been stolen.'

Most of the animals were marked in some way. Clipped tags poked out of cattle ears, coloured numbers streaked the backs of sheep. By the middle of the day, when hundreds of sales had been made, there was a mass confusion of colour. Newly assembled flocks sported three or four different shades of paint, while contented-looking owners cradled the strays in their arms, legs strung together to stop them returning to their old herds.

Axle deep in the muddy hill above the market were trucks to take the stock back to the mountains. Hands of Fatima hung from the windscreens of Hiluxes and Mitsubishis, between pictures of the king and tasselled verses from the Quran. By noon, they were packed. Animals squeezed together like rows of *babouches* in a leather store, the luckier ones plugging their mouths to the openings, sucking in diesel instead of the stench of shit inside. The rattling of engines and lock-bars were the only sounds that matched the sheep: a reminder that humans were in control, however much the animals might protest.

Like the sellers I had met in the skin market near Fez, they all spoke dialects of Tamazight. Some of them were farmers who cultivated fields, but many were nomads who lived in the mountains, grazing their animals on the available pasture. I told them my plans – heading up mountain towards the village of Ain Leuh – and they tipped their heads in approval. 'There is good grazing in that area,' one of them said. I wondered how they had brought their animals to the market. Presumably they didn't have cars?

'We come with the farmers from the village,' explained an elderly *bedawi* in a woollen burnous. 'There are three of us in one truck and at the end of the day we take back the animals we haven't sold. We paint different colours on their backs, so we can't mistake them.'

'Besides,' said his friend, 'they are ours. We don't need paint to recognise them.'

I thought of Lamina and other nomads I had met, their animals so bound up in their lives they were as familiar as household pets.

So many herders were milling about, surrounded by so much live-stock, embroiled in such a roaring trade, it seemed the country was in rude health. But strolling back into town, I met a *kilim* seller who told a different story. Ahmed Zahid was in a good position to know – he ran the Bazaar Salama, one of Azrou's top carpet emporia, stocked with loom-woven textiles from nomad camps all over the region, which he personally visited to seek out their products.

'Look at all the houses they're building in town,' he said. 'There's so much pressure on nomads to bring their children to school – and then how do they continue their life? So they take work in a café, or selling mobile phone credit, or helping to build all the houses. Being a nomad has never been harder, because now so much land is privately owned. The government has arrangements with most of the tribes, but the land for grazing is much less than it used to be, so even if they are living in the mountains, people can't move around as much.'

❧

I saw what Ahmed was talking about when I strolled out of Azrou the next morning. Unpainted breezeblock pronged the sky with rebars. Mounds of cement lolled beside stacks of pipes and a brick hod that was acting as a lookout post for ravens. The red bottlecap of Coca-Cola flashed on the wall of a distribution centre, making the tufted grass look pale and anaemic. A shepherd was leading his flock nearby. I waved to him, and he seemed to stop and look at me; until I realised he was looking at the billboard behind me. It was advertising a new five-storey condominium and the logo read: 'For a comfortable and happy life'. I wondered how long he would hold out.

At last I was in the countryside: a taste of sweet, cool air, laced with animal sulphides. Yet I was still far from nomad terrain. Compartmentalisation was everywhere: chickenwire and picket fences, drystone walls and barriers made from rows of Barbary figs, guarded by green cladode pads bristling with barbs. The freedom of the open country was nowhere to be seen. You couldn't even stray off the roadside without being heckled by dogs. Apoplectic barks flailed my ears, dishing out canine threats that didn't take much imagination to translate: '*You son of a whore, get away from my master's cherry orchard or I'll spray the road with your ankleblood!*' '*One more step towards this fig grove and the next time you see your toes they'll be coming out of my arse!*'

The humans were more welcoming. A farmer in an olive grove showed me a spring. The water drummed in my bottle and stung my palate with freshness. A teenager on a tractor threw a hearty wave from his cab. And when I sat on the wall of a sheepfold to eat my lunch, a couple of children beckoned me inside their limestone cottage, where their mother chatted away, telling of her visit to Fez nine years previously, while unbuttoning her shift to feed her newest (and eleventh) baby. Without ever losing the thread of the conversation, she massaged and kneaded her breast to make her milk more accessible. All this time she kept her headscarf on, and carefully put it back in place when it was in danger of slipping. Sitting beside this garrulous lady, tucking into my goat's-cheese sandwich while her lactating nipple quivered in the corner of my eye, I had already learned more (about how maternal needs override the modesty prescribed in Islam – or, to put it another way, how nature trumps religion when you are living so close to it) than hours on the urban *passegiata* could teach me.

The land was growing rougher. Knobs and tendons burst through the sillion, shedding fences like King Kong snapping his chains. Mantled with cypresses, blue juniper and giant cedars a hundred feet high, the hills tilted ever steeper. Behind oleander shrubs and picnic rugs of poppies, sheep tumbled down the slope like scree. The metamorphosis was exciting, but the gradient was exhausting. My thighs were stiffening, my heart beating to the altitude. A shared taxi squiggled up the road from Azrou and I stuck out my thumb, pinching back the shame. *Save your feet for tomorrow.*

Ain Leuh was a pretty village of winding alleys and limestone guesthouses, tucked beneath a pinnacle of cedars that looked like a CGI backdrop projected from the Alps. I took a bed above a tea-house for just under £2. There were cigarette butts floating in the communal basin and the mattress felt like it had been chipped out of a nearby tor. All in all, I would say the price was spot on.

In the evening, men in hooded gowns filled the piazza like attendees at a *Star Wars* convention, ringed in spinning circuits of teenage roller-bladers. A street-corner rotisserie dished up spicy 'Berber omelettes'. I ended up sharing one with a jittery *keef* addict who displayed the scars he had earned from fighting for scraps with the local cats. If I wasn't on a mission, who knows what friendship might have emerged? But he summed up Ain Leuh's atmosphere for me: a paradise lost. Villages were too much like towns; I needed a clean break. Tomorrow night, I promised myself, would be spent in the hills.

9

The Hunt for Aziza's Lost Cattle

THE NEXT MORNING, I COULD HEAR THE PLAINTIVE HOO-HOO-HOO OF WOOD pigeons. There was an azure rustle in the trees, but the African blue tits were acting coy. Hopefully, the nomads would prove less elusive.

Switchback roads cleaved the forests of the Aguelmouss massif. The hills tilted sharply, as if they were trying to push me back to the village. I had set out with firm intentions straight after breakfast. But it wasn't until an hour's strolling in the cool shade of the cedars that I was struck by one of those Homer Simpson 'doh!' moments: I had managed to evacuate town with only a small bottle of water and not a crumb of food. Hmmmm.... After congratulating myself on my immaculate preparations, I decided to cross my fingers for rural hospitality. Going backwards always feels wrong. And, like the ping of good chance in a fairytale, the path offered encouragement. Sliding downslope to pick a handful of cherries, I piled them into my backpack pocket, in case they were the landscape's only freebie.

The road was as smooth as a bowling alley, and the air hurled by the trucks nearly skittled me. In the interests of avoiding my impending fate as roadkill, I clambered up a knoll. Scree threaded the grass-coated hills like gingerbread crumbs laid down by giants. I picked my way carefully, wary of tearing my boots. This was a land that ran by its own rules, and I had yet to learn what they were.

Across a valley, there was a fluctuation of light, a warping in the texture of the hills. Igneous rock burst through the greenery in tough, serrated shoulders. It took a few more steps to interpret the warping – man-made material, grafted to the native skin of the rock. Slowly, more material accumulated: a palisade of thorns, ribbed plastic sheeting held down with stones, cotton gowns hung to dry from strings lashed to wooden poles. I stepped closer, pausing to flick through the Tamazight phrases I had scribbled in my notebook. They were already forming on my lips when my presence was registered by the household guard.

'*Get the hell out of here, you pasty-faced turd-brain!*'

So barked the dog. Furious yellow eyes flashed above slavering fangs, driving me to the safe haven of a hilltop. There was another dwelling nearby, rice sacks rattling in the wind above a drystone sheep pen. I sucked in my breath and bellowed the Islamic greeting.

'*Salaam-u aleykum!* Peace be upon you!'

Above a limestone crag flashed a pair of dark eyes. Two hands, tattooed with henna, gripped the feldspar. My tentative steps acted like the pressure on an alarm sensor. A dog pounced over the ridge. He was barely a leap from my ankles when the girl stilled him with a single command, and he turned back on his track, head dipping in disappointment. She didn't move or make any other gesture of welcome, but watched me, her smooth, coppery brow creased with caution.

'*Azul! M'nik a'atgeed?* Hello! How are you?'

She returned the greeting warily. I stepped a little closer. She looked about 12 or 13. There was a flash of pink further back; another child in a tracksuit.

'Do you have bread?' I asked in Arabic.

A few coins gleamed on my palm. A chance to stock up on food, perhaps. I reached forward to offer them, but she clicked her teeth.

'*Hashuma.*'

The Berber honour code. I was in luck! If this family subscribed to *hashuma*, they were unlikely to set the dogs on me. The pink tracksuit belonged to a curly-haired boy called Sufyan. His sister's name was Khadija. They stared at me for what felt like a really long time, eyes wide with fascination. Eventually, Khadija whispered something to Sufyan and he sat down on the crag, rolling up his tracksuit trousers. There was a burst blister on his ankle.

'*Tibb*,' said Khadija. 'Medicine.'

So I got to work. Unzipping my medical kit from my backpack, I scissored off an alcohol pad, wiped off the dirt, applied a few drops of antibiotic ointment and sealed the wound with a plaster. Later, Khadija brought a teapot and some hard bread, cooked in a clay stove at the back of their hut, and showed me some black granules of cumin. Like generations of Berbers, they had been using natural resources to keep their bodies together.

In all Morocco's major towns there are 'Berber pharmacies', where you can find jars of saffron (to increase the blood flow) and cayenne pepper (to fight bacteria), along with jaguar powder breast-firming cream, hair-repairing snake oil and packets of ostrich fat to relieve back pains. Back in Fez, I had often browsed the shadowy stalls of the 'Witches' Market', across the street from Leo Africanus's old hospital. I peered into rusty cages, locking eyes with chameleons and tortoises and dusty-spined hedgehogs. Once I passed a woman in full *niqab*, carrying a packet of rhino horn powder to the counter ('*traitement le faiblesse sexuelle*' read the label). Another time I met an old lady who needed help pulling down a long-tailed skink hanging over a spice jar. She was buying it, she told me, to help her husband's diabetes. Judging by the weary lines on her face, I suspect it was a last resort.

Neither the rhino powder nor the skink was likely to solve the customers' problems. The popularity of such remedies (and their unfortunate impact on endangered species) is boosted by tradition and the efficacy of other natural cures. Wandering around the Atlas and meeting Berbers in the desert, I came across people using argan oil to treat skin complaints, inhaling cumin seeds to clear their sinuses, using ginger as an anti-inflammatory and cleaning their teeth with sticks of fibrous, antiseptic miswak. In communities that can't depend on social welfare or access to city hospitals, knowing the uses of the local botany can be the difference between life and death.

Sufyan's injury wasn't serious, and in such a craggy environment there would be plenty more. Still, the medicine was a way of bonding, and Khadija thanked me with a glass of tea and a much appreciated flatbread. I wished I could say more than the Tamazight greeting, but as a first encounter it fired me up for the day.

I felt marvellous: I had managed to hold down half a conversation with two Berber children. I marched out of there like I had slain a dragon. The stony valley slid beneath my feet, scree crumbled down the plain, my feet dug into a rocky divot. Then, like a trapdoor sprung by a secret button, the earth came walloping up and slapped me in the face.

One advantage of being in the open country is there are few people to witness your pratfalls. A herdsman was striding in the distance, but

I don't think he noticed. There were a few sheep nearby. A couple of them glanced up, like readers in a library when your phone goes off, but most were busy with the knoll they were mowing. I scrambled up an outcrop and, sitting in the knotty shade of a holm oak, tasted the iron on my lip. There was a bump on my forehead, but it didn't hurt particularly. Besides, it pimpled into insignificance when I looked up.

Rippling around me was the northwestern cusp of a real wound: a mighty tumescence caused by the collision between Africa and Europe around 80 million years ago. Shadow lapped the clefts of the valleys under smooth-skirted limestone façades, which gathered in tidy peaks like tagine pots in a craft store. Mountain spurs shouldered above them, receding and overlapping, fading through indigo and delphinium blue to milky invisibilities. If it weren't for the sting in my face, I would have felt like a god, or an eagle, hovering over valleys and villages, sharply cut terraces and cataracts of tumbling stone. Sprawling southwards were the vast, violet-bruised limbs of Atlas himself, condemned after a glimpse of Medusa's head to an eternity of being crawled on by ruminants. The Berbers have given these peaks a more direct but equally dramatic name: they are the *idraren draren*, the 'mountains of mountains'.

Clouds were scudding out of clefts in the hills, shadowing barley fields and fortified *kasbah* terraces; battering rams ready for battle. The sun rapiered between the viscous membranes of the clouds, slicing the colour from the uplands, turning the sheep to fleets of silhouettes. I saw a dozen herders in the course of that afternoon. They were still and watchful: teenage boys in tracksuits, a couple of thick-browed middle-agers, an old man in pinstripe trousers and a double-breasted jacket. He let me wander with him for a while, although not long enough to work out how on earth he managed to keep his sheep so close together (he had nearly a hundred of them), which he seemed to do by flicking his tongue off his top teeth: order maintained by alveolar click. His back was tent-pole straight, but his skin was as creased as the untreated hides I had handled in Fez, cross-hatched around his eyes from a lifetime of squinting at wind and sun.

'How long have you been herding?' I asked.

'Oh... it's a long time now. I was herding when the French were here.' Nearly 60 years ago. 'It was better then. Why don't you bring them back?'

We both laughed, but he shook his head, his eyes limpid and weary. 'There are too many thieves now. Yes, yes, you had them in the past, but they went by foot. Now they come with trucks and they can take away the whole flock.' He turned towards the woods and the road. 'I'm going to sell this lot in Ain Leuh. The hills are no place for us old ones.'

I was amazed he had lasted this long. The wind was whistling in my ears, but it was the heat that threw the sucker punch. Layers of air quivered at the tips of the hills and the earth was tessellated with cracks where the flocks had munched it bare. I swung my legs over a bastion of limestone, following a dragonfly the size of a toy helicopter. Sitting down, I gobbled up the bread Khadija had given me, along with the rest of my cherries, squandering their juice on my fingers. From the top of the knoll, the old man was still visible. He looked so small now, a pin-striped blob surrounded by cream-yellow thumb prints.

The sun was westering and the sky was turning a sallow, stormy colour, with tinges of violet in the gullies. It was time to find somewhere to stay, or to think about hitching a lift back to Ain Leuh. Feeling a little anxious, I worked my way back to the road through puddles of cloud shadow, until a slab of pink blocked the path.

'*Attay!* Tea!'

In front of me was little Sufyan. Like an angel, or a genie that turns up just when you need it, he was inviting me home for refreshment. Except... there was a little bit of work to do first. A flock of sheep was mincing behind him, herded by a woman in a sombrero and a red smock. A string belt tucked her smock inside a pair of baggy trousers, which were sequinned with pine needles, flakes and seed wings and strands of wool, stuck to the glue of grease and tree sap. She was Sufyan's mother Aziza, and she looked like a queen surrounded by her entourage. She teetered out of her woolly company, eyes dancing under a rim of frayed straw. Rubbing the dust from her smock, she blew on her hands to cool her skin. I pressed a hand on my heart in greeting, but she reached out to hold it, then kissed her fingertips and uttered a ritual phrase.

'We have a hundred sheep,' she told me. 'We also have three cows and two calves – but they have gone.'

'Stolen?'

'We don't know.' She tipped her head so the hat almost fell off and rolled her eyes at the heavens. 'It is all by the reckoning of God.'

And so began the hunt for Aziza's missing cattle.

The nutmeggy tang of bark, the ginny aroma of junipers, the pong of decaying mulch – a smorgasbord of sylvan smells. The canopy thickened and it was hard to see at times, but the glades were bright with an underwater kind of light, sucked down through the hoods of the saplings. Aziza led the way (she moved faster in her plastic slip-ons than I did in my rubber-soled boots), pausing to steady her hat or peer at the forest floor. Eventually she called a halt with a determined blast of breath. I crouched to see, my eyes rolling over pine needles and cedar mast, acorns and curved leaves that still held the recent rain. At last I saw it, impressed in the grassy mud: a pair of kidney-shaped pug marks.

'*Alhamdulillah!* Thanks be to God!'

Aziza led the way along the warp of the trail. We scrambled between the trees, under the yellow bustle of a woodpecker, descending around a pile of stones – an old sheepfold fallen into disuse – and followed the chime of water to a spring. Limey with algae, the concrete-rimmed drinking trough dribbled over a sward as green as pistachio.

To the hum of chatter and the splash of play, women were washing clothes and feeding their children. With bright scarves and tattooed chins, they were from the Aït Mouli tribe, and their faces shone with friendly welcome. Aziza knew them. After a seesaw of greetings, she asked if they had seen her cows. One of them had a clue – a calf spotted in a field on the other side of the wood. So Aziza adjusted her sombrero and bade them farewell.

'The water is good?' I asked, pointing to the spring.

'*Bezzaft!* Excellent!'

I refilled my bottle and took an icy glug, before following Aziza back on the trail.

Trees. Road. Scree. A few stray goats from another herd. Aziza pointed out the differences between the pug marks: goats like pairs of tapering rabbit ears; the sheep more jammed together; a pair of longer cleavings with tiny grooves at the base like the dots of exclamation marks (going by Aziza's widened expression, I think these were deer foylings).

I had learned some of the patterns in the Sahara, from watching Lamina and Jadullah. The fauna was different, but the discipline was transferable: eyes focused on the ground, quick to detect the slightest indentation, analysing depth and frequency for additional clues. It is one of the most important skills in the school of nomadic life – and one of the most fun, like solving a crossword or assembling a jigsaw puzzle. It was an echo of Lamina's tutelage, a link to the nomads I had left behind in Timbuktu. For a moment, it felt as if they were walking beside me.

We plunged deep into the woodland. The canopy shuffled the air above us, drops of light seeping through like rain. I could hear nothing out of the ordinary, but Aziza trotted ahead, cupping a hand to her ear. Suddenly, she pulled up and let out a blast: a run of yodels so fast they had the force of a trumpet. There was a rustle in the trees. The boughs parted and the leaves swung aside like a curtain. Rolling towards us, blithe as teenagers sauntering down a high street, were three cows and two calves. Aziza didn't ululate or stamp the ground in triumph or anything like that, but there was a bounce in her step all the way back to her tent, and I felt a little thrilled myself to see her reunited with her cattle.

Sufyan had invited me to join the family for tea. But I couldn't simply step inside: there was a protocol to follow. I would have to wait until Aziza's husband Rasheed came back with the rest of the flock. He loped down the hill, shoulders drooping with fatigue, his burnt coppery face smeared with sweat. Nodding to Aziza's explanation, he sat down on a boulder to ask me a few questions about my background and what I was doing here.

'It will rain tonight.' A bony finger pointed skywards, where the clouds had grown as fat as cattle ready to calve. 'You must stay somewhere warm.'

I assured him I would be fine – hey, I had a woolly jumper in my backpack! After a few words with Aziza, and much muttering about *hashuma*, he gestured to a barrel of water. Rasheed went ahead, driving in the sheep and calling off the dogs, helped by his older son Mohammed, while the other children showed me where to set the water. Phewww! For a nervous while, I had feared I might have to sleep rough on the hills. I felt like one of those down-and-outs from *The Thousand and One Nights*, picked up by a whimsical princess and carried to the family palace.

The palace, in this case, was a cuboid frame of poplar poles roofed and walled with stretched-out flour sacks. There was a drystone sheepfold at the back and a grouchy mastiff – my old nemesis from earlier – prowling by the door. Spirited past slavering jaws, I sat down on a musty-smelling deep-pile rug, beside a tin packing trunk, a pile of *kilims* and a tumulus of cooking pots. To my surprise, a pinewood wardrobe hovered behind me, heaped with clothes.

It was a wonderful evening. The children – Khadija, Mohammed, little Sufyan and his twin Maria – encircled me to stare, flick my face, pull my beard or (when they got really comfortable with me) take all the stuff out of my bag. 'Um – could I have it back now?' I asked, followed by a long-winded search around the tent, during the course of which various presents were distributed: my sun cream for Aziza, a hat for Mohammed, pens for the little ones. I could hardly begrudge them, especially when Aziza had waved off any talk of payment. '*Hashuma*,' she decreed. '*Hashuma*!' I rallied, a little less sincerely, watching her pasting her face with Ambre Solaire.

While the children gathered round to look at the pictures on my phone, Aziza bustled about, shaking a stick at a couple of chickens, sweeping a pair of cats away from the cooking pots. In the heart of the room, dead fir roots burned in a stove: a tin box on a slab of scree, speared by a steel flue pipe, which burrowed through a confluence of sacks, supporting the roof like a tent pole. An earthenware tagine pot was warming on the stovetop, adjusting the salty animal odours with the rooty smell of steamed carrots. When it was ready, Aziza emptied out a basket of bread, baked in a clay oven outside.

Later, Sufyan took me out to show me his slide – a wooden washing pallet slanting off the sheep pen. I wanted to wander about, but the dogs were really ticked off by my presence and snarled bitterly whenever I went out to pee. Ushering me back, Rasheed cut the horizon with dark looks, telling me to stay inside 'for safety'.

He wasn't comfortable with his neighbours. Some of them only pitched here briefly, he said, and 'we don't know if we can trust them'. This wasn't the solidarity of the historical sources, the *asabiyyah* that Ibn Khaldun associated with tribal people. Later, wrapped under woollen blankets inside, Rasheed talked about it.

'When my father was a child, the *jamaa* (the gathering of tribal elders) decided everything.' He wolfed down some bread and swiped his palms against each other, a mime of atrophy. 'But now it is all in the hands of the government and the district court. The *jamaa* cannot help us any more.'[20]

This was one of the reasons so many people were moving to the villages. Tribal institutions and traditional welfare, developed over centuries, were becoming impotent.

'And everyone tells us', Rasheed added, 'it is better to live in the towns.'

'But would you prefer to live in Ain Leuh?' I asked, while we soaked up the remains of the tagine.

'No! There is no work there, and where would our animals go? Anyway, this house is strong, isn't it?'

He was right. With the arrival of the stars, the heavens unleashed hell. Hammer blows of thunder drummed against the chanting of the rain. The dogs took it as a declaration of hostilities, and threw so much back they barely had any voice left to curse me in the morning. Yet, despite the ferocity of the storm, not a drop breached the tent.

---

20 Anthropologist John Shoup describes this process: 'Decision making power was taken from tribal councils and placed in the hands of elected commune councils ... Among the results of the weakening of corporate tribal cooperation has been to open common "tribal" resources to both private and commune interests. In the Middle Atlas this has resulted in serious problems of overgrazing by private flock owners (some from Meknes and Fez) and deforestation as a result of logging and demands for fuel.'

In an annexe behind the main room stood Aziza's loom. Two thick logs shouldered the warp, the yarn as tight as violin strings, with straight boughs hung as bars and string knotted to the frame at the top of the weft. Bristling across the bottom of the loom, indigo and black, the carpet-so-far looked like the skin of a mythical creature that is already half flayed. I had visited many artisanats in Fez and other cities and had heard of the 'nomad women' who wove these loop-pile carpets. Now I was looking at the proof. It was like going backstage and peeking into an actor's dressing room.

Aziza used her own wool, locking it away for several weeks after the shearing, carding it and blessing it with chants against the *djinn*. Black represented fecundity, being the colour of storm clouds; blue was the colour of wisdom. Black crosses (symbols of the earth's four corners) swooped along the weft, like the routeline on a map, girdling a trail of lozenges (which represent the vulva and sexual union).

I sat scratching my head for a while, remembering what Yusuf the pastry seller had told me in Fez: 'You see things too literally.' If a butchered camel could act as a symbol, even more so a carpet. Long after the others had gone to sleep, I sat there, holding my phone to light up the loom, wondering and thinking... imagining an epic of fecundity and fucking all over the world.

The School for Nomads

Lesson Three: Tracking

THE FIJAR, THE FIRST LIGHT OF DAWN, HAS CRESTED THE HORIZON. I SHAKE myself free of my blanket and clamber up the dune, pulled towards a burn line of pale orange. Hovering on the crest is a silhouette, still and squat like a monolith. Slowly, this resolves itself into Jadullah. His face is a bearded mask, sealed against the expressive muscularity of his body.

'*Sabah al-khair*, good morning.'

'*Sabah an-nur*,' he replies. 'Morning of light.'

Underneath him, at the bottom of the slope, is a white pavilion tent. Tugged by the wind, the flaps flare around its west-facing entrance like the hood of a cobra.

'Do you know them?' I ask.

Jadullah turns, his small brown eyes hidden deep in their hollows.

'Let us find the camels.' He springs down the slope, down towards the well and the silvery waste beyond.

The animals have roamed far in the night, driven by hunger between the wide-spaced acacias and the odd patch of bristlegrass. Standing at the foot of the dune, we can't see them across the plain, so Jadullah bends to the earth, disentangling the web of heart-shaped hoof tracks by what he knows of their habits. I am a fast walker usually, but I have a job matching him. Years of practice have taught Jadullah to slide and trench his heels, shifting his weight according to the surface. It is like trying to keep up with a goat in the Atlas. Where the earth is firm I find it easier, but the sand is sucking my feet like a marsh and my heavy breathing seems to be the only sound for miles. I can feel the blood sloshing in my head, pulsing in my fingers and toes.

'Here,' says Jadullah.

He gives no other sign. It is a good 50 metres further on before my eyes pick out what he has already detected: two of the camels, munching on an acacia bush. Approaching the nearest of them, he curls his lips, forming the magic sound 'oooooshhh'. The creature's legs buckle, his belly plunges and his knee briskets shift across the sand.

'I'll look for the other one.' Jadullah throws down a couple of ropes; his foot kicks against the swerving camel's side. 'You tie Naksheh.'

The light holds him for a lingering moment, as if he is still beside me, when I know he is already halfway across the plain. I close my eyes against the brightness and kaleidoscopes blaze inside the lids. When I open them again, Jadullah has shrunk to a dot. I turn back to Naksheh, fizzing with an uncomfortable mixture of pride – at the responsibility with which he has entrusted me – and terror. *Better not screw this up.*

Holding the rope, I slide towards Naksheh. I take a deep breath, click my teeth and lunge for his mouth. The camel's response is unequivocal: he swings out of reach and bats me away with his backside, uttering a deep-throated bray. I try again, with no more success, so I change tack, tiptoeing to the other side like a pantomime burglar. The work is painstaking, somewhere between trial and error and blind chance, but eventually the rope snags between his muscle-thickened lips. A furious, intestinal gurgle blasts my cheeks while I am tying the halter; his pink throat sac, the *doula*, glistens in his mouth like some putrid monster in a cave. Rolling under imperious brows, his enormous eyes flash disdain, as if to say: '*Who the hell are you, upstart? You think you could possibly take charge of me?*' I remember the trouble I've been having when we gallop; the embarrassment when I have to rely on Abdul-Hakim. Naksheh's legs still need to be unhobbled, but I can see them twitching, signalling an imminent kick. Crouching between front and hind quarters, I reach in, grabbing a braid of twisted grass-rope.

'You didn't finish?'

Well before he reaches me, Jadullah's face is as crisp as the camel beside me. He is riding at a trot, the stray lolloping beside him like the sidecar to a motorbike.

'I'm nearly there,' I say, a bit tetchily. I finish the job and draw myself up. No response from Jadullah, and for a few moments I hate him. He swings off his mount and busies himself around the rope I've tied, fastening the noose much tighter at the jaw.

'Next time it must be perfect,' he says, flexing a rope to tether the stray.

'Ah, Yusuf, you are making good tea now.'

Although he didn't say so at the time, now Lamina admits my first attempt was a disaster: 'You had the wrong amount of sugar and the top was very short.' He went soft on me because he didn't want me to feel discouraged.

He and Abdul-Hakim are both laughing: apparently they've been joking about my terrible tea making for the last couple of days, so it's a good thing I've moved up a grade. Jadullah doesn't join in the banter. He just drains his glass, passes it to Abdul-Hakim and strides off to feed the camels.

I am still finding Jadullah hard to crack. He is the broody one, like the Clint Eastwood character in a 1960s Western. Basilic veins wrap his forearms like rope, giving him plenty of muscle to swing himself onto the camels. Sometimes in my more paranoid moments at night, I imagine a rival tribe attacking us all, Jadullah leading our defence and picking off our assailants one by one, breaking their necks with a steely look and a ruthless twist of his wrists.

His movements have a clockwork precision: he epitomises the value of energy conservation in the desert. When he saddles the camels, each flick of his wrist secures another binding, each step propels him to another knotting point. I am in awe of the way he mounts his camel. He kicks his heels and ascends in a whip-like swirl, shaping his body to the dromedary, landing over the hump. With a hum in the mouse-like ears, he rubs the beast's neck and turns them both into a shrinking keyhole on the horizon.

Among his many skills, Jadullah is an expert tracker. Today, after we have eaten our lunch, I wander across the dune with him, on our way to unhobble the camels, and he points out some of our neighbours in this patch of desert. Judging by his burly tone, they are more welcome than the strangers in the white tent.

'*Shuf*, look!' The embroidery of scarab tracks. '*Shuf!*' The scratchy indentations of a scorpion. '*Shuf!*' The tracks of a hare (after forensic analysis of the sand, Jadullah locates a burrow and the likelihood it is still there – there are no tracks on the other side). 'The ground is all memoranda and signatures', wrote Ralph Waldo Emerson, and nowhere is this more true than the desert.

One afternoon, we spot sand-coloured carapaces flecked with brown, like miniaturised soldiers in camouflage gear: grasshoppers in an acacia bush, with very little grass to hop. Another day shows us the shallow heart prints of someone else's camels, slung between the dunes like endless valentines. I learn later that Jadullah can estimate, by the depth of the prints and the distances between them, how fast the camels are travelling and how much luggage they're carrying. We find deep-fronted hoof marks near a grove of acacias and wild donkeys braying nearby; hieroglyphic birdfoot, inscribed in the sand with the enigma of clandestine coding; the ridged wavy lines of snakes. Added together, they represent a secret survival manual for anyone who can read them.

Morning's apricot deepens to terracotta; noontime's cinnamon darkens to umber. I wander around the dunes by myself, trying to see if I can pick out the tracks, to consolidate what I have learned. Disappointingly, the sand never seems as crowded when I am alone. A few camel tracks and some donkey hooves later, I stroll back to the others. The land has withered to an ashy grey and my companions are performing the evening prayer, etching the sand with knee divots and handprints and the grooves of their smooth, domed brows, signatures left behind for the next travellers who pass by.

Tonight we are making for Lamina's encampment in an area called Dar al-Beida. Night-time riding requires a different kind of tracking – and it's one in which Lamina is especially skilled. Every once in a while he stops, twitching his fingers, recalibrating our position according to the stars. These blink and flash, their lights squealing at the tips of our noses, occasionally blurred by clouds of solar gas. I remember a line from René Caillié's *Travels*: 'though without a compass or any instrument for observation,' he noted of his Saharan guides, 'they possess so completely the habit of noticing the most minute things, that they never go astray.' Lamina points out Alnilam, listing to one side like the mast of a boat, and Al-Kaïd, at the head of a bridge of five stars. The names are familiar from books on Arabic science – the appellations used by medieval pioneers like al-Khwarizmi (who introduced Ptolemaic concepts into Islamic astronomy) or al-Shatir (whose model of the cosmos influenced the star gazers of Renaissance Europe). The stars are 'translucent, luminous, pure, free from turbidness and any kind of vileness,' wrote Ibn Tufail in the twelfth century, in a passage that reads like an ideal of nomadism, '… some of them moving around their own centre and some around the centre of another'. No wonder the people of the desert understand them so well.

For Lamina and Jadullah, the stars' names are less important than the shifting patterns. They are hazy on nomenclature, but they know which formations will guide them. Except tonight their usual expertise is failing them. Signposts may stay put, but stars and tents are rarely so obliging. The brothers shrug at each other, click their teeth and swing the camels back along our track, tacking between the dunes before a shake of Jadullah's finger shows a squat black shape in the distance. They have been away for a couple of weeks, so the camp has moved in search of new grazing: the grass is too sparse to stay in the same place for a fortnight.

Dismounting, I stroke Naksheh's flossy mane and dig out my water bottle. Lamina is clasping his hands together. He bows his head and addresses me in a voice as magnificent as the desert itself.

'*Marhaba bek al-usrah.* Welcome to the family.'

One of the tents is already up – low pitched but high peaked, a pyramid of cotton. The other lies collapsed on the ground. This is the guest tent – the nomadic living-room. Two women bustle around, hitching guy-lines with acacia pegs, lifting the T-shaped pole, carrying over a pot for the tea and a blanket for me to lie on. They look like ravens with their black get-up, their dipping, rocking movements. I want to approach them, to introduce myself. Yet a pang of anxiety holds me back. I don't want to offend Lamina by appearing too forward. Stiff from the ride, I drift into the strange pleasure of aching joints, knowing we have a few restful hours ahead. I lie down to scribble in my diary, fringed in the murmur of chatter, and fall asleep with the pen still in my...

Part Four

Dunes

The lion slumbers in his lair,
The serpent shuns the noontide glare:
But slowly wind the patient train
Of camels o'er the blasted plain,
Where they and man may brave alone
The terrors of the burning zone.

Felicia Hemans, *The Caravan in the Desert*

10

Poets of the Sahara

IMAGINE YOU ARE A SPANISH SHEPHERD IN THE YEAR 1086 AD, TRUDGING along in your braided espadrilles, your shoulders covered by a dusty cape. You've counted your sheep out of the fold, they've cropped their way up the hills of Badajoz, and now you're mounting the crest. '*Dios es misericordioso!*' you cry. For down below, the Sagrajas river looks like it is on fire.

Assembled along its banks are 70,000 Christian soldiers. Sunlight sparks off breastplates, elbow cods and the polished cruppers of their horses. Alfonso the Brave, King of Leon and Castile, is riding high, having recently captured Toledo. As for his enemy, the once-mighty Caliphate of Cordoba, it has melted into a stew of 23 antagonistic emirates, whose squabbling is as handy to the Christians as Toledo's famed steel. Yet a drumbeat is throbbing from the south. A sea of javelins and iron-spiked shields surges forward, catching a flame of its own. Its leader is a black-eyed, curly-haired, eagle-nosed warrior-king.

His name is Yusuf Ibn Tafshin. He is King of Morocco and chief of the Almoravids (*Al-mourabitoun* in the original Arabic). With his simple woollen robes, his diet of barley, meat and camel's milk, his cavalry of camel riders and the pounding beat of his drummers, his identity is nomadic to the core. It is said that his force includes representatives from every tribe in the Western Sahara. They tear the field to shreds, leaving barely a fifth of the Christian forces alive, spilling so much blood the place is renamed *az-Zallaqah* or 'slippery ground'.

Such a victory should bring plenty of spoils, but Yusuf doesn't bother hanging around. A true nomad, he has no wish to burden himself with excess baggage. 'I came not to this country for the sake of booty,' he declares. 'I came to wage jihad against the infidel and to merit the rewards promised to those who fight for the cause of God.'

Nearly a millennium later, Yusuf's capital stands where he built it,[21] on the site of an old brigands' lair near the foothills of the Atlas. Its name comes from the Tamazight root *mur* and translates as 'land of God' – 'Marrakesh'. One imagines the puritanical Yusuf would be shaking in his shroud if he knew what has become of his old bivouac: a hangout for hippies and Moschino-clad revellers, where Brad Pitt and Nicolas Sarkozy celebrate New Year and roadside billboards advertise the latest golf courses. Here is Ibn Khaldun's theory in action: several generations after sedentarisation, the tough shell of nomadic life has rubbed away, leaving a feathery surface that is easily breached.[22] It was this process that did for Ibn Tafshin's successors. Court bred and pampered, they failed to hold his gains. The last of them was decapitated by the Almohads (a tribe of mountain Berbers who formed the next wave of Maghrebi conquest) after falling off a cliff.

Nevertheless the Almoravids' legacy has survived, retaining enough juice to interest North Africa's most notorious jihadist. In 2013, after falling out with Al-Qaeda in the Maghreb, the one-eyed bandit chief Mokhtar Belmokhtar needed a name for his new faction. He chose Al-Mourabitoun, invoking Ibn Tafshin's victories against the West and his austere Islamic principles. Whether Ibn Tafshin would approve, however, of a hot-tempered ex-cigarette smuggler who sends his minions to slaughter unarmed civilians (27 hotel guests at the Radisson Blu in Bamako, for example, murdered in November 2015) and never places himself in the crossfire is another matter.

Marrakesh may be Morocco's modern-day Land of Cockaigne, but in Ibn Tafshin's day it still had the atmosphere of a nomad camp. Animals whined in the dust and knobbly ridge poles held up goat-hair tents, stabbing the ferruginous soil that gives the region its name

---

21 It was founded by his cousin, Abu Bakr Ibn 'Umar, but Yusuf oversaw the construction. 'He girded himself with a belt,' records the fourteenth-century *Rawd al-Qirtas* (the 'Garden of Pages'), 'and worked in the relay and at the building work along with the labourers out of humility towards God.'

22 'Indeed, we may say', the historian tells us, 'that the qualities of character resulting from sedentary culture and luxury are identical with corruption.' This certainly holds with the Almoravids: although their leaders maintained Yusuf's puritanism, the courts became increasingly decadent. 'Even worse,' reported the contemporary chronicler Abd-Wahid al-Marrakshi, 'their wives took charge, involving themselves in every vice, not least the drinking of wine and prostitution.'

– *Blad al-Hamra*, the 'Red Country'. But urban development is hardly
a keynote of nomadic culture: Ibn Tafshin's Marrakesh has long fallen
under the dust and only one Almoravid structure ranks high on the
roster of Marrakeshi architecture. I was itching to see it.

Rolling down the Atlas, I made my way towards an interlude of urban
sloth. Juniper hills bristled below sawtooth mountains seething with
cloud like cannon smoke. Cedar forests slid aside for bald cliffs and
canyons where the state slogan was inscribed in white stone and chalk
(*Allah al-Malik al-Watan*, 'God, the King, the Country'[23]). Blue rollers wheeled over the palmeries and chaffinches hopped around dusty
fields. They looked more stimulated than the people in the flaky pink
villages, where the boredom level could be measured by the volume of
pistachio shells on the stoops of the houses.

At times, the slopes were so steep that whenever we stopped, the
bus boy ran out and piled stones behind the wheels; and so sinuous
that he handed round plastic bags in case anyone was sick. Stumbling
out at the other end, I teetered like a sailor on shore leave, keeling
between mud-plastered walls, and entered the city under a groined
arch. Scalloped and ribbed hemispheres framed the gateway, curves
joining concave to convex, communicating a drama of opposition, a
suggestion of movement as dynamic as a caravan. The gate was built
under the auspices of Yusuf Ibn Tafshin and is the only architectural
residue of his era still standing in Marrakesh. But there is another
Almoravid gem, on the other side of the lively Djemaa al-Fnaa, and
after putting down my backpack in a dusty *riad* I went to seek it out.

The marble domed tomb or *koubba* rises from a courtyard several
feet down from the current level of the city (testifying to the depth of
urban development since Ibn Tafshin's day). It was built under the
direction of his son, Ali, who had grown up in the courts of Andalusia,

---

23 This slogan is displayed on hillsides all over Morocco, although not with everyone's
endorsement. A Berber in the High Atlas told me about his mischievous friends, who had
climbed up one of the hillsides and added some stones to the first letter of the declaration,
transforming it into *kul* – 'eat' – so the slogan now read: 'The King eats the country.' In a
case of unusually rapid state efficiency, it was renovated within days.

so the vitality of its design – lobed and horseshoe arches smearing the sides with light and shadow, honeycomb squinches seizing attention when you stand inside – owes as much to the sophisticated urban culture that produced the Al-Hambra as any desert influence. But I was struck by the abundance of vegetal imagery – knotted over the dome and spandrels, creeping up the walls inside.

During my trips in the mountains and across the desert, people pointed out dozens of plants to me. They were alive to vegetation, to every visible root and branch, in a way I struggled to emulate. With its palm and acanthus leaves and its pine-cone motifs, its dome sprouting between stepped merlons like a bushel rooting out of the ground, the *koubba* is a celebration of fertility. It has been identified as a prayer fountain, drawing water from the upland aquifers for worshippers' ablutions. Its design celebrates that most precious of resources, through a dizzying range of motifs associated with it.

The rest of Almoravid Marrakesh is lost. Like stones added to a desert cairn, succeeding dynasties made their mark, although none matched the military achievements of Yusuf and his clan. By the time Leo Africanus wandered through in the early sixteenth century, the city's prime was past and, being from Fez (which is famous across the nation for its snobbery), he was unable to resist a sneer:

> *I have heard that in old time here was great abundance of students, but at my being there I found but five in all; and they have now a most senseless professor, and one that is quite void of all humanity.*

Not that modern Fassis (people of Fez) were any more positive. 'Why do you want to go there?' Mansur had asked me. 'People go to Marrakesh to relax, not to learn.' Still, I had heard about an octogenarian scholar who might be able to teach me what nomads do leave behind, in the place of grand palaces and towering mosques.

Behind the Djemaa al-Fnaa, moped fuel mingled with the stench of donkey shit. Trolleys and pack beasts carried freshly tanned skins, jars of spices and plastic figures of President Obama in cardboard boxes. In a narrow alley, a bossed wooden door creaked open and tiled steps swooped up to rooms stacked with nomadic clobber. Light peeled off the display glass, tugging you around the exhibits for the best angle of observation; smudges on the explanation cards made you lean a little closer. Sometimes there was a click and a flash, and instead of looking at a wooden sugar hammer or an antelope-horn pipe, you saw the reflection of the photographer beside you. So it goes with museums – they rarely suck you in.

Yet the deeper I found myself in Bert Flint's cavern, the more the display items inched forward, pulling loose from their plinths and shelves. Tassles hung from a tobacco bag that had once been the scrotum of a goat; jagged suns wheeled across camel-leather bags designed for Tuareg brides. Zigzag stitching corkscrewed up the slit robes worn by Wodaabe herdsmen for the Gerewol beauty pageant in Niger, next to sky-blue Mauritanian *boubous* (wide-sleeved overshirts on the pattern of a poncho) and ridged doors from Timbuktu, etched with the intricacy of literary texts waiting to be deciphered.

'I have sold the museum to the university,' explained Mr Flint, guiding me along the covered rooftop to his dining salon (I had emailed in advance and he invited me for lunch). 'I don't mind being a refugee in my own home – if it is my own choice!'

He had the clear blue eyes of a man half his age, sparkling with adventure in a patchwork of wrinkles and liver spots. We sat down on a pair of goatskin saddle covers, drinking bowls of sweetened buttermilk and spooning couscous from a large clay bowl.

He was born in Holland, but had lived in Marrakesh since the 1950s. He had taught Spanish, run his own clothing line, set up the museum, and he told of his experiences with the meandering rhythm of a true magpie. It was hard to keep up. One moment he was narrating an ox-cart adventure from Mali to Burkina Faso; the next we were debating the eighteenth-century Dutch–British rivalry over the East Indies. No question had a simple answer. When I asked if he thought nomadism was on its last legs, he tilted his earpiece, nodding to the *amesh-shaghab* at the back of the room – the wooden frame of a nomad's baggage carrier, built on two round crossbars, which was acting as a side table.

'You know,' said Flint, 'I thought these *amesh-shaghabs* went back centuries, but I have learned they only began to make them in the 1950s. And now they are changing again, because the people who use them are settling in the towns. But instead of adopting the furniture of the people around them, they adapt their own. So now you have *amesh-shaghabs* that are used exclusively in people's houses.'

'As a sort of trunk?'

'Exactly. And because they have no need to move them, they make them bigger. So the new kind of *amesh-shaghab* is no good for a nomad – because you wouldn't be able to fit it on a camel!'

He chuckled over the couscous, gleaming with a scholar's delight in muddy waters. Nomadism was evolving, the pure pastoralism of the past interfusing with aspects of sedentary life. I thought of the housing blocks I had seen in Azrou, the billboards inviting country folk to join the urban utopia. These were the kind of people Flint was talking about: the first generation of ex-nomads, amphibiously caught between two ways of life.

When Flint shuffled off for his afternoon nap, I wandered back through the house, sucking up the beauty of the artefacts like a child gargling every last drop through a straw. I stopped for a moment beside an *amesh-shaghab* – scrolled motifs and diamonds, fringed at the neck seams with ribbons of kidskin; a pungent whiff of old leather. A voluptuous nude, girdled with cowrie shells, torpedoed her acacia breasts towards it. There was a shock of chiaroscuro: these two cultures side by side, expressions of the desert and the land that hugs its belly. I felt as if I were being bombarded by premonitions of my journey, fragments pulled out of the future, whispering of what to expect along the way.

The world was changing. A couple of hours south of Marrakesh, signposts and hoardings faded away and the roads tapered into gullies of dust-powdered tar. We were well beyond the reach of celebrity golf courses now. The air was sharpening, biting through the windows of the bus. I was leaving the cliffs and cataracts of the Atlas for the 'River of Sand', *Solitudines Africae*, Pliny's 'torrid zone ... where the sun's orbit is ... scorched by its flames and burnt up by the proximity of its heat'.

In my Arabic–English copy of *Gulliver's Travels*, the hero found himself marooned on the island of Brobdingnag, lifted 20 metres high on a giant farmer's palm. Surrounded by the vastness of the desert, I felt dwarfed myself; I wouldn't have been surprised to see a Brobdingnagian leap over the hilltops towards us. After all, this was the land of magic, a depository for all the wildest chimerae of the medieval fabulists: howling quadrupeds, hominids with eyes in their chests, basilisks who could stare you to stone. It is any wonder that Aladdin's sorcerous nemesis was 'a Moorman from Inner Marocco ... a magician who could upheap by his magic hill upon hill'? Or that Musa Ibn Nusayr, the governor of North Africa, searched the Sahara (in another tale from *The Thousand and One Nights*) for the Valley of the Ruby, the City of Brass and the Tower of Lead? My travels among the dunes and *wadis* would teach me more about these supernatural powers; but for now, the world seemed to be losing its youthful enchantment – a Faust in reverse. The freshness of the north was giving way to a boiled lethargy, receding hair and the liver spots of baked earth.

My neighbour on the bus was a travelling salesman from Senegal. Tall and smooth of scalp, he had large, soft hands and a caramel warmth in his eyes.

'I want to sell a few things in Dakhla,' he said. 'There's a good market for mobile phones. I'll pick up a few things, then I'll go back to Agadir.'

Here was the old merchant's way: exploiting demand and seeking out local commodities to sell for profit further along the road.

'That's a lot of travelling,' I said.

'I like it this way.' He nodded at the broken plastic rubbish holder in front of him; we were too close for eye contact. 'I used to work in a hotel in Agadir. Can you imagine how boring it is? Sitting in the same place every day. I hated it!'

He seemed happy-go-lucky enough to get by. Seated on plastic stools at an Afriqiya petrol station (one of the Libyan-run fuel stops dotted around southern Morocco), we stretched our legs, enjoying relief from the cramp in the bus. Next time, we declared, we would both go with the more capacious Supratours, although we knew the cheaper price of Satas would keep reeling us in.

'I like this life,' said Mohammed. 'I'm free. I go and come back, I see things, I make friends in many places, I do what I like.'

'You're a nomad,' I joked.

But after we had said goodbye, I thought: *he is!* An intercity nomad, carrying his leather holdall instead of livestock, taking it wherever the grazing is good.

I had arrived in Goulmime, the so-called Gate of the Sahara, where Berbers and Arabs from the north have been mixing with Saharawis (literally, 'people of the desert') from the south for centuries. A sprawl of low buildings (their rooflines suggesting the tents in which their owners used to dwell), it still handles plenty of trans-Saharan merchandise, including thousands of smuggled livestock (according to anthropologist Mohamed Oudada, 3600 Malian and Nigerien camels passed this way in 2006–07) from well-worn routes along the Drâa Valley and the Anti-Atlas.[24]

Contraband was not my focus today – I had already picked up a Mauritanian SIM card from Mohammed. I wanted bards rather than bootleggers. I had stopped here on the advice of an activist in London, a Saharawi ex-pat who told me: 'You will find many of our best poets there.'

Yusuf Ibn Tafshin wasn't fond of poets. When he heard the sycophantic rhymes in the courts of Andalusia, he muttered, 'All I understood was that their composers were in need of bread.' But his antipathy is uncharacteristic. For those nomads who aren't packing all their energy into battle, poetry is the glue of life. Leo Africanus (a skilled rhymer in his own right[25]) was charmed whenever he encountered verse. Writing of the Numidian Arabs, he tells us, 'they take great delight in poetry, and will pen most excellent verses; their language being very pure and elegant. If any worthy poet is found among them,

---

24 This has become a major source of revenue for many nomads. As Oudada points out, the tightening of borders encourages smugglers to lean on older techniques: 'Camels have again become the most favoured means of transport, because they can penetrate the tighter chain of frontier posts silently and by night, and also because they are able to cover short distances, thus reducing the risk of capture for the smugglers themselves.'

25 He tells us, with disarming pride, of his recital for a mountain chief: 'and being as then but fifteen years of age, the prince gave right joyful and diligent ear unto me; and whatsoever he understood not sufficiently, he would cause it to be interpreted.'

he is accepted by their governors with great honour and liberality.' I wondered if such rewards were to be met by poets of the Sahara today.

A breezeblock house on a street of rubble and hardcore. Inside, a lush carpet, tendrils the colour of stewed damsons. A pair of poets in gowns of wide-sleeved homespun – the *dara'a*, the formal jacket of the Saharan gentleman. We were all sprayed with perfume (a Saharawi custom) and refreshed with glasses of milk, while our intermediary, a kindly friend of one of my Saharawi contacts in London, brewed the tea.

The poets' names were Jaghagha and Ga'in. They both hailed from the same tribe, the Aït Oussa,[26] but the similarities did not stretch much further. Jaghagha, with his suitcase and toothbrush moustache and horn-rimmed spectacles, had something of the schoolmaster about him. Ga'in was earthier, his face as rimpled as the folds of his *dara'a*, his voice heavier and crisper.

'Poets,' said Jaghagha, 'are the blood of our culture. I speak about everything – religion, social justice, the situation for Arabs in the world. I write when I travel. Poetry comes to me when I see the mountains and the sea and the desert.'

He recited several pieces, in a voice that popped and trilled with classical precision. Among these was a poem about nomadic life: a 150-line *qasida* (ode) written in three-foot rhyming couplets, depicting the life of the encampment – from the games played by children using painted stones to the *faqihs* (Islamic teachers) giving Quranic lessons in the tents.

'I wrote this one for the *moussem* at Tan Tan,' he explained. 'The organisers asked me to write about our nomads. So I wrote the poem and went to the competition. There were more than 800 people in the municipal hall – men, women, young and old, people from different states. Because of the *moussem*, a lot of people had come to Tan Tan and they all wanted to see the poets. There were 30 poems that day,

---

26 A branch of the Tekna confederation and descended from the Bani Hillal, the pastoralists whom historians like Ibn Khaldun have blamed for devastating the Maghrib after their arrival from Arabia in the eleventh century AD.

but some of the poets didn't make it so they sent their poems by fax. When it came to my turn, the people responded with delight. They clapped, they shouted "bravo!", many of the women trilled.'

How else could the result have gone? Jaghagha won the competition, of course!

Ga'in was harder to draw out. Unlike Jaghagha, he had grown up entirely in a nomadic encampment, and he believed this was crucial to his poetic identity.

'To be a poet,' he said, 'you need to come from the desert. There, you can see all around you, but in the city your vision is limited by four walls. I grew up in a camp near Assa. I write about the land, the grass and cold water, all the things we want from this life.'

He was less technical than Jaghagha, more earthy and instinctive. He illustrated this by telling how he had responded to a severe drought.

'It was the day of the Prophet Mohammed's birthday and I saw the situation was not good for our people, so I went up the mountain behind Assa and recited a poem. I felt scared, but I was hoping for mercy. And thank God, after that day the situation became better.'

Ga'in didn't need any papers to recite. His voice was deep and bristly, quivering high notes plunging to long-drawn semibreves, wheeling to a circular rhythm. It was emotive and shamanistic, and I could well imagine its capacity to mediate between God and the earth. This was hardly the kind of poetry Ibn Tafshin scorned at the Spanish courts. It was rugged and pure, poetry as a way of marking one's connection to the earth.

This rootedness, this rapport with nature, is a common thread I witnessed in every nomadic community I visited. We are mistaken when we think of nomads as rootless – for isn't it by walking around a place, rolling in its dust, branching out and returning, that you grow to know it, to love it? Hence *tariqa*, a way or path, is the Sufi *tariqa*, 'the Way' to communion with God, the beloved.

11

The Last Colony in Africa

'I KNOW WHAT YOU ARE THINKING.'

I turned from the window of the bus. I had been watching the world strip itself down, slinging off its furs like an ageing beauty at the end of a long night. The mountains had shrunk early on. The trees fell soon after, and before the inkspots of night had swallowed up the land, the buildings sank to blisters on the wounded earth. Other than the goats, gathering like gangster squads to see off the last patches of vegetation, we could have been sliding over the surface of the moon.

'You come here for the Saharawis,' said my neighbour, between mouthfuls of fried chicken, 'you want to know about their situation?' Globs of greasy sauce splattered his hands, and he rubbed irritably with a tissue. 'They will tell you they don't have jobs, they don't have money, "this is unfair, help us please..." They are liars! Who has developed the land? Did the Saharawis find the phosphate mines? Of course not! And now they want to enjoy the benefits of it.'

I thought about the nomads of northern Morocco, driven higher and deeper into the mountains. Was the same principle in operation here? Sedentarists claiming the benefits of 'development', ignoring the disadvantages heaped on the people who used these lands for pasture? Far from damaging the land, nomads were victims of the lightness of their footprints. They had left no marks – no mines, no cultivated fields – to which a claim of ownership could be pinned.

Around Laayoune, signs of the development appeared. A wind turbine sliced the air near a cement factory. A road-building machine tooled up the highway like a giant tarantula. A cow – not an animal likely to thrive in this pastureless landscape – was painted on the wall of a dairy farm. More suited to the world around us were the camels, skulking beside acacia groves and farmsteads built from the abundant local stone. They matched the tawny colours around them, unlike the deceptively welcoming pink of the ever-recurring military kiosks.

I stepped inside one of these cabins, following the beckoning finger of a shiny *gendarme royale*. Gold stars decorated his shoulders and a holster at his waist reeled a thread of sunlight. He dropped onto a cracked plastic chair behind a tatty ledger and a tea tray buzzing with flies, to scribble down my details.

'Coochy-coo-coo,' I said – not to the soldier but to a tiny puppy sitting in a corner of the kiosk. After the snarlers of the Atlas, it was nice to meet a gentler canine, although I was only using the puppy for my own ends. It gave me a chance to look at the '*rechercher et arrêter*' posters, in which local 'miscreants' were depicted in grainy black and white above brief descriptions of their crimes ('*terrorisme*', '*deux actes de violence contre l'état*'). Mugshots drain the personality out of people, stripping them to thuggish jaws and hollowed eye sockets. They were a cipher of the political tensions shimmering across the Western Sahara, visible but opaque, like the midges of dust lit across the doorway by the slanting sunbeams.

On the outskirts of Laayoune, red and green starred flags tussled with the breeze to flaunt Moroccan sovereignty. Seashell patterns grooved the spandrels of an archway, hovering pink and welcoming above the dry *Sakiya al-Hamra* (Red River). White *Sûreté Nationale* vans and green military trucks rattled around us, the noses of their artillery probed by sun rays like giant needles to clean out the dirt.

I was travelling light. Flinging my backpack over a shoulder, I tilted down the pavement, between watchful soldiers with twitching helmets and women in wraparound *melhfa* drapes, carrying bags of fruit from the early-morning cart stalls. I didn't have to search for long: tucked above a downtown café, a drab little hostel had rusty metal doors and bedbugs. It was perfect for my budget. There was a crowd in the café on my first night, jammed around the television to watch Chelsea take on Barcelona, and the stubbly hotelier asked me which team I supported.

'Um... Barcelona?'

'What? You must support Chelsea!'

I only found out later why he was so passionate about the blues. It wasn't that he wanted Chelsea to win, more that he was desperate for Barcelona to lose.

'All Moroccans in Laayoune like Real,' a Saharawi activist told me the next day, 'because Morocco has a king and "Real" means "royal". And Saharawis all support Barcelona, because we have sympathy for the Basques. They are fighting for independence, just like us.'

In almost every teahouse I passed, a match was playing. Young men huddled over heaps of fag ash, fists pumping at the glimmer of a goal. Football had become a parallel to political reality, a valve through which they could pour their allegiances with passion and impunity. It was one of many examples, communicating Saharawi identity through a secret code.

The Western Sahara was the crucible from which Yusuf Ibn Tafshin's drum-beating Almoravids emerged. Sanhaja Berbers like the Tuareg, their men wore veils and looked with contempt at the uncovered 'fly catchers' around them. In the centuries after the birth of Islam, as Arab tribes emigrated across the Sahara, they raided, traded and inter-married with the Berber natives, forming a network of more than 120 tribes, which today range from the Berber-descended Reguibat to the Oulad Delim, who claim the blood of the Prophet Mohammed.

The latter were described by Leo Africanus: 'They have neither dominion nor yet any stipend, wherefore they are very poor and given to robbery: they travel unto Dara, and exchange cattle for dates with the inhabitants there.' Although many of the tribes developed monop-olies in trans-Saharan commerce (the Oulad Bou Sba became special-ists in tea and gunpowder, for example, while the Aït Lahsen were the people to talk to if you were after tobacco or wool), they remained diffi-cult to subdue, rugged products of the terrestrial furnace in which they were bred. The Moroccan sultans never managed it (one of the reasons why independence is so passionately claimed today) and labelled the area *Blad as-Siba* – 'land of dissidence'. Not until the Spanish colonists started mining for phosphate in the twentieth century was any kind of administrative control imposed.

The Spanish had been loitering in the area since the fifteenth cen-tury, when they made a deal with the Portuguese to split the Atlantic

African coast and launched slave-hunting missions from the Canary Islands. So successful were they that a Saharan jihad was launched against them. In 1517 and 1524, tribesmen besieged the Spanish fort, and a plague in the Canaries helped to keep the Christians out. Preoccupied with their discoveries on the other side of the Atlantic, the Spanish would establish no further settlement until 1884. Even then, they paid so little interest that by 1952 there were only 24 subscribers to the Spanish Saharan telephone service and only 130 wells across the whole territory by 1960.

It was the discovery of phosphate reserves that changed the narrative. Now the 'Spanish Sahara' was a colony worth pulping. Profits from the mines, investment and cheap credit from the Spanish government began to fund development. But resistance was evolving. The old nomadic skills turned out to be well suited to guerrilla tactics. Raiding missions put lighthouses out of action, outlying Spanish posts were sacked and Spanish officers were kidnapped. The guerrilla campaign fizzled out in leadership disputes and a 1959 drought. Yet a Saharawi political identity had been moulded, and the United Nations gave it a jolt of motivation with a call for decolonisation in 1965. In the run-up to the Spanish withdrawal, a new pan-tribal organisation emerged, replacing the old *jamaa* or gathering of tribal leaders: the Polisario. Independence was within reach.

Except that 226,000 square kilometres (an area roughly the size of Britain), not only rich in phosphate and fishing but also uranium, titanium and iron ore, was never likely to ease into a smooth independence. Not with its recently liberated neighbours (Morocco, Mauritania and Algeria) all licking their chops for a taste of the other side of colonialism. Ignoring a UN Resolution guaranteeing Saharawi self-determination,[27] they all made a lunge. Morocco came out on top, thanks in part to the Green March: a spectacular mass ramble, inspired by King Hassan's pledge to 'reunite' Western Sahara 'with the motherland'. Driven by patriotic zeal and the promise of subsidies,

---

27 This resolution was backed by the International Court of Justice, which categorically refuted Moroccan claims to sovereignty: 'the court has not found legal ties of such nature as might affect the application of resolution 1514 (XV) in the decolonisation of Western Sahara and, in particular, of the principle of self-determination through the free and genuine expression of the will of the peoples of the Territory.'

350,000 Moroccans hauled their national flags, copies of the Quran and portraits of the King across the desert.

The ploy worked. Fighting raged on, but Morocco was able to chain its gains with military patrols and sow the borders with landmines. By the time a ceasefire was declared in 1991, more than 100,000 Saharawis had been driven from their homes, forced to languish in an area of Algeria so inhospitable it was known as 'the Devil's Garden'. Living off international aid and using car batteries for electricity, they were separated from their relatives across the border by the *berm* – a 2-metre high, 1500-mile long sand wall (the world's longest continuous minefield, framed in an estimated 5 million explosives – around 3000 for every mile). The terms of the ceasefire pledged a referendum to be held among the indigenous population – a pledge that, two-and-a-half decades later, has yet to be honoured.

I heard an eye-witness account of the war when I joined a Spanish charter flight to Algeria to visit the Devil's Garden. There I met several veterans of the 1975 conflict, including a middle-aged Saharawi called *Hajji* Hodud. Grey bearded, sallow featured, with a sharp look under his heavy eyelids, he took me by the hand, leading me between the tents and mud huts of his rugged camp.

'I was just a boy of 12,' he said. 'The Moroccans were in the north and the Mauritanians were attacking in the south. They were flying French Jaguars and dropping napalm bombs on us. My family was in a place called Oued Modraiya. It was surrounded by mountains so they thought it was safe. About 40,000 people went there to escape from the Moroccans, people from Smaara, Laayoune, from all over Western Sahara, as well as some of our fighters who were travelling in a big lorry. Then one morning, we saw the surveillance plane and we knew we were in trouble.'

It came in the form of napalm and phosphorus bombs, dropped by the Jaguars. The attack lasted three days and hundreds died.

'Our family tent was burned and some of my relatives were killed,' *Hajji* Hodud continued. 'There was panic everywhere. People went around distributing food and trying to help the others, but by the third day our resources were finished and we had very little to eat. We had run out of equipment so we had to use traditional medicine

– plants for stomach problems, camel fat instead of bandages for people who had to be amputated. After the third day, we climbed into the Polisario lorry and drove to this place.'

He waved a dismissive hand. Goats were scrambling around solar panels, under mud huts shaped like tents. *Hajji* Hodud had lived in the Devil's Garden for three-quarters of his life, but still he thought of the dunes around Laayoune as his home.

'There was nothing here,' he said. 'We had to live on aid, and we still do. I stayed with my mother, and we used the soil to make bricks and build houses, while our fathers went back across the desert to fight.'

※

Laayoune is a paradise compared to the camps. Linked to the phosphate mines by a conveyance pipe, with the fishing ports only a few miles to the west, it shines with the glitter of development. But once you've rubbed the sand out of your eyes, the military presence is hard to ignore. Every corner produces another wooden military kiosk, and I was perpetually warned against crossing the road by the roar of another artillery-loaded truck. With a garrison of 160,000, there are nearly half as many Moroccan military personnel as there are Saharawis.

The most telling details were the seemingly innocuous ones: uncracked roads, the lack of young men loitering around street corners, unpeopled public squares, with their immaculate bougainvillea. Sometimes more specific signs of the political situation seeped through – gated compounds festooned with flowers (the property of rich Moroccans at the top of the food chain); pink Lux minivans, with taped signs on their back windows from the UNHCR Saharawi Family Visits Programme.

Unsurprisingly, the people I met on the streets were edgy and evasive. But my contacts in London had put me in touch with a group of underground activists. I was hoping they would peel back Laayoune's surface for me. So I made my way down a sun-drained street of rosy-pink hardware stores, where the air pulsed to the heat of the sun and the beat of jackhammering.

'You chose the right day.'

Firas was a stocky graduate, with hooded eyes deep in their sockets, mismatched against the rounded warmth of his face. Like most of his peers he was unemployed, despite being fluent in five languages.

'There's a demonstration this afternoon, so you can see what goes on here.' He looked at his friends, before adding, with a wry puckering of lips: 'But it would be the same if we met you tomorrow. Most days there's a demonstration.'

This one took place on Avenue Smaara, one of the longest roads in the city. I sat in the back of a scuffed Renault driven by Firas's spiky-haired brother Abdullah. The rear window was splintered and foam was bubbling out of cracks in the vinyl. The passenger beside me was called Maimuna. Intense eyes flashed under spidery lashes and strands of nut-brown hair leaked out of her midnight-blue *melhfa*. She fitted a pair of gloves over her hands and tightened the cotton around her face, so she wouldn't be easy to identify.

'Wrap your turban better,' she said, in the tone of a mother telling her child to buckle his seatbelt.

I had been given a black headcloth to hide my face and told to keep my giveaway white hands away from the window. Lining the road around us were a dozen dark blue police trucks; the white vans of the auxiliary forces were parked in the side alleys. Helmeted officers held plastic shields and batons; plain-dressed policemen mingled in the crowd, giving themselves away when their back pockets crackled with static. All around us, jaws were stiffening, lips were clamped tight, brows were creasing.

'You see the men on the motorbikes,' said Firas, 'that's the secret police – watch out. If they find out about you they're gonna give you hell.'

We drove past a group chanting slogans, but Firas didn't think it would be wise to linger with a foreigner in the car.

'That's the guys at the front,' he said, tapping his phone. 'Our friend Malainin just got his arm broken.' He turned to Abdullah and told him to take the back streets, changing direction when we heard a motorbike gunning behind us.

It was some relief to get back to Abdullah's house. I sat back against a bolster and sipped Coca-Cola while Firas filled my lap with snaps.

They were bright polaroids, vivid with the blues and reds of *dara'a* robes and women's *melhfas*, as well as the blues and reds of bruised legs and bleeding heads. There was an old man with a split lip whom I had met in the house earlier; a woman's bare back, ridged with welts; a crowd of women, clapping their hands defiantly in front of a line of soldiers; a youth with a gash on his forehead from a stone thrown by a policeman. The pictures were intense and unsettling. Yet there were so many, along with the flipcam footage playing on a laptop, that I found them hard to digest. It was only when people told me their stories that I felt I was stepping into the Saharawi abyss.

'For us as women,' said Maimuna, 'it is really important to take part in the demonstrations.'

She knelt beside me, arms folded across her chest. She wanted to make a point, not friends.

'It is our land,' she said, 'women's as well as men's. And a lot of the men can't take part because they lose their job if they are seen at the demonstrations, or maybe they are already in prison. You must understand, we are different from women in Morocco. We have respect in society. In Morocco, their husbands beat them all the time and they cannot complain. But in our culture, if a man beats his wife it is shameful. She will return to her family and the man must do a lot to get her back.'

She had taken part in countless demonstrations, always careful, always wearing her *melhfa* tight, but never holding back from the front line.

'Once, I stood in front of 50 policemen. We were demanding freedom, work, the opportunity to bury our martyrs. They shouted back at us. They said "you are mercenaries", and the deputy police chief struck me with his baton. I fell to the ground and they kicked me and pulled off my *melhfa*. You know, in our society, this is very shameful. They surrounded me and dragged me away from the others. They pulled me by the hair and threatened to rape me.'

'Does it ever make you nervous?' I asked.

'Never! When 50 policemen are facing you and I am only a single woman, I don't feel scared, I feel hatred for them.'

She looked straight at me as she said this, eyes burning with righteous defiance.

Many of the demonstrators shared Maimuna's intensity. They moved thriftily, cautiously, used to sliding round corners; speaking in carefully modulated whispers, then raising their voices to the level of protest chant. That afternoon, and several others, I heard dozens of stories. Some people sought me out, desperate for a link to the outside world. Others sat more quietly, cosseting their stories until they were ready to unfold them.

An activist friend of Firas's described being picked off the street, just a few months before, to spend several days in a cell, 'strung up like a chicken'. Families told how they were forced to leave their villages in the fighting of 1975. A student called Ahmed showed me the scars on his leg from driving over a landmine, travelling with a nomadic herder who was inspecting his flock. The herder's feet were ripped open and a toe had to be amputated. As a result, he could no longer walk steadily and had to sell his flock; another nomad taken from the land.

One of the most emotive subjects was the protest camp of Gudaym Izik. It took place in October 2010, predating the self-immolation of Tunisian street vendor Mohamed Bouazizi by a couple of months. Although the camp attracted little interest from the Western media, several observers have credited it as the first spark of the Arab Spring.[28] It took place about 12 kilometres into the desert and at its peak numbered an estimated 20,000 people.

'It was a utopia,' said Salim.

He was crouching over a gas stove, preparing the tea: lanky and dark skinned, frizzy haired, with a look of acrid intensity. While he talked, we could hear the water chuckling on the stove.

'Before the camp,' he said, 'I was unemployed and unhappy. But I found freedom there. Living in those tents... it took us back to our roots as a society. We wanted to show the world we can live on our own, we can live away from civilisation, we belong to the desert.'

---

28 'The Arab Spring', claimed Noam Chomsky in a speech in October 2012, 'began in November 2010 when the people of Western Sahara revolted against their Moroccan occupiers.' Mohammed Lamine, the Saharawi UK ambassador, put it this way: 'If you're talking about the ingredients – marginalisation, poverty, lack of rights – the Arab Spring started in Laayoune. But if you do this in Laayoune, no one cares. If you do it in Cairo, then people start to notice.'

All over the world – from Tahrir Square to St Paul's Cathedral – protesters use tents, broadcasting their campaigns from makeshift camps. Protesters are always nomads, pitching camp where they can, hoping their voices will be heard, holding on until the authorities kick them on. For the Saharawis this analogy goes deeper, protest merging with heritage, the very act of defiance drilling back to their origins. No wonder the protesters talked about the camp as if it were a primordial idyll.

'It was a protest against social marginalisation,' said Salim, 'the lack of jobs, decent housing, legal rights. We showed we can make our own society. There was no crime, no complaining. I was in the security committee, I was like a sheriff.'

Twenty-eight days after the camp was established, everyone was awoken by the sound of the army: helicopters whirring overhead, tanks roaring over the dunes, military orders ringing the camp like a cordon.

'You could smell gas,' said Salim. 'You could hear gunshots – bang, bang! I saw two policemen picking up an old woman and beating her with batons, dragging her by the hair. I saw them grab a woman with an infant and throw her into a truck. They were shouting at us: "You dirty Saharawis." They called the women bitches. They used shameful words, they didn't care, they kicked the women with their boots.'

'How did you get out?' I asked.

'I ran. There was a Land Rover heading out, so I jumped inside. We were packed together, so many of us, and we were angry. When we got to Laayoune we marched on the police station. They didn't care, of course. We shouted outside the station, and you know what they did? Bang, bang! Bullet in the shoulder! Five other guys got hit too. I went to the hospital but they refused to treat me, so I had to use traditional medicine to ease the pain – sheep's fat and maggots. Have you any idea how much it hurt? I could barely move my arm. I didn't get a doctor to look at it until a few weeks ago, when I went on the UN programme to the camps in Algeria.'

For centuries the Moroccan sultans ignored the Sahara. They wanted gold to mint their coins and revenue from the caravan trade, but they didn't want trouble from the tribes, so they left well alone. Occasionally a chief would pledge allegiance in return for the title of *caid*, to bolster his status within the desert *jamaa*. But such pledges were rare, and usually short. Before the era of colonialism, only one Moroccan sultan had much success in taming the desert – and even then he had to suffer plenty of reverses before his famous victory.

That was Sultan Ahmed Al-Mansur, 'the triumphant'. Emboldened by the 'Battle of Three Kings' in 1578 (at which the King of Portugal, a rival claimant to the throne and his own brother all died), he sent a force towards the Niger, hoping to secure the fruits of the trans-Saharan trade. However, the desert was at its most capricious, preying on the entire Moroccan army and justifying the warnings of the Sultan's advisers: 'There is an immense desert, which is devoid of water and vegetation, and so hard to traverse that the very birds lose their way there.' It was only after he seized the salt mines of Teghazza that Al-Mansur decided to brave another crossing, sending 3000 men to subdue the Kingdom of the Songhay in 1590. This was the 'event collapse' that tore Timbuktu to shreds. From the Moroccan point of view, this was a victory not only over a rival power, but over the desert itself.

Yet the tribes of the Western Sahara were less easily corralled than the Songhay. Mobility remained their chief asset: as long as they could run away and raid, they were impossible to subdue. Many of their origin legends emphasise their independence, often by contrasting them to the sultans whose powers they evaded. Take the Arosien tribe, for example, which derives from a preacher called Sidi Ahmed al-Arosi. According to the story, he was accused of sorcery in Marrakesh and thrown into a dungeon. In the way of such tales, a long-dead saint came to his rescue, spirited him out of his cell and carried him over the desert by the belt of his trousers. Eventually the belt gave way and Sidi Ahmed crashed into the sand. The spot where he landed became the heartland of his tribe.

Similar tales bolster other tribes (the Aït Lahsen, for example, say their founder was threatened with the amputation of his hand unless he paid off the sultan – heaps of gold magically appeared and he was able to ride away to freedom). Such stories not only appeal to deep, atavistic feelings of independence, they frame tribal identity in terms of its opposition to the central Moroccan authority. Literally, Saharawi means 'from the desert'; in narrative terms, it also means 'not Moroccan'. No wonder Saharawis have developed such an astonishing capacity to resist and endure, sometimes against the most appalling privations.

Imagine a man of middle years. Soft brown eyes, pallid behind bifocal lenses, a dark moustache brushing over his thick grey beard. His *dara'a* robe hung loose around his tight-drawn frame, because 20 years of freedom hadn't been enough to recover his former vigour. His name was Mohammed Fadl and, of all the stories I heard in Laayoune, his was the one that sucked me deepest into the Saharawi nightmare.

'It was 1975,' he said, 'and I was doing my baccalaureate in Tan Tan. That's when they abducted me. There was a bad atmosphere in the town. The Moroccan forces had invaded and some of us would gather to discuss the issues. I was only 15 but the Polisario leaders were young too, so they figured I was part of the movement. My mother was anxious about the surveillance and told me not to go out, there were curfews and patrols and we saw a lot of our neighbours' houses being raided.

'One day I was cornered in an empty street. They blindfolded and handcuffed me, put me in a black *djellaba* and kicked me into a car, locking me to the bar inside. I was in solitary confinement for 15 days while they questioned me. Then I was taken to a house and given a number: 72. That's what they called me. I didn't have a name anymore, just a number: 72.

'That's when the torture began. I was blindfolded, hung in the air for hours, or they made me sit on the floor and kicked me. They shaved off my hair and beard. They deprived us of food for days, then gave us lentils or chickpeas with insects in it. There were other Saharawis with me, and other groups the government didn't like. We were like brothers, all together in this ordeal.

'One day they transported us in the cars they use to round up wild dogs. Officially, we were "captured Algerian petroleum workers". We were taken to Agdes, an old French prison in the mountains. We had to eat the leftovers after they'd fed the dogs and the whole place was full of cow manure. People got diseases easily. There were women with us. I remember one of them, her name was Naj Ibrahim, she died of sickness. If I close my eyes, I can still hear the sounds of her suffering.'

Mohammed and his fellow prisoners were hardly unusual – since the war of 1975, up to 2000 Saharawis had gone missing. As far as the Moroccan authorities were concerned, these prisoners were a huge logistical burden. To avoid press attention when King Hassan was making an official visit to nearby Ouarzazate, they were transported to the hill fort of Skoura in the High Atlas. Another time they were moved to an old French prison called Meguna ('I saw an owl when we came off the truck,' said Mohammed, 'so I knew it was an abandoned place, and you could tell from the smell of the air we were on top of a hill'). The journeys were hellish and, for some, fatal. Mohammed spoke of a fellow prisoner who asked to go to the toilet: 'They stamped on his groin until his bladder ruptured. He died a few days later.'

Mohammed's incarceration took place during the 'Years of Lead', the long period of state oppression under Hassan II. But in the twilight of the old king's reign, there was a shift in policy. Mohammed experienced this when he was transported to a hospital and later a residency in Ouarzazate.

'We frightened everyone who saw us, because we were so thin. They said we looked like skeletons coming out of hell. We were released at last in 1991, after 16 years, and on the journey back we saw a woman on a camel. She asked, "Are you the prisoners?" She trilled and gave us milk. I went back to my home and saw my parents. They couldn't believe it. My mother just sat there staring at me, and my father kept repeating "*alhamdulillah*" (thanks to God). It was the only thing he said for a week. My sister was grown up now with her own family. My brother's children had grown up, I didn't recognise them.'

It was like the Quranic tale of the 'People of the Cave', a group of youths who hid from persecution and only emerged three centuries later, to find the whole world had changed around them. But instead of sleep Mohammed had endured torture, beatings and three decades of confinement. I wondered if it angered him at all, having missed out on so much. He tipped his head, looking away for a moment. His expression was phlegmatic, his cheeks drawn under his lucid brown eyes.

'This is God's will. Nobody wants it to happen, but it is God's will.'

These were the moments when I glimpsed the power of Islam. Far more than any of the Quranic tenets my friends in Fez had taught me, it was this ability to process the worst life can throw at you, a philosophy born out of the rigours of nomadic life, that showed the consolation, and the power, of the faith.

12

Picnic in the Desert

ONE MORNING, WHEN DAWN WAS STILL PAINTING A VIOLET SLUR OVER THE breezeblock apartments, I wandered out to the edge of Laayoune. Near the Souq Djemal, the grand bazaar, the houses shrunk to tent-shaped bungalows, ridged with dormer windows and bracketed with gas flues. Behind them sprawled the dunes, dipping and rising like rolls of brocade on a cloth seller's table, sliding down to the glassy meander of the *Sakiya al-Hamra*. Palmwood logs poked out of the basins, rigged with plastic sheeting to protect the town from the greedy sands.

I walked longer than I had intended, enjoying the press of my feet in the sand, the suck of the grain on my boots. The further I went, the more cautious I became, because whenever I mentioned the desert to Saharawis, they asked me: 'Do you know how many landmines there are?' (Answer: 9 million either side of the *berm*.) So close to town, I was probably safe. There were footprints to follow, signs of cultivation nearby, broken green bottles left by Saharawi youths who had fallen for the classic vice of the newly urbanised. Still, the free-floating pleasures of a ramble are slightly dented by the prospect of blowing yourself up, so after a while I decided to head back.

It was not till my final evening in Laayoune that I was able to visit the desert. I had been invited to join some friends of Firas's, who had a tent and a herd of camels a few miles east. Since they knew the land pretty well, I was crossing my fingers they would keep us free from the mines.

That was one obstacle. Another – and the first to negotiate – was the difficulty of simply getting out of Laayoune. I was instructed to present myself at Firas's activist HQ, but my phone buzzed the moment I slipped out of the taxi.

'U R followed. Walk round block & back in 5.'

Further texts advised me to sit on a step outside the block, wait on a bench, go inside a shop and ask for the back door. *I've stumbled into the* Bourne Identity! It took half an hour of cat-and-mouse before

I was given the all clear, guided by cryptic texts to a Land Rover with darkened windows a couple of blocks away.

'Welcome to Saharawi life!'

Bubbling inside was a group of men in loose, crisp robes. Their festive smiles struck a surreal contrast to the fraught atmosphere outside. They were a cheerful, well-connected gang – one of them was related to the former Polisario president, another was the sheikh of his tribe. The latter's name was Abdellatif. He was amply built, tucked inside his blankets, chain smoking Marlboro Reds.

'My tribe is the Oulad al-Assad,' he said. The name means Sons of the Lion. 'We're a famous tribe in Western Sahara, because we're the only ones who fought against every single one of the others!'

He ran his own camel dairy, with all the milk and cheese coming from the camels.

'When we are in the desert, you will drink camel's milk. There isn't as much fat or sugar as cow and goat milk, so we have a lot of customers who are diabetics. And some of our best customers are ladies, because it is good for the skin.'

An hour out of town, fields of moraine tilted the Land Rover and topsand nibbled at the tyres. The earth swayed below, guiding us into a ring of modest dunes, where a couple of tents were pitched beside a rug of palm-reed matting. Rags on wooden stakes shielded the brazier, stoked to boil the tea and keep us warm. The coals crackled and flashed, jetting sparks and tattooing our faces with shadow, while Saharawi music tinkled through the window of the Land Rover.

The men around me were not only friends, they were also business partners in a camel-herding co-operative. The camels lounged around us, legs folded and necks bowed, unobtrusive as clumps of bunchgrass. I stepped away from the others to look at them. I hadn't seen so many camels since Timbuktu, and I could feel my heart beating a little faster. *Oh my God, I'm welling up at the sight of artiodactylic retromingent ungulates!* They reminded me of Naksheh, who had carried me so gently (or was that just how I remembered it?) across the southern Sahara. I wanted to stroke them, saddle them and ride them. I wanted to try out the skills I'd been taught by Lamina and Jadullah. I wondered if I remembered them all.

Moishin, the chief herdsman, was wrapped in a woollen cloak. His wiry hair jiggled when he laughed – which was often, in response to my Arabic. Slowly, he adjusted to my level and invited me to join him for the milking.

'Now, hold this bowl, will you? The bosses are here, so I've got to make sure there's plenty to drink… In the name of God! You never drank camel's milk before? It is as if you were never born! Come on, give me the bowl.'

Snood-like nets of cord webbed the females' udders, preventing the calves from sucking the milk. Moishin crouched in his plastic slip-ons, kneading the teats, while I held the aluminium bowl on the other side. Camels have multiple milk canals in every teat (one of their advantages for a dairy farmer) and can produce up to 24 pints of milk in a single day. The calves lingered nearby, eager for sippings of the warm, sputtering juice; when the bowl was full, Moishin showed mercy and let them through.

'Drink!' he commanded. 'Camel's milk is the best milk in the world, and if you are travelling you will need to be healthy.'

This was *it*! So much of Western Sahara is out of bounds to outsiders, thanks to the landmines and the army presence. To be here in the desert, milking camels with a Saharawi nomad: this was what I'd come for! A few generations ago, there was no other kind of Saharawi. But against the ever-rising tide of war, landmines, military occupation and plain old economics, Moishin was a member of an increasingly exclusive club – just 4 per cent of the modern Saharawi population. Standing next to him, holding the warm, foamy bowl in my hands, I was absorbing a new lesson among nomads. I had learned about goat milking with Lamina's family near Timbuktu. Now I could add camel milking to the list.

It was getting dark, so Moishin wrapped his cloak around my shoulders and helped me back to the others. He had been herding for several years, but it wasn't a hereditary role.

'When I was younger my family went to the Canary Islands.'[29] He took my hand to stop me from tripping over the resting camels. 'I

---

29 Where there is a sizeable Saharawi population, comprised largely of refugees and asylum seekers. People are not the only exchange with the Canary Islands, which import Western

was going to live in the town with my family. But I decided to come back here, and you know what? I am happy I did! Living in the desert is the best life – I wish I lived in earlier times when this was more widespread.'

It was a refreshing point of view. Nomadism is usually characterised as a lifestyle of the desperate, TE Lawrence's 'death in life'. But for Moishin, it was life itself. I wondered what in particular attracted him.

'That's easy. It's the camels, of course! They are much cleverer than people realise. I swear by God, people have no idea. For example, a month ago we lost two of our camels, but I knew they'd go back to the watering place even though it was 50 kilometres away. So we took the rest of the camels back to the watering place, and there we found them, just as I predicted.'

Over by the windbreaker, the camel's milk was passed between us – salty tasting and frothy, as hot as if it had come out of a samovar. My hosts were enjoying themselves, relaxing by the fire. They all lived in town, but like every Saharawi they had nomadic roots and still identified themselves through this heritage.

'It isn't just living in the desert that makes you a nomad,' said Abdellatif. 'You can tell a nomad from other things. For example, in the tea-house many of us shout, because that's how it is in the desert. You have so much space and you get used to talking across big distances.'

'But it is our nomadic identity that makes life difficult for us,' said Abdullah, Firas's brother. 'When the Spanish did their census, many Saharawis were looking for pasture. So they weren't included in the census.'

When Moishin appeared with the meal – a stewed goat carcase on a bed of rice – we all clustered round. A bowl of water was passed between us, hands were wiped and God was praised. Then everybody dived in and ripped into the meat.

'Don't be shy,' said Abdellatif. 'Here in the desert you have to fight for your food!'

Saharan sand to top up their beaches, although much of it is blown back on the prevailing wind.

I struggled to keep up: eating with your right hand can be a hard task for a leftie, and I am not the nimblest of crouchers. The others could tear off pieces of flesh with one hand, sponging the juices with tufts of bread; and unlike me, their clothes remained unsplattered. I kept eating until only Abdullah and I were left mopping the last remains on a second tray, patting the rice into greasy balls in our palms.

'It's Barcelona against Chelsea,' joked Abdullah.

Even in the desert, the 'code' prevailed. We both laughed as we claimed our allegiances, taking turns to pull at the last vestiges of flesh.

Driving back that night, the headlights picked out silvery rocks and the odd spectral rabbit. A guitar tune played on the Land Rover's CD system and we swayed to the rhythm. Abdellatif clapped and hummed, and Firas plucked at the shoulders of his *dara'a*. According to an old Arabic proverb, 'a man can only be free in the desert'. For the Saharawis, there is a melancholy truth to these words. The song was about the late Polisario leader Mazhoub, a figure widely admired by my companions, less so by the Moroccan authorities. So, when Abdullatif turned down the volume dial, I sensed there was trouble ahead.

A checkpoint swung towards us and a soldier darted out of his kiosk. I felt my lips shaping a curse. I could see it now: *we're going to be hoicked into the police station, hauled over the coals, kept in for hours. Luckily I'm planning on leaving this country, but what about my companions? Having relatives among the Polisario heavyweights may not bode well.*

The soldier flicked through my passport, puckering his lips over my Mauritanian visa. He asked for my companions' ID cards. Still unsatisfied, he demanded to see the car documents. That was when Abdellatif decided to launch a charm offensive.

'*Lebas! Bekheir?... Yek lebas. Bekheir? Barakallah! Yek bekheir! Wa usratak?... Alhamdulillah! Yeksalmim!... Lebas! Bekheir?... Barakallah! Alhamdulillah!* No evil. How are you?... No evil! How are you? Praise God! And how are you? And your family?... Thanks be to God! May you and yours be safe!... No evil! How are you?... Praise God! Thanks be to God!'

The greetings were garrulous but also genealogical (Firas told me later he only knew the tide was turning when Abdellatif teased out the soldier's tribe). Well-worn implements in the nomadic toolkit, these salutations have been developed and deployed at wells and crossing points over the ages. Abdellatif rattled them out so fast I was lost after three or four sallies. He carried on, lobbing expressions through the window, attacking the soldier with clasped hands, magnetic smiles and flowery language. At last, his victim wobbled. A quick glance at the kiosk, and he posted my passport back through the window. More phrases were flourished, families were blessed, God and the prophets were invoked and eternal happiness became a bathtub for our souls, but it was all drowned by the squeal of Abdullah's foot on the pedal. Relief was so palpable you could taste it. Along with the revived beat of the music, it tingled all the way back to the city.

∾

The other end of Western Sahara. Dakhla: a sun-baked frontier town where truckers in greasy vests played cards on the piazzas and sinewy black men crouched over ripped-open hessian sacks. They were Mauritanians, Senegalese and Malians, their massive bodies reflecting the physical challenges of Africa's terrain. They offered batteries, mobile phones, sunglasses, bootleg Afropop, 12-inch steel knives for the forthcoming Eid festival, a night with the waitress at the café round the corner, a joint of '*chocolat*', and rides to the Mauritanian border. I went for two of the first and one of the last. The driver was a fixed pole in a lavender-blue *boubou*. His name was Iselmu and he was a *beidane* (a white Moor), with a shiny-finned Merc and one place left.

'You will reach Nouadhibou', he declared, 'at the time of dusk, God willing.'

His head didn't so much as twitch. His sunglasses shielded his eyes so completely, I couldn't even tell if he was looking at me. But the sharply gathered syllables admitted no doubt – which was exactly what I needed.

Since leaving Laayoune, anxiety had been scooping a cavern in my stomach. What did I *know* about Mauritania? Hmmm... there was its knack for military coups (five since independence, including two in the last decade)... the ongoing slave trade... the bandits infesting its deserts... Apart from a genteel French monograph about the birdlife on the Banc d'Arguin, nothing I had read about the country inspired any confidence. Like WB Yeats enlisting Leo Africanus's 'undoubting impulse', I was in need of a boost. So to put myself in the hands of someone who looked like he knew what he was doing – it was all I could hope for.

Tomorrow would mark my first official border crossing since I started my journey in Fez. The return to Timbuktu was now well under way.

The School for Nomads

Lesson Four: Camp

THE POUNDING OF MILLET AND THE CRACKLE OF GRAINS STIR ME INTO THE day. Against the 360-degree solar attack, flaps of canvas are lifted and dropped, levered by hooked sticks and acacia pegs. Constant adjustment is required to keep us unstifled and burn-free, despite being deep in the heat like chips in a scuttle.

I hear yowling all around me. My early morning half-brain mistakes it for some kind of exotic wind, before I realise it's the mewling of a baby. By the time I'm sitting up, there are naked, blubbering, drooling children everywhere. Fingers probe the air around my nose; eyes expand to the size of karité nuts. The women scoop the babies up, swaddle them, sing to them, plug them to their breasts and wipe their bums with strips of old clothing. At the same time, they putter about, tending the teapot, preparing the millet, performing the dozens of tasks that comprise the daily life of a camp. One of them is carrying a bowl of speckled milk eked from the goats while bearing a 1-year-old in a sling across her back.

I go out later with Abdul-Hakim to watch. She caresses the nanny goats and strokes their underbellies, while Abdul-Hakim hamshackles the calves. The udders are nagged and slanted towards the bowl like a fireman's hose. The calves bleat in protest as their mothers are drained; and when it's over, they dive in for the slops.

The children are both Lamina's and Jadullah's. I would like to identify the women (ideally, I would like to talk to them), but Lamina is evasive when I ask about them, and I don't want to cause offence. Whenever I turn towards them, a head turns or a veil lifts across the face, a process of concealment so automatic it barely disrupts their chores.

'You are a wonder for the children,' says Lamina.

The mothers may avoid eye contact, but the children are under no such restraints. They stand around and ray-gun me with stares. I pull a silly face and one of them explodes with laughter; another bursts into tears and a little girl hides behind her brother's legs, poking her head round when her courage is up. Lamina is more familiar territory. They throw themselves around him with glee, bouncing on his knees, turning his legs into a mobile climbing frame.

Jadullah, characteristically, is more reserved. He pats a couple of toddlers, but he's in need of sleep. After spending most of the day under a blanket, he wanders to the fringe of the camp, to pick at the grass and peer at the sky, where harriers swirl like tea leaves seen from under a stirred glass.

'Is Jadullah watching out for something?' I ask Lamina.

He has already warned me not to stray too far from the camp. When I try to go to the toilet, he sends Abdul-Hakim to follow me. I remember the white tent I saw Jadullah peering at yesterday. I sense Lamina is nervous about something.

'There is an encampment near here.' The creases thicken on his brow. 'They are strangers.'

To Lamina, the desert is no wilderness or labyrinth, but a village where he knows everyone and is on good terms with most of them. But new arrivals are multiplying around the dunes. 'They are *ishumar*,' he tells me. Tuareg exiles, traditionally uncommon in this part of the Azawad; war veterans from Libya, returning to their homeland after the demise of their patron, Colonel Gaddafi. What their arrival augurs is for the future to decide.

I am thinking of the Tuareg when I wander away from the camp for a pee. 'What has no arms or legs but can still make a hole in the ground?' A favourite Tuareg riddle: the answer is carving a shallow runnel in the sand between my legs. Suitably relieved, I retie my pantaloons and go back to Abdul-Hakim. He's standing on duty a few yards away, assigned by Lamina to make sure nobody sees me who shouldn't.

'Come, Yusuf,' he says, 'we drink *dukhun*.'

This is a staple of desert diet, described in the fourteenth century by Ibn Battuta as 'water containing some pounded millet mixed with a little honey or milk'. We sip it from a common bowl, passed around the tent. Later, I am offered a handful of dried dates – the travel sweets of the desert caravan. They taste, lavishly, of honey and pepper.

I like these communal rituals. They help connect me to everyone else and are much easier to master than the dialect or the camel riding. When I get something right for the first time, Lamina gives me a smile, whether it's a complicated task like saddling or a no-brainer like sipping *dukhun*. The schoolboy in me is thrilled by these marks of approval: each smile is like a big tick on a test paper.

This far from town, the nomads have to be self-sufficient. They have a few sacks of rice, which the women start boiling for lunch, but the rest of the menu is homemade. The most delicious item is the *khubz ar-ramla* (literally 'sand bread'). I'm intrigued to watch them prepare it.

A pit is dug under the embers of the fire and a paste of millet flour dropped down the bore, covered with the embers until it cooks on top. After half an hour, the dough is turned over. Finally, it is scooped out of its warren and shared out with the rice and a black bean sauce. The crust has a bitter, charcoal taste, but the pith is rich and chewy, mealy as sourdough fresh off a griddle.

We eat the bread with rice, but my fumbling efforts leave plenty of flecks on the sand. No wonder the goats are eyeing me so attentively. As soon as I'm up, they dive in to swipe my remains, like conscientious waiters clearing the table for the next customer.

'Thank you,' I say to the wife I have identified as the maître d'. She doesn't reply, but she does look at me, and that feels significant. Her face is laced with wrinkles; she looks older than the others, strands of grey trickling under her scarf. Lamina relays my compliments and she opens her mouth, revealing half a dozen pointy black teeth between wide, blank spaces.

'She is happy,' says Lamina.

Part Five

Plateau

Wherein I spake of most disastrous chances,
Of moving accidents by flood and field;
Of hair-breadth 'scapes i' the imminent deadly breach;
Of being taken by the insolent foe
And sold to slavery; of my redemption thence,
And portance in my travel's history:
Wherein of antres vast, and deserts idle,
Rough quarries, rocks, and hills whose heads touch heaven,
It was my hint to speak.

William Shakespeare, *The Tragedy of Othello, the Moor of Venice*

13

Iron-Ore Train to the Adrar

BORDERS ARE THE GROINS OF NATIONS. IF ALL IS GOING WELL, THEY ARE jammed together like a couple of happy honeymooners. But when the frost sets in... that's when the chastity belts come out. Kuwait is sealed from Iraq by electrified fencing; India and Pakistan tease each other with silly walks and fanned turbans; Israel holds off Palestinians with 8-metre high slabs of concrete fitted with electric sensors. As for Morocco and Mauritania – bitter rivals since the 1975 war over Western Sahara, routinely shutting down their embassies, accusing each other of supporting their insurrectionists – they watch each other across 3 kilometres of landmined no-man's-land. Sandblasted truck cadavers, fleeced of their coats by the solar paint stripper, twisted piping and blistered body mouldings: it's an automobile graveyard. Some of the vehicles have been ripped open by landmines, their gunwales battered out of shape, their dashboards springy with mechanical entrails. Others have been abandoned by frustrated drivers mid-trip (their conditions suggested by flat tyres or bonnets still open for inspection) or dumped out of Morocco to avoid import duties.

I set out from Dakhla in Iselmu's Merc, one of four passengers. Palm trees and sand; tyre-grooved pistes; Atlantic breakers sapping the dunes like miners in a siege. At the checkpoints, light sparkled off epaulettes and collar studs and five-point star cap badges. Surrounded by the entropy of so much dead machinery, I could feel my confidence waning – *should have got a berth in one of the 4WDs, you fool!* – so I was relieved when we rolled onto asphalt at the back of the queue for the border. The cars bottlenecking at the front were shimmering in heat haze, bonnets quivering like jelly, as if the barrier had some supernatural power. A few trucks hovered among them: open-top Isuzus, stocked with freezer compartments to fill up with fish in Nouadhibou.

Most borders feel artificial, terrier efforts to piss a line on the sand. This one was different. Outside the tin-roofed customs hut, one of my companions took a couple of banknotes out of his wallet and handed them to the clerk, like a cloakroom ticket. He noticed my expression and his lips curled, the wry smile of a veteran.

'This is Africa.'

Over the coming weeks, I would hear this phrase many times. But what is it? A hardboiled shrug? Submission to pragmatism? A refusal to let dirty reality grind you down?

The name 'Africa' was given by the Romans. It refers to the Afri, a Berber tribe near Carthage. It has also been linked to the Phoenician word for dust. Leo Africanus traces it to 'the word Faraca, which signifieth ... to divide' or an Arabian king 'who is said to have been the first that ever inhabited these parts'. Whatever its derivation, there is an emotional heft to the word, lifted by those stressed vowels at either end. It means a thousand things to the people who claim it, but I do wonder if the spell it exerts is benign. What power those three potent syllables hold to pull people back, crushing them on centuries of thwarted hopes, shackling them to the cruel expectations of history.

Nouadhibou is Mauritania's second largest city, although it feels more like a village that keeps going. The lack of tall buildings, the single high street, the young men loitering: here is where the African Wild West begins. I sat in the hotel gatehouse, sipping tea with the security guard. 'Don't go on the street,' he warned, adding in a stagey whisper, 'Al-Qaeda!' But I was already cross with myself for not talking more to my neighbours on the car ride.

Outside, I wandered among men in flowing wide-sleeved *boubous*, plantain grillers and mobile phone credit sellers. I kept peering over my shoulder, too fresh in Mauritania to be trusting. There was warmth in the people I met, and after an evening of light conversation, snack chats and tea tattle, I was ready to plunge into a part of the journey that had excited me ever since I started planning it.

As part of their many grand plans for the Sahara, the French colonialists dreamed of a trans-Saharan railway. Steam was at its peak when they spread their conquest, and what better way to underline their authority than by dissecting the desert with tracks and signal

Tanners working in Fez: depilating goat and sheep skins in lime pits and drenching them in vegetable dyes.

The author at work in the tannery of Ain Azletoun, using a *sadriya* knife to smooth a freshly dyed goat skin.

Worshippers inside the Kairaouine mosque, the beating heart of Fez, whose university preceded Oxford's oldest college by four centuries.

Zagora, southern Morocco: 'Timbuktu 51 days', indicates
the traditional duration of the camel caravans.

Riding near the Black Mountain in the Moroccan Sahara, led by Salim, a Berber cameleer.

Saharawi girls in the Dakhla refugee camp: 165,000 refugees have been living in the 'Devil's garden' of south-west Algeria since the conflict of 1975.

Jaghagha and Ga'in, poets of the Aït Oussa tribe, regular victors in regional poetry contests in southern Morocco.

Ghazi (a *beidane* or 'white moor') leading his camel near Chinguetti, Mauritania.

Women dancing at a wedding party in Ouadane, Mauritania, stirred by the drumming and lute-playing of hereditary *iggawen* musicians.

Iman, a Fulani herder, leads his flock on the Séno-Gondo plain, Mali.

Iman's brother Suleiman rides a camel to draw water near the village of Tiogoro.

Ali *Hajji* and family: chief of the Fulani community in Djoungiani, Ali *Hajji*'s experiences have brought him into conflict with lions, bandits and the ravages of climate change.

Ibrahim, a Bozo
fisherman, drops his
net in the Bani river,
Mali: another day of
lean pickings.

The Great Mosque of Djenné: built in 1907 and annually replastered
by the whole community, it is Mali's most famous mud mosque.

Drawing water at the nomad encampment of Tayshak, five miles north of Timbuktu.

A Tuareg *enad* (blacksmith) prepares tea in Timbuktu.

Guns embedded in the
Flamme de la Paix (Flame
of Peace) in Timbuktu, a
monument erected after the
Tuareg rebellion of 1996.

Alladi, a corporal
in the Malian army,
an active pursuer of
jihadists.

The author outside the Djingereyber mosque in Timbuktu. Built in the fourteenth
century by an Andalusian poet, it was vandalised in 2012 by jihadists
who objected to the rituals taking place there.

points? The idea is irresistible. Sometimes, hugging my knees in buses or shared taxis, I thought wistfully of a railride across the Sahara. The French dream came to nought: investment faltered, profit calculations missed their targets, maritime trade routes were too dominant; and when Colonel Paul Flatters set out to chart a route in 1881, he and his men were slain by Tuareg tribesmen.

The French did, however, manage to lay 437 miles of track in Mauritania, linking the iron mines in the desert with the Atlantic Coast. The line still runs, conveying ore and supplies, as well as hundreds of passengers who pile into hoppers and cram the single passenger carriage. As a fan of rail travel, I couldn't wait to give it a try.

The station was a single hut on the dunes. People camped on suitcases and hessian sacks, rolling them over the sand to get in position. Waiting under the peeling blue plaster, a refuge from the sun, I watched the women presiding over their snack tables – wooden planks set on tyres, loaded with bottles of lukewarm water, packets of biscuits and cheese. A pneumatic-armed *vendeuse* punctuated her cheery monologue with puffs of squirrely laughter, while a wiry girl, wrapped in gauzy pink, counted the change. Floating behind them was a thick-bearded tea seller, bare chested under a cagoule. He was carrying a brass *théière* on a tray, pouring glasses from so high up you had to gulp several fingers of froth before you reached fluid – the sign of a really proficient pourer.

'*Allaaaah-u akbaaar!* God is great!'

Across the desert, the men gathered to pray, packed together like a wedding photo. Apart from myself, there was only one male who didn't join them. He was a twentysomething in a stiff-collared shirt, his face long and hollow cheeked, his nose a lordly beak, and I found him talking to one of the snack sellers. The vibe coming off him was haughty, possibly even hostile, but something encouraged me to approach him. I think it was the wing tips on his collar, which were as pointy as the ears of a fennec fox.

'*Dhalik al-makan huwa harr li as-salaat!*' I said. 'That's a hot spot to pray.'

His eyes moved right to left: first the top of my head, then my face, all the way down, then back again.

'*Isma*, listen!' His voice was low: the sort of tone you'd expect from a fellow seditionist if you were hiding in a cellar waiting to blow up parliament. 'You must not trust anyone. You understand? You are a white man. It is very dangerous for you.'

His name was Yisslam and he came from a village in the Adrar, although he wouldn't tell me its name.

'I am going to watch out for you,' he said.

Was this a pledge of protection, or a threat? Before I had a chance to find out, he drifted away, apparently to join the end of the prayers.

The freight train to Zouerat is an electromotive diesel, constructed to carry up to 84 tonnes of iron ore. Although preparations for the line started in 1940, the standard-gauge track was not laid until the 1960s, so the colonialists reaped little benefit. Negotiations repeatedly broke down with the Spanish to share resources and cut across Western Sahara (proof the colonial powers were just as snarky with each other as African states are today). As a result it is a curious hybrid, a fruit of colonialism that has proven more profitable to the postcolonial state (which has a 78 per cent shareholding). Today, it was scheduled to arrive 'some time in the afternoon'. We heard its first roar an hour after sunset: a mile and a half of cast-iron wagons on screeching, sparking bogies. Bolts rattled, doors clanked, people hurled themselves against the sheet-metal side.

According to James Joyce, travelling by train is one of the easiest things in the world: 'you get into those waggons called railway coaches,' he wrote to his friend Frank Budgen, 'which are behind the locomotive. This is done by opening a door and gently projecting into the compartment yourself and your valise.'

Joyce, of course, never made it to Nouadhibou.

A man with a hessian sack biffed a small girl out of the way. A woman passed her son through a tiny hatch. A behemoth built like a heavyweight carried his wife over his shoulder like a rag doll, face-palming anyone who came near him on the stepladder. Blinded by torch flash, deafened by the roars of competition, I was resigning myself to failure (*would it be safe to spend the night in the station hut? Or should I jump into one of the hoppers, along with some of the other stragglers?*) when my wrists were seized and my boots clattered on the edges of the steps.

'You want to sleep on the sand?' Yisslam hauled me through a mash of shawls and *boubous*, elbows in our ribs, tails of turbans brushing our ears, and parked me in the train's only seated compartment. 'This is Africa – you have to fight!'

Over the hubbub in the carriage, you could still hear fists slamming at the sides, slowly drowned by the racket of the train's departure. I was relieved, and a little humbled; I would never have made it under my own steam. Not that Yisslam was claiming any credit: with only one space left in the compartment, he left me there to join the sardines in the corridor.

I caught up with him later, but first I got to know my neighbours. A veiled lady beside me tried to empty her son's potty through the window, but the wind was feeling generous and threw it straight back. Perfumed in toddler pee, we did at least all smell the same, and it didn't stop my neighbour on the opposite plank from asking if I would like to marry his daughter (having softened me up for the deal with some delicious dates and a Winston). My excuse that I hadn't met her was countered by the presence of a taciturn-looking girl beside him. 'Look,' he said, shining his phone light, 'she is very beautiful – and fat!' I rallied back that I was already spoken for. But that didn't deter him either, so I made a tactical retreat to the corridor and sought out Yisslam.

He was standing in smoke fug and crowd mesh, his mouth plugged to a crack in the window. He reminded me of the caged market sheep in the Middle Atlas, panting in their buyers' trucks.

We talked for most of the night, about politics, Hollywood movies, laptop manufacturers, but mostly about money. Yisslam complained about the cost of study books and lessons, the extortions of his landlord in Nouadhibou, the inconsistent rates for electricity and food.

'Everyone wants to cheat,' he moaned. 'This is the problem in Africa, everyone wants to screw up everyone else.'

There was only one cost he didn't complain about. 'If you go back to Nouadhibou, you must ask for the Chinese one. She's the best. But be careful – when they see you are a white man, they will want to charge you double. Actually, it's better if you don't go on your own. You will call me and I can take you there.'

It sounded like a fascinating subject to learn more about, but any further insight would have to make way for refreshment: a tea seller was approaching. He squeezed through the crowd, balancing his glasses with astonishing dexterity. If anyone ever decides to launch a Mauritanian national circus, he's got to be a shoo-in. While we sipped our lukewarm glasses, another, less welcome figure was circulating, although calling him the ticket inspector makes him sound far more formidable than he really was. Sunk in his studded jacket, he looked overwhelmed – not only by the morass of ticketless passengers, but also by his jacket, which was several sizes too big for him.

'Why must I pay him?' Yisslam thrust his nose at all the limbs entwining us. 'I must pay for *this*?'

The inspector didn't have the spirit to muster a counter-argument. With each refusal his shoulders sagged a little more and he continued on his way, as if the whole process was some tortuous penance and he couldn't wait to get to the end.

Later, I squeezed back into the compartment and huddled down on the boards, inhaling the ammoniac smell of the blown-back potty. Most of the passengers had managed to close their eyes. Snore blasts harmonised with the melody of the couplings and the clacking of the wheels on the joints. How strangely soothing the mantra of a train can be, when all other transport comes off as such a cacophony. I suppose it has to do with the rhyme between train sounds and the human body. Close your eyes and it feels like you're inside some gentle mother giant, listening to her heartbeat and the pumping of her blood.

Unfortunately, on this particular train closing your eyes required the sort of concentration I had to apply to the pronunciation of the most awkward Arabic letters. Yisslam's knees cantilevered under my back and someone's head rocked against my knees. So distended was the journey – 14 lurching hours, at a speed never more than 30 miles an hour – that by morning I only had the haziest memory of a time when I hadn't been entangled in this matrix of interlocking bodies. It was as if we had metamorphosed into some kind of giant amoeba from which it required a concentrated effort of will to extract oneself.

Inside, the train was a contortion of limbs worthy of Hieronymous Bosch. Outside was its opposite: a pale golden void. The colours of *boubous* and robes, the sparkle of gold teeth and silver necklaces, the hoarse morning cry of newborns and men arguing over deals thrashed out in the dark – they were all pounded to insignificance by the sheer scale of that smooth, untrammelled sand. I tried to count how many freight wagons there were. Standing next to Yisslam on a bank of sand, I made it to 126. Yet against the backdrop of that unimpeded desert, every single one of them was tiny. The train was a caterpillar towing itself through a cornfield.

We were on a granite spur of the Adrar ('the mountains'), a tableland of dunes and sandstone cliffs that spawned the Almoravids and raised caravan towns on the trans-Saharan trade route, luring Portuguese merchants as early as the fifteenth century and holding off the French throughout most of the nineteenth. I jumped alongside Yisslam into a Toyota Hilux, carving a path through the dust to Choum, a warren of mud-brick houses and children skipping with broken wires. I was figuring on some haggling time to fix a ride to Atar, the regional hub; but Yisslam reeled me back from the drivers with a curved finger.

'You will stay with me.' His tone suggested less an invitation than a carefully studied forecast.

Conical thatched huts mushroomed between jaundiced tufts of grass on hard rocky *hammada*. Open-shirted officers leaned out of checkpoint huts, their hands embedded in bowls of rice and goat offal. We arrowed between the high grey cliffs of a gorge where vegetation flashed momentarily, a squall of green, before reverting to the greys and browns of the crusty *hammada* and the halogen gleam of shell-rock. We were up in the highlands now, where scarps scissor the plains into broad sandstone plateaus, curdled like overcooked custard.

'You know we have our festival tomorrow?' asked Yisslam.

Back in Fez, my friend Najib had invited me to join his family for Eid. I would have loved to take up the invitation, but I had to keep an eye on the calendar. To spend Eid with a family after all – what a prospect! Although, when I asked Yisslam about his background, he was curiously unresponsive. He spoke only in broad terms, informing me he was a *beidane*, a 'White Moor'.

'We are the chief people of Mauritania.' He flicked a finger towards one of the huts, pointing out a couple of darker-skinned men standing nearby. 'You see, those are *haratines* (Black Moors), they are not as handsome as us, or as clever.'

He might be haughty, but I was delighted to be in the company of a Moor. They were the main reason I was visiting Mauritania – the land of the 'Mauri', or Moors. Although the term 'Moor' is associated with colonial identity labels (their own term *beidane* simply means 'white'), there were people calling themselves Mauri back in Roman times. They were the Berber tribespeople who dominated northwest Africa when the Romans invaded, mentioned in Strabo's first-century *Geographica* and the 'obnoxia Mauris' of Calpurnius's *Eclogues*. Sometimes vassals of the Empire, sometimes allies of Carthage, they kept their independence when military means allowed, succumbing only sporadically to Arab rule.

These days, a 'Moor' is typically a Hassaniya Arabic speaker of Berber extraction, mostly confined to Mauritania (with small populations in Mali, Morocco and Senegal) and living further south than the ancient Mauris. But the term has been used more widely in the past. Employed as a catch-all for the Arabic-speaking populations of North Africa and the Iberian peninsula, it has been applied to philosophers and thinkers like Averroes, Ibn Tufail and of course Leo Africanus, whose adventuring and cultivated reputation may have inspired the most famous Moor of all (at least, from the perspective of Western literature): that 'honourable murderer', Othello.

Before Shakespeare's extraordinary tragedy made its debut in 1604, representation of Moors in English culture had been one-dimensional, 'black in his look, and bloody in his deeds'. So why did Shakespeare invest Othello with so much depth and nuance? 'We have still', wrote the literary scholar Lois Whitney, 'to explain not only the simplicity, frankness, and nobility of the character of Othello in spite of his sudden fit of passionate jealousy, but the whole colourful background of Othello's past: his connection with "men of royal siege", his wanderings from country to country that made it possible for Roderigo to describe him as "an extravagant and wheeling stranger Of here and everywhere"; his conversion to Christianity; and his captivity and "most disastrous chances". Is there any source for all this? I think there is.'

In 1600, three years before Shakespeare wrote *Othello*, John Pory's English translation of Leo Africanus's *Description of Africa* was published in London. Like Othello, Leo was captured, sold into slavery and later converted to Christianity. Like the Moors in Leo's account, Othello is 'valiant', but also 'credulous', 'proud and high-minded' and, 'by reason of jealousy', Leo tells us (like a plot spoiler at the Globe Theatre), 'you may see [the Moors] daily one to be the death and destruction of another'. Given that Leo was known to so many of Shakespeare's contemporaries (Ben Jonson references him in his *Masque of Blackness*), the bard's voracious reading and his familiarity with Richard Hakluyt (the preeminent Elizabethan publisher of exotic travel narratives, who encouraged Pory to translate Leo from the Italian), it is highly probable that Shakespeare was familiar, in some form, with Leo's *Description*.

Yet there is a significant difference. Leo's account of the 'white, or tawny Moors' is much more complimentary than Shakespeare's rash hero. They are 'steadfast in friendship,' he tells us, 'as likewise they indifferently and favourably esteem of other nations, and wholly endeavour themselves in this one thing; namely, that they may lead a most pleasant and jocund life. Moreover, they maintain most learned professors of liberal arts, and such men are most devout in their religion. Neither is there any people in all Africa that lead a more happy and honourable life.'

Remembering Leo's description, I thanked God for my luck (or, as it would be defined locally, my *baraka*, the divine blessing necessary to all travellers). Bring on the pleasantness! Sprinkle me with jocundity! Basalt ran down the sandstone cliffs, as if molten pitch had spilled down the fissures. The huts behind them were dwarfed by geology: bungalows of mud, squatting in swamps of sand. I climbed down behind Yisslam, wondering what kind of home a modern-day Moor might have.

We were standing in a film set for the Book of Genesis. Granted, there were no cameras or dolly tracks or clapperboards, but in all other respects it was perfect. In a rocky combe stripped of all but the last few tufts of bleached grass, around 400 livestock were holding pow-wows with high-pitched bleats and whines. Men in dust-stained robes leaped out of pick-up trucks and 4WDs, picking out the healthiest-looking animals and handing over 20,000 *ouguiya* (about €50) per beast. There were no tea marquees, no walls to pen the herds behind, no contracts. It made the livestock market in the Middle Atlas look like a state-of-the-art department store.

'My driver will meet us here.' Yisslam scanned the scene with narrowed eyes. 'But he is late.'

There was reason for his impatience: the plumpest of the goats had already been snaffled. When his driver arrived at last – tall and bow-legged, dust spilling from his turban – they set to work at once. Gliding down the hillside, they grabbed a pair of legs each, slinging the fattest goat they could find into the back of a pick-up. Particularly close attention was paid to the pendulous scrotum and the rigidity of the ears. Four animals were secured, under the watch of a boy with a swollen lip, before the introductions were made.

'This is Abidine.' Yisslam slung an arm across the tall man's shoulder. 'He is my slave.'

The man who brushed his hand against mine was beaming, a single yellow tooth poking from his gummy mouth, a look of laid-back warmth in his small dark eyes. He was a member of a notorious club – half a million Mauritanians still in bondage (the highest per capita slave population in the world). Abidine's family had been retainers to Yisslam's for so long that neither could tell how many generations were spanned. Yisslam tipped his head back – an instruction to get moving – and Abidine swung over to the driver's seat.

The relationship between white and black (definitions that draw on ancestry more than appearance) is a knotty feature of Mauritania's modern history. Although French armies marched across the Adrar, the *colons* only made a superficial impression on the area's long-standing social structures. Administering the colony from the comfort of Senegal, unable to impose agriculture on a land dominated by rocky plateaus and sand dunes, they never dug as deep as in their other African colonies.

As a result, Mauritania was an exception to the prevailing post-colonial rule: it was the traditionally nomadic *beidane* who held the reins of power, and for more than half a century, despite increasing sedentarisation, they haven't let go. Of nine heads of state, only one has been black, and he was an interim president who held the post for just four months.

Nevertheless, events outside the corridors of power suggest a popular will to break this status quo. In 1979, discrimination against blacks in government posts led to widespread unrest and the fall of Colonel Ould Salek. A decade later, a dispute over grazing rights on the Senegal river unleashed a storm of bloodshed (characterised by shootings, arson attacks and several beheadings) and a blitz of oppression from the Mauritanian government, leading to a population shift of around 170,000 people. More recently, in 2011, seven black protesters were shot in a march about citizenship rights. In Mauritania's hierarchical, Manichean system, race remains a tinderbox. Yet what made the relationship between *beidane* and *haratine* (former slaves, many of whom continue to work for their 'masters' on terms little changed from those imposed on their ancestors) so disturbing to me was the lack of antagonism; the phlegmatic acceptance. Colour-coordinated social status was so deeply entrenched that I found myself questioning my own right to evaluate it.

We rattled over to Yisslam's pied-à-terre: a mud-brick hut squatting in a yard where the sand was so high it blocked the door and had to be cleared. Abidine and the boy with the split lip crouched around the doorway, shovelling the sand with their hands. It was going to take a while, so I stepped forward to help. I think I made it about halfway across the yard before I found myself stalling. I still don't understand why I couldn't move. It felt like an invisible wall, a barrier mortared by anxiety... a fear of displeasing my host... cowardice, I suppose. I was conscious of being an alien, in a culture I had scarcely begun to know. But how I wish – when I think back to that moment – how I wish I could have broken down that invisible wall and got down in the dirt with Yisslam's slaves.

Inside the hut, sunlight swamped a cellophane window, fuzzing the air around the boy with the swollen lip. He never spoke, and when I thanked him for the tea, he kept his eyes resolutely on the mat. It was a wonderful glass – generously frothed and poured from an astonishing height. I never heard him speak. Yisslam moved across him, received a glass from him, but never acknowledged him. It was only when we were leaving that the boy looked up. His eyes were limpid, grey-brown pools, impossible to read because I never knew him; but I can still see them, gleaming with what I think was an unsatisfied curiosity.

We boarded the pick-up truck to drive to Yisslam's village. The boy strapped a couple of plastic water *bidons* over the running board to collect the overflow from the radiator, and lowered himself into the back with the goats. Whenever we stopped, I turned and looked his way; but he was well trained and didn't lift his eyes again. Abidine's status was more ambiguous. He had his own house (a 'gift' from Yisslam's family) and was not required to show deference all the time. When we climbed out of the car for breaks, he dusted the sand from Yisslam's cloak; but he also took cigarettes from Yisslam's pack without needing to ask; and when his master made a joke, he low-fived him as loudly as a boon companion. He drove with his turban tucked over his nose to keep out the dust and his left foot, bare and bunioned, slung over the lip of the window. It was a posture that would have given me aches and pains for weeks, but Abidine was clearly well used to it.

Slavery has been active in West Africa for centuries, if not millennia. Still rife in Mauritania and Mali, the trade has a devious capacity to evolve and adapt. Not every slave is aware of their rights. As a campaigner for Anti-Slavery International told me before my trip, 'It can be very hard for slaves psychologically. They have to break the chains themselves, otherwise they can never be free.'

Religious tradition offered justification for apologists: the sin of Ham, whose descendants were traditionally cursed with blackness after he saw his father Noah naked and drunk. Ibn Khaldun dismissed this argument in a forceful passage in the *Muqaddimah*,[30] but that did not shake the idea off its stubborn perch; and for those seeking alternative justifications, others were available. 'You know', wrote Ahmad Baba

---

30 'Genealogists who had no knowledge of the true nature of things imagined that Negroes are the children of Ham,' he wrote, '... and that they were singled out to be black as the result of Noah's curse ... The curse included no more than that Ham's descendants should be the slaves of his brothers' descendants. To attribute the blackness of the Negroes to Ham, reveals disregard of the true nature of heat and cold and of the influence they exercise upon the air [climate] and upon the creatures that come into being in it.'

in the sixteenth century, 'that the cause of enslavement is unbelief ... whoever is enslaved in a state of unbelief may rightly be owned.'

Leo Africanus sheds some light on the practicalities of the trans-Saharan slave trade, enumerating the value accorded to black slaves in inventories of tribute. In Bornu, you would need 15–20 slaves to cover the price of a horse; but by the time they had crossed the Sahara, they had earned a little VAT. Inventorying the tribute sent to Fez by a prince of the Drâa valley, Leo tells us male and female slaves retailed at 'twenty ducats a piece', compared to 50 for a camel. Even at their most costly, slaves were rarely considered more precious than a manuscript, or a bar of salt.

The numbers of the medieval slave trade are hard to estimate, but they were sufficiently gargantuan for Ibn Batutta to be unfazed by a caravan with 600 female slaves in the fourteenth century. By the time René Caillié crossed the desert half a millennium later, slave raiding was on the wane, although he saw plenty of slaves on his travels and was appalled by the treatment of the child slaves: 'Exhausted by their sufferings and their lamentations, those unhappy creatures fell on the ground, and seemed to have no power to rise; but the Moors did not suffer them to continue there long when travelling. Insensible to the sufferings which childhood is so little fitted to support, these barbarians dragged them along with violence, beating them incessantly, till they had overtaken the camels.' These days it is rare to witness such public abuse, and the most vicious treatment tends to take place in the walled confinement of cities. The term 'slave' drips with so much emotional baggage that many anthropologists insist on using more specific local terminology. I would discover more about slavery in Mali, and the more I learned, the murkier the subject appeared.

We were driving along the Adrar escarpment, flanked by scrub desert where acacias and balanites offered intermittent shade. Knuckles of granite gripped the plain, grouted with sand, while desert larks skittered over the scrub in search of insects, and the pointy ears of a fennec poked out of a narrow dugout. People were scarce, although the odd low-lying tent grazed the sky. So even without such bright clothing, the hitchhikers would have stood out. They were waiting under the raggedy parasol of a balanite, he in a white suit as shiny as sharkskin, she in a multicoloured headdress decorated with coins. Recently married, they were on their way to celebrate Eid in his family's tent. The man looked really proud. When they disembarked a couple of miles down the road, I guessed why from the way his wife's hand curled over her stomach.

Soon after that, we left the blacktop. Rock jolted the wheels and played havoc with the suspension. You could hear the scraping of thorns and the rattle of acacia branches whipping the gunwales. There was only one way for Abidine to make progress: fly with open throttle, gripping the steering wheel with all his might. A couple of times, I thought we might topple. Once, we slid over the edge of a well. The window beside me was jammed open, so I was stung by the sun, lashed by gusts and pelted by dust at the same time (Abidine had to use the windscreen wipers to clear his view), but thanks to the mesmerising sight ahead, it was possible to ignore all that.

Tapering skywards in the windscreen was a jagged black pyramid. Sand cascaded around its base in smooth glassy cliffs, under fluted walls of coppery rock and lone-standing yardangs that provided look-out posts for falcons. It would be an exaggeration to compare Mount Zarga to the great wonders of the earth, but it had something of their brute majesty – a landform you could revere.

Yisslam had said little about the village, insisting: 'You will find your answers when we arrive.' But I had naively assumed, when he spoke of a village, that he meant a place with houses. It was only now that I realised...

Squatting ahead of us, webbed with rope, ringed with thorny palisades, were dozens of tents. They were black and peaked, as if in homage to the mount. Goats loitered between them, feeding out of bisected car tyres. All that talk of laptops and movies and Chinese prostitutes had misdirected me. Without even being aware of it, I had stumbled on an invitation to a nomad encampment!

We pulled up beside one of the tents. Around 30 logs, some forked, others bent to form arches, lifted a roof of stitched goatskins. Rugs and palm-reed mats stretched across the ground, ridged with utensils – a steel bowl with a sieve on top, a pile of lambskin blankets, a Dunlop tennis ball tube filled with herbs. More tools and bric-à-brac hung above us, from a pair of trestles lashed by leather thongs. Seen from a distance, you might have sketched the dwelling with three straight lines. Close up, it was an intricately layered hive.

Several women were sitting inside the tent, gathered round a kettle. The younger ones had knotted plastic around their fingers to protect their henna decorations. At their centre was a moon-faced woman with dark tattooed lips, in a full red gown, presiding over a double-tiered tray with a bag of tea leaves and several thimble-shaped glasses. Given her posture and position, I assumed she must be important, but I was still taken by surprise when Yisslam introduced her.

'Mr Nicholas,' he announced, 'this is my wife.'

14

Dancing with Nomads

SOME LESSONS ARE SO PARTICULAR YOU CAN NEVER USE THEM OUTSIDE of their immediate context; others are adaptable all over the world. Among the nomads of North Africa, one lesson had a wider application than any other. No wonder it was one of the first lessons Lamina had taught me. Because, until you have this string to your bow, how can you even call yourself an apprentice? Now was my opportunity to show what I had learned.

That's right: I was brewing the tea.

Yisslam's grandmother made sure I did it correctly. Her face was seamed and riddled with so many grades and textures, it recalled the mountain cliffs we had passed on the journey from Atar. It brought out all the more vividly the delicate beauty of her eyes, which were a shade of brown so pale they could almost be described as gold.

She had started the fire, dropping lumps of charcoal onto a brazier, stoked with dry leaves. Following her guidance, I scooped a handful of tea leaves into a metal pot, poured a few drops of water from a *guerba* and placed the pot on the coals. When bubbles of water started wrestling with the lid, I took three glasses, filled them with water, then emptied the water back into the pot. This process was repeated three times. When the pot was bubbling over again, I tipped sugar into one of the glasses and poured it back. Then I filled the de-sugared glass with water, raising my arm high over my head to increase the froth, before knocking back the lid and emptying the glass again.

'*Jawdah*,' said the old lady. 'Quality.'

She wasn't one for short-cuts. When I decided the water was ready, she wagged a finger, nudging me to fill the glasses again, until she was satisfied with the level of saccharification. Pinning her mouth with a narrow silver pipe, she tilted her head at the pot until the tea was steeped; and only when the required standard was met did she let out a triumphant puff, her lips curling in a narrow arc around the smoke. I set the glasses before her and she poured out three servings, calling over to Amina, Yisslam's wife, so we could all have a sip.

'The first glass,' said Amina, 'is bitter, like death. The second is strong, like life, and the third is sweet, like love.'

I had heard the same ritual saying in Timbuktu; and I would hear it all the way back there. As Noël Coward once said, 'Wouldn't it be dreadful to live in a country where they didn't have tea?' All across the Sahara, there is no fear of that.

Yisslam's grandmother spent her days making silver bracelets, using metal from the mines of Zouerat. Unplugging the lid from a painted wooden box, she showed me bead necklaces, camel-hair bowls and satchels made of painted goatskin. I wondered who she made them for: we were an hour's drive from the main road, in a country that was hardly thronging with tourists.

'Chinguetti,' she said, as if reading my mind.

The seventh most sacred city of Islam, storehouse of learning and pilgrims' launchpad for the region. On the route map I'd squiggled into the back page of my diary, it was marked by a big red star, matched only by the ones for Timbuktu and Djenné. I asked her to tell me about it.

'*Medeeena kabeeeera*, a big city.' She stretched out the words, her brown-gold eyes glittering against her wrinkles. 'Everything is there. Vegetables and fruit... tobacco, silver, cloth...' She listed several other items I couldn't fathom, before completing the account with a marvelling slide of the head: '*Makan al-dhahul*, a place of amazement.'

When Yisslam awoke from his nap, we all sat around to eat. Oil was poured into the couscous so we could fasten it in our hands. The girls were allowed to use spoons to avoid ruining the decorative henna patterns on their hands and arms, but I tried to follow the men. As usual my place was the messiest by the end of the meal.

At least I was in good company. In 1828, travelling in disguise on his journey to Timbuktu, René Caillié told his hosts he had escaped from Christian captivity. Without this excuse, his food handling would have been a giveaway. 'Though I had been accustomed to take my food by handfuls,' he wrote, 'I was still far from being as expert as they. I sometimes let part of the mess fall on the ground which gave them great offence, and made them vent their anger in maledictions on the Christians, who, they observed, had not even taught me how to eat decently.'

I wasn't conscious of maledictions, but a few amused glances were certainly exchanged. If anything, they helped me feel more welcome. Like my Arabic howlers, they were a great way to entertain my hosts.

After dinner the girls gathered around me, asking my name, the size of my family and various other questions. One of them, Yisslam's 10-year-old niece Hady, showed me her *Al-Kafi* Arabic textbook and I read a few sentences with her. Her school was near the road but she was staying with her grandfather for Eid, while her parents were in the bush. Like the other girls, she was thrilled with her henna decorations. They were all keen to admire each other's patterns, which had been applied to celebrate the imminent holy day.

'It is a blessing for us', said one of them, 'to have a guest for Eid.'

All eyes turned to the grandmother, the way eyes in other parts of the world turn to the television screen when a favourite show is about to start. She pressed her wrists in the sand, levering herself back from the bowl. Clasping her hands together, she looked up towards the roof of the tent and narrated the story behind Eid.

'The Prophet Ibrahim wanted to have a son. But for many years God did not grant his wish. His wife was barren and she had reached the age when women no longer bear children. But God is all-powerful and one day a son was born to Ibrahim and they named him Ishmael. When Ishmael was old enough to work, Ibrahim had a dream that God wanted his son as a sacrifice. So he told Ishmael and asked if he agreed, and Ishmael said he would do as the Lord commanded. So Ibrahim took his only son to the top of Mount Moriah to kill him. But God stayed his hand at the last moment and told him to keep his son. A ram appeared nearby and Ibrahim took it to the altar to sacrifice instead.'

Looked at with a modern eye, this is a troubling story: it reads like child abuse and an early example of the Nuremberg Defence. But it is understood differently in Muslim societies. So absolute is Ibrahim's submission to God that he is prepared to give up the most precious thing in his life. However crude the story's narrative elements, they provide the framework, as stark as the desert in which the story takes place, for a parable about humility. Coming from a society that emphasises individualism, I found it hard to engage with the story in the same way as Yisslam's relatives. They listened to the telling with glowing smiles, their admiration for their fellow nomad renewed by their grandmother's crackly voiced rendition.

Time's elastic stretch can give an impression of universality to scriptural stories. It is easy to forget they were written and recorded in a particular time and place. In the case of the Quran, this is the mercantile world inhabited by the Prophet Mohammed. The *surat* are rife with references to 'accounts' and 'balances', to men's deeds being 'weighed', the Last Judgment as a 'reckoning'. If this is the word of God, it is the word specifically directed at the merchant class to which Mohammed belonged.

Yet there is another world, underneath this one, which inspired many of Islam's most enduring symbols and ideas. This is the world of nomadism. We see it in the mention of wells, caravan routes, herds, blood revenge. We see it in the theme of fatalism, accepting cruel twists of fortune, be it marauding tribes, dried-up wells or vicious sandstorms, which is rooted in the practicalities of energy conservation in the desert. And we see it in the faith's most abiding symbol: topping every mosque, curling across the flags of Islamic states or the sides of their ambulances. Nomads are lunar people, grateful to the kindly beacon that lights their caravan trails. Their hearts are with the moon; and so, it follows, is Islam's.

Yisslam's family emphasised their religious credentials with their interest in the story of Ishmael's almost-sacrifice. But a lighter form of entertainment was awaiting us, and the first stirrings of its music had already breached the tent. When the meal was over, Yisslam led me across the plain, yelling through the awning of a neighbouring tent. Taking care not to trip over the guy-ropes, I followed him inside.

Imagine bright lights, a dark vault above you, the performers shining in the glare. The lights are torches held by the men, a ring around the edge of the tent; the performers are four girls in patterned gowns and sequinned headscarves. They have an upturned couscous bowl and a water barrel between them, which they rap in sharp, rhythmic hand beats. One of them has loosened the shift around her chest, her baby suckling while she leads the beat.

Was this the 'pleasant and jocund life' that Leo Africanus noted? One of the girls beckoned me over to play with them, so I knee-walked across the rug and crouched behind the couscous bowl. I don't think anyone could accuse me of injecting any rhythm into the tune, but I thumped with plenty of enthusiasm and that seemed to please them. They were indulgent hosts, trilling me along while they tattooed the other side of the barrel, conjuring lyrics out of the air, chanting an old rhyme that, according to Yisslam, was 'a praise song for the blessing of a stranger in our tent'.

Later, some of the men punted me to the middle of the tent. 'Raqs!' they commanded. 'Dance!' I was a novelty for them, and they wanted to see my moves. Oh dear, if only they'd asked for something else! I managed a few pirouettes, an arm twist or two... I jangled my wrists and twerked my shoulders. I tried out some of the moves I'd learned from Najib in Fez – stutter-stepping and arm chopping like a hip-hop robot – but I was running out of ideas. *Can somebody help me out here?*

After they had seen enough of my solo turn, the girls sprang up, melting my staccato dance with the languid sway of hips and curling, coiling arms. One of them lassoed my shoulders with a folded turban and towed me towards her, then minced backwards, her feet covered by the hem of her dress, her scarf held tight over her face, like a *yashmak*. *Is she flirting with me?* There was a ritual atmosphere to the choreography, as if it contained layers of hidden meaning – a courtship dance, perhaps – matched by the slower, more deliberate tempo of the drumming. All around the tent I could hear the clapping and laughter of the men and the other women; it was the perfect balance of high spirits and relaxation. It was one of those miracles that, if you travel long enough, occasionally pulls you in – a magical evening in the bosom of this welcoming nomad family.

As Yisslam led me back to his tent, deep into the night, I felt like I was drunk. When I started looking into the world of nomads, I never imagined I would be dancing with them in the middle of the Sahara. The beat of the couscous bowl, the lassoing of the turbans, those marvellous girls and their flashing, toothy smiles, would all stay with me, long, long into my journey through their desert.

'Congratulations for Eid!'

All over the village, there was a merry exchange of good wishes and hard-boiled sweets. Yisslam took me on a morning strollabout: we extended our hands and pressed them to our hearts, batting the greeting phrases back and forth. Each extended arm, each swaying of our robes, was echoed on the ground, where the sun stencilled our shadows with the black precision of steel etchings.

Between the tents there were patches of vegetation, shrivelled capers on twisting pink stems and fleshy honeycombs of euphorbia. One old woman presided over a bed of colocynths (or 'Sodom's apples'), the toxic green fruits ballooning from wide-lobed leaves. She was boiling their seeds to make flour. She offered us untreated goat's milk – bluish and rancid smelling but much esteemed by everyone around me – while her husband lay in the shade of their tent, whooping at some unseen vision.

'He is crazy.' The woman's shoulders lifted in a flinty shrug. 'The *djinn* ate his mind.'

Crazy – *majnun*. Literally 'bedjinned': taken by the magical spirits that haunt wastelands and ruins throughout Islamic culture. I had heard plenty about the *djinn* in Fez – one of Mansur's friends had described being possessed by a *djinn*, after loitering in an abandoned house to drink alcohol and sleep with tourists. He was only exorcised when his father slaughtered a sheep, distributed the meat to the poor, and read the *sura* of the *djinn* from the Quran. After passing out, he woke up, feeling 'cleaned out, like a cooking pot', and ever since he had been a passionate, born-again Muslim.

Desert dwellers are just as vulnerable as city slickers. The old lady's husband may not have stooped to drinking alcohol or picking up foreign girls (fat chance round here), but he had exposed himself to the *djinn* all the same, in a way that makes nomads especially susceptible: he had spent too much time on his own.

'He was always in the desert with his camels,' said Yisslam later, in the unforgiving tone of an Old Testament patriarch. 'It is not good to be alone in the desert, away from other men. Everybody knows that.'

We were back at his tent. His wife Amina had pulled a plate off the kitchen shelf (a hammock swinging from the roof) in preparation for lunch. After another round of goat's milk, we were given goat's cream with dates, followed by goat's stomach. I think, during my stint as Yisslam's guest, I tried every part of a goat you can eat. Leo Africanus would not have been surprised by the way we ate them: he notes of the Saharan Arabs that 'for supper they have certain dried flesh steeped in butter and milk, whereof each one taking his share, eateth it out of his fist'. Despite my earlier lessons in bare-knuckle banqueting, I remained a rank amateur. I fumbled my crouching, struggled to use my right hand as a spoon, and unlike everyone else I still had nerves in my fingertips, so I kept dropping the meat back on the platter.

'What is the problem?' asked Yisslam, giving me one of his right-to-left scans. 'Do you not like the food?'

'Oh, I do.' I threw him a pleading look, but he didn't catch it. 'It's just... very hot.'

'You don't like it?'

'No, I do, honestly.'

'Then please eat it, Nicholas.'

I bit my tongue and dug in, trying to hide my winces. I could feel the heat burning through my palm. Presumably, after a few years in the desert, I too would be able to pick up these pyroclasts of flesh as nonchalantly as everyone else. But for now, I was an embarrassment: the clumsy foreigner who dribbled his couscous and couldn't even hold a morsel of freshly cooked goat without having to suck his fingers.

Hospitality is one of the great provisions of the desert; but 'the dues of hospitality extend for three days', as *The Thousand and One Nights* reminds us. I had read enough stories about the subtle measures taken by put-upon hosts, so on the third day I asked Yisslam if he could help me back to the blacktop.

'Of course,' he said confidently. 'We will make sure you reach Chinguetti.'

I was glad at the prospect of continuing the journey, but a little saddened by his readiness to help me on my way.

The next afternoon, as I was saying my farewells, he presented me with a *boubou*, full sleeved with a V-line of gold thread around the collar. I felt like Alice when she offers her thimble to the dodo: I didn't have anything adequate to give in return. So I tore a sheet out of my diary and scribbled a thickly dotted thank-you note. It was handed to 10-year-old Hady. She scanned it carefully, mouthing the words to herself, then read it aloud to the assembled gathering, looking up through her eyelashes to see if her elders approved. Yisslam's wife and aunt bowed their heads, and his grandmother spread her hands in benediction: '*Alhamdulillah*, thanks to God.' I could wish for no greater seal of approval. Although, as Yisslam escorted me to the edge of the village, he did point out that I had misconjugated one of my verbs.

'I think you are only a beginner in Arabic,' he said.

Mohammed-Amin was an old friend of Yisslam's family. His ridged face looked like it had been made out of the local mud by a moulder whose nails needed paring, and he wore a 4-metre-long turban that could double as a mattress. He was heading to the road that afternoon with his donkey, so he would be able to point me in the right direction. I was in luck: it wasn't every day someone from the camp ventured this far.

'How long do you think it will take us?' I asked, while Mohammed-Amin was strapping my backpack onto his donkey.

The animal's mane was short and springy, threaded with sand. Boils pustuled on the skin at the top of his hind legs, tracking the bitter history of previous burdens.

Mohammed-Amin shrugged. 'One hour, God willing.'

God was not willing. Three and a half hours later, with only a slither of moonlight to show the way, we were still deep in the bush.

We kept behind the donkey because, as Mohammed-Amin explained, 'The donkey always wants to be the leader.' If you walked in front, he stopped; and whichever side you went, he veered towards the other. Occasionally Mohammed-Amin gave the animal a tap with his stick, but mostly he communicated by clicking his tongue between his teeth and making groaning sounds.

'I don't like to hit the donkey,' he said. 'You can talk to a donkey, just as you can talk to a man. You only use the stick when you failed at talking.'

More problematic than the donkey's stubbornness was the lack of a path. Fortunately, Mohammed-Amin had a solution for this. He would stop at a caper bush, running a hand down the springy leaves; or let out a whoop when he spotted a familiar hanza bush, its marble-shaped fruits hidden under leathery fronds. There was enough vegetation to tow us all the way, recognised from countless traverses, each shrub or well like a knot in Theseus's thread through the labyrinth.

'People will come,' Mohammed-Amin said when we finally made it to the road. 'There are always people coming this way.'

He was right. We only had to wait two and a half hours before a pair of headlights burned through the horizon like low-hanging stars. It was a pick-up truck, with a full cab and a dozen sheep in the bed, squeezed under a cargo net.

'Have you got... space?' I asked.

Of course they did! Within moments, I was ensconced in my seat: a dozen ovine heads for cushions and a couple of rams' horns poking between my legs.

'May God protect you!' called Mohammed-Amin.

He glowed in the taillights, hands clasped over his head.

The road was only tarred for a mile. After that it swung across the curving surface, lurching over rogue boulders, sucking me down among the sheep. It was cool outside, but the heat of the animals scorched through me, like I was bouncing on top of a bread oven. Every time I pulled myself upright, another lurch siphoned me into the net, then a bump and I was a flipped pancake. Sometimes I rankled – from the lurching, a crossbar digging in my back, the tupping of the sheep at my arse. But I only had to remind myself 'I'm riding a sheep truck on the road to Chinguetti!' and I couldn't help smiling.

Except, this wasn't quite the road to Chinguetti. At a turn-off, the pick-up came to a juddering stop. The bleating of the sheep vocalised their relief: *good riddance to Mr Big Fat Intruder*.

'Where is Chinguetti?' I asked the driver.

He was impatient to be moving on. 'There!'

It was only visible after the dust cloud of the truck's departure had dissolved: a flicker of electric light, 10 miles across the horizon.

Perhaps a car would stop... I'd meet some tardy 4WDer rushing home for Eid... I'd be invited to a feast! I trudged along the road hopefully, but an hour's stagger was as much as I could manage. The truth might as well have been scrawled across the sky: *your luck's run out*. Banking down in the sand, I opened my backpack to release the *boubou* Yisslam had given me. It made a pretty decent mattress. With my Moroccan *djellaba* as a coverlet (the same one I had bought for the camel sacrifice in Fez – there were still a few brown bloodstains on the hem), I lay down for the first of many nights under the stars, praying there wouldn't be any hungry hyenas doing the rounds tonight. Or vipers. Or deathstalker scorpions. Or bandits.

I can't say it was the best night's sleep I have ever had.

15

Libraries in the Sand

IN JANUARY 1833, AN UNUSUAL VISITOR APPEARED ON THE ROCK OF Gibraltar. His name was Sidi Ahmed and he was (according to the *Gibraltar Chronicle and Commercial Intelligencer*) 'the Tributary King of Changuiti'.

'The African King landed', the report informs us, 'under a salute, at the Ragged Staff where a Guard of Honour and Band were in attendance.' Carried around Gibraltar in the Lieutenant-Governor's official carriage, Sidi Ahmed visited the Grand Arsenal, attended the Guard Mounting on Alameda Parade, and was guest of honour at a soirée held by the Lieutenant-Governor's wife, as well as a ball at which he 'expressed his unbounded admiration of the beauty and graceful-ness of the ladies'. So warmly was he received that he was reported to declare 'that Gibraltar was the wonder of the world'.

The joke was on Gibraltar: Sidi Ahmed was no king. He was just a humble scholar from the Adrar, heading back home after the *hajj*. Like many Mauritanian scholars, he had been picking up books along the way (in Tunis, the stepson of the Bey gave him more than 60 vol-umes because Sidi Ahmed said, 'There is nothing I love better than books') and he would add his own to the collection: *The Pilgrimage of Ahmed, Son of the Little Bird of Paradise*. One of the most mercurial travelogues of its period, it spins from audiences with the Sultans of Morocco and Tripoli to encounters with clairvoyants, visits to the tombs of Sufi saints and a pilgrimage to Mecca under the shadow of a plague. Along the way, Sidi Ahmed is visited with bundles of luck (in Cairo, he manages to retrieve his impounded goods from the 'Tithing House'; in Algiers, his brig is loaded with provisions by the French consul), all of which he attributes to 'the *Baraka* of the Messenger of God' – the blessing necessary for the success of any journey.

Sidi Ahmed is not unique. That is what makes his story so intrigu-ing: he bears the standard for a wider phenomenon, lifting the lid on the little-known world of Saharan bibliophilia. While in Chinguetti, I hoped for a glimpse of the harvest.

After a straggle of homesteads half swallowed by sand – iron-domed enclosures with stone walls – a giant sandpit sweeps across the valley. Teetering up the dune are reddish-grey drystone walls, precariously balanced like a giant domino set. Here is Chinguetti, pearl of the Adrar and the seventh most sacred city of Islam, the hub from which pilgrims in the region used to set off on the *hajj*.

There was barely a soul knocking about: a girl with a sack of rice on her head, a small boy with a toy car ingeniously made from twisted wires and drink-can cut-outs. A group of 9- and 10-year-olds invited me to join their game. They had a small pile of coins, which they hid under the sand, taking it in turns to strike the sand with their flip-flops. Once the coins had been uncovered, the winner was the one who knocked the coins out first.

'*Mabruk*, well done!' they yelled, slapping the sand when – after a dogged run of defeats – I finally emerged triumphant. I decided to retire at my peak, and wandered into the stone maze with their congratulations ringing in my ears.

I wondered that coins were all they uncovered from a sweep of the sand. I half expected the last sally to reveal the tattered fringe of some ancient manuscript; for Chinguetti is the great library town of the Moors, the place that bears out Leo Africanus's assertion about their 'learned professors' and men 'devout in religion'.

'The reason we have so many books here', explained Ahmed Mahmoud, 'is because of the caravan trade. Thousands of caravans used to pass through, because we are one of the holiest cities in Islam and the chief place on the caravan trail in this part of the desert.'

Mahmoud was one of the town's best-known librarians: tidy of beard, high of brow, with the ramrod spine so common among the *beidane*. I met him by appointment in the doorway of his family's limestone house, and he led me across the courtyard, holding a block of wood pierced by six nails. It looked like a toothbrush for a steel-fanged giant. It was a suitably mythic key for his collection, which was locked behind a thick acacia door. He jammed the key in the hole and twisted open his ancestral heirloom. Sunlight spread around us like a stain, filling up a tenebrous chamber roofed with palm trunks, as dusty and book crammed as a wizard's study.

Chronicles. Quranic commentaries. Grammar books. Works on mathematics and astronomy. Property deeds. Dictionaries. Shelves sagged under lever-arch files, leather portfolios and stuffed manila folders. A large wooden case hovered beside them, containing the showpieces: a goatskin copy of the *Hadiths* of Bukhari, a crinkly tome by an eighteenth-century Andalusian astrologer, a poetry anthology in which different coloured inks (iron oxide for red, indigo for blue, charcoal for black) indicated the different authors, their verses threading the deckled pages like singers' voices in a trio. I was standing in a time capsule, peering into an era when books were so precious that a single dictionary could be exchanged for two horses and the average book fetched a higher price than a slave.

'Our family has 700 books in total,' explained Ahmed. 'They collected them on *hajj* or on trading journeys. It was unusual to come back from a journey without something new.'

It wasn't nomadism in the pastoral sense, but it followed the same principles: intellectual grazing, coming back to the old watering holes richer than before. What is more, these collections were gathered by men who were trading in salt, camels and other merchandise (in another room at the back of the house, Ahmed showed me camel-milking boards, cassiawood inkpot carriers and *amesh-shaghabs* for women and children to sit on top of the camels, similar to the ones I saw in Bert Flint's house in Marrakesh). Books were one precious feature among the many traded across the desert.

Over several days in Chinguetti I visited many of its libraries: dry-stone homesteads where the termite-nibbled tomes looked like cabbage patches after a caterpillar rampage. The guardians were used to visitors, so they had an eye for quirks and celebrities: a Quran written by ostrich feather; judicial scrolls kept in bamboo stalks; a fourteenth-century astronomy tome that shows Arabic scientists engaging with a heliocentric solar system two centuries before Copernicus; a volume of verse elegies to the Prophet, recited by an egg-headed custodian in a voice as low and musty as the shelves from which he picked out the book.[31] Although the dryness of the desert has helped to preserve the paper, few of the books have survived without blemish. The edges of the pages were jagged, the binding wax dry, the leaves as brittle as onionskin. The books were like Chinguetti itself, battered and sunk in the desert sands, barely surviving against the odds, its character intact even if its hinges are loose.

In his *Pilgrimage*, Sidi Ahmed tells of his encounter with the Sultan of Morocco. Asked 'Is there scholarship in your land?' he replies: 'My lord, all the sciences are to be found there, both exegesis and principles of law, logic and rhetoric and the study of Arabic, its grammar and its rules and its syntax.' This could be taken as a catalogue for the genres contained in Chinguetti's family libraries.

What both the *Pilgrimage* and the libraries underline is that intellectual pursuits have never been exclusive to urban living. Al-Mutannabi, the classical Arab poet, honed his craft among the Bedouin of the Syrian desert; Ibn Khaldun wrote his *Muqaddimah* in a mountain cave. In Mauritania, for centuries itinerant teachers have moved along the pasture trails, integrating Sufi *tariqas* with the nomad encampments. As the nineteenth-century Saharan scholar Mohammed Wuld Buna sang, 'We have taken the back of she-camels as a school where we expiate God's religion.' Deserts have long been famous as places for contemplation and intellectual retreat; Chinguetti reminds us they can be hives of scholarship as well.

∽

I stayed in Chinguetti for a week, taking a mud-walled room in a guest-less guesthouse, where sand lapped at the painted camel on the façade, swallowing it up to the knees. I wandered between the drystone houses in the old town, chatted to *boubou* sellers and store owners, who sat

---

31 The poem he recited, the *Burdat ash-Shifa'*, is known for its healing properties. 'It happens,' wrote Sidi Ahmed in his *Pilgrimage* (because he heard this poem too, in Alexandria), 'that the mimiya ode possesses a great secret, and mighty Baraka.'

below lonely shelves of Weetabix and Casa Italia peas, and I marvelled as my underwear steam-dried in the sun in a matter of seconds.

When I wasn't burrowing into the book collections, I went on trips around the Adrar. A cameleer called Ghazi, who was friends with the hotel owner, took me out for a couple of days. Riding a snarling bull-camel, whose grunting sounded like Chewbacca with a poker up his arse, I crested sharp-ridged *seif* ('sword') dunes, leaning back on the downhill runs. Bouncing to the camel's grumblings, shuddering when his narrow legs jackhammered on the crusty *hammada*, I thought longingly of Naksheh, the lovely camel I had ridden out of Timbuktu.

One morning, we hobbled the dromedaries near an old French fort at the Amougjar Pass. The odd skeletal bush groped the black rock as if to suck out the minerals, and crag martins made careful study of the gaps between them. Above a locked gate, we levered ourselves over a limestone bluff, and dropped in on an astonishing menagerie.

There were horned cattle, an antelope, even a spotty giraffe. Inches from my fingers, a lion swung its tail and a crocodile snapped its jaws. They were Neolithic portraits, fashioned out of mineral pigments and animal fat, so pale in parts, absorbed by the crust and colouring of the bruised rock face, they seemed to be emanations of nature. It was as if we were witnessing the mountain's dreams – or, more precisely, its memories – bleeding to the surface.

Although not on the scale of the Sahara's most celebrated rupestral art (such as Tassili N'Ajjer in Algeria or the Cave of Swimmers in the Gilf Kebir), they articulate the same point. As Lloyd Cabot Briggs wrote in *Tribes of the Sahara*, 'Long, long ago, during the prehistoric ages before the dawn of written history, the Sahara was very different from what it is today, for much of it was fertile and relatively thickly populated.' Oak, elm and alder furred the mountaintops, bone harpoons were fashioned to catch freshwater fish and mud-turtle shells enthroned tribal chiefs. A shift in the earth's orbit, the melting of glaciers in northern Europe and the subsequent retreat of the monsoon rains withered the landscape, already pressurised by large, voracious herds. It was in the wake of these dramatic climactic changes that nomadism became the primary mode of survival, and the sedentary black populations fell under the lordship of horse-riding and cattle-droving tribesmen – the ancestors of the Berbers.

'*Ajib*,' said Ghazi, his leathery face swinging across his rounded shoulders. 'A wonder.' The same word Yisslam's grandmother had used for Chinguetti. When we left, he pressed a cheek to the rock, as if to kiss it.

I saw the rock paintings as something ancient and remote, almost magical in their antiquity. But for Ghazi, I think, their importance was mnemonic. They reminded him this area was not always so arid. That, even in his own parents' lifetimes, the land around Chinguetti had been kinder. Sitting in a grove of date palms, making our evening fire, Ghazi told me about the drought that brought that time to an end – the nightmare of the 1960s and 1970s, when Saharan nomads lost their last foothold on prosperity.

'I was not born at this time,' he said. 'But my father and grandfather told me about it. There were many different kinds of grass and we had hundreds of camels. Life was so much easier then. Now we cannot say we even have 20 camels.'

The drought was a blitzkrieg, stripping thousands of nomadic families of their animals. There have been other droughts in more recent years, as the Sahara continues to suffer the effect of increased greenhouse gases and associated feedback mechanisms, but none has been as devastating as the drought of 1968–74.[32] Globally, it was the worst drought of the twentieth century, killing around 100,000 people through famine and disease, and slashing livestock numbers by at least a third.

'I know many people who lost all their herd,' said Ghazi. 'Not in a year – in just a few days. Even now it is happening. When there is no rain and people lose their animals, some of them go to the town and take work in a shop, or they go to Zouerat to work in the mines. And usually, they don't come back to the desert.'

Statistics bear out what Ghazi was telling me: the decline of nomadism in Mauritania is one of the most dramatic in the world. At the

---

32 Although there were comparable disasters in earlier eras, such as a sixteenth-century drought around the time of the Moroccan conquest, and a terrible drought in 1913, which cost thousands of lives, caused the evacuation of colonial outposts, and led to a Tuareg uprising in Niger.

dawn of independence in 1960, 85 per cent of the population was nomadic; by 2000 that figure had slumped to less than 6 per cent. Like any demographic mutation, it is an amalgam of different factors – the loosening of the tribal system under the French administration; the development of a bureaucratic class; the growth of the agricultural and mining industries. Arguably, the abolition (or more accurately, reduction) of slavery has had an impact too, preventing nomads from exploiting free labour for food. Yet the drought is paramount among all these factors, one of those periodic events when nature bares its teeth and shows how deep it can bite.

From the Neolithic to the nineteenth century: another day took me with a cold drinks merchant to Ouadane, one of the most historically significant towns on the plateau. We rolled across plains the colour of burnt umber, shadowed by tangerine cliffs and the vermiculated wings of falcons. It was a furnace world, where valleys misted in the distance and pools of watery light glistened near the ground; and when we stuck our hands out of the windows, we could feel the same dragons-breath winds that sculpted surreal fan shapes on the crests of the cliffs.

Built over an oasis of green sward and date palms, Ouadane's walled town cascaded into the valley, biscuity and piecemeal, like 'a colony of barnacles on the bottom of an upturned boat'.[33] It is a genuine ruin, uninhabited among the arches and watchtowers of its old town, arranged by archaeologists in tantalising patterns that hint at the lives once lived there. It was founded in 1141 by a group of religious scholars, after whom its most famous street is named. I walked down this crumbly alley, 'the Street of Forty Scholars', peering inside the dry-stone huts. Palm trunks straddled pits that functioned as toilets; triangular niches signified dressers. Now, the principal inhabitants are rock hyraxes and ruminants who have marked their territory with dung; but a couple of centuries earlier, that wonderful scholar Sidi Ahmed (the 'son of the little bird of paradise') lived along this street. I sat down in

---

33 So wrote Sidi Ahmed's translator, HT Norris, who discovered *The Pilgrimage of Ahmed* in Ouadane in the 1960s.

one of the houses and imagined him here, poring through the books he had amassed on his travels, scribbling the tales of his *Pilgrimage*.

That night in Ouadane was one of my wildest so far. I was staying at another guest-less guesthouse. The owner, Zayda, invited me to join her and some of her friends for the evening – they were off to a wedding. We rattled into the old town and joined the crowd gathering in the floodlit courtyard of a large stone house.

A band of roaming, hereditary musicians (members of the *iggawen* caste) set down a couple of goblet drums and plugged their electric guitars into a generator, while the yard bubbled with blue and white *boubous* and a rainbow's spectrum of headscarves. As the night progressed, the music swelled, hypnotising the crowd with its coaxing measures. Men quivered at the edges, eyes on stalks and arms in loops. Women's hips jerked and swayed, wrists and elbows tracing elegant shapes in air that prickled with henna and perfume, scarves melting in the glare of the downlights, like thumb prints on sand-coloured card. It reminded me of the dancing at Yisslam's camp on the night before Eid: it was the women who performed, while the men's role was mainly to watch.

The musicians made up for the inactivity of their sex. One of them was playing a *tidinit*, a Moorish lute with four strings and a soundboard made of sheepskin. Raw notes thrumbled, pegged to the beat of the drums... deeper, louder, growlier... a song of exaltation and celebration... inflamed and sexy and sweating with life. At the climax, the lead singer strutted like a Moorish Mick Jagger, jamming the microphone to his crotch, pumping his pelvis in fast spasmodic wrenches, drawing enough trills and screams to drown a hen night with the Chippendales.

'Mmmmm...' Zayda made a diffident moue on the way back. '*Actuellement, c'était trop tranquille ce soir.*'

The plateau may be dry – in every sense – but its people sure know how to party.

The School for Nomads

Lesson Five: Study and Play

'Yusuf! Oh, Yusuf, you need to keep still! Don't move, Yusuf! Keep still!'

Abdul-Hakim and his friends are conducting an experiment: they have found a scarab beetle and they are taking turns to set it down in the sand, trying to predict whose legs it will pass under. I feel like a croquet hoop.

There are plenty of other games. We play a version of Connect Four, with divots in the sand and counters of camel dung. We kneel to watch dung beetles processing a donkey turd, like state employees tidying up for a presidential visit. We pass my compass like a 'hot potato' and play variations of peekaboo (for which our turbans are well designed). Abdul-Hakim is having a super time, mucking about with his cousins, whooping and arm wrestling and looking for animal tracks. Occasionally, Jadullah warns him to keep his voice down. Later, Lamina calls him over to help with the baggage. His head sinks a little under his shoulders, but his father rubs his head and they stand together for a moment, molten to a single silhouette. It is impossible to tell whose hands are untying the knots.

We are staying with a kinsman of Lamina's called Salih, who wears a double-breasted woollen jacket over his *djellaba*, pioneering a look that could be branded 'Saharan Piccadilly'. There are a couple of chickens, a troop of goats, two boys with spiky mohawks and amulets around their necks, and a headscarved wife with jauntily bare shoulders. She approaches me when I'm digging out my diary and shows me a Mauritanian banknote. 'Do you have this?' Her expression is flat, the lines so tight around her eyes it's impossible to guess her age. Later, as we are about to leave, I put a couple of banknotes beside her, and the look of gratitude on her face is heart-breaking.

The children are fascinated by anything I pull out of my pack: my diary, my phone, a compass with a verse by Robert Burns inscribed on the base. It was a present for my trip, but I try not to look at it when

I'm with other people. It makes me float a little out of my journey, imagining the features I long for: soft brown hair tickling my cheeks, eyes so close I can drink up their blueness, and a voice I can only hear on the crackling, irregular line in town. The children take it in turns to hold the compass; they tap the dome and place it against their ears like a seashell. I try to play along, but looking at it makes me grumpy, so after a while I put it away.

How easy it is to get swept away by the outdoorsy freedom of nomadic life. I hear no tiffs between Abdul-Hakim and his cousins. I think of panicky op-eds in British newspapers about hyperactive attention deficit disorders, neuroscientific research about chemical imbalance, outbursts against computer games, laments to the death of nature walks. Hardly problems for parents to worry about round here; and nobody can say these kids are missing out on Vitamin D.

I think of my own childhood on the edge of a wood in Hertfordshire. Running between gnarled oaks, turning their branches into climbing frames. Decorating stones and sticks, and the oddest-shaped objects my brother and I could forage, pitting them in a long-running adventure with a tribe of mischievous plants. Nomad children like Abdul-Hakim are basking in nature, literate in the languages of tracking and star mapping, as multilingual as Dr Doolittle. If camping outdoors is one of the treats of childhood, these are surely children to envy.

Moments with children in the Sahel. Throwing stones at a jujube tree with Fulani kids in the bush, each falling fruit as thrilling as a goal. Climbing out of a canoe on a holm in the Niger, to the boggle-eyed dancing of boisterous Bozos. Watching a Tuareg boy sitting on a dune in Timbuktu, pretending to ride a camel, holding a couple of rice straws for reins.

It would be disingenuous to say nomad children miss nothing from a structured education (and for this reason, schools have been built in many of the larger fixed camps). There are choices they will never have, ideas they will never learn. Nobody who loves books can truly envy a child who is unlikely to have meaningful access to the pleasure of reading. And the number of protective amulets some of them are wearing (one of Salih's boys has three leather pouches slung over his chest) reminds me they have limited recourse to scientific medicine.

Yet hanging out with Abdul-Hakim and his cousins does make me wonder.

I remember a study I've read, conducted in 2005 by the anthropologist Elliot Fratkin in northern Kenya. Among the communities he visited, Fratkin concluded that the nomadic children enjoyed significant advantages over their sedentary neighbours, because of their access to fresh milk and a cleaner environment. As a result, they had lower rates of malnutrition and stunting, diaorrhea and respiratory illness. But this was mitigated by the sedentary children's access to health care, food security, education and physical security. It is hard to know which way the scales truly tip.

The advantage of a rural childhood is a theme in one of Arab literature's most enduring tales: the philosophical fable of *Hayy Ibn Yaqdhan*, written in the twelfth century. Hayy (whose name means 'Awake, Son of Alive') grows up on a desert island, raised by a gazelle. When his foster mother dies, he dissects her body, performing an accurate autopsy and setting off on a journey of 'scientific speculation'. Although he is a little confused to note that he doesn't have gazelle horns of his own, he slowly teases out the answers to his questions, from the cultivation of plants and the tending of animals to more 'sublunary' matters; all without any need for language. When his travels carry him to the city, he is shocked to learn that most men 'are like irrational animals', driven by 'riches to collect, pleasures to partake of, lusts to satisfy'. Spurning their materialism, he determines to return to his desert island and 'his previous sublime station'.

The story was written by an Andalusian vizier called Ibn Tufail. Iconic in the Arab-speaking world, it has also had a huge impact in the West, where it is cited as an early *Bildungsroman* and an influence on *Robinson Crusoe*. Yet there is a telling difference. Daniel Defoe's hero is a townsman surviving outside the protective shell of civilisation. Hayy is coming from the other side: a feral child nurtured at nature's bosom. For Ibn Tufail, education is subjective, depending on the individual's 'natural curiosity to look for the truth of things'.

'It should be known', writes Ibn Khaldun, 'that the storehouse of human science is the soul of man. In it, God has implanted perception enabling it to think and, thus, to acquire.' The tale of Hayy gives fictional expression to this idea, which is borne out by the sparky curiosity of nomad children like Abdul-Hakim.

I am getting into the routine: our twilight departures, riding across the plains, gentle conversations around the evening fire, the childlike pleasure of life under the stars. Life feels purer, stripped of clutter and distractions. Perhaps Roger Deakin put his finger on it when he wrote, 'There's more truth about a camp because that is the position we are in ... a camp represents the true reality of things: we're just passing through.'

I am always ready to sleep as soon as the opportunity comes – exhausted mentally as much as physically, from the linguistic challenges and all the lessons I am trying to absorb: strapping the luggage, hobbling the camels, tying the ropes around their legs (always keeping yourself behind to avoid a lethal kick), fastening the rope inside the camel's mouth, tight over the gums, locked with a small twig under the chin.

Today, we set off well before sunset, so I have a good opportunity to see the land we are crossing. Bunchgrass and mimosa show up like smudges on a sheet of paper. Sometimes the wind thickens and sky and sand interfuse in a wheezy brown haze, before cleaving, allowing us to continue. It is hardly the glorious desert promised by Hollywood – Tatooine's golden swathes or Lawrence's sculpted *barchans*. Rugged, unpristine, this is an honest desert that few would bother to photograph.

Eventually, Jadullah calls out. He has spotted a tent. He calls it an *imbar*, as opposed to the *khaymah* we stayed in last night. An armature tent, built around a frame, it pokes the sky like a lone tooth in an elder's mouth. It looks only a short trot away. But we still haven't reached it an hour later. Its promise of rest and food tantalises, like a neon-lit motel on the brink of a highway.

'Who lives there?' I ask.

A rattle of laughter: something has tickled Lamina.

'Oh, Yusuf, tonight is a special one for you, God willing!'

We gallop into an ashy tunnel of dusk. Trying to keep up with the others, I dig my heels into Naksheh's flanks, slapping the reins against his neck, like a cowboy. The wind lashes our sides, raising will-o'-the-wisps around the camels' hooves. The sand churns beneath us.

At last, we couch and climb up a dune. A stooped, raggedy figure emerges from an awning of goatskins. His face is cracked and mottled, his chin filigreed with light beard like fonio grass, his eyes sunk in deep-ribbed sockets. He looks at least a hundred years old.

'I praise God a thousand times! Oh, what a blessing! God is great, God is great, God is great! Truly, this is a blessing! God is great, God is great, God is great!'

We have arrived at the home of Lamina's chatterbox cousin, the mercurial Ismail.

Part Six

Urban Nomads

The great affair is to move; to feel the needs and hitches of our life more nearly; to come down off this feather-bed of civilization, and find the globe granite underfoot and strewn with cutting flints.

Robert Louis Stevenson, *Travels with a Donkey in the Cévennes*

16

*Fishing and F***ing*

LOW SLUNG AND DUST CHOKED, NOUAKCHOTT HAD THE ATMOSPHERE OF an open-air warehouse, spiced with the reek of sewage and cooked fuel. I stayed for a few days, revelling in the luxury of a guidebook-recommended, French-run hostel. A guard toted his machine gun at the gate; the storekeeper suggested the best insect repellent; a concierge printed out routemaps under a smoothly reeling fan. Rocking on a wicker chair in a yard that smelled of freshly watered bougainvillea, I chatted to a French couple I'd bumped into weeks earlier, queuing for visas in Rabat. Like most of the guests, they were shiny and happy and on their way to the beaches of Senegal.

'*Allez-vous au Mali?*' The girl puckered her lips in disapproval. '*Ouf!* You must go by plane, it's too dangerous to cross the desert.'

'Don't you know about the jihadists?' asked her boyfriend.

'Oh, I'll just take the bus.' I made breezy, laissez-faire strokes in the air. I was sure I was very convincing. 'I figure the jihadists won't attack the locals, so it should be fine really.'

But as I spoke, the incredulity in their faces became airborne. I could feel their doubts breaking through my defences like a germ.

Anxiety makes its nest in the belly. It stretches its claws across the stomach and pulls everything tight around itself, like a rodent keeping itself warm. I needed a distraction – and what better way to relax than an afternoon at the seaside?

Slewing past a string of brick depots, a taxi rattled along dusty unpaved lanes where men were kneeling to pray outside their shops and women in shimmering dresses were balancing trays of mullet on their heads. The salty breeze did the job of signposts, guiding us through the wreckage of Nouakchott's outskirts, towards a bustling market on the last dune before the sea.

What a wonderful place! The Port de Pêche is Whitstable meets Brighton Pier, boiled in the pith of Africa. Red mullet spilled out of a pick-up truck, dribbling over the gunwales, while men in sweat-stained vests heaved it through the golden sand, bannered in a smell of tar and fish scales. Women in cotton prints flashed past bearded men in grand *boubous* orchestrating the sales. There were so many vivid colours in the pure, gloopy light before dusk that I sat there mesmerised, like a toddler bewitched by Teletubbies or Tombliboos.

Along the strand, women were chatting and haggling over sardines on sand-furred nets. Behind them was a band of rippled mercury, hardening near the horizon to fresh-cast lead. I edited the sun with a hand on my brow; the glare slid back, revealing a row of dinghies, flaking rinds of ebonywood, like *babouche* slippers fashioned for Brobdingnagians. Men with brine-cured faces shouldered them against the tug of the tide, like Lilliputian workmen. Veterans clambered over the prows and tightrope-walked down the hulls. Apprentices waded in the shallows, towing the nets back to shore, skipping over salty turf and bladderwrack.

'Hey, *blanc*, you want to join us?'

Mohammed was a 21-year-old fisherman, his bare, drum-tight chest varnished by seawater and sweat. His face wore the serene calm of recent activity, lips pouting around a tooth-cleaning stick. He sat on a hummock of seashells, telling me about his latest trip – working the lines for a week, poling south towards Senegal.

'Are your arms tired?' I asked.

'I'm used to it.'

He shrugged, picking a soggy pack of Winstons out of his shorts. I offered him a dry one.

'It's my back that hurts. You can't sleep on those boats, there's no space and the bottom's too curved.'

Still, he had pulled in a good haul, and wasn't planning on going out again for a few days.

'We wanted mullet,' he explained. 'You get more money from mullet, but they're hard. Sometimes we go for the sardines. They're easy, you catch them in the net, but if you want something more expensive, you need to use the lines. It's easier in the summer. That's when the hake come along. They swim up from Senegal, but in the winter they go back because it's too cold for them here.'

This was the nomadic instinct – seasonal migration. Rich in nutrients, 'upwelled' from the depths of the ocean, the North African

Atlantic is one of the world's last great fishing zones. Its annual catch (which ranges from octopus and squid to shrimp, black hake and tuna) is worth an estimated $14 billion a year.[34] But the fishing industry is being sucked dry. Leviathans from thousands of miles away hover near Mauritania's coastline. Armed with sonar equipment, mid-water trawls and sophisticated freezing compartments, they hoover up the best of the catch, breaching the 12-mile zone reserved for local fishermen, who are left to trawl the shallows, like down-and-outs picking through the bins. The sweatshop crews crawling inside these trawlers (such as 200 Senegalese fishermen sleeping on cardboard mattresses in a Korean vessel searched in 2006) are too desperate to notice the terrible irony of their underpaid, dangerous employment.

'My grandfather used to go to sea for half a day – and he caught enough fish for a week.' Mohammed's eyelids drooped in bitterness. 'Life was so easy in those days! Now we have to travel three days or more, and even then we don't find as many.'

I thought of the Berbers, hedged into the least hospitable corners of the Atlas; I thought of Lamina and his fellow caravaneers, competing with trucks and the lower prices of sea salt. Why was it always the same equation? Local, traditional techniques competing with internationally funded big business. Well, maybe the answer is not so hard to fathom; but that doesn't make it any less depressing. We muddy the water with talk of 'modern life', 'competition' and 'progress'. Yet in the end there is one stark and frankly dirty word to explain why so many traditional lifestyles are falling away: capitalism.

❧

The bus station at Nouakchott: seashells crunched under my boots. Hessian sacks, cardboard boxes and strapped-up bags tumbled over each other in shapeless mounds that were slowly deflated by the baggage boy, a marker pen between his teeth to scribble down the ticket numbers.

---

34 So valuable are Mauritanian waters that in November 2015, the European Union signed its biggest fisheries deal with an African country to date, worth €59.125 million, allowing EU fleets to fish up to 281,500 tonnes a year.

The shells were a last whiff of the sea. From now on, I would be gnashing at Africa's interior, riding the Route d'Espoir. Forget the French couple's warnings – when the road's called 'Hope' you know you're in danger! Sliding southeast, my route should carry me into Mali, to follow the Niger river all the way to Timbuktu.

I slumped in my seat, flicking through my Arabic–English *Gulliver's Travels*. The journey to the South Seas and the green fields of the Houyhnhnms did not exactly chime with the dust-rinsed streets I was passing through. As for my erratically progressing Arabic, it would be even less useful with Mauritania at my back. I dropped the book on the seat beside me and focused on the view.

'Hey, man!'

Square shoulders strained against a dusty linen jacket. A lantern jaw and frizzy hair boxed in a pugilist's face. A silver crocodile was gleaming on his belt buckle, almost as shiny as the cocky glint in his eyes. He looked like Lennox Lewis dressed up as Toad of Toad Hall.

'You're English, man? Hey, I don't mind, English or French. You see, I'm from Cameroon.'

His name was Freddy. He plonked himself beside me, picking up *Gulliver's Travels* and using it to fan himself. I was still waking up after tipping out of bed at half past four, but Freddy shook me out of my torpor. Within a few minutes, it was like we had been travelling buddies for weeks.

'See that – *that's* Mauritania!' He snapped a wrist at the colourless scrub through the window. 'I can't wait to get out of this place. Man, I'm from the forests, you know what I'm saying? All this desert, it's killing me.'

His story was an unlikely one (although he told it consistently over the next couple of days). He had been living in China, working as a judo instructor, and had come back to Africa to visit his mother in Cameroon.

'I was only gonna be here a few weeks. Once you leave Africa – man, you never want to come back!'

But he had lost his passport, and with it his Chinese visa. He had already been to Algeria, squeezed in a pick-up on the old caravan route, down to Benin, across to Nigeria, all in the hope of securing the elusive visa to magic him back to China. He had been mugged in Lagos, broken a rib in a car crash outside Ougadougou and nearly got stabbed in the neck after sleeping with someone's girlfriend in Algiers. His journey sounded like a horror-comedy *Odyssey*, with Algerian thugs taking the role of the Cyclops and a brothel in Burkina Faso stepping in for Circe's lair. His Penelope was back in China – although in Freddy's case it got complicated, because there were two sons by different mothers and he wasn't 100 per cent about which way to go.

'That's the crazy thing. I thought my problem was choosing *between* them – now I don't even know if I *get* to choose!'

This thought seemed to sap his spirits. His face melted into sunken cheeks and puppy-dog eyes. Maybe looking out of the window wasn't the best idea. There was a patch of sorghum, some acacias, and we did pass some toxic Sodom's apples. The rest of the country was as bald as a prisoner's scalp. We averted our eyes from the sand-clogged villages to tell each other stories from our travels; and if there were any more exciting details in the landscape, I'm afraid they were lost in Freddy's detailed description of a five-times-in-one-night romp with a Nigerian pizza waitress in Porto-Novo.

'Man, there's nothing in this whole country as juicy as that chick's ass!'

In the looser definition of nomads, Freddy was a classic case: *nomos* – 'roaming'. Swooping across West Africa in search of a visa, he was a twenty-first-century neo-nomad, hurled from land to land to recover his identity. His body language underlined this somehow – his steps were loose and there was a roll in his shoulders when he moved. He floated, like many of the nomads I met. But his charm and ready smile, his regular knuckle crunching, his crocodile-skin belt and his slick chat-up techniques, all marked him out as a townsman. An urban nomad, currently of no fixed abode.

Air rushed through the open windows, hot and gritty like invisible smoke. When we stepped outside on the periodic rests, you could feel it rolling over you like lava. In this punishing climate, dusk is a reprieve. I was grateful for the cooler air, the paring of the sun's teeth. Yet the darkness brought trouble of its own: a sinister atmosphere, laced with all the bogeymen I had been imagining since Dakhla.

Eighteen hours after leaving Nouakchott, slowed down by the endless gauntlet of checkpoints, the scouring of passports and ID cards and details triplicated on tea-stained ledgers, we arrived at the frontier.

Night dropped, soon after our arrival, like the scrim at a play: dark and velvety, announcing an interval until the new scene would be revealed in the morning. People climbed out of the bus to bed down in the sand, where the multipurpose nature of Mauritanian couture was turned to account: turban pillows, *boubou* sleeping bags, veils that doubled as sleep masks. I was one of the few to stay in the bus. Stretching across a row of seats, I counted rivet holes in the roof to lull myself to sleep.

Borderlands are to bandits what unclean sheets are to bedbugs. I dreamed of them all through the night: smugglers, kidnappers, thieves and murderers – the reason for all the checkpoints we had passed through. Al-Qaeda in the Maghreb, the Salafist Group for Preaching and Combat, the Movement for Oneness and Jihad in West Africa, the Sons of the Sahara, the Masked Men Brigade... Experts in 'double-think', who can profit from cocaine smuggling and bootleg cigarettes, while preaching abstinence and holy war at the same time.

I dreamed especially of Mokhtar Belmokhtar, the one-eyed bandit king nicknamed 'Mr Marlboro' for his role in the trans-Saharan fag trade. In 2003, he masterminded the kidnapping of 32 European hostages, for which he earned $6.5 million (even more than the $5 million American bounty on his head) and started the craze for kidnapping tourists in the Sahara. Since then, a spate of lethal attacks had swollen his notoriety, including the murder of 5 French picnickers near Nouakchott in 2007, the slaughter of 38 hostages at the Algerian gas facility of In Amanas in 2013, and the killing of 27 westerners in a Bamako hotel in November 2015. He was often mentioned by people in Timbuktu – 'he only has one eye, but it sees everything.' Yet he was such a volatile character that he couldn't even keep the peace with his fellow jihadists. Falling out with Al-Qaeda in the Maghreb, he founded his own group in 2013, naming it Al-Mourabitoun, after the nomadic warriors led by Yusuf ibn Tafshin to blood-soaked glory in medieval Spain.

Belmokhtar epitomises the dark side of twenty-first-century nomadism. Born to an Algerian herding family, he used clan connections and desert know-how to help him up the ranks of the region's jihadist hierarchy, recruiting disenfranchised nomads to his cause. Raiders and robbers, smugglers and thieves: if Belmokhtar had his way, Saharan pastoralists would start to look like the tribesmen pilloried by the French colonialists more than a century ago.

The vulnerability of nomads to jihadism – and their significance to tackling it – has been illustrated in the heartbreaking misfortunes of Iraq. In 2006, an embryonic Islamic State infested the tribal region of Anbar, muscling in on long-established smuggling networks. The tribes were provoked, and succeeded in driving out the jihadists. But the sectarian bias of Nouri al-Maliki's government (a legacy of US policies in the country) drilled into tribal hegemony, opening fracture lines through which the jihadists were able to pour their influence. Revitalised, Islamic State returned to a more porous Anbar, overwhelming the area and co-opting its sheikhs with deadly effect.

The same principle is visible in the Sahara. With militant groups like Boko Haram pledging *bayah* (allegiance) to Abu Bakr al-Baghdadi's so-called Caliphate, and Middle Eastern jihadist groups active in Libya, the knotty connections between North Africa and the Middle East should never be underestimated. In Iraq and Mali, an analogous situation can be observed: disenfranchised nomads, and recently sedentarised, out-of-work ex-nomads, co-opted by shady organisations offering self-worth and salaries that are tantalisingly elusive elsewhere. This calamitous dynamic would be spelled out for me, on my return to Timbuktu, when a schoolteacher told me the tragic tale of his nomadic ex-students who had been lured to battle.

Ideology and identity rarely make snug bedfellows. The links between nomadism and jihadism are thornily inconsistent. North Africa's jihadist leaders hail from a range of backgrounds (the 'emir' of Al-Qaeda in the Maghreb at this time, Abdelmalek Droukdel, was a mathematics graduate from the Bay of Algiers; while Hamada Ould Khairy, leader of the Movement for Oneness and Jihad in West Africa, grew up in Nouakchott). When it comes to jihadism, town and country know no border. It is their ubiquity, their fluency in the many networks of North Africa, that makes the jihadists so dangerous, and that is why they loomed so large in my darkest dreams.

'Hey, man, have some breakfast.'

Sunlight clawed my eyes open and I jolted upright. In spite of the limited sleep, Freddy's eyes had lost none of their swank, although he had taken off his linen jacket and was dusting it down with a tissue. Sitting on a bench beside the bus, we breakfasted on a plastic beaker of Nescafé and a Styrofoam tray of dates.

If you were to compile a list of highlights from any African journey, I doubt border crossings would feature high up. But today I was in luck. After my bag had been emptied into the sand, I was signalled through with a shake of the hand and a '*profitez-vous au Mali*'. For Freddy, the process was significantly more gruelling. Half an hour after me, he staggered under the shade below a locust-bean tree, looking like he had just played touch rugby with a team of wildebeest.

'This is the problem in Africa,' he muttered. 'It's the way Africans treat other Africans.'

He had lost his watch, 10,000 *ouguiyas* and, worst of all, his silver-crocodile-buckled belt.

'Man, I loved that belt.' His head shook from side to side, unsoothed by the remains of the dates. 'And so did the chicks!'

New countries usually announce themselves slowly, but crossing into Mali the difference was immediate: the whole mise-en-scène had shifted. Curly horned *zebu* cattle congregated around lakes that caught the sun like fully operational heliostats. Hats of woven palm and goatskin gripped the coppery heads of the herders, whose arms stretched across their goads, turning them into elongated scarecrows. They were Fulanis, and they intrigued me, with their stiltwalker postures, their hair braids and the tattoos on the women's faces. They were nomads in the purest sense. On my last visit, I had managed no more than fleeting encounters, so I was hoping to learn more this time.

It wasn't only the people: the landscape was changing too. There were more trees – jackalberries, umbrella-shaped kapoks and tamarinds. Most spectacular of all were the baobabs. Broad as elephants, they lashed the air with their twisting branches, like the tentacles of electrocuted octopuses. In Mauritania they were rare sights, but now the world was growing back again, and this reflected itself in the village markets. They were more crowded, more thick with produce and activity – women pounding yams or grinding pepper, picking the weevils out of the beans and turning the white, gourd-like pods of the baobab into 'monkey bread'. Whenever we stopped, hoarse-voiced women levered themselves onto the bus, nudging out small boys with tomato-tin begging cans. They had ginger beer and mango juice in refrigerated sachets, twists of newspaper filled with hard-boiled eggs, grilled plantains, bruised bananas and any rootstock you cared for: ginger, manioc, baobab, cassava. Freddy dived into the pockets of his linen jacket for change. He hugged a lump of cassava to his chest, purring over it, as if it made up for the loss of his belt.

'I want to take this for tonight,' he said, pulling off a chunk and peeling it with his teeth.

'Why?' It looked like it would make a good doorstop.

'Because it makes your dick go hard all night!'[35]

I got the feeling Freddy needed to get off the bus – pretty soon. We had been on the road too long and were both suffering from that feeling of encapsulation that tightens on a long journey. Dusk was sucking out the light, blue ribbons of smoke coiling over the forests. Half-shrouded by their braziers, people sat on the stoops of thatched huts or lay down on bedsteads. Women carried piles of firewood on their heads; men hacked at them with axes; stick-like children with runny eyes and umbilical hernias waved their hands against the flies. Slowly, concrete and cement stamped down the flora, flyovers swung into carriageways blurry with taillights and the Niger spewed beneath us, a tar-like soup, 'as broad as the Thames at Westminster, and flowing *to the eastward*', as Mungo Park described his first sighting in the eighteenth century; although the buildings around us were a little less gilded.

Bamako is never going to steal the beauty prizes, but it makes up for its looks with verve. In the markets, diesel and dust reacted with the

---

35   Like Freddy, Leo Africanus delved into the use of rootstocks as a form of natural Viagra. He identified a root called *surnag* in the *Atlas*, which is 'said to be very comfortable and preservative unto the privy parts of man, and being drunk in an electuary, to stir up venereal lust'. This sounds pretty much like the method Freddy was planning on.

sickly odour of the offal sold in butchers' tubs, the rotten fruit, sun-pulped sweat and hundreds of other pongs to blast the nostrils with the full olfactory spectrum – a synthesised smell you could market as '100% alive'. It was Freddy's kind of place. I checked into the same hostel where I had stayed a couple of years ago, greeting Boucoum, the laid-back owner, who was brewing coffee under a mango tree.

'So you came back?' He slid a Dunhill out of his pack and called over to one of his boys to fill the pot. 'Look at this place! No tourists, no peace. You should be careful.'

Most of his rooms had been turned into dormitories for boys from the villages, sleeping side by side on the floor, scrapping around for work. After Boucoum set me up with a bed and a mosquito net, one of his tenants took me on his moped to the market. Behind a gauzy curtain, Chinese businessmen were dabbing their chins with their napkins. We passed their striplit restaurant and dived into a tunnel of Afro-funk.

The central market was a labyrinth of clanking poles and rustling burlap, greasy with acrid stenches, hidden like a trap street from any kind of inspector. Slumped around a zinc counter, traders and bargain hunters fuelled themselves on tin bowls of *bissam*, a soup of split peas and cumin with a disc of olive oil floating on top.

'Man, life's too short to waste it.' Freddy dropped a Winston in the dregs of his dinner. 'You and me, we're gonna party!'

The place he had in mind looked from the outside like a saloon bar in the Wild West – swinging doors between plasterboard walls and drunks stumbling off the porch, crashing into a cigarette trolley. Inside, the atmosphere was like you'd expect if the end of the world had just been announced on *News at Ten*. Men and women were shouting at each other, kicking each other, spilling Castel beer down half-unbuttoned tops, jostling with each other to get to the bar. But mostly, they were fucking each other.

'Man,' yelled Freddy, 'this is my favourite place in the whole city!'

On the dancefloor, breasts and thighs and buttocks shook with blue and purple light, sweaty and sizzling like the ingredients of a cannibal's cauldron. Big-hipped girls in tiny skirts were taking turns to rule – spidering arms and bodies convulsing, like baobab trees uprooted in an earthquake. Guys in coloured trousers bucked around the sides, shaking their legs like sprinters on the starting blocks, beer drool sliding down their chins. Stabbing cigarettes into heaped bowls, they picked out their paramours with a few sparky preliminaries, and led them behind a bamboo-cane screen in the yard. All that was left to negotiate was the shrill-voiced woman who managed a row of short-stay cabins, which she advertised with a couple of fob keys dangling from her wrists.

'I told her, "come with me girl!"' said Freddy, 'But she says she's gotta work. Man, some chicks need to relax!'

I know there are classier places in Bamako, but I'm glad that's the bar I went to. It was a place for the hard-up, a chance to unwind, on cheap girls and cheaper beer. For some of the girls, it could earn them enough to get through another week, which I guess is as far ahead as most Malians can afford to plan. And it was a place where people talked, where I heard one or two tales that made me realise the nomads aren't just in the desert – they're right over the whole continent.

'*Je gagne!*'

I was leaning forward on a wooden stool, ears ringing like stamped metal. Somehow, I'd got myself embroiled in a thumb war. My opponent was a guy in polka-dot trousers called Moussa, who presented himself as the 'good guy' of the bar. He was wearing a *gris-gris*, a prayer sewn into a strip of sheepskin, wrapped around his upper arm. When it rolled down to his elbow, I asked about it.

'It gives me power,' he said, 'and God's protection.'

'Even here?' I was a little surprised by the religious emphasis, given our surroundings.

'Of course,' said Moussa, 'but I must be careful. If I do *glu-glu* with the girls, then my *gris-gris* is finished, and I like my *gris-gris*. I got it from a famous *marabout* in Djenné.'

'So no *glu-glu* in that case!'

I was planning to visit Djenné and wanted to learn more about its *marabouts*, so I hoped Moussa could give me an info dump. But when his inevitable victory came, he thundered at the open sky '*Je suis champion!*' and tore across the dancefloor like he'd won the Paris–Dakkar Rally.

Tossing another swig of Castel down my throat, I shuffled over to the bar. There was a Cameroonian girl with dyed red cornrows leaning over the counter. Her name was Ashley and Freddy had already introduced us.

'You still don't want to marry me?'

'Sorry, like I said, I've got somebody...

'Back home. Yeah...'

'But I could buy you a beer.'

'Okay. But I don't think you want to marry me, so why should I drink it?'

She had come up with her sister, who had married a tailor from southern Mali. Ashley had trained as a masseuse and travelled as far as Casablanca in search of work.

'But they don't like black people in Morocco,' she said. 'The Arabs are the most racist people in the world, they think we're lower than donkeys.'

Back in Bamako, she had briefly secured a restaurant job – 'waiting at the tables and looking after the clients'. But the restaurant had closed down and now she was here, hanging out among all the other girls who came to the bar to make a buck.

'Anyway, they're all sex workers.' She drew on a Dunhill, tipping her head behind a cataract of smoke. 'They're from Guinea mostly, dirty girls, no education. They want to get a job in a restaurant but they can't find anything. So they come to this bar, then when it's too crowded they try somewhere else. Malian men are animals. As long as you don't look like a goat you're gonna find something.'

I thought of the depressing tales that circulated – the brothels near the gold mines in Kayes, with abortion clinics next door, the foetuses sold to traditional healers to use in rituals; the STDs that were spreading round West Africa faster than the rate of urbanisation. I looked at the faces around us. Was there no room for romance in a place like this?

A couple was sitting behind us, hands clasped on the edge of their table. The girl looked into the boy's face and smiled, pressing a hand flat against his chest. He smiled back and she reached forward to plant a kiss on his cheek. Their body language seemed so connected, so much sweeter than the way Ashley described it. The boy edged over to the bar, to start negotiations for a cabin. The girl's lazy lover's smile disappeared in a moment, wiped away like a stray crumb, and she pulled out her mobile phone. A few moments later, arms around each other's waists, they rolled in a bubble of mutual rapture towards the bamboo-cane screen.

'What are you going to do?' Two more Castels arrived, and we clinked. 'Stay here in Bamako or go somewhere else?'

'When I was a child,' said Ashley, 'I thought, "I will go to Europe." I thought, "I will reach Spain or France and live a wonderful life." I knew it cannot be easy, but I thought, "This is possible, if I try hard and I'm lucky."' She tugged at the bottle and threw her head back. 'Now I know it was only a dream.'

My previous visit to Mali had been curtailed by a deadly attack in Timbuktu. Three Western travellers had been taken hostage and another shot dead. That incident was like the hornbill's squawk in an African folktale – the warning cry that must be heeded at all costs. A few weeks later, the country collapsed, like a mud-brick wall that hasn't been resurfaced for decades. Insurgency fractured the north and a military coup spun out of the barracks in Bamako. Renegade 'green berets' overran the state television studios and the presidential palace, ousted President Touré and installed a military junta. Meanwhile, the MNLA[36] grabbed its opportunity like a cattle thief stumbling on an unmanned corral. With the country's borders frozen, aid suspended and the land scorched with looting like a bush fire, the situation was ripe for rebellion.

Driven by Libyan arms, an inept opposition and the *asabiyyah* (solidarity) cited by Ibn Khaldun as the most precious tribal weapon against sedentary opposition, the Tuareg militants swatted Malian forces out of one base after another, until they seized control of Gao and encircled Timbuktu. It was April Fool's Day, and there was no doubt who were the fools. A day later, Timbuktu was under the charge of Iyad

---

36 The Mouvement National pour la Libération de l'Azawad – the Tuareg independence movement whose armed insurrection launched the Malian crisis in late 2011.

Ag Ghali's Ansar ad-Dine, erstwhile allies of the Tuareg secessionists. *Shariah* law was their goal, and Azawad was merely one patch among the many to be collected in the neverending fanatic's game of Risk.

Abandoned by its soldiers, Timbuktu bowed to the guns of the Islamists. Algerians, Libyans, Pakistanis, Afghans, even a French convert – an international hodgepodge of mania – screamed their slogans out of their jeeps, wheeling around town to implement their half-baked version of the *shariah*. Socialising between men and women, alcohol, smoking and dancing were forbidden; basically, all the universally accepted ingredients for a party. Women were instructed to lower dresses over ankles and veils over faces; men to lift the hems of their trousers so their ankles were showing; and swords were selected as the most judicious way to lop off the hands of thieves. In barely a month, the majority of Timbuktu's population had voted with their feet, seeking sanctuary further south.

They were part of a nationwide displacement of nearly half a million people – the largest migration ever witnessed in the Sahara. Refugee camps in neighbouring countries absorbed some of them, but many could be found in the capital. Bamako was bursting at the seams, stuffed with every northerner who could spare themselves the insalubrity of the camps. They all had a story to tell. There was Mammy, a married man in his 20s, beaten for smoking. There was Abdullai, who lived behind the BMS Bank in the centre of Timbuktu, which had been transformed into a correctional facility, 'so we could hear the screams of the people inside'. There was Nady Haidara, scion of a celebrated Timbuktu family, who had taken a bus out of town soon after the jihadists arrived. Now she was sitting in a damp, poky flat pining for her hometown.

'I miss Timbuktu,' she said. 'It's calmer there. You can visit people on foot, you can buy things on credit in the shop. I miss the sand. The red colour of the earth here annoys me. People in Bamako are greedier, more aggressive, they don't help you like they do in Timbuktu. I don't find them easy to talk to.'

Nady, like many of the refugees I met, was planning to return (and she did – I met her several weeks later, in Timbuktu). Her family was an example of circular migration, which is often overlooked by demographic experts focusing on the prevailing patterns of urbanisation. Yet even when people returned, it would be optimistic to imagine nothing had been lost, or broken.

Among the refugees I met were many from nomadic communities, including a Tuareg family who had spent several squalid months in a refugee camp in Burkina Faso. Selling off most of their possessions, they had rustled up enough cash to make it to Bamako, where they were living on wasteland near the airport.

'The life was too hard in the camp,' said Mohammed Ali, the family chief. 'The UNHCR gave rice and beans and coverings to keep us warm. But there was a lot of sickness and the water pump was dirty. It's better here, but I can't find any work. There are organisations, but they only took our names and numbers, they don't do anything.'

Equally fraught were the cultural tensions they had to negotiate. Since the crisis, people in Bamako had become less tolerant of the Tuareg, blaming them for starting the conflict. In a barbershop near my hostel, a couple of local Bambara guys showed me a clip on their phones while I was getting my beard trimmed: a dead man in an indigo turban, lying at the feet of a Malian soldier. Hundreds of clips, photos and stories were circulating, like football cards swapped by kids, reinforcing centuries-old antagonisms. So, for families like Mohammed Ali's, it had become impractical to go about in traditional dress.

'We get bad looks from people when we dress in our traditional way,' said his wife. 'We have to hide our Tuareg identity or people might attack us.'

Mohammed Ali himself didn't wear his *tamelgoust* any more. 'This is only temporary,' he said. 'When we go back home, I will dress like I did before. It's the young people I worry about. The longer we stay down here, the more they lose their culture and traditions.'

The drought of the 1960s and 1970s had taken away their nomadic lifestyle, but they had retained many of its trappings. Now, in the wake of the Sahara's biggest crisis since those ruthless years of desiccation, the last vestiges of their heritage were being lost as well. They were a microcosm for the nomadic culture that was bleeding dry all over the region.

According to the politicians, at least, the crisis was over. French troops and fighter jets, erratically supported by the Malian army, had swept the MNLA and the jihadists out of Northern Mali's key towns. F-1 Mirage fighter jets wheeled over the desert, dropping bombs on terrorist camps and hunting down the ringleaders like desert trackers rounding up stray camels. That was the media narrative, at least. Many people believed the situation was still precarious, but there was a sense the tide had turned.

I was now approaching the home straight on my journey, potentially the most dangerous and unpredictable stretch. I wanted to find out how Timbuktu had fared; I wanted to catch up with old friends. Throughout the crisis, I had read so many commentaries and analyses and seen the words 'nomadic' and 'militant' jammed together like a forced marriage. There were clearly many nomads involved in the fighting, but the media images were hard to reconcile with the people I had met in the desert. I wanted to find Lamina. Emails from friends in Timbuktu offered a few clues: some said that he was in a camp north of Timbuktu, others that he had escaped to Mauritania or Burkina Faso. I hoped by travelling to Timbuktu I might be able to find out.

'Don't go,' said Abdramane.

He was a friend from my previous journey. We had met on a boat up the Niger and shared stories and cigarettes. Later, he hosted me in his family home in the desert town of Goundam, and helped me when the danger signals were flaring. Now he was living in Bamako, sleeping at his sister's house in the unpaved, dusty Lafiabougou district.

We sat on the rooftop, hemisphered by the sandstone parapets of the Manding mountains. A brazier was burning behind us. Abdramane's wonderful big sister, always smiling, greeting me with vivid Songhay phrases, was peeling onions and slicing up plantain to fry. The meal was delicious, the most wholesome I had eaten in weeks, my plate ladled with celery, garlic and tangy green peppers. I wolfed the vegetables down, relishing their rooty taste.

Underneath us, on the other side of the street, sparks were flashing from a tailor's brazier, swung and stoked to heat his iron. Next door, a coiffeuse was washing her scissors in a bowl, before emptying the water in the street. There was a melancholy atmosphere that night, a moon-silvered brittleness, stirred by the matter we were discussing.

Abdramane had prospered since we last met. Which is to say: he had qualified as a teacher and now worked a punishing schedule for three different schools in Bamako, which earned him enough money to run a motorbike. He invited me back to his sister's house every evening I was in Bamako, and in the daytime I squeezed behind him for rides around town. He was a wonderful companion, cheerful and incredibly generous, an antidote to my anxieties. Yet he was nursing a broken heart: for a girl he had hoped to marry.

'I did everything properly,' he told me. 'I sent cola nuts and a *griot* (storyteller) to her parents to ask for the engagement. But they didn't accept me – I'm too poor, they want a rich husband for her. As long as she's in Bamako, they knew she won't forget me. So they sent her to Spain. They had contacts there, some distant relative. The problem is, she is so beautiful, and when she arrived in Spain, she got too much attention from her host. His wife didn't like this, she accused her of trying something, and she ended up on the street. Now she's living with some guy she met on the plane. Her visa's expired, and she can't find any work, so she's stuck in Malaga, dependent on this guy and there's only one business he's going to find for her.'

It was the old story – a version of the tales I had heard in Freddy's favourite bar: the scramble for a better life, which was turning so much of Africa into a demographic whirlpool. Economic mobility has a patchy history in Mali, but increasingly people were daring to dream. It was the same impulse that was luring so many nomads out of the dunes and pasturelands in search of employment in town, driving Mali's extraordinary rate of urban growth (which at 5.08 per cent was substantially higher than the continent's rising average). I hoped to learn more about these issues on the way to Timbuktu, as well as to meet another branch of urban nomads, a group that I had already seen lining the road to Bamako, panhandling to paradise. Whether a journey in that direction was a sensible option, though, was another matter.

'My family in Goundam tell me things are getting back to normal,' said Abdramane, 'but there is still a lot of suspicion. People don't know where the jihadists are. Maybe some are still hiding in the towns. You heard about the bomb at the military barracks in Timbuktu last month? So you see, the situation is very unstable.'

This was the refrain that kept tolling in my ears. *If you've got any sense, you'll stay in Bamako.* Absolutely, that was sound advice – *stay put, don't stray out of the capital.* After all, there were plenty of refugees to interview, and places to visit in the south of the country. *Who needs to go to Timbuktu anyway?*

One evening, Abdramane took me to meet his *marabout*, an elderly preacher in a cotton cap, with sprigs of silver hair in his ears. He was the man Abdramane consulted whenever he had an important decision to make. He sat, hugging his knees and tipping his head, while Abdramane explained where I was planning to go. The *marabout* scribbled down some markings on a sheet of paper, ruminated over them for a few moments, then told me to buy three guineafowl and a sheep, and offer them to the poor.

'That seems like a lot!' I said, mentally adding up how much I would have to shell out.

'Well...' He tipped his head, the shadow masking his inscrutable expression. 'To keep out of danger, you will need a lot of help. The blessing you ask is not a simple one.'

17

City of Spells

THE MORNING BUS TO DJENNÉ ROCKED LIKE A SHIP IN A STORM. POTHOLES sucked down the wheels, then spat them back out, and herds of scrawny cattle yo-yoed in the corners of my eyes. It was barely six o'clock when we set out, but like a hiker determined on the best view, the impatient sun muscled its way over the low-standing trees. A bank of eucalyptus held firm for a while, until the syrupy light oozed between the leathery leaves and splashed over the canopies. I envied the French soldiers, sitting in the back of an army truck, knees braced under their machine guns. They might be heading to mortal danger, but at least they had shade.

The road to Djenné was a fixed anvil under the solar hammer. Still, a few crops had survived the blast. Watermelons glowed the brightest, bubbling on beds of dark leaves or rolling off trestle tables in the villages, among heaps of shrivelled fruit that looked even more pallid against the colours of the *vendeuses'* dresses: tomato reds, tangerines and cyans, dappled with shadow from the skeletal shade of a tree or spotted with maculae of sliding sunlight.

Women were doing all the work: pounding millet with pestles the size of baseball bats, drawing buckets of water, with babies tucked into *pagnes* wraps knotted under their breasts. Living caryatids, they were able to support impossible loads – buckets and baskets perched on rings of twisted head-cloth, the weight balanced on the columns of their spines, held in place without any muscular effort. Like René Caillié, I was in awe of them. 'They go to distant places for water,' he wrote, 'their husbands make them sow, weed the cultivated fields, and gather in the harvest.'

Plus ça change...

The bus dropped me at a dusty crossroads, where a grouchy Slovenian backpacker in combat trousers was already waiting beside a Japanese photojournalist, strapped into his gear like a modern-day White Knight. We huddled in the shade of an abandoned pick-up truck, like raiders waiting for their chance, until an eight-seater mini-van trundled off the main road to carry us – along with thirteen adults and five babies – down to the river.

'This is the last time I come to Africa!' vowed Jos, the Slovenian.

He clamped a handkerchief over his face to keep out the dust. Beside him, the photojournalist held one of the window bars to keep himself still, eyeing up another thatched granary for a snap.

Sliding across the vista, silvery and abrupt, the river forced a dust-clouded swerve. We had reached the Bani, a tributary of the Niger. The afternoon haze was shimmering on the water, draining the light out of the odd pirogue (a traditional fishing punt), catching the skirt of a ferry raft and sparkling in the froth that bubbled round its edges.

'You think everyone can fit?' asked Jos, scrutinising the crocodile's tail of traffic.

A flock of sheep had joined the queue, scraggly coated and anxiously bleating, along with a chestnut-brown stallion, his god-like head floating above us.

'I wouldn't put it past them,' I said.

The current shone beneath us like molten glass. Behind it hovered a jagged crest of mud, pitched above banks of matted grass and cropped rice fields. Djenné appeared like the enchanted isle in a romance; or, as the French journalist-explorer Félix Dubois put it in 1910, 'Jenne in her island has remained as completely herself as if she had been enclosed in a tower of ivory.' Hardly surprising for a place whose name echoes the word for a magical spirit, a *djinn*. You half expected there would be some price to pay – a riddle or a sacrifice – before you could plant your feet on such hallowed ground. As if you had left the real world behind and were entering the land of fable.

The price was a leap of faith – or, if your legs didn't stretch, a wade. Reaching the other side, the minivan hurtled down a steel ramp and splashed to the banktop, leaving the passengers to lurch through the shallows. The locals had no fear. Unencumbered by socks and shoes, they hitched their skirts and rolled up trouser legs, while the rest of us fumbled with buckles and laces before crashing behind them, taking part in the bilharzia lucky dip. 'This is bloody ridiculous,' fumed Jos, while the photojournalist snapped away, knee deep in zen.

'This place exceedingly aboundeth in barley, rice, cattle, fishes, and cotton,' wrote Leo Africanus. A couple of generations later, the chronicler As-Sadi described Djenné as 'the reason why caravans come to Timbuktu from all quarters – north, south, east and west' and 'one of the great markets of the Muslims'. Every Monday, it still lives up to that billing.

Pitched logs and sacking canopied the animals – pack donkeys, cart ponies, sheep and goats – as well as spatula-wielding women frying galettes of karité butter.[37] Bozo fisherwomen presided with the flies over black heaps of carp and capitaine fish, while robed men from the north hawked boxes of 'Tuareg' green tea or bags of dates, and Bambara women sat behind piles of red peppers, which glistened like firecrackers on their hessian sacks. It was a thrilling place to wander – to the trill of anxious goats, the bisyllabic boasting of guineafowl, the languorous call to prayer, the pop and rumble of truck engines, the chatter of people sipping tea over braziers. Even Jos was enjoying it: I found him beaming in a snack shack, dipping bread into salted eggs and honey.

'Isn't this a marvellous place?' He shook his head at the wonder of it all, his fingers icky with yolk.

Towering over us, impressively and a little pompously, was the Grand Mosque. Ostrich eggs blinged its towers and rodier palms spiked its sides. Its walls were high buttressed and swollen: a muscular, steady contrast to the nimble colours flickering beneath. Félix Dubois (who saw it when the clay façade was still fresh) unflatteringly described it as 'an hysterical mass drawn from a hedgehog and a church organ'. Softened by the market, I was easier to please: I thought it was marvellous.

Although it is Mali's most iconic monument, that doesn't mean the tourists can swamp it. Ever since a truckload of scantily clad models paraded under the vaults for a *Vogue* magazine photoshoot in 1996,

---

37 Also known as 'shea butter', this is the fat from the nut of the shea tree, and is used in cooking and washing as well as being rubbed into the skin to protect it from the sun and smeared in women's hair to give it lustre.

foreigners have been strictly forbidden.[38] It took me four days to find a breach. Every morning I lingered in the square, angling for an opening. Above me, workmen scaled the walls as nimbly as lizards, toes curled over the palm spikes or the splintered rungs of ladders, pasting cracks in the wall with plaster made out of river mud and rice husks. After asking around and being rebuffed each time, I wasn't holding out much hope for a peep until I got chatting with a cheery water seller, who claimed to be a nephew of the imam.

'You want to look inside? Sure you can!'

'But I thought it was forbidden.'

'Forbidden? What is this word? You want to look inside or not?' All that remained was to work out his fee.

Next day at dawn, droopy eyed and a little poorer, I followed him up a ramp behind the southern wall, crossed a courtyard and scuttled into a jungle of mud pillars as wide as baobabs. Through the gaps under the pointed arches, you could make out the odd prayer rug... a carpet brush hanging off a nail... the figures of worshippers, who seemed in the semi-dark to be part of the building, breaking away from their prayers as if a section of pillar had come loose.

There is often a feeling of disappointment when you have made it inside a forbidden building. How can it match the promise that lured you through the breach? Djenné's Grand Mosque is no Kairaouine. It has the shadowy atmosphere of a cavern, a place well suited to prayerful repose. The men kneeling in the corners of the mosque were as silent as monks at vespers, prostrating on the rugs or resting against the pillars, squinting at Qurans as tattered as the manuscripts in the libraries of Chinguetti. They were all men: the undecorated corridor that functioned as the women's area was empty. I guess they were too busy doing all the work.

---

38 Although the association of sexual licence with the Djenné mosque is hardly as foreign as all that. Back in the early nineteenth century, 'dancers sauntered about the galleries of the mosque itself' (according to Félix Dubois) and a young Quranic scholar was so affronted by the carnal activities taking place around the mosque that when he emerged as a regional conqueror, under the name Sekou Amadou, he had it torn down and rebuilt from scratch.

I took a room in a nineteenth-century villa: a buttressed fort with a high porch, triangular battlements and delicately carved wooden shutters battened over the windows. There was a well in the courtyard and a billowing neem tree, occupied by carolling sparrows. The house had the double identity so common along the Niger's banks: a stronghold ready for a siege (complete with its own water supply) and a sprawling mansion fit for a wedding party.

It dwarfed the people walking outside. Among them, I met two religious students called Yunus and Adama. Weighed down with wooden prayer tablets and tomato-can begging tins, they were *garabouts*, come to Djenné for the sake of learning, inspired by its status as the Oxbridge of the Malian *madrassah* system. They hailed from Diré, a river town about 200 miles north, on the way to Timbuktu.

'Our fathers brought us here', said Yunus, 'so we can learn the Quran.'

They had been in Djenné for three years now. In all this time, they had seen no one from their families. I walked alongside them to their school in the Kanafa district, a mud-brick house hanging over the banks of the Bani.

'We beg from eight in the morning till twelve,' said Yunus. 'Then we go to the school to learn Quran.'

'Do you get enough to eat?' I asked.

'Sometimes. But whatever we find, we always come together at the school and share it out, so everyone has something.'

It sounded like a West End musical – the plucky kids tramping across their shattered country, surviving on solidarity and thrift and sheer good-heartedness.

> *Oh, to be a garabout!*
> *It may not seem a lot,*
> *There's not much food, and never fruit,*
> *But one thing that we've got...*
> *Each other, yes it's true, so when you're running out of pennies,*
> *You'll find a brother here amongst the garabouts of Djenné!*

That evening I sat on the steps of the school, trying to disentangle the Southern Cross, watching watery streaks of moonshine to the beat of croaking bullfrogs. It was all very idyllic. I thought I could stay here forever; although I would definitely have to leave by Friday. I soaked it all up, all this fine beauty, then I turned back to the paupers behind me and asked them more questions.

'Do you ever get homesick?'

Yunus had tugged his straw sleeping mat to the doorway to carry on talking.

'Not now, but sometimes... I did, at the beginning. But if you have bad feelings, the *marabout* can do something. He knows a special verse to help you forget.'

'Forget?' I leaned closer, trying to make sense of his words. 'What do you mean, forget?'

But Yunus was tired, and so was I. Like any initiate, I would have to be patient.

Over my week in Djenné, I met dozens of *garabouts*. Hamadou, thin as a reed, was characteristic. He had left his village with his friend Ali to follow a popular *marabout* who had been preaching in their neighbourhood. They walked for six days to Djenné, sleeping on the ground, with no possessions except their clothes. That was 11 years earlier. In the intervening time, each had been home just a couple of times.

'I hope I can be a *marabout* myself one day,' said Hamadou. 'I already know a lot of secrets, but I want to learn more.'

'What sort of secrets?' I asked.

'Well, for example, I know how to save someone from the police.'

'By reciting a verse?' I was intrigued. I wanted to know the technical details. Whether or not it worked seemed less important than how you arranged it.

'It isn't only by reciting,' said Hamadou. 'You can say the verse into your hands, then you spit on them and rub your hands down the person's face. Or you make them drink the verse. Or you write it out in a special way on a piece of paper, and the person wears it, wrapped in an animal skin. We call that a *gris-gris*. It's the best way if you want to protect yourself.'

I thought of my thumb war with Moussa in Bamako, his *gris-gris* rolling down his arm. I had seen other *gris-gris*, poking out of ripped shirts and lumping people's sleeves everywhere I had travelled in Mali.

'If you are going on a big journey,' said Hamadou, 'maybe you should ask the *marabout* for a *gris-gris*. I think you will regret it if you don't.'

The cynic in me wondered if he was touting for business. *Haven't I already forked out on three guineafowl and a sheep?* But his eyes were fixed on me, his cheeks lifted in warm consideration. I was too worried about the coming journey to turn him down: incredulity is a luxury for people who know they are safe.

❧

In the daytime, I wandered through the stew of the town, down narrow alleys where high mud walls fended off the sun. Goats and chickens rootled among broken calabashes and plastic bags, hopping over gravel-bottomed sewage trenches so thick with gunk they looked solid. I would spot a yellow-headed lizard on a downpipe, dewlaps dilating over its shadow; or a pair of doves, cooing in the recess of a rooftop battlement. It was that kind of place, where people and animals live cheek by jowl, too busy with their own affairs to mind any other species unless they are planning to eat it.

In one of these neighbourhoods, I sat down beside a mud-brick hut under a cluster of rodier palms. Boys kicked off flip-flops before stepping inside. Each of them carried a tablet made from the wood of the karité tree. One of them was balancing a reed basket on his head. He crouched in the lee of the hut next to another boy, who was holding a pen chiselled from a bamboo stick, carefully tapered into a nib. The first boy lowered his basket and pulled out a tub of charcoal ink, which he uncapped for the other boy. I was entranced. I had a flashback to Fez and all my Arabic lessons, trying to weave those sinuous patterns, the most beautiful script I know.

The *marabout* was sitting inside, his belly slumped over his lap, his legs crossed over a sheepskin. He held up his bamboo pen like a wand. Known as Bamoyé, he had worked as a religious teacher for the last 20 years, having risen through the same Quranic school himself. There were more than 60 boys in the hut with him, but less than a dozen in the inner circle, bending in turn to recite from their tablets. The other students sat in pools of shadow around the room, peering at the verses, swiping mosquitoes or fanning themselves, waiting for their turn to join the inner sanctum.[39]

Marabouts possess two kinds of knowledge: a public tradition (known as *bayanu*) and a secret one (known as *siri*). The former allows them to teach the Quran, while the latter is used for the esoteric practices that supply most of their income. Any student with ambitions to prosper would certainly hope to be inducted in *siri*. I saw an example of it later in the afternoon. The *marabout* was sitting in the shade beside the wall of his school, filling a piece of paper with a grid of neatly written Arabic verses.

'We call it *kawateen*,' he explained. 'It is for somebody who is struggling in life. Maybe they need a job, or they would like their wife to bear a son. Either you wash the ink into a cup and drink it, or you use it when you are cooking. Sometimes you use it for washing and there are also herbs I advise at the same time.'

Later, Hamadou took me to the market to see the stalls where these special herbs were sold. Among bags of kola nuts and tennis ball–sized cakes of traditional soap were green bottles of Bint al-Sudan or 'Black Girl' ('it's good for getting you a wife,' he explained); black bottles of Aroura ('this helps you get your baccalaureate'); black-green bottles called Al-Hajj ('this gets you respect') and numerous other potions, concocted by quacks and pharma-fraudsters whose trade is one of the most recession resistant across the region.

Hamadou had used these potions many times himself. There was a girl in his neighbourhood who had spurned his advances, and her

---

39 There has been no huge change from the Quranic schools René Caillié described in his nineteenth-century journey. 'By the light of a great fire,' he wrote, 'they recite some verses of the Koran, chanting them in a loud tone; these verses the master writes upon their boards and they have to learn them by heart. At night they meet again at the master's tent to repeat the lesson.' Western educators tend to be dismissive of rote learning, but it can be a useful tool and helps to develop the faculty of memory.

rejection was making him feel sick. 'She is very beautiful', he said, 'and she has a kind heart. I cannot imagine my life with anyone else. So I went to my *marabout* and told him my problem. He didn't give me the answer straightaway, he needed time to think about it. Then he told me to recite a verse and throw three eggs in the path where she goes to school.' His dreamy smile sharpened for the denouement. 'A week later, she wrote me a letter and now her father has accepted me to marry her.'

The longer I spent with Hamadou and his friends, the more stories I heard of how the *marabouts* had helped them. There was the guy possessed by a *djinn*, who had been exorcised by washing in the ink from a Quranic verse mixed with crushed palm leaves. There was the one who found love thanks to a judicious combination of a holy verse and the Bint as-Sudan herb. And there was the story of a friend saved from the law. 'He drank alcohol and caused a really bad accident in his car', Hamadou explained, 'and many people were injured. So he was arrested and they sentenced him to two years in jail. But his mother visited a *marabout* and asked for help. He wrote out a verse and gave her the ink, telling her to use it to cook the meals she took to the prison. Just three days later, the sentence was reduced to two months.'

Everybody in Djenné had a story about *marabouts*. Their faith was contagious. I felt naked, surrounded by all these enchanted people. One afternoon, I made my way back to Bamoyé the *marabout* and handed over a few banknotes. Later that evening, he gave me a rolled-up scroll bound in sheepskin, pasted with glue from the baobab tree, ready to wear on my arm like a sweatband. Its contents were 'a mixture of verses from all through the Quran, they will make sure you are safe'.

The *gris-gris* contained no words to which I could attach any belief, but wearing it gave me comfort. It was a transmission of local faith, a link to the people around me. I was taking part in an old tradition of European travellers procuring native charms. René Caillié did something similar, paying 'a few charges of gunpowder' for his own *gris-gris*. 'As long as I kept it about me,' he was told, 'I might travel in safety and without fear of illness.' *If it's good enough for René*, I thought, *then it's good enough for me.*

The School for Nomads

Lesson Six: Lore

ISMAIL'S HOME LOOKS MORE LIKE A CAVERN THAN A TENT. IT IS A FRAME TENT, made from a patchwork of skins as threadbare and tattered as its owner's clothes. Forked corner posts of acacia give it shape, lashed to crossbars and horizontal arch pieces, bearing the weight of the skins and mats of plaited palm leaves. An organic extension of Ismail himself, it feels more permanent and charismatic than Lamina's streamlined, flexible pavilion.

Two white kittens scuttle out of the aperture, scratching at palm-reed matting and pawing the ring pull on a tin of sardines. One of them glares at me, eyes narrowed, as if it is subjecting me to a proper scrutiny and is a bit miffed that nobody else has done so already. Abdul-Hakim scoops it up and strokes the silky coat; a head turns and nuzzles his shoulder. A couple of chicks circumambulate the tent, like patrol guards, embroidering the sand with jagged lines of arrowheads. Apparently, they are very good at getting rid of scorpions. Ismail pats down the sand and I sit down beside him, accepting a hanky full of snuff, while Lamina takes over the brazier to prepare our dinner.

'This is God's blessing,' says Ismail. 'Take it and praise him. Oh, God is great! God is great!'

He looks impossibly old. His skull is palped, the smile on his lips only distinct from his mandibles by the palest integument. Liver spots tattoo his skin, which is crumpled like tissue paper, as ragged as the mesh of cotton folded over the bare hollow of his stomach. Whether this was once some kind of gown or not, it certainly isn't any more. Hemless, sleeveless, neckless, it is patched with nothing but air, and over the course of our stay I notice pieces of it tacked around tent pegs or binding the handles of cooking pots.

Ismail crouches on the windward side of the brazier, receiving the warmth of the flames while Lamina stokes it. Sometimes, he lifts it up by a rag-knotted handle and swings it, like a priest with a thurible. He lives up here on his own, a mystical old man of the dune. He is too lame to go on the caravan trail any more, but he doesn't want to give up the desert, so he has found the ideal compromise: taking care of the well, a couple of days' ride from Timbuktu.

'Oh, the old days were hard,' he says. 'Praise God for his mercy! There was a single well, all the way to Taoudenni. Can you believe this? These youngsters have no idea how blessed they are. Do you know, there was a journey I made, we got a lot of salt that time, it must have been the beginning of the season... but oh, say the oneness of God! We set out with fourteen men and only eight returned. We buried the dead in the sand and made piles of rocks to mark the graves. And all the money we gave to the widows, so we had to set out again or our own families would go hungry.'

I think of Leo Africanus, who also experienced the desert's cruelty: 'many are found lying dead upon the same way', he writes of the tract north of Timbuktu, 'in regard of extreme thirst'. Ismail's memories are a glimpse into the ruthless ferocity of the Sahara, but I feel like I'm peering through the window of an ion chamber. The sado-masochist inside me wishes I could experience more of this hardship for myself.

The tent sits on an elevated hump. In Saharan tradition, the entrance faces due south, so in the evening we look towards Timbuktu: the red blip of its transmission mast, its houses like termite mounds. The town is more than 20 miles away, but seeing it reminds me of our circular, meandering journey, which must soon come to an end.

Still, there are plenty more lessons to absorb. The teapot squeaks and gurgles, and so does our host, matching every glass of tea with another tale. He hasn't read the *Tarikh as-Sudan*, or the chronicle of Ahmad Baba, or Leo Africanus's *Description of Africa*. But he knows plenty of history all the same, and he lectures me in paragraphs as spidery as an essay crammed with footnotes.

He tells of the kinship between the Berabish and the religious Kounta tribe; of the arrival of the French (and how everyone was amazed by the shortness of their hair). He tells of a French officer who married an Arab chieftain's daughter; of a chief called Sidi Mohammed, who fought against the *colons*. He conjures up a dizzying whirl of characters, drifting into genealogical digressions, side anecdotes about tent size, enumeration of sons, a bizarre story that sounds like a parable, about a man who ran for two weeks through the desert, all the way to Arouane, because he mistook a jackal for a *djinn*. Of all these characters, the one who sticks in my memory is Mahmoud Ould Dahman, a wily old chief who advised against direct conflict with the French and held a key role in Berabish politics until his death, in the early years of Malian independence, at the age of 101.

The picture Ismail draws is a surreal mix of divine magic and realpolitik: a people of rigid religious observance, cannier and more cautious than the Tuareg. He speaks with the philosophical good humour that is a hallmark of Arabic conversation, sprinkling his talk with proverbs and bon mots and ecstatic declarations of *tawhid*, the oneness of God. He is absolutely thrilling to listen to.

Woolly headed but all ears, I scribble down as much as I can absorb. Abdul-Hakim holds up a torch to help, and every so often points at a word, asking me to say it aloud. The men exclaim at my English – '*barak allah*, God's blessings' – and Lamina laughs, quietly, into his beard. Yet I can feel my head drooping, snapping back with a slosh of cooling blood. I need to physically concentrate to keep awake. So, after a weary patch in which I have understood very little, I excuse myself to lie down.

It will take more than sleep to discourage Ismail. He carries on gabbling, and I am not sure if he still thinks I'm listening, or if he has turned his attention to Jadullah, who throws him the occasional grunt. But the old man's voice is soothing, smoothly continuous. I get the feeling he hasn't had anyone to talk to for a very long time. Occasionally, his chatter breaks off and the air tingles to a delicate chant – '*La illaha ill'allah w Mohammed resul allah*', there is no God but God and Mohammed is his prophet – the refrain to which I feel myself falling into slumber.

Part Seven

Plain

In the Maghreb, sedentaries and nomads have never tried to live together without the one disgorging the other.

EF Gautier, *Le Passé de l'Afrique du Nord*

18

Paradise Lost

STARLINGS SKITTERED OVER THE STUBBLE FIELDS IN SEARCH OF GRAIN AND goats tiptoed to reach the lower branches of the balanzans. I was moving south, taking a detour away from the riverlands to visit some of the most distinctive nomads in the region. As the gap from the Niger widened, the trees began to narrow, their trunks became crooked and shields of rock battened the earth from the sun. Two rows of neem trees formed an entry parade to Bandiagara, but the signboards for European NGOs and micro-financing consortia underlined the challenges in this tricksy region.

Known as Pays de Dogon, this is a plateau of hand-tilled rice fields and onion farms, where produce clusters in panniers woven from the stubble. The Dogon are a fascinating people, traditionally animist, whose creation myth conceives the universe from an exploded grain of fonio. Now mostly Islamised, they retain their heritage in zoomorphic masks, intricately carved statuary and a matrix of customs that has drawn anthropologists for decades. I was hoping to meet some of them, but it was their neighbours who had lured me here: the nomadic herders who roam the bone-dry plains below their cliffs.

I had come across Fulani before, selling calabashes of milk in the market of Djenné, herding cattle with dewlaps as droopy as Italian gangsters'. Of all the nomadic communities I visited, they come closest to the literal definition of nomadism: 'roaming' with their herds; 'beginning people', entangled in the murky roots of Africa's earliest tribes.

Spanning the breadth of Africa, hedged by the pastureless dunes of the Sahara and the tse-tse flies in the forests of the south, the Fulani number around 30 million, the world's largest traditionally nomadic ethnic group. In Mali alone, they account for 17 per cent of the population, although the majority have sedentarised. Easy to identify – by the men's wide-brimmed hats, made from woven palm reeds and dyed goatskin, or the women's braided hair and mouth tattoos – they have been mesmerising explorers and anthropologists for centuries (although not all their visitors gave happy reports of them – Fulani bandits seized Mungo Park in 1796 and 'stripped me quite naked', while Heinrich Barth in the 1850s accused them of 'destroying the little commerce still existing in these unfortunate regions').

Like Africa's other nomads, the Fulani have been battered by the myriad crises of the last century – war, drought, famine, desertification. Many have lost their herds and been forced to make do in the towns and cities. For those who stick with it, their lives continue to harden, like the hide of a dead cow left to rot in the sun. Where once they roamed the plains unchecked, now they have the full apparatus of the modern African state against them: development projects, farmland expansion, land sales. This has led to violent conflicts all over their range, from massacres on the Jos plateau of Nigeria to entanglements with sinister groups like Boko Haram, or police crackdowns on cross-border roaming in Guinea and Ghana.

Fulani origins remain a mystery, shrouded by a largely unwritten culture. Their physical characteristics – slim and sinewy with long oval faces (the technical term is dolichocephalous), small lips, almond-shaped eyes and copper-brown skin – invite comparison with East Africans. But their language, Fulfulde, shares roots with Wolof and other West African tongues. Different theories, swinging in and out of fashion, have suggested ancestry from the Prophet Jacob,[40] Aramaic-speaking Syrians, Berbers, Indians and even (according to the nineteenth-century French ethnologist Gustave d'Eichthal) Polynesians from the race of Phout. The most intriguing clue is a cave painting in Tassili N'Ajjer, in southern Algeria: a crowd of herdsmen roam among their cattle, their elongated silhouettes and the lyre-shaped horns of their cattle suggesting a proto-Fulani presence dating back to the fourth millennium BC.

Their own mythology, as revealing as the Dogon's, derives creation from a single drop of milk. But history furnishes few particulars until the sixteenth century. Five years after Leo Africanus's visit to

---

40 According to this interpretation, they were one of the Tribes of Israel, who emigrated south of Egypt to escape the cruelty of the Pharaohs and took their name from the word *foudh*, meaning 'those who left'.

Timbuktu, a Fulani chief called Tenguella revolted against Mohammed Askiya, the Songhay king. Tenguella was slain in battle but many other chiefs rose in his wake, seizing land, power and grazing rights throughout the precolonial period.

'The most dramatic political development in the Sahel after the Moroccan invasion of the Niger Bend', writes historian Bruce S Hall, 'was the rise of Fulbe Muslim reformist movements beginning in the 18th century.' One of the most famous of these was led by Osman dan Fodio, who preached jihad against the Hausa Kings of Nigeria and founded the Caliphate of Sokoto, which lasted for a century until it was absorbed by the British in 1903. In Mali, the most iconic of Fulani leaders was Sekou Amadou, a theocratic warrior-king of the early nineteenth century, who established a kingdom between Djenné and Timbuktu, spanning the Niger's northern crook. Underlining his religious credentials, he named it Hamdullahi, or 'thanks to God'.

A strict Muslim who banned alcohol and tobacco, but also set up social welfare for widows, Amadou prioritised religion over race. His ruling system, known as Diina, or 'faith', is described by Katherine Homewood as a 'theocratic natural resource management system', which 'established a detailed record of resource use, listing fish dams, transhumance routes, village grazing grounds and markets within the (Niger) Delta'. For many Fulani his epoch was a golden age (and he is still remembered with affection in the Fulani community at large), but it wasn't the pastoralist paradise it has been painted by nostalgia. 'It subjected everybody, Fulbe and non-Fulbe, nobles and non-nobles, to the same unitary power', writes Han Van Dijk, 'and made everybody part of the same social project, under the guidance of a sedentary, preferably religious, Fulbe, elite.' The feudal system instituted by Sekou Amadou had far-reaching effects, not least in the divisions it sowed between the ethnic groups of Central Mali, encouraging an atmosphere of mutual distrust that facilitated French colonialism, much like the Northern crisis of 2012 that led to the latest French intervention. Another of Ibn Khaldun's timeless drops of water.

Contacts in the UK had given me an introduction. After a night in Bandiagara, I was picked up by a rusty 4x4 and carried on the bouncy journey to the plain, along with a carton of bottled water and a sack of spuds in case I didn't take to the distinctive Fulani diet. Considering the wear and tear it had to suffer, the 4x4 was surprisingly robust. At least, it made the journey without conking out.

The first part of the trip rattled us along the cliff, the Dogon plateau where sandstone smothers the soil, leaving precious little space to plough. Dogon farmers were bending over the arable patches, using long hoses to divert stream water onto onions and rice paddies. Balanites twisted out of fissures in the rock, their branches fiery with the hooks of hornbills; hawks and other birds of prey glided blackly over the cliffs. We tilted between ironstone ridges and tumbled down runnels in the sandstone, rocking about like a ship in a tempest, until a gorge bottlenecked us to the scarp and, for a breathless moment, we hovered in mid-air. The rockface peeled back behind us and the plain of Séno-Gondo yawned below, 100 metres down. An abyss, a pit, the bottom of the barrel. After the bumpy ride along the escarpment, the change was abrupt: an eerie flatness, running all the way to Burkina Faso.

The high broad mass of the cliff surged behind us like a wave. Hump-backed eolic dunes floated on either side. Encased in tawny membranes of dust, the villages had the faded tones of old sepia photographs. They were widely spaced, so low slung you only noticed them when you were almost upon them, like scenery flats rolled on stage just in time. Many were stamped with the marks of Dogon culture – carved wooden figures, pendulous of beard and breast, holding up the roofs of the *togunas* (meeting places for Dogon elders, low ceilinged so no one could stand up in anger), the thatched millet-stalk granaries raised on mud-brick stilts. But the Fulani presence was equally conspicuous in the sandy plains between the villages: hemispherical huts matted in millet stalks, men resting on their staffs, shielded from the sun by their pointy hats; women with inky mouths and nose-rings, their braids half-concealed by calabashes of milk.

My fixed point was Djoungiani, a mixed village at the edge of the bush. Mud-brick Dogon huts crowded the northern side, near a water tower and the Friday mosque; Fulani tents bubbled to the south, ringed in thorn-bush stockades. At the village's fringe, women were drawing water from a well, tugging at the ropes like bell chimers ringing the hours. We crossed the Dogon side to the edge of the Fulani neighbourhood, and pulled in beside a mud-brick house with a cane mat slung across the doorway. Chickens were clucking around a solar panel, led by an imperious speckled hen, and a couple of sparrows were chirping in the branches of a neem. Underneath them, hunched over a bowl of rice, was a local herd owner in traditional homespun. Small eyes beamed in an owlish face lashed by the elements.

'Now listen, Boureima,' he was told. 'Nicholas is your responsibility. We've heard about the bandits in the bush, so you better take care.'

The prospect of being bandit fodder was raised again when Boureima took me on a tour of the village to make the necessary introductions. After we had salaamed the mayor, the schoolmistress and the local rep for the Ministry of Water and Forests, we sat down in front of the office of the *sous-préfet*, the local administrator.

'Oh, you're safe here in the village.' He rocked on a plastic chair, wrapped in purple cloaks, hands steepled under his lips. 'But don't go into the bush on Thursdays. Or Fridays. Actually, I'd be very careful about going into the bush at all. You see, there's a group of bandits operating in the area at the moment and we haven't been able to catch them. They're particularly active on market days.'

Swallowing down a bubble of panic, I tried to think of the most practical questions: 'So... are they armed?'

'Of course. They are probably from the MNLA. So if you do meet them, I would advise you not to resist.'

Given that I was hoping to move between the villages and explore the bush, this wasn't quite the welcome I had been hoping for. I was anaesthetised by the introductory rounds: passing from one millet-stalk hut to the next, trying out the greeting phrases Boureima taught me, which drew merry, toothless laughs and gleaming welcomes from women with wrinkles as deep as the ceremonial scars around their eyes and mouths. It was a warm introduction to Fulani society, although there were too many for me to absorb their stories in detail. But the next day, the 'real talk' would begin in earnest, with a visit to the village chief.

'Life used to be easy,' said Ali *Hajji*, 'but now everything is hard!'

Top dog in the hierarchy of Djoungiani's Fulani, he was sitting on a stool beside his mud-brick house. He leaned forward, stroking a spade-shaped beard, while his tattoo-mouthed daughter worked a millet pestle in the yard.

'The water is very deep,' he said, 'so we can only reach it if the foreigners come with their equipment and pumps. The taps keep breaking down and there are too many people using the wells.'

It was a far cry from the paradise of his youth. Growing up, he was used to a land of plenty, with fruit available all around.

'There were jujubes, and plenty of baobab fruits. If you took your animals into the bush you didn't need to bring any food with you. You could find a guineafowl, a partridge or wild goat. There was always something to cook.'

Rhapsodies on life in the old days were a recurring theme. On my first night in Djoungiani, Boureima's 86-year-old mother waxed lyrical to the same strain, her eyes bright and timid in deep hollows of bone. 'We used to pick fruit from the bushes and trees,' said Khadija, 'we collected wild honey and helped ourselves to the jujubes.' Among the elders I met, two major causes were cited for the decline: the Great Drought of the 1970s[41] and the arrival of the Dogon farmers.

'The plain used to be for the cattle breeders', said Ali *Hajji*, 'and the farmers were up on the cliff. Even when they first started coming down, they only farmed a small area, so it didn't affect our passageways

---

41 This was the same drought, spanning 1968–74, that spread disaster across Mauritania. My guide there, Ghazi, had told me about its impact. Its nightmare shadow similarly hung over the nomadic communities I met in Mali. For the Fulani, its effect was especially severe, as cattle are less resistant to drought than many other animals such as camels (in the cool season, a cow can last only 3 days without water, compared with 90 for a camel). Equally damaging was the impact on the land. 'Everything died,' said Hamidou Bouki, an elder in the village of Yoru, 'the animals, the grass, the trees. The government brought us wheat and red sorghum but there wasn't enough to go around. We were only saved by the fruit of the gigilé bushes.' Bouki listed seven different grasses that could no longer be found in the area around his village. Other people talked about the death of the baobabs and the disappearance of the fauna. The drought acted as a courier for the desert, bringing sand dunes and acres of arid flatness where there used to be lakes and forests, establishing a vicious cycle of desiccation from which the land has yet to untangle itself.

very much. But now they have carts to carry their tools, camels to draw the water, new techniques to cultivate large areas of land. So their fields have become much bigger than before and there isn't as much space for us.'

This was the Fulani point of view. An NGO worker later told me that many Dogon had been brought to the plain as slaves for the herders, and Islamic preachers certainly counted them among the peoples it was lawful to raid; but after Malian independence, their success in cultivation, and the government's prioritisation of agriculture over pastoral husbandry, had contributed to the eminence many Dogon now enjoyed on the plain. For the Fulani, the loss of pasture and access to the best water sources had drastically reduced the productivity of their animals. Boureima's mother pointed out that it was rare to squeeze much milk out of the cows these days.

'In my youth, you could feed three people for a whole day from a single cow, but they can't do that any more. They don't eat enough grass.'

It was hard to tally the dry landscape around us with the technicolor Eden of the remembered past. Even more so when the elders talked about the plain's most fearsome visitor – because the bush may have been generous, but in those days of plenty it wasn't always kind.

'One good thing', said chief Ali *Hajji*, 'is we don't get attacked by lions any longer. When I was young, we had to protect our herds all the time. If you were out in the bush you lit a fire and kept it burning all night, and stayed awake watching out for them.'

'Did they eat your cattle?' I asked.

'Not just the cattle! Many people were maimed by the lions and we didn't have much medicine in those days, so we had to treat the wounds with cooked cow butter. I remember one lion, a really big fellow, this was in 1973. He came into our area and caused a lot of damage. You know how many cows I lost? Twelve! All over the village, people were talking about their losses, so we decided something had to be done.'

There was a famous hunter in Burkina Faso at this time, known as Bi Biga. He was invited to stay in the neighbourhood of Djoungiani, waiting four months until the beast let down his guard.

'One night,' explained the chief, 'we hung up cow meat on a tree and Bi Biga climbed up the tree next to it. Well, when the lion came to eat the meat, he snapped a twig and the lion looked up. That's what Bi Biga wanted – his rifle was ready and he shot him in the shoulder. But the lion was big and one shot wasn't enough. He ran into the forest, and in the morning when it was light, we all went in there with our guns and stakes. We knew where the lion was, so we set a fire around him and when the lion tried to escape, that's when Bi Biga shot him again. Can you imagine the celebration? It lasted two days, as long as a marriage feast! We danced, ate, celebrated. The lion's skin was brought to the district chief and we hung it from the wall of the *sous-préfet*'s office.'

The Fulani never call a lion by its name. They use nicknames such as *mawdou ladde*, 'big one of the bush', or *laddeeru*, 'bush dweller'. The lion is too powerful to be addressed directly – a god of the bush, a dark talisman of a mightier, more abundant world.

'Now we don't have lions to worry about,' said the chief, 'but we do have bandits.'

'Which is more dangerous?' I asked.

'Well, lions were dangerous for our animals, but for people the bandits are more dangerous, because they have guns and if you resist they will probably shoot you.'

19

Cowboys and Animists

BOUREIMA WAS IN HIS 40S, A CHILD OF THE GREAT DROUGHT, SO FOR HIM the elders' stories belonged to a historical idyll, just out of reach of his own experience.

Highbrowed, with a tuft of beard, he had pointy front teeth that made me think of a merry beaver when he laughed. He took it as a point of pride to show me every aspect of his culture, and answered all my questions, even when they were incessant or intrusive. Every morning, he parked his Sanya motorcycle outside my hut, and pelted greetings through the cane-mat door.

'*Djumwali! Arasele? Koori basa walla?* Good morning! How are you? Is everything OK?'

'*Mirasele! Ooru ma na sele? Basi fu walla!* I'm fine. How's your family? Everything's OK.'

Fulani greetings are wonderful, generously elasticated, full of operatic vowels; and much to my delight, people in Djoungiani never seemed to tire of hearing their language assaulted by an idiot.

Boureima had been appointed to look after me because he was one of the few Fulani on the plain who spoke good French. Although he had grown up in the bush, he had been sent to Koro, the chief town of the plain, for schooling. This was a rare opportunity for a nomadic Fulani, which he was unable to extend to his own children.

'We were in charge of the herd when my children were growing up,' he explained one night. He stoked the brazier with a twig, his face glowing to a coppery mask. 'So I had to stay with the herd and keep my sons with me. Sometimes I think they would have a better life if I sent them to school. You'll meet them when we go to the camp – my son Iman, he's the one who does the herding. He's got a brightness in his eyes, but unfortunately he doesn't have any schooling.'

Thanks to his education, Boureima was aware of what lay beyond. But career opportunities were rare on the plain. I wondered if he had ever thought of migrating.

'Oh no,' he exclaimed. 'I'm Fulani! I come from the plain. My mother and father are here, my children are here.'

Like so many of the Fulani I met, Boureima was rooted in his culture. He taught me the code of *pulaaku*, which emphasises the importance of self-restraint and maintaining dignity. A good Fulani should never give public utterance to discomfort, should make no show of grief, and should always drink his milk by holding the calabash in both hands. Boureima talked proudly of these traditions, as of the many festivals, and complained (without, of course, showing undue passion) that so many of his neighbours had to miss the celebrations.

'We used to have many people during Eid and *Tabaski*,' he said. 'When I was a child, we all gathered round, eating buttered rice, listening to the recitals of the *griots*, dancing to the tam-tam. But now everyone's looking for pasture, so the village is empty.'

Wandering between the millet-stalk huts with Boureima, I could see what he meant. Few voices piped around us. It had the atmosphere of a retirement village, populated by those too long in the tooth to live on the hoof.

I was keen to visit Boureima's camp, to meet his family and see the life of the bush. We decided to take the slow path. We would visit some of the other villages along the way, so that I could learn about the conflict over land and the narrowing of the pasture trails, which was forcing so many of Boureima's people to travel so deep into the bush. These problems are rooted in the particularities of the plain, but they are linked to the wider nomadic experience across the region.

༄

In December 2012, when the Malian state was in tatters and jihadists were threatening to push even deeper into the country, something terrible happened in a village called Sari, 9 miles from the border with Burkina Faso.

'There was a Fulani thief', said Boureima's friend Abdullai, 'who stole a Dogon's herd and disappeared. They say the Dogon community caught him, but they never released a body. There had been tensions between the Dogon and the Fulani in that area for a while. They were like a tent with no pole: it was just a matter of time before everything collapsed.'

In the early hours one morning, before the watering of the animals, a gang of Dogon farmers fell on the Fulani camp at the edge of their village. They were armed with iron-barrelled hunting rifles. Most of their victims could only defend themselves with the knives at the end of their goads.

'The chief did his best to defend the community,' narrated Abdullai. 'He only had a few balls in his gun so he couldn't do a lot. But he refused to run away, that would be shameful, so he and his family died fighting.'

Around 30 casualties were recorded. The rest of the Fulani community fled into the bush and made their way to the border, seeking refuge in Burkina Faso. They were unlikely to return any time soon.

The story of Sari sat at the heart of the Dogon–Fulani conflict, a battle for land control that had troubled the plain, with increasing intensity, since the Dogon started coming down from the cliffs in the 1950s. Not every conflict was a straightforward inter-racial dust-up. There have been fights pitting Dogon against Dogon, and Fulani against Fulani, for it is the resources that are at stake more than identity. But the stories I heard during my stay shed some light on the devious ways in which identity politics wheedles its way into the desperate plight of people scrambling for survival. I wanted to learn about the substance of these conflicts, which drilled to the core of the modern-day nomadic challenge: the difficulty of movement when so much land is fixed. So, one morning I put my feet on the steel footrests of Boureima's Sanya and wrapped my arms around his hips.

We rode fast. Sometimes, launched by ruts in the track, we took to the air. Knobbed baobab branches stretched towards us and flowering gigilé bushes (*Boscia Senegalensis*, the plant that saved many people in the drought) hung clusters of marble-shaped fruits. Hornbills and desert sparrows nattered in the trees, whose trunks were shaken by the hooves of clambering goats. In a moment like a flash of lightning, a rusty red squirrel plunged across our track, seeking refuge in the coppery fastness of a combretum bush. All around us, the land was deceptively peaceful, dusty and dry and still. Like a torture victim, whose skin has been flayed and his tongue pulled out, so you can't hear him screaming.

'You see!'

Beside a row of acacias, Boureima pulled to a stop with a huff of tender outrage. Inside this natural boundary, planted to mark the droving path, were patches of millet stalks.

'They've been sowing their crops here even though it's forbidden. This is the problem – people don't respect the agreements!'

Hamid Barri concurred. He was a gaunt-looking Fulani elder in the nearby village of Gorti, where we found him sitting on a millet-stalk mat. I presented a bag of cola nuts (the standard visitor's offering) and he welcomed me with a beaker of milk. Hamid had a disturbing story to tell, for his son had been one of the conflict's recent victims.

'A couple of months ago,' he narrated, 'my son Suleiman was taking the goats to pasture. He went to a place called Peta, which isn't far from here, but there was a Dogon farmer harvesting the millet. Well, Suleiman saw that a part of the field had already been harvested, so he and his younger brothers led the flock across it. The Dogon called out to him, "What are you doing here? Go away!" "There's no problem," said Suleiman, "you've already harvested this part."

'But the Dogon wouldn't let him pass. He called out to his neighbours and they came along. There were three of them, armed with axes and sticks. They took hold of Suleiman and beat him. My other sons brought back the herd and Suleiman stumbled back into the village a little later. He was injured very badly and we had to take him to the health centre. Actually, we didn't have enough money to pay for the medicine, but fortunately the Dogon boy's father found out what his son had done and he came and offered his apologies and paid for the medicine.'

During my stay in Gondo, I heard many similar stories: fights breaking out between Dogon and Fulani, ignited by the history of conflict and the fact that most of the manual work is done by teenage boys – not always natural peacemakers. The roots of this conflict are both impossibly ancient and surprisingly recent. Their antiquity was illustrated by the film director Cheik Oumar Sissoko, when he made a film called *La Genèse* in 1999, retelling the scriptural conflict between the sons of Isaac as a dust-rinsed, cattle-rustling battle between herders, hunters and farmers in the Malian bush. Past and present are fused in Sissoko's vision, jammed together like Ibn Khaldun's drops of water.

Recorded history backs this stance. Disagreements over pasturing rights were a key incitement for some of the dramatic jihads that characterised the period before colonisation. 'The problem with the agricultural communities', writes the historian AA Batran, 'always centred around the payment of taxes and fines for damages caused by Fulbe cattle on crops.' So the jihad 'offered the Fulbe freedom from the burden of taxes and fines, and security from Tuareg raids'. Seen in this light, Sekou Amadou's conquest of the Niger Bend wasn't simply an act of aggressive evangelism – it was an elaborate tax dodge. No wonder the nineteenth-century jihadists are so fondly recalled in Fulani culture. So much so that Sekou Amadou is regularly name-checked by jihadists trying to lure young Fulani into their ranks.[42]

Yet there are other, recent factors stirring the conflict. Chief among these is the Malian government's attitude to cultivation. Maintaining the agricultural prejudices and fixed boundaries of the colonialists, they have chipped away at customary rights, enshrining 'the creed of private property'.[43] Mali's first president Modibo Keita believed pastoral nomadism was incompatible with effective resource management and made the settlement of nomads a state priority. This attitude is embedded in a legal system that favours the cultivator – the one who can mark the land with his presence, even if he is paying no more for its use than the herders who pass through it.

One Friday, Boureima took me to the weekly market of Duma. It was the biggest barterfest on the plain, drawing traders from as far as Gao to take advantage of the cheaper prices. I met a Songhay merchant from Goundam who had come here because 'the Fulani cattle give the richest milk'. Another, a trader from Djenné, belonged to a consortium that was hoping to buy some cows and sell them on for

---

42 In a December 2011 video, the Movement for Oneness and Jihad in West Africa claimed inspiration from Sekou Amadou and Osman dan Fodio, alongside Osama bin Laden. In February 2014, while I was in another part of Mali, this group was responsible for a devastating attack in the Gao region, in which 31 Tuaregs were killed on their way back from a fair. The attackers were later identified as Fulani.

43 'State institutions', writes Charles Grémont, 'clearly considered agriculture as the only real work, while raising stock was seen as a marginal and transitional activity, if not as an ecological threat and a potential source of conflict.'

profit. But most of the traders were Fulani. They swirled among each other, rustling banknotes and resting on their goads, picking out the longest-eared sheep, the bulls with the biggest humps, the most magnificently horned of the moufflons and the billy goats with the biggest scrotums. Whereas sheep dominated the Atlas markets and goats reigned in Mauritania, here the cattle had the spotlight. As Mungo Park wrote in 1797, they 'constitute the chief wealth of the Foulahs'.

Near the market, in a sprawling house of mud brick and millet thatch, lived 78-year-old Mahmedu Ahmedu, a local celebrity. His inherited livelihood had kept him away from herding and enabled him to observe the conflicts from a position of detachment.

'Oh no, our family never herds,' he said.

Peering through a dim, glassy eye, Ahmedu clasped his thickly veined hands around a cut-down goad that he used as a walking stick. He was sitting on a reed-covered bed in the yard outside his mud-brick house, shaded by a matting of millet stalks.

'We are *griots*, we tell stories, we sing praises, we record the history. That is our role. I inherited it from my parents, and I've passed it down to my sons and my grandchildren.'

Although the demands of a *griot*'s life – singing at weddings and religious feasts, travelling from one village to another to perform – kept him too busy to herd, he was still fully immersed in the herding culture.

'When my songs are well received, the people present me with a cow. If they are very happy, they might even give me a bull. I tell you, my last performance, it was for the chief of a village called Nawooge for his son's wedding, and he was so happy with my songs he gave me a 2-year-old bull and a 4-year-old cow at the end.'

He smiled with the contentment of a man who knows he has lived a useful life. I suspect, if the whole day had been available, he could have enumerated the many cattle he had been awarded over the years. Yet he never amassed his own herd. Part of the wider community, and apart from it, he had become far more than just a wedding crooner.

'We are guardians of the culture,' he explained. 'We can understand things that other people are unable to realise. We help the people to celebrate, but we also help to bring them together. And God be praised, I have been called to do this many times in my life.'

'You mean to resolve disputes?'

'That is a mild word!' The *griot* laughed, shaking his head over his stick. 'I speak of wars!'

'Between Fulani and Dogon?'

'Oh, no. Even before the problems with the Dogon, our lives were hard. Let me tell you a story. There is a village called Bana. They have a lake behind the village, but there is another village nearby called Bodoval. Well, many years ago, they were arguing over who had the right to the lake. They couldn't reach an agreement, so they took up wooden stakes and fought each other in the field. By the time I heard about it, many people had been injured. I got on my horse and rode out to the lake. They were fighting hard, with axes in their hands and blood pouring from their mouths.

'"My brothers," I called out – I did this in song because that is my way to get people's attention – "my brothers, you are sons of the same fathers and mothers, why are you fighting like this?" I played my *kora* and sang to them, and thank God they listened to my words and put down their stakes. They agreed to discuss the situation and we found an agreement to share the lake between the villages. God be praised, this accord is still in place.'

It had been a challenge to secure agreement when both sides were Fulani, united by culture, ancestry and language. So how much harder must it be when the only common ground was the land they were fighting over? Fulani and Dogon 'always marry our own kind', as Boureima put it. I certainly didn't hear any examples of exogamy on the plain. When Dogon and Fulani fell into dispute, if the situation didn't spiral immediately into violence, it went to arbitration, and that could prove costly for the guilty party – which was usually the herder.

∽

But what was the Dogon point of view? One afternoon, I wandered over to the other side of Djoungiani, feeling like a West Side Jet scurrying to a secret meeting with the Sharks. Brima Guindo, chief of the local Dogon community, was sitting in his yard, among piled millet wands and water *bidons*.

'Actually,' he said, 'our biggest problem is water. The rain only comes for a short period. It used to be three months of the year, but now we're lucky if it's one.'

As for cattle, there were other creatures that caused more trouble to his crops. 'Insects are a bigger problem and the birds are even worse. They eat the seed as soon as it's sown, and the millet when it comes up. We have to harvest it all very quickly, to stop them from ruining it. I'm growing peanuts and black-eyed peas now, because the birds don't eat them so they're my safety net.'

Listening to Guindo underlined how difficult farming life can be. In Africa, only gangsters and dictators get to walk the Mickey Mouse path. For the farmers, conflict with herders was only one obstacle among the dozens of others they had to deal with.

'The problem with cattle is only a month or so, because in the rainy season the breeders are in the bush, so it's only when the lakes dry up and they come back to the villages to use the wells. But actually, we welcome the cattle. We need them to fertilise the fields, and they need us for the millet, so we work together really. It's only a few cases where there are problems.'

As with many of the higher-ranking Fulani, Guindo was keen to downplay the tensions. But a little more chat brought the skirmishes to the surface: tortuous negotiations when Fulani herders couldn't pay the reparations; Dogon farmers demanding justice for their crops.

'We had a tough time persuading the Fulani to pay,' he said of one recent incident. 'Sometimes it can be decided without any problems, but in this case it was the farmer's only livelihood. That's the problem for our farmers. If there is a bad harvest like this year, they have to find a way to survive all the way through to the next year. They don't have any cows to sell, so if their crops fail they have nothing.'

We tend to think of rural life as more 'simple' than urban living. Yet time and again, I had learned how untrue that is: how complicated life can be when the margins of survival are so tight. Tomorrow would take us deep into the bush, and I wondered if life there might be closer to a pastoral idyll. It had been out of reach everywhere else I had visited... but when you're travelling in strange parts, who's to say paradise isn't just around the corner?

20

A Short Walk in the Gondo Bush

BRAIDED HAIR SWUNG FROM HER SCALP AND LIGHT CAUGHT ON THE RING of gold under her nose. Her cheeks were decorated with black stars, gouged into her skin like the decorative patterns on a woodcut. We sputtered towards her, teetering along the furrows of the stubble field, and she pulled herself up, tall and majestic and thin as a tent pole. She looked like some exotic princess off the cover of a pulp thriller. She raised a pestle, holding it over a wooden tub of millet husks. Then she buckled over, her black mouth tattoo crashing open with laughter.

'You are the first white man she has met,' said Boureima. 'For her it is like something out of a story.'

She was Aisha, Boureima's oldest daughter. She had married the previous year, but was still living with her family until her 18th birthday, when her husband would come to collect her. Shy and spiky at the same time, she covered her mouth when she laughed, but rattled with chatter as much as anyone else. Like other Fulani women I met, she was always involved in some task, bustling between grain pounding, stalk stripping and food preparing. It was only around the evening fire that she was able to relax.

Aisha's laughter brought out the others: Boureima's wife Buhaisah and three daughters-in-law. Two of them were breastfeeding, so their T-shirts were rolled up over their chests, the babies cradled in one arm while they carried millet stalks and calabashes in the other. Buhaisah came over, a wry smile flickering across her narrow face.

'The *toubob* must eat!' she announced, in a kindly, slightly husky voice. Wrists snapped, fingers pointed, and her daughters-in-law scurried about to fulfil her commands.

I was guest of honour in a millet-stalk palace. I enjoyed it shamelessly. Slouching beside Boureima on a mat of knotted millet stalks, I sipped from a calabash of milk, while my host magically turned into a funfair ride. Running forward, leaping back, diving onto grandpa's chest, the children filled the air with whoops and giggles – except when their eyes settled on the strange-looking *toubob* and they burst into tears.

Meanwhile, Buhaisah's orders had been obeyed. The calabash of milk was followed by a bowl of water and a lump of soap made from cow's milk. Our hands were washed, our appetites whetted – it was time for a feast.

'The *toubob* eats *toh*!' Boureima declared. '*Iniamo, allah berdujam!* Eat and may God increase your strength!'

Buhaisah stood above me, awaiting my response. I wish I could have satisfied her, I really do. But my God, it was hard! The metal bowl contained a dry green paste of pounded millet, with the consistency of plasticine. We dredged it in the hand, and moistened it in a bowl of sticky, dribbly sauce made from crushed baobab leaves. It had a fetid taste, which you could feel in your stomach for hours afterwards. I was grateful for the first, bitter glass of tea. I smiled weakly at Buhaisah – '*gassi*, good!' – but the rest of my face let me down. After a stilted nod, she turned away.

Behind the camp, there was a low pulse of steady groaning, the beat of hooves on dry earth. Through the smoke-yellow glare, we could see the approaching herd: 50 cattle, spanning the full spectrum of malnourishment. Some had thoracic humps drooping over their backs, others were bow kneed, pocked with tick bites, ribbed like radiators. In the middle of them, leaning against a 10-foot staff, his face half-hidden under a pointy red hat, was Boureima's second son, Iman. He rounded up the piebald sheep and a straggle of brindled goats, then sank onto the mat to slake his thirst. Dust stained every inch of his shift, but his eyes were as bright as torches. He picked out lumps of *toh* and tossed them into the calabash, raising his knuckles on trails of milk, revitalising himself after a day in the furnace.

'*Djumiali, ladé ma na selé?*' I asked him, using one of the Fulfulde phrases Boureima had taught me. 'Good afternoon, how was the herding?'

'*Gassi.*'

He was being polite. Outside of the rainy season, herding was never good. The goats and sheep had to eat from the trees and, apart from a few lacy patches of fonio grass, there was little for the cattle.

'Look at how thin they are,' said Boureima later. His older son Ayyub was squatting beside the largest of the milch cows, a calabash poised between his knees. 'In the past, you were guaranteed two litres of milk every time you put your calabash down. Now, we're happy if they give us a quarter of a litre.'

Iman only had a moment to rest. There was still work to do and the sun was dropping to the horizon. Muffled in a pair of headphones, plugged into the tunes on his phone, Iman knelt beside a camel, which was tied to a cart at the side of the camp, and untied its braided grass hobble.

'Where's he off to now?' I asked.

'Where do you think? Come on.' Boureima took me by the arm and nudged me onto the cart. 'You can help us with the watering.'

Like some infernal tyrant who has dealt with all the business of the court and wants to get back to his harem, the Malian sun doesn't hang around. After a day's ruthless incineration, it beats a hasty exit – so the short journey to Tiogoro, the nearest village, was too far to outrace it. The animals made their way ahead of us, following the scent of earlier trips; while Boureima and I bounced on the cart, driven by a donkey with the camel juddering behind. Peering into the dark, I followed the spin of torchlight – a glimmer of wet cement and the warped flash of a forked prong. I could hear the well more easily than see it: the slurp of cows at the troughs, the crack of sticks on donkeys' backs, the rattle of hawsers, the ringing of water dripping back into the bore.

'Suleiman, get on the camel!' called out Boureima.

Wiping any trace of fear from his face, his youngest son clicked his teeth and leaped onto the camel's back. Meanwhile, Iman was busy attaching a hook to the well pole, tying the waterskin and feeding out the hawser. Once everything was secure, Suleiman clucked a command, his bare legs vibrating against the camel's ribs, spinning into the dark nearly 100 metres away, spelling out just how deep you have to go to draw water on the plain. Scooped-out logs provided troughs around the well and once Iman had filled them up, the cows jostled for a drink, rubbing at each other's sides like rowdy punters in a West End bar.

That first night I stuck with Boureima, who hurled out shouts and calls – '*Iye! Ti Tig!*' – to keep the cows in line. On later visits I leaned over the coping with Iman to swing the skins over the toothed rim, or held the plastic filter cone over the *bidons*, or strode around with Ayyub, bearing bowls of salt under the snouts of the cattle. I had learned well drawing first under Ismail, Lamina's garrulous cousin in the desert near Timbuktu; over the course of my journey, I had plenty of opportunity to learn more.

There was always plenty to do, and with other herds turning up, there was pressure to water the animals as fast as possible. But the atmosphere of bustle went hand in hand with the chatter and gossip for which wells have always been famous. Iman, spotting a friend on the other side of the troughs, would share a clip on his mobile phone, or rock on his heels at some tall tale, while Boureima pointed out the various herders and villagers, where their camps or huts were situated, and to whom they were related.

'That boy with the scruffy hair, he's one of Abdullah's. You know, the herder I pointed out to you, with the camp behind us... And over there, that's Guindo's lad. You know Guindo, he's the one who sold us the cola nuts you gave to the chief...'

Back at the camp, a fire had been lit. The women were sitting around it, pouring millet chaff onto the embers, swatting flies with palm-reed pot covers. On the horizon you could track the nomads heading home by the amber beams of their motorbikes. A button of moon clasped the sky, silvering the stalks of millet at the tips of the tents.

I hunched down beside Iman, rubbing my hands over the flames. He was playing a clip on his phone: a horse-riding contest at a party for a famous *marabout*. A couple of his friends from a neighbouring camp had come to hang out. One of them wore a sword, slung over his shoulder in a goatskin baldric. They swapped pictures (goggling their eyes at the beautiful girls from Burkina Faso, as well as the really big humps of the fat-looking herds) as well as stories and gossip. One old favourite, a cautionary tale for 'picky' girls, told of a young woman who refuses a string of respectable suitors, insisting 'the perfect man' is just around the corner. When Mr Perfect finally arrives, he turns out to be a hyena in human guise, which the unwitting bride only discovers after the marriage ceremony. She steps inside her husband's tent to find it crammed with human bones, and he transforms himself back into animal form, a zoomorphic Bluebeard, adding to his blood-stained ossuary.

'We told Aisha this story many times,' said Iman, laughing, 'until she finally accepted a husband last year.'

She turned a wrinkled nose at him and tossed more chaff on the fire. 'So if you hear no greeting from me, then you know you gave me to a hyena!'

At this, Buhaisah and Ayyub's wives burst into cackles, blowing so hard across the fire that for several moments the flames disappeared.

It was rare to see Ayyub's wives sitting together. There wasn't open hostility between them, but they rarely took part in the same chore. Often I saw Tameen, the second wife, nursing her baby at the back of the camp, or sitting on her own with a bundle of millet stalks. She had left her first husband to be with Ayyub, who was something of a player back in Djoungiani. Haala, the first wife, was not best pleased when she learned she would be sharing Ayyub with another woman; although according to her mother (whom I met when we returned to Djoungiani), 'she is happy to be part of a bigger family'.

Under the circumstances, it is as well the tents belong to the women. Husbands are allowed inside as their invited guests, but construction and maintenance are in the hands of the wives.[44] I was curious to see inside a tent, so I asked Buhaisah if she might grant me admission, and after much laughter about this double entendre, she pushed me through the opening. Five horizontal rings, from bundled stalks of Sodom's apple, formed the horizontal frame, lashed to vertical stems of millet with threads of dried grass. So intricate was the construction, there was no need for a pole in the middle: the hooped stalks supported each other's arcs, as well as shelves rigged out of more stalks, on which pots and cloths were

---

44 This principle is followed in many nomadic communities. In Mauritania, Yisslam's wife owned the tent I stayed in. In Tuareg culture, women traditionally own the tents. Nomadism, generally though not exclusively, offers a more equal share of power between the sexes. Women are less confined, have a greater share of property, and in some cases (such as the Fulani) they have broader sexual freedom. Broaching this subject in *African Nomadic Architecture*, Labelle Prussin writes: 'If a woman's reproductive potential, with its guarantee of social continuity, is embedded in the material components of nomadic life, then sedentarisation has far more dire emotional and cognitive consequences than we have yet to realise.'

piled. Combs of millet poked between the interstices, hanging there like decorative beads.

The politics of tent ownership presented something of a dilemma when it came to turning in. Having no Fulani wife of my own, I had no tent to sleep in.

'Hmmm... so you will have to marry someone,' said Boureima, his smile half-hidden in the mist of the fireplace.

'But everyone's taken!'

'Well... we could go and talk to the neighbours.'

'Isn't it a bit late? And I don't own any cows. So I don't think I'd be much of a catch.'

'That is true.'

After a little joshing, I was introduced to my accommodation: a storage hut, where the water *bidons* and millet wands were kept. It was spacious enough, and I had a couple of blankets to keep me warm. Iman was still playing tunes on his mobile. The hooting of reed flutes washed over me like a lullaby, along with the rustle of stalk stripping and the chatter around the fire. I picked out Orion – *Babaradji* to the Fulani, 'the knife holder' – part of a vivid starscape in the gaps between the stalks (among the others were *al-Hanah*, the brand, and *Sadalachlia*, the 'lucky star of the tents'). They were another component to the magic of the camp, flashing around us like the gold coins woven into the women's braids and the rings in their nostrils.

Lie-ins aren't an option in the bush, not with so many alarm clocks around you. There is the pounding of the millet pestles (around 5.30), the foghorn of lowing cattle (5.45), the panicky bleating of hungry young – both animal and human (6.00 if you're lucky). As soon as Iman and Suleiman returned from the well, Ayyub would squat down with his calabash, gently massaging the cows' underbellies. Sometimes he brought a calf to draw the milk, letting it suck the first foamy drops before pushing it into the hands of one of the children. Every so often, he dipped his fingers in the calabash, moistening his fingers to reduce friction on the teats.

'Milking is the eldest son's job,' Boureima explained. 'He is in charge of the camp, so he must provide the milk. And the cows are used to him. If anyone else tries to milk them, it is much harder to get anything out of them.'

The accommodation may not have been en suite, but I only had to walk a few yards to reach the shower facility. Hanging a towel from the branch of a jujube tree and draping my clothes on the pegs of various boughs, I rinsed myself in a pan of fire-warmed water and rubbed off yesterday's dirt with a lump of cow's-milk soap. A couple of the children had come out to watch me, but Boureima reeled them back, so I was able to shower in relative privacy, freshening up for the day.

Breakfast – which was the same indigestible *toh* and baobab sauce as all the other meals – was a hurried affair for Iman. Soon after the watering, the animals were impatient to set off. Iman had to be brisk: if he didn't accompany them, they would stroll away on their own. He made sure his flask was full, slung it over his shoulder, picked up his staff and set off. I went along with him a couple of times, turbanned against the sun, chanting the phrases Boureima had taught me, trying to pick up the individual names of the cattle.

'*Ti Tig! Ti Siga! Ti Wagey!*'

'Nicholas the herder!' Iman bellowed from the other side of the herd, lips parted in a broad grin. He was a super guide to the bush, pointing out the different trees and plants, handing me the staff from time to time, laughing me along the day's slog as blades of sunlight pronged a merciful buffer of cloud.

Little Suleiman was in charge of the sheep. We could see him a couple of fields away, running in a blur of woolly specks. Iman and I hung back with the goats, while the cattle plodded ahead, slowing down whenever their names were called. Watching Iman at work, I thought of Mungo Park's comment: 'They display great skill in the management of their cattle, making them gentle by kindness and familiarity.' For the Fulani, the cow is a peer, individualised by name, treated affectionately, if firmly. They move in a fleet, with only one stud to a herd. He was easily identified by his spiralling horns and slabbish hump, and the withering snorts he directed at the geldings; although the miserly pasturage didn't give him much strength to run amok.

The slosh and sigh of Iman's water flask, the crackle of millet stalks underhoof, the rustle of the breeze between the logs of the millet ricks: these were the sounds of a day in the bush. A knife gleamed on Iman's staff, slotted into the tip, and when we reached a wild acacia he speared a branch, hacking it down with a double-handed twist. There was no grass, but it is hardly great news for the long term when the little shade that is left is being pulled down.[45] At least the goats were content. Assembling like animals at a trough, they mashed their jaws and stripped the branches, beards swinging against the barbs as they nibbled.

The land behind Boureima's camp was millet and sesame fields – sun-crusted ridges, stubbly with the stems left over from the harvest. Traversable now, they would be an invitation for skirmishes in a few months' time: the paths between them were too narrow for a 50-strong herd. With no live crops to worry about, our passage was at least unfraught. On the other hand, in the heart of the dry season there was little pasturage other than the stalks.

At the edge of the fields, a pair of baobabs fingered the air with contorting branches, a few furred fruits hanging out of reach on the higher boughs. We stepped between them as if we were passing through some monumental gateway, leaving farmland for the freedom of the bush. Acacias divided our journey like wells on a caravan trail, their snapped-off branches providing the only food the goats would accept. They hung close to Iman, aware of their dependence on his staff. The cows were less needy. Strolling at their own pace, they munched on spikes and panicles of fonio grass, wandering en masse until Iman reined them in.

It was an achromatic world – tan and ochre, brindled earthy tones, the pea-green of the acacias. There was no gloss anywhere. The sun hurled its light down, but there was nothing – no pool, no waxed leaves or fruit skins – to rally it back. By our third tree stop, our party had grown. Two teenage herders, rubber sandaled and pointy hatted, strode over from their own quest for pasturage, their goats following

---

45　This was the vicious cycle inflicted by the Great Drought. Without adequate vegetation, the animals turn to the trees; the destruction of the trees leaves the ground with no shade (and reduces ground moisture), so it is even harder for vegetation to grow back; and the soil is left open to the wind, which blows the topsoil away to create desert.

at a distance. One of them was an impish 14-year-old called Hami. He wore a whistle round his neck, which he blew with all his might whenever his herd was on the brink of wandering out of sight. We sat together, taking a rest in the shade of an acacia, nibbling the peanuts we found on the ground. In front of me, Hami and his companion were statues with hanging jaws. As soon as I wandered off, they collapsed into hoots of laughter and giggling chatter. They reminded me that however well I thought I was doing, however much I told myself I was getting on with Iman and his family, I was still an alien here. I would need to stay a lot longer among the Fulani to become anything more.

I had stepped away to watch a couple of billy goats. They were digging up the dust with their hooves, circling each other with tilted heads. At last, their horns locked. They ran and passed each other, like medieval knights at a jousting.

'*Iye! Iye!*'

Iman sucked his teeth and waded in with his stick, sending off the warring goats in different directions. Fights in the flock were rare, but they could get vicious pretty fast. Normally, the animals jostled together without too much trouble, lining up around the fallen boughs like customers sidling into a diner. Each goat ripped her own section, waiting for Iman to turn the bough so they could access the leaves on the other side. When the bough had been picked as clean as a chicken bone, he called out '*Iye! Iye!*' and the goats scrambled behind him, jogging towards their next snack.

While we crouched in the narrow shade of a balanite, taking a breather and swigging our water, a moment of magic took place. It was a glimpse, a thrilling glimpse, into the inner workings of nature's oily machine. A pregnant goat called Torda had edged away from the herd. Digging her black hooves into the soil, she scratched the air with labour cries. Strings of viscid white slipped between her legs, followed by a red haematic sac. The air rang with bleats, and a hoof breached the blood-slicked lips of her vagina. Another followed, then a head, slicked down with fluid. When the baby tumbled onto the sand, Torda bent to lick him clean, rolling him around with her tongue, cawling him in saliva and sand. Cheeping and squeaks were met with gentle blurps, a sound so sweet, so elemental, it scrubbed out the difference in species. They were simply a mother and her baby.

I was aware that my response was wildly sentimental. I couldn't help it. It was the first time I had seen a calving. Iman gave Torda a few moments – he was more absorbed by my response than the birth itself – before seizing the baby by the neck. It was time to move on. Torda was allowed to canter beside him, and occasionally he lowered the calf for her to lick. Her placenta fell out like an afterthought, landing among sand-crusted gobbets of blood. By our next tree stop the calf was standing up and reaching for her teats; but the nursing process was going to hold us up, so Iman called out to Suleiman and sent him back to the camp with the newborn. Poor Torda spent most of the day crying in motherly anguish, and it was a lovely moment to see her reunited with her calf later in the afternoon.

Sitting on a mat of coppery leaves, picking out the spines of cram-cram sticking to our ankles, we swigged our water and watched the cows munching away at the fonio grass. They didn't demand much of Iman's attention, which was focused mostly on the goats.

'When the pasturage is better I can go with the other animals,' he explained. 'But there's nothing for the goats to eat here. They can't eat the fonio so I have to get the branches down for them.'

Talk like this was translated for me afterwards, back at the camp with Boureima. During the walk itself, Iman and I communicated in phrases – Fulfulde sayings gleaned from Boureima, along with some new ones, passed between us like a ball, which every so often I would clumsily drop: '*wa wa enadoga ananyanyo*' (you can't go two ways at once), '*eniali ney bey bali erine qorte*' (we're bringing the cows, sheep and goats back to the camp). We weren't going to be discussing the intricacies of pan-African pastoral politics, but for a few days in the bush it was okay.

The slim pickings of the fonio were as much as the cows could hope for. Stripped of its fur and shorn to its rootstocks, the plain is no longer a place for large herds. But small herds are no good for the Fulani: ambition and self-esteem are entwined with herd size. To ask them to cut down is like asking someone in the West to close their investments. Back in Djoungiani, I had bumped into the local representative for the Ministry for Water and Forests, Amadou Dicko. 'The people increase,' he told me, 'the animals increase, and the forest shrinks.' He shook his head, cradling it in his palm. 'If we don't resolve this situation in the next 15–20 years, there is no hope.'[46]

Now the sun was starting to dip, muffled by a kindly froth of cloud, and the animals were towing long shadows. It was time to head back to camp. We took a different route, shortcutting across a millet field, where a Dogon farmboy was piling stalks onto a donkey cart, to be used for roofing in the nearby village.

'*Y a un blanc à la brousse!* There's a white man in the bush!'

He raced over, swinging my hand like a newly installed water pump. Between him and Iman, there was no greeting; only a perfunctory grunt.

'You came to see our agricultural life?' he asked. 'You should stay in the village, then we can show you. It's safer there. You shouldn't be out in the bush on your own.'

'I'm not, I'm with my friend.'

I nodded to Iman, but the farmboy didn't look at him, and Iman made no step forward. Wearing an expression of serene detachment, he loped down the furrow. I thought he was just going to relax, or maybe do a spot of tooth picking, but after a while he smoothed down the earth and knelt with his back to the sun, a hum of Arabic prayer floating over our shoulders.

'It's very hard round here, you know,' said Alysson, the farmboy. 'Especially at harvest time. We have to work all day when the crops are ready. But now we've got nothing to do, we're just waiting to grow the crops again.'

I asked what kind of relations he had with the herders. He slid his eyes toward Iman, just for a moment, before turning back to me.

---

46 Dicko's concern echoed the ecologist Garrett Hardin's 1968 essay, *The Tragedy of the Commons*: 'Therein is the tragedy. Each man is locked into a system that compels him to increase his herd without limit – in a world that is limited. Ruin is the destruction to which all men rush, each pursuing his own best interest in a society that believes in the freedom of the commons.' This distinction (which has had a massive impact on the way governments around the world treat their pastoralists) assumes there is land that is *not* common – which, under the neo-liberal policies of twenty-first-century Africa, is the growing majority. Pastoralism depends on the sharing of land; on the agreement that those who pass through it have the same rights as those who mark it with their tools.

'We're friends with them, especially at this time of year. We like the animals because they fertilise our fields.'

'What about later in the year?'

'Well, we don't see them so much. They go further into the bush because they can't be here when we're planting our crops. Only the lazy ones stay, and we have a few problems with them.'

All the time we were talking, Alysson was looking over his shoulder, his eyes tight in a face pinched with worry lines. Iman was very different. When he strode back over, he was picking his teeth, like a cool kid chewing gum. He seemed to express the freedom of the nomad: the one who doesn't have much to lose.

In the light of the elders' tales of past fertility, the plain felt terribly empty. Its fur had been fleeced, exposing every muscle and knob of bone. But I was slowly learning to read what was left. Ants and termites were hard at battle on hills of laterite soil, bearing corpses and chaff out of ribbed orifices in the ruddy earth. Millet stalks crunched under the animals' hooves, and the odd starling glided down from the lopsided trees. The sun had been gentle on us, a pewter gleam through the clouds rather than the usual hammerbeam, but still I was tired, ready for refreshment. It came, in the magical way of the bush, with a slop of plastic slip-ons and the appearance of Hami, our whistleblowing companion from earlier in the day.

'The *toubob* drinks goat milk!' yelled Iman.

I took a slurp from Hami's calabash and handed it back: 'Hmmmmm.... *anavelli*, delicious!'

Launching himself on a farewell smile, Hami disappeared into the brake, his whistle tapping against the gourd. I turned to Iman and we both shook our heads, merry with laughter. The walk had been wonderful. Sure, my legs were a little stiff, but I was already looking forward to the next one.

There were more greetings, more invitations to hospitality. We stopped frequently, sipping milk and exchanging laughter, congratulating a family Iman knew who were wainscoting their new tent with bundles of millet stalks. The bush is a village, and I felt the joy of a straggler who has been admitted inside its walls. By the time we reached

Boureima's camp, I was hungry and tired and eager for a sit-down. Yet I was still buzzing, high on the camaraderie of the bush.

'You survived!'

Boureima was hopping in the furrow, clapping his hands together. The beat of millet pounding and the crackle of stalk stripping chimed around us, like a familiar tune on the radio. Torda the new mum bleated in relief, trotting over to lick her newborn. A clatter of pots turned me towards the millet-stalk mat, where Aisha was laying down a worryingly large bowl of *toh*. A calabash of baobab sauce glistened beside it: a feast was being threatened. She took one look at my expression and flung a hand against her mouth, to shield her laugh.

'Come on, Nicholas.' Boureima wrapped an arm around my shoulder and led me towards the food. 'After a day in the bush, you must be starving. Eat – and God give you strength!'

The School for Nomads

Lesson Seven: Water

'YUSUF, FOR SHAME!'

Old Ismail pulls back the mirror, grasping it with translucent, waxy fingers. He has ferreted it out of a burlap sack, after I complained of grit in my eye. I am struggling to blink out the dirt, but he won't give me the mirror until I follow the protocol.

'Did the Prophet, on him be peace, take things with his left hand?'

Finally, I get it right and the mirror is released, but I still can't excavate the grit. A handful of black grains is offered – Ismail says I should drop them in my eye, 'and God will bring an end to your problem'. But I don't have his faith, so I decide to let time, and lots of blinking, do the healing.

It is another day of lounging: sipping coffee, snacking on peppery dates, listening to Ismail's chatter and ecstatic declarations of the *shahada*. I spend the afternoon wandering around the dune, never straying far, while the others take it in turns to pray and Abdul-Hakim frolics with the kittens. One of them is still cutting me, slitting its eyes as if it is the only one who knows the truth about me, waiting for the others to catch up.

Halfway through the morning, Ismail takes me and Abdul-Hakim down to the well at the foot of the dune. Poles of acacia spur a square hole braced by logs of palmwood, surrounded by a cement coping as smooth as cake icing. A rusty winch dangles from the crosspole like a fishing rod, carrying the weight of the *guerbas*.

'Do you know how to draw the water?' asks Ismail.

'I've never tried before. At home we have...' I don't know the Arabic word for a tap, so I mime it.

'Like a pump well?' Ismail wonders.

'Yes. But they're smaller, and we have them inside.'

He mutters something about God's glorious works, and repeats the word *ajib* ('wonder') several times. I wish I could show him a picture of my kitchen in Borough. I don't imagine he would be envious, I think he would just say it was *ajib*.

Abdul-Hakim has brought down Ismail's donkey, who does the bulk of the work. A flabby goatskin *guerba* is hooked to a hawser rope dangling from the cross-pole, which rotates and lowers the skin into the *aiun* – the 'eye' of the well. When the *guerba* has reached the bottom, we hear a slurp and Ismail calls out to Abdul-Hakim, who shouts at the donkey. Sand puffing round its hooves, it shrinks across the sand, its movements growing slower as the waterskin rises. When we pull the swollen, dribbling *guerba* over the lip, Ismail offers up a satisfied cry of 'bravo!' It is an oddly secular word to hear from his mouth, but he makes up for it when we carry the *guerbas* back to the tent.

'Oh, Yusuf, give praise to God! God is great! Oh, God is great!'

He is pleased, I think, to show his well to an outsider. As its keeper, he is proud of the quality of his upkeep, and the quality of the water.

'What reason is there', he asks, sitting in the shade on the north side of the tent, 'for a well to fall out of use? As long as someone with good character is nearby, the well remains in good condition and everyone is able to drink from it. Why should anybody thirst in the desert? The water here is pure. By the truth of God, it is better than the dirtwater they force down themselves in the city!'

By late afternoon, we are packing our gear and saddling the camels once again. Time for one last prayer before we go. The sun is already sinking, turning the sky a pale, burnished copper. The distant hills are ashen and opaque, outlines in charcoal. The Islamic calendar may be lunar, but when it comes to prayer, the schedule is solar. These divisions structure the day, as precise as the astral signpostings of night.

Jadullah, Lamina and Abdul-Hakim line up behind Ismail, who leads them in their prostrations. I am sitting only a couple of feet away, and I feel caught up in their prayer. I follow the movements with my eyes, absorbing them, responding to them: standing upright, bending forward with their hands on their knees, kneeling, bowing until their foreheads touch the sand. I have watched them do these movements so many times over the last few days, I feel as if my own body is moving with them. The cats have come out to observe, and one of them settles beside me, fluffing my leg with its tail. The other cat holds back a few feet, still wary of me.

'May God grant you the wisdom you seek.' Ismail grasps my shoulder in his hand; it has a vigour that belies his age. 'May he guide you to the truth.'

I smile back at him. We both know what he means.

'Say God is great,' he whispers, one last evangelical push. 'Say Mohammed is his prophet.'

'Thank you, Ismail. I promise, I have my Quran and I will read it carefully.'

His pale lips curl at the compromise. I suppose he doesn't often get the chance to win a new follower to the faith.

I am sad to be leaving Ismail. He has an energy that is entirely his own – garrulous, pious, kindly, good-humoured – and I fear this sketch will capture no more than his shadow. But he saves the best for last:

Allah-humma inna nasaluka fi safarna
hadha al-birra wa at-taqwa
wa min al-amali ma tarda

Oh God, we ask you on our journey
for goodness and piety,
and for works that please you.

We are mounted on our camels now. Jadullah bobs to the front, while Lamina takes the rear. Ismail lingers halfway up the slope, singing the blessing for our journey, his torn rags tugged by the wind. A part of me itches for a camera or a phone to record him; the other part is determined not to spoil the moment. His words cling to us, as if by some paranormal acoustic, amplified far beyond an old man's natural reach.

Halfway across the plain, crossed by quick eclipses of sunlight, the dune is still visible. Ismail has become a flickering speck, although his antiphonal singing lingers among us: words filled with faith and feeling, with all that is best, all that is purest about the desert. It is a song so warm hearted that I feel my own heart swelling to the sound of it. I think it may be the most beautiful thing I have ever heard:

Oh God, make our journey light
And its distance easy for us.
Oh God, you are our companion on the journey
And the one in whose care we leave our family.
Oh God, we seek refuge in you
from the hardships of this journey
And evil visions, and from finding on our return
Our family and our property in misfortune.

I 'ooooshhhh' Naksheh over the dunes, leaning back on the descent, hands tight on the headrope. Scrub bristles around us, acacias teeter and we skim across the bending earth, as night plunges and Ismail's words are licked away by the air.

Part Eight

River

*The land of Negros is extremely hot, having some store of moisture
also, by reason of the river of Niger running through the midst thereof.*

Leo Africanus, *The Description of Africa and the Things
Therein Contained*

21

Masters of the River

THE MARKET OF MOPTI LACKS THE ROMANCE OF DJENNÉ'S ALL-ROUND SENSE assault – but it's just as exciting. Dogon women carry wicker baskets on their heads, bubbling with pounded onion. Fulani herders balance water gourds on the tips of their staffs, kid-goats and lambs bundled in their arms. In the heat of the day, light splinters the jagged edges of rock salt from the mines of Taoudenni, waxes the peppers and shimmers in buckets of reticulated fish scales. Baskets gleam with silver dogfish, crescents of stingray or 3-foot-long black-eyed capitaines, as the Nile perch is known locally. The smell of brine spices the waterfront, where stevedores leap between the bobbing prows and tiptoe up the gangplanks, bearing saturated rice sacks, drums of petrol, 10-foot-high wardrobes, Super No 1 motorbikes. The din thickens with shouted orders and near misses, the odd splash when a stray papaya tumbles out of a pail, and high above them the spars whistle to the beat of the breeze.

'Are there any spaces to Timbuktu?' I asked.

'*Bien sur!*'

A hardy veteran in a ribbed beanie as grey as his beard welcomed me onto a 100-foot pinasse (a multidecked longboat). The 20,000 CFA (about £25) he asked for was substantially more than the locals would be paying, but it was a lot more practical than the 1500 cowrie shells Félix Dubois had to stump up for his Niger passage a century earlier.

'And so... when do we leave?' I asked.

'Soon.'

He turned away to deal with a consignment of onions, before spinning back round when I asked if he could be a little more specific. Feet rang on sheet-metal plates. He stepped towards me with flashing eyes, indulging the whim of a pedant.

'Tomorrow after the noon prayer.'

With time to spare, I decided to seek out one more group of nomads. Timbuktu was a few days away. There, I would meet Tuareg and Arabic-speaking herders – as long as the conflict had left any in town. But on my journey up the Niger, I was sure to pass another branch of roamers. I was keen to meet these 'masters of the river' and learn what it is like to be a nomad who floats.

Ten thousand years ago, when the region we know as the Sahara was gushing with rivers and swaled with marsh, a civilisation of foragers flourished, leaving their signatures in small blades and ceramic pots decorated by fish spine. In spite of the region's desiccation, some vestiges of this culture endure.

'The Bozo fishing people', writes ecologist Katherine Homewood, 'are generally acknowledged as the first inhabitants of the region.' Distinguished from other nomads by their riparian setting, they still have much in common with them: moving about in a symbiotic relationship with the wildlife around them, often spending weeks away from any village, driven by seasonal change.

It is to the Bozo that the founding of both Djenné and Mopti is credited. Great spirit consulters, they turned to their *marabouts* when their first efforts to build a town were wracked by collapsing walls. Evil forces were at work, the *marabouts* decided. There was only one solution – to sacrifice a virgin. So a girl called Tapama was interred and the city flourished. While I was staying in Djenné, I used to pass Tapama's clay tomb every day on my way to the market.

While some Bozo settled in towns like Djenné, the true river rats were at home in their dugouts, harpooning crocodiles and hunting the plentiful hippopotami. These days, most Bozo live in villages, in huts of mud brick or bamboo (their name derives from the Bambara for 'bamboo hut'), stilted over the banks to protect them from seasonal floods. But there are some who still wend the riverways, tracking the fish with the stealth of huntsmen following game, their knowledge of fish migration so intricate they can tell where the best haul will be at any time of year.

Introductions in Mali can be complex. My friend Mahmoud, who lived in Timbuktu, had put me in touch with a friendly Dogon in Sevaré (a town near Mopti), who gave me a bed for the night and the name of a Bozo fisherman called Ibrahim. Dogon and Bozo are linked by a code of inter-ethnic kinship (known as *sanankuya*, which is usually translated into French as *cousinage*), stretching back to the legend of a Bozo fisherman who fed a starving Dogon family by cutting slices off his own flesh. To find my contact, it was just a matter of asking about on the waterfront.

I was directed to a breakfast shack, a tent of poles under a canvas hood. Eggs were frying in a pan and the steam was so thick it hid the faces of the men sitting behind the cook's table. They were merchants and fishmongers, munching and smoking, waiting to be summoned to their boats. Among them was Ibrahim.

Tall and thick armed, with long fingers crusty from ropework, he nodded over a beaker of coffee, murmuring softly in French. I explained that I wanted to meet some of the nomadic fishermen working the river, and suggested a price. Eyes narrowed, as if I were an unexpected pool whose murky depths would need to be assessed. He placed his beaker on the table, and made his way soundlessly out of the shack.

'Let us pick up supplies.'

Ibrahim's boat was a pirogue, made from fire-curved boards, caulked with old rags soaked in karité butter. Poling across the fuel slicks around the port, we swung across the current to Masa Daga, a narrow islet jagged with prows and fuzzy with bundled nets.

The houses near the shore were barrel-shaped tents, easily dismantled when the river is in spate. Higher up, stones pinned down iron roofs on hilltop huts. It was an unusually windy day: the breeze ruffled the plastic sheets knotted to the roofs, tugged a kite tethered to a hut, unpeeled the clothes laid out to dry. Women were picking through a haul of carp, gutting them with rusty knives. Ibrahim muttered a greeting, which they received with a whispering reply. His wife was waiting outside a small hut on top of the hill, holding out the items we needed: a wire-coil brazier, a sack of charcoal, a rug to sleep on. I pronounced a greeting, and she replied with a silent tilt of the head.

The plan was to follow the Bani, the Niger's largest tributary, which flows for nearly 700 miles southwest of Mopti. Conditions for river travel were perfect – if you happened to have a wide sail or an outboard motor. A northwesterly had raised a swell, pinching the water like customers in the market picking out cloth. Pirogues punted valiantly, the rowers slumped over their poles with hangdog shoulders, while diesel scent drifted from motorboats whose operators had good reason to look content. One skiff was using the wind to its advantage: a couple of poles had been lashed, a dozen millet sacks stitched together for a sail, with old net cordage for stays. Inflated by the breeze, it was working a treat, scudding the boat along the current.

Ibrahim stood rod straight on the stern, hauling the river behind us like a trench digger with a spade. We rounded Masa Daga and nosed between a pair of tawny cliffs crested by palm-reed huts. To the west uncoiled the Bani, flowing north from the direction of Djenné. There were only a few driftnets out; most of the fishing was being done by the waterfowl. Cattle egrets stood in the shallows, impersonating reeds, lifting off as we approached. A fish-eagle glided on its kill path, the broad planks of its wings kissed by the sun. Less subtle were the kingfishers: pied and hyperactive, with spiked head crests. They used bamboo-net cages as springboards and rattled the air, before diving down to snatch a dragonfly or skewer the carp.

Whether we could replicate the birds' fishing success for ourselves was another matter. At first, the signs were auspicious – we caught something before we even dropped a net. It was a tiny capitaine, a fingerling. It hopped over the side of the boat, flapping among packets of tea and a bag of sugar. With barely a glance, Ibrahim scooped it up and dropped it back in the water.

'It can grow to be a big capitaine,' he said. 'This is one of the problems these days. Too many people, they catch the small capitaine and eat it, but they should give it back to the river until it is ready.'

Luck (or baraka, at least) was less generous when we tried to fish in earnest. Splashing the bundled net, Ibrahim tossed a jerry can into the water as a marker buoy and fed out the rope. Gouts of water hung to the fibres of the net as he straightened them. Dropping a plastic bottle to mark the other end, we slid to the bank, floating beside the beehive-shaped bamboo cages, which were coned with side funnels to draw the fish.

'It's the current that brings them,' said Ibrahim, 'so we must wait for them to come, then we can pull up the net.'

He sat, legs apart, the pole between his feet, relaxing with a cigarette. The silence was long and lavish and strangely relaxing. Rather than digging around in panic for some topic to break the pause, I just let it wash over me. People in cities get used to squawking at each other, but out in the bush or the dunes, or floating up the river, you are alone with your thoughts for long stretches of time. It teaches you to be reflective, but also to listen more broadly.

What I took for silence was nothing of the sort for Ibrahim. What is sound, after all, but the driving of compression waves through billions of molecules of air? And there were plenty of compression waves pulsing that morning. There was the beat of wing-strike, like the rustle of a money changer's banknotes, the riffle of wind in the boat cover, the creak of the hull in the shallows, the ultrasonic of gliding fish and the occasional splash to remind us of the shoals on the move. 'When you listen with exactness,' a Berber cameleer in southern Morocco had told me, 'you understand the world is full of music.' If I had learned anything on these travels, it was to listen better, so I was starting to hear some of these sounds for myself.

Even when he spoke, Ibrahim's voice was carefully modulated, a cat-like purr. Like many of the Bozos I met, he was used to whispering on board, to avoid disturbing the fish below. He had been working the river since boyhood, having honed his skills, in the usual way, by watching his father.

'I got my own boat when I was 20,' he said. 'That's when I became a fisherman. I've caught everything there is to catch in the river: carp, dogfish, capitaine, stingray. It varies year to year. Some years I do well, some not so much, but I've got a lot of experience and I usually know where to find something.'

This patch of the river, however, was no longer the place for a grand haul. 'The season's over round here,' said Ibrahim. 'Gao's the best place at this time of year, the water's higher up there.'

Drips of water spilled off the cord as he reeled in the net. The pile rose, blocking out the view of the river between his legs, but there wasn't even the glint of a tiny petrocephalus. Ibrahim pulled up the jerry can and tossed it on the bundle, signalling our failure with a shrug, the patient gesture of a gambler who knows the casino will still be open tomorrow.

'Should we wait a little longer?' I asked.

'No. It's often like this. You can stay out all day and only catch one or two. It used to be much easier.'

Here was the common lament, repeated in every branch of nomadic life on my journey, as constant as tea rituals and plastic slip-ons: the glory days of yesteryear, in bitter contrast to today's slim pickings.

'When I was younger,' said Ibrahim, 'you could get 20, 30 fish in one haul. You didn't even have to go very far. You went out for the day and you would catch 25,000 CFA (about £30). Now I go on long trips. I know where they are, because the fish go by a calendar, just like people. I take a small tent, a torch, my brazier, some coal and my net. Sometimes I stop in villages and camps along the way. I give some money to the chief, and he grants me permission to sleep in all the villages in his area.'

He dropped the pole back in the water. We still had several hours to go, so I sat on a thwart, feeling the suck of the paddle, the air on its tips, the pull of the river. The sun was at the zenith, pixellating the current, twinkling the froth at the edge of the sand. Dry, wrinkled banks rolled alongside us, blanched by guano and netting fluff, dappled by the shadow of wing spread. We passed the odd fisherman, sitting patiently above his net; and near the villages we heard the chatter of women washing. Soapy water frothed out of cooking pots and sparkled down bare chests and backs, sunlight jewelling their skin in gem-like suds. Sometimes they covered themselves as we approached, or dropped down to their necks in the water; sometimes they raised a hand and smiled.

'Go on,' said Ibrahim, 'why did you learn the phrases if you aren't going to use them?'

'*Mayha!*' I called out. '*Hiya bana? Nyingola?* Hello! How are you? How is the fishing?'

I felt awkward addressing them, when most of the women were wearing nothing more than a rag around their hips. It was like wandering into the wrong changing room at a swimming pool. Most of them laughed at my halting phrases and called back '*Funogulima*' (good fishing). A few turned away or covered their breasts. I was glad when we had passed them.

The banks were spongy where the water lapped, soft blades of grass moistly entwining. But the stalks on their crests were yellow and dry, stiffened to palisades, a sign of how quickly the sun makes its claim. The tips of the *bourgou* (or hippo-grass) were uneven, chomped away in patches, which was explained by the cattle hovering on the horizon, pricking the sky with their horns.

'There are many Fulani here,' said Ibrahim. 'They come for the *bourgou* so their cows can eat.'

'Do you have good relations with them?' I asked.

Ibrahim tipped his head to the side. 'They give us milk and we give them fish. We can be useful to each other.'

'But you don't live together?'

He looked at his pole, dragging it through the current. 'It is better to stay with your own people.'

In that respect, the hammering tattoo around another loop of the river was welcome. It tugged us like a siren's call, chiming our arrival at the island of Kona Daga. Upturned boats hummocked the shore like beached whales, jacked up on barrels so the workers could probe their underparts. We moored between a couple of half-hulled pirogues and clambered off the bow. All around us was the orchestra of work: the thump of hammers on nails, the nasal back-and-forth of saws, the crunch of torn wood. After the gentle sounds of the river, there was something exciting about these staccato poundings: a lively chiaroscuro of sound.

We had arrived at one of the river's best-known boatyards, which supplies pirogues and pinasses to many of the top traders in Mopti. Peppered with shavings, tangy with sawdust and sweat, the men looked up from their work: sawing along charcoal lines, drawing nails with screwdrivers heated on boxes of coal. A couple of them returned my wave. One of them was Khalil, a friend of Ibrahim's. He had a tent where we could stay and a chicken for supper. Lines of dirt streaked his face, which was tough-looking and shiny with sweat. His arms were as thick as a boxer's, bare under his dust-stained vest.

'I've been doing this work for 36 years.' He lay down his adze and took a glass of tea from his teenage son. 'I learned it from my father.

It's hard work. You need at least three men to make a big pinasse. Me, I cut the wood. There's another fellow who does the joining, and another for the metal. Then there's others to do the painting.'

I noticed a bandage around his thumb. 'Is it dangerous work?'

'Oh, we're always getting injuries.' A grizzled laugh rumbled over the hammerbeat. 'Once I had to go to the hospital in Mopti. Another time, I put a saw through my hand and it took a month to stop the pain. The problem is we don't have any medicine here, so we just have to live with it.'

If you dropped out of the sky and crash landed in the village, it wouldn't take you long to work out the local trade. You can see it in the damp trousers drying on millet-stalk walls, the bamboo cages hanging off the mango trees, the dewy, stretched-out nets under mop-headed doum palms, the fluffs of torn netting underfoot.

Khalil's hut was at the back of the village, conveniently located behind a pump well. Ibrahim set down his brazier, while I went inside the rice-stalk tent to hang my mosquito net and lay down the rugs. When I came back out, Ibrahim was drawing his blade across the throat of a chicken. Thick spurts of blood guttered from its throat, turning to dark pebbles of sand. Ibrahim warmed the chicken on the fire, then plucked the feathers, skinned it and stuffed it in a pot. As for me, well, who's to say peeling the onions with a penknife isn't a mighty task?

'I thought we might be eating fish tonight,' I said.

Ibrahim shrugged. 'Then we needed to catch some.'

That evening, after we had ripped up the fleshy chicken and scalded our fists in rice, a couple of old river hands came to meet us. One of them, Mohammed, had damaged his wrists, so he was mostly village bound; but the other, Galina, still roamed like Ibrahim. His eyes were gleaming like polished oar hooks and his arms were ropy with muscle, hanging from the broad loom of his shoulders. He sat restlessly, hands clasped at his waist, as if that were the only way to stop himself from charging back to his boat.

'The best haul I ever caught? Hmmm, I'd say it was about 12 years ago.' His lips curled a little, winched up by fond memories. 'I went away for weeks. Oh, I can't remember, it might have been months. I ended up at the frontier with Burkina Faso and I put out my net one day and after three hours it was too heavy to lift.'

He ended up with a sack load of carp, which earned him 100,000 CFA (about £125) – enough to buy a motorbike.

'We had a big celebration when I came back,' he said. 'People danced, there were blessings from the elders, I bought a couple of sheep and everyone ate really well. It was a wonderful night.'

The fishermen all agreed that to pull in the best hauls, you needed to be versed in the ways of the river from childhood. Nobody but a Bozo could be a truly successful fisherman. It wasn't just a matter of knowledge, it was something else, something in their bones and blood. And there was another source of fishing success – non-Bozos didn't really get it, but the fishermen round here swore by it.

'We have in our river', said Galina, 'a powerful genie. We call her Maryama. Whenever I set out, I take aubergines and a ball made from rice or millet mixed with groundnuts. I go to the middle of the river and give my offering.'

'We all do,' said Mohammed. 'I used to fish a lot in the Bafing area, and round there the genie is called Koria. You have to ask her help and you have to give her something.'

This, Galina explained, was the reason we had failed to net any fish earlier in the day. He turned up his nose at Ibrahim, expressing the elder's disapproval for the younger generation's negligence.

Mohammed was less hard on Ibrahim. 'The problem is,' he said, 'the imams keep telling them not to do this. They tell them it is against Islam.'

This is one of many traditions criticised by conservative clerics, along with eating drowned animals and holding exorcisms conducted by *gaws* or spirit masters. Vituperating in mosques built on shady funds from the Middle East, these puritanical preachers have been netting young Bozos in towns like Mopti, rinsing the culture of its uniqueness.

'But we don't agree with all that.' Galina threw back his head, wagging a finger against orthodoxy. 'We are Bozo. When we marry, we have pirogue races and carry our brides on our boats, we beat the tam-tam and the women sing the *faranga*. That's our culture, it's what our parents handed down to us, and it's the same with the genies.'

I would have liked to join Galina on his boat that night. There is no better time for fishing, he told me. When the river is quieter and there is less noise on the banks, the shoals begin to relax. But I needed to be back in Mopti by noon tomorrow, and he was heading in the other direction. So I contented myself with helping to push him out.

As we approached the shore, he touched my shoulder and I looked up. A magnesium flare was glowing in the sky, like a comet. A French fighter jet, I think, lighting a raid. A reminder that even here, on these peaceful islands on a tributary of the Niger, the conflict wasn't so far away.

'This life is not easy.' Galina tipped his head, a gesture of acceptance, while I helped to pile his gear in the hull. 'There's a lot to think about. You have to change the nets every couple of months, there's often problems with the boat and it can be expensive to repair. Then there's the mosquitoes, and it can be lonely at night, and cold.'

'And your children?' I asked. 'Will they do the same?'

'My son sold a capitaine last week for 2000 CFA (about £2.50). I am happy my boys are starting to do this.'

He smiled, his eyes moonshine bright, a man at peace with himself.

'The Fulani herd, the Bozos fish. This is our life, you understand? This is what we are.'

22

Spirits of the Niger

IT WAS JUST AS THE BOATSWAIN PREDICTED. AROUND THE TIME OF THE NOON prayer, more than a hundred people squeezed onto the top deck of the *Tikambo*, and plenty more tumbled into steerage. Then, for nearly four hours, they all stayed put, waiting for a sign of departure.

The covered part of the deck was taken over by women. They gathered on the floorboards, feeding their children, curling to the diesel-smelling warmth inside. Pirogues and dugouts poled out from the shore to sell them snacks while we waited, skiffs twisting between the dribbling cascades of poured-out potties.

The steering wheel was in the prow, connected to the rudder by chains running outside, so there was plenty of space on the foredeck. It had the atmosphere of an old-fashioned pub or a working men's club. Men were slouching on packing cases or lying across spaghetti coils of rope, smoking cigarettes, drinking tea and laughing in low, piratical hoots.

We made steady progress, churning the river to a rooster's tail. Pirogues arrowed beneath us, packed to the gunnels with silver heaps of dogfish, like the swag of some river-king, while fishermen plounced in the shallows with driftnets. Bozo fishing hamlets huddled over dim clusterings of pirogues, until fens of hippo-grass closed them off. Three branches fingered out of Lake Debo, and we followed the most permanently navigable, the Issa Ber. We were gliding into Songhay country – the land of the ethnic group that dominated when Leo Africanus came this way.

I stood over the railing, taking it all in, watching out for the 'multitudes of ... water-birds, which inhabit these marshes, and brood undisturbed by the people of the surrounding countries', which René Caillié had led me to expect. The birdlife of the Niger has certainly felt the impact of the two tempestuous centuries since René's visit, but diversity endures: every year, three to four million waterfowl use the Inner Niger Delta as a wintering area.

Raggedy herons parachute to the banks on stiltwalker legs, breast feathers trickling down their necks like beards made out of dish-cloths. Kingfishers poke out of tunnels in the banks. Weaverbird nests hang from the bushes, echoes of the spindly thatching on the Dogon granaries. Most of the birds blend into the riverside col-our scheme, but occasionally a more daring tincture – the rump of a golden bishop, a bee-eater's sulphurous throat – dazzles like a flashing light. It was the lack of reptiles and freshwater mammals that disappointed. This far west hippos are rare, and hunters have stripped the Upper Bend of manatees and caimans. Although this was actually quite reassuring when I found myself receiving urgent signals from my bladder.

'Um... is there a toilet on the boat?'

I quickly regretted asking. The toilet was a rag-guarded hole near the stern. To reach it you had to climb along the freeboard, holding the grab rail and hoping no one jerked out an ill-timed elbow. I'd seen what the mothers did with their potties, so I was anxious not to mis-step. It was the scariest toilet I had ever tried to use.

'Come on!' called out a Fulani dairy merchant sitting on the roof. 'You're a man, aren't you?'

It was like stumbling onto a pirate ship and being ordered to walk the plank. The rail grew slipperier, a little spray reached my shins, and I dived through the gap, feeling like I was carrying a barrel under my belly.

There was one more level to the boat – the liveliest of all. Up on the roof, raggedy men with flashing gypsy eyes sprawled under mattresses and coverlets. A couple of them were playing dice; one had a hip flask. They said it was cold, but to me the weather was perfect, a balm after the burning heat of day. When my designated sleeping space was swal-lowed by the families below, I went up and joined the top squatters, using a sack of charcoal as a step and someone's hand as a guiding rope.

A sugar seller from Niafunké curled around my feet. My hip nudged against the belly of the dairy merchant. It was dark, but everything around me was clear – the stars, the fires in the hamlets, most of all the sounds. Perching birds churred and bullfrogs blasted to a distant thump of tam-tams. Water susurrated at the freeboard. I turned from the sharpness of the sky to the grooved skin of the river, tooled like a book cover by the fractured silver of the moon.

'You must pray to God the river genies are merciful tonight.' The sugar seller smiled behind a floret of smoke.

I told him about my conversation with Galina and the other fishermen in Kona Daga.

'They are wise to make the sacrifices,' he said.

That night was full of genie lore, embroidered no doubt to deliver its full shock effect on the goggle-eyed *toubob*. There was the genie who stole a royal horse and hid it in an underground city; the genie who stitched a girl back together after her unforgiving parents cut her to pieces; the genies who stole the eyes of people they had drowned and used them as delicacies in underwater festivities. The men who channeled these spirits were just as remarkable – *gaws* or 'knowing ones', wizards regarded with awe by the riverfolk, brought at great expense to the bedsides of the ailing.

One of the greatest of these wizards was Waada Samba, who cast his spells during the early nineteenth century. He was summoned one day by the Fulani theocrat Sekou Amadou to drive out the demons from his mad daughter's mind. Samba held a *batou* – an all-singing, all-dancing exorcism – and the king's daughter broke down the door to her chamber, throwing herself at his feet in a trance. The demons fled, recognising Samba's power, and the princess collapsed, exhausted but exorcised. For Sekou Amadou, it was a turning point. He had distrusted the *gaw* until that time, but now he was forced to acknowledge their value. He loosened his persecution and sent Samba back to his village loaded with gifts.

What this story expresses, like many of the tales associated with the *djinn*, is the tricky relationship between Islam and the occult practices that preceded it. No wonder the *marabouts* had been trying to monopolise magic. Everywhere I travelled in North Africa, there were pre-Islamic beliefs lurking under the surface. They were like the shoals of carp you saw if you squinted long enough when leaning over the railing of the *pinasse*.

2600 miles in length, the Niger is Africa's most improbable river. It begins in the rainforests of Guinea, cutting through swampland before it hacks a life-giving loop through the Sahara. Subdued for a few miles, the sands slowly launch their reprisals and the river curls back in retreat, winding south through Niger and Nigeria, scissoring mangrove swamps and jungle until it spends itself in the Atlantic at the Bight of Benin.

Leo Africanus would tell you it runs the other way. 'This land of Negros', he writes, 'hath a mighty river, which taking his name of the region, is called Niger: this river taketh his original from the east out of a certain desert called by the foresaid Negros "Seu". Others will have this river to spring out of a certain lake, and so to run westward till it exonerateth itself into the Ocean sea.'

Did Leo even travel on the Niger? Was he wearing blinders at the time? His misorientation has provoked some damning criticism. EW Bovill (author of the historical classic *The Golden Trade of the Moors*) called it 'a blunder of almost incredible magnitude'. It certainly didn't do the European explorers any favours, leading them into all kinds of confusion until Mungo Park settled the matter in 1796 (although ancient authors like Pliny and Herodotus had long ago speculated correctly). Still, this does underline how seriously Leo was taken by European geographers for more than two centuries.

For those who traded on the river, there was never any doubt about its direction; and there were a great many who used it for trade. To the Arabs it was *Nahr al-Abeed*, 'River of Slaves'. Gold diggers and salt merchants could just as easily have named it for their wares, so abundant were they on the riverways. Together, they underline the chief historical role of this remarkable thoroughfare: a marketplace luring desert tribes and sub-Saharans together.

Roads have challenged its primacy, but the river will never lose its significance in a land where water is so precious. The passage to Timbuktu, although several times slower, is widely preferred to the desert road, thanks to the frequency of bandit hold-ups on the latter (I did travel by the desert on my return journey, and every time a motorbike flashed near the truck, fear stirred in my belly like the early warnings of dysyntery). Pirogues pole out from every village, loaded with goods for sale – rice, millet, watermelons, bananas – and return with cargo or passengers. On this trip, the *Tikambo* was specialising in sacks of Dutch quality onions and crystal sugar, much of it kept in the hull, doubling as ballast.

Up on the roof, I had the perfect lookout. I watched the king-fishers launching their diving raids from Bozo fishing cages, barred by bamboo verticals and my own sleepy lashes. Nimble stevedores passed goods along the gangplanks and swung out of the hull. Naked children turned themselves into balls, throwing themselves off the breakwaters, cracking the polished soapstone of the river. Grown-up men waded more gingerly, one hand cupped over privates, while bare-breasted laundresses kept their own quarter, scrubbing and squeezing T-shirts and *boubous* that only needed a few minutes in the sun to dry. They underlined the Niger's other great role: as a giant bath-house, drawing people together for the camaraderie of the early-morning wash, like the *hammams* I visited in Fez.

I revelled in the riverside life, until the sting of the sun drove me under the covers. My fellow passengers were less bothered. Most of them treated the river with the same insouciance as the egrets floating out of the hippo-grass, or the reeds that swayed and dipped to our rip-ples. Yet every so often, the Niger reminded us it could bite. Rips and creases broke through waxy boils, a swell broadsided the *Tikambo* and waves pawed at the gunwales to squeals in the hull.

'Our river is angry,' said the sugar seller.

As night plunged, firelight danced on the banks, smoke unfurl-ing banners over villages and fishing hamlets. A cheer went up at the sound of a splash – someone had braved the river for an evening bath, his skin varnished by moonshine. Speakers were placed on the roof and hooked to a Walkman to play a song by the blind albino Salif Keita. We sat on the packing cases, nodding to the rhythm, a few of the passengers clicking their fingers.

The camaraderie of the boat was exhilarating, even when I couldn't follow any of the half a dozen languages in which the con-versations were held. Scooping up fistfuls of rice from a communal dish, I broke into the crusty bread I still had left, before giving myself over to the insects.

We had passed the junction of the Issa-Ber and its sister branch, the Bara-Issa. You could tell we were near Timbuktu because the architecture of the villages was changing. Fretted parapets stretched across the glassy mirror of the river, under the buttressed walls that bore the originals. Echoing back through time, they were a dirge for the troubled history of the Niger; the fortress homes of a settled people protecting themselves against the menace of the desert.

It was still dark when we moored at the port of Koriumé. We would have to wait until transport arrived on the car ferry from the other bank. I had barely slept, but I felt wide awake, fuelled as much by anxiety as adrenalin. I wished there was a little further to go; I wished I could have another day on the river and go to Timbuktu tomorrow.

Clambering down the gangplank, I lay on the foreshore and watched the early Bozos out with their driftnets. They were sliding around an isle of reeds in the middle of the river, indifferent to the bustle around the banks. Riverlife was carrying on with only a passing nod to the landlubbers.

The peace was broken by truck horns and human shouting. Nosing out of the rose-bleach of dawn, a ferry glided over the plate-glass water, carrying passengers who had followed the desert track from Douentza. Along with a couple of jeeps and dozens of livestock was a Malian army SUV with a mounted gun.

There was some business with the driver, so the soldiers planted themselves on the slope, digging into their cigarette packets, balancing their guns between their legs. I wondered if they might be able to advise me. They would know about the bandits and the danger in the desert; maybe they could give me some tips. They didn't look surprised when I approached them, so I sat down and offered a light.

It took a while to start the conversation. I wasn't sure how many questions I could get away with; I was wary of annoying them. But the corporal beside me was affable and surprisingly frank. Each question he considered for a few moments, then replied in clear, rapid spurts.

'We've been in the bush around Gourma,' he said. 'There are lots of bandits. They've been living in the bush for years so they know the best places to hide. It's difficult to surprise them.' He nodded towards the SUV. 'Too much noise. One mission, we drove in convoy, but by the time we reached their camp, they were gone. We found only their provisions – medicine, macaroni, water, flour. It seems they were living pretty well.'

The bandits had superior desert know-how. That was why the army was starting to lean on the one group who knew the desert even better.

'Many of the bandits', said the corporal, 'try to hide in the camps of the nomads. But the nomads are tired of them, so they come to us and tell us where to find them. We give them medicine, water, food, whatever we can, and they tell us what they've seen – trucks that passed, how many, which direction they took.'

This point of view is not shared by everyone: in Timbuktu I would hear of extrajudicial killings and nomads dragged out of camps. But for the corporal, nomads and soldiers were united by a shared goal.

'The nomads are fatigued by the jihadists. Their food's been robbed, their animals have been taken. They want an end to this. They know if they cooperate with us, we can help get their lives back to normal.'

He talked about busting a gang of bandits who had kidnapped a group of Qatari bird hunters; manning checkpoints against suicide bombings; taking part in a shootout in the desert town of Goundam. The latter ended in chaotic success for the army. It was one of those anecdotes that bring the jihadists to life, reminding you that for every murderous psychopath there is a clown as hapless as a Keystone Cop.

'We tracked the jihadists to a building in the centre of town, and we were winning the shootout. Only two of them were still alive. One of them escaped. We shot him in the leg but, before we could catch him, the other one ran out of the building. He had a bomb belt and was going to explode himself. He had enough to blow us all up. But one of my colleagues had taken off his helmet and laid it near the door – and the jihadist tripped over it when he ran outside. He blew up straightaway! It was very lucky for us, no one was injured.'

'What about the other jihadist?' I asked.

'Oh.' The corporal drew on his cigarette and flicked it along the foreshore. 'He was bleeding very heavily, so it was easy to find him. We just followed the trail of blood until we found him under a tree. Then we shot him dead.'

The road from the port seemed to tumble out of my memory. Bony eucalypti drained the shallows, weeping shade onto the road, where river traders rested in palm-reed tents. Workers were bending in the rice fields, their legs stolen by the lush green blades. The truck ahead of us disappeared behind its own particulate contrails, and a couple of passerines dived through the fug, to emerge untroubled on the other side. The track was lumpy and soggy, the bonnet seesawing in the windscreen and a tasselled prayer swinging under the rear-view mirror.

It didn't take long for the land to dry. Sand bullied everything out of the way, letting only a few thorn bushes share its territory. This was the 'Passage of the Fate of the Virgins', named for a group of fifteenth-century slave girls who were slain because they didn't move fast enough to entertain the soldiers of the tyrant Sunni Ali. It was an early example of the heartache and blood that have been pestled into the sand between Timbuktu and its port.

We jolted onto tar, gliding to a stop at an oil-drum checkpoint. Further ahead were a billboard for Orange phones, signs for USAid, warnings against HIV ('Fidelité, Abstinence, Preservatif'): the gamut of international billboards, heralding the most mysterious city on earth. When I first visited Timbuktu, these billboards had been pale and dust skinned; now they were battered and misshapen and gouged with bullet holes. One of them – for Colonel Gaddafi's Fond Libye – lay flat in the sand. They had become ciphers for the condition of Timbuktu, rather than the organisations they were supposed to be promoting; as telling as the rows of sand-filled barricades and gun emplacements behind them. Light roared through the ripped-open doors; gun stocks rattled on the fender. Moody, early-morning soldiers' eyes scanned the truck, and we lifted our legs so they could poke under the benches, in case we were hiding any weapons.

Ahead lay Timbuktu, slung low like a nomad snoozing under an acacia. Frayed palm-reed tents lined the road; walls of mud and lime-stone thickened, knitting a maze in the heart of town. Across the road from the wreck of the Al-Farook monument stood a row of soldiers on high alert, weapons braced in the gateway of their barracks.

I had thought often of Timbuktu over the last couple of years. I felt like I was visiting some old, sickly friend who's just been let out of hospital – unsteady on his feet and barely out of danger, but alive.

I looked around, almost pinching myself. For a long time, I wasn't sure if I would come back. The sun tickled the edges of my T-shirt, but I couldn't stop the shiver in my spine. A memory sensation, an echo of the terrible dread I had felt when I was last here. When it all went so horribly wrong.

The School for Nomads

Lesson Eight: Score

THE DESERT SPREADS AROUND US, A RUMPLED CARPET OF FIRE. WE HAVE been riding for several hours and I can feel the scorch of the rope on my hands. My lips are chapped and my throat has the texture of dry kindling. The light spins off the sand at ruthless angles, stabbing me like a crazed stalker, jabbing my shoulders and stinging my eyes. The wind is no relief: in cahoots with the sun, it lifts the tail of my turban and whiplashes my neck. A peculiar thought flashes through me and makes me burst out laughing. At last, the desert has got under my skin. Right under! It is in my ears, my mouth, my eyes; it has dug under my fingernails and smeared behind my ears.

Only a few hours' riding lie between us and Timbuktu, but we will spend one last night in the desert. There is a tinge of green in the distance, so we scythe between the dunes. It may not be verdure, but it is certainly pasture, and the camels tuck in with relish, trails of green slaver dribbling down their chins.

'I don't like it when I'm near the city,' grumbles Lamina.

'You prefer to sleep in the desert?'

'Of course! We are Berabish. The town is not our place. It has too much noise.'

There's a blowout on the edge of the desert, a couple of miles out of town. This time, I am able to build the fire without any help. I collect a bundle of sticks and make a lattice over a small pit, crouching behind the flame to shield it from the wind. Jadullah leaves me in charge while he goes to hobble the camels and I tend the ashes, fanning them to keep the heat for the pot.

'Do you think I could do the *azalai*?' I ask, later.

We are squatting around the bowl, filling our palms with the fluffy rice. Jadullah looks at me, the most intense, most intimate gaze he has given me. 'Yes,' he mutters. Our eyes lock for a second, then he turns back to the food and digs out a fistful of rice.

Lamina's answer is more detailed. He clasps his hands together and rubs his beard against the knuckles, tipping his head from side to side.

'I am a serious man,' he says. 'I do not say this if there is no truth in it. I see you are a serious man too, and I believe you can do this.'

I want to jump up and punch the air. I want to give Lamina a hug. I want to grab Jadullah and kiss his beard. I stay exactly where I am and nod.

We carry on eating, and I ask for more information about the *azalai*. Every detail is a precious addition to my store of learning. It feels as if the caravan trail could be within reach. Is it too elegiac? A magic carpet-ride adventure, too distant from the real lives of nomads around the Sahara? If so, I don't care – the romance has snared me already. I lie down on my blanket, daring to imagine myself as part of a desert caravan: strapping my cargo in grass-twine ropes, loading it onto my camel, riding the long path to Taoudenni, and coming back with a slab of salt as big as a tombstone.

Naksheh gives me a lovely last ride, a smooth glide between the dunes in the apricot bloom of dawn. It is the kind of ride you never want to end. You could carry on for ever, drifting between the dunes with this wonderful creature, all your struggles veiled by a dreamy pall of amnesia.

We couch outside the high metal gate and Lamina strides inside, Jadullah following, while Abdul-Hakim stays with the camels. He gives me a high five and his eyes follow me, puckishly, to the gate. Inside, Berabish traders are lolling on the carpet. My host comes over and clasps my shoulders, greetings are rallied, and we settle across the rug to enjoy a soothing glass of tea.

My training is at an end. I lie back, enjoying the tenderness around my temples, the perverse pleasure of fatigue. If I were a character in a comic strip, there would be a bubble of Zs already gathering over my head. But one more thing needs to be settled. Because now, lolling my head on a bolster, I am to be told my score.

'Oh! I'm going to be marked?'

I feel a pinch of apprehension. I tried my best, but some of the lessons were hard. Will I lose points for all my mistakes, my erratic riding, my poorly brewed tea? I've been fascinated by the lifestyle, but I am not cut from the same cloth as nomads like Lamina and Jadullah. Besides, I feel content with the trip. I don't want to be deflated by some unsatisfactory number!

'Before now,' says Lamina, sitting down on the carpet, 'no one would have scored more than 15 out of 20, but you have scored 18.'

I feel stars swimming around my head. Is it fatigue or excitement? It is becoming hard to tell them apart. Given my mediocrity as a cub-scout and the bollockings that fell on my head in the Combined Cadet Force at school, I never expected this. I have passed with flying colours! I can go on the *azalai*!

'In the lists of our tribe, your name is now added,' continues Lamina, 'and even if you do not return for ten years, your name will always be there.'

I sit there, smiling gormlessly, too happy to say anything in reply.

It is two weeks until the next *azalai* – the last of the season. I can stock up on provisions, fatten myself up and prepare mentally for the journey. I will go and visit my friend Abdramane in the desert town of Goundam. It will be a great way to while away the time, before meandering back to join the caravan; the chance of a rest and some mental preparation. The timing could hardly be better. The desert is safe, the Tuareg rebellions are in the past, I am fit and healthy, and my guru believes I can do it.

'Your place is ready,' says Lamina.

His grip on my hand is tight and warm. I remember how bewildered I felt at our first meeting. Traditional phrases pop and trill, hands clasp tight and palms press against chests. I drop among the bolsters, watching the brothers floating out through the gate. Next time I see them, we will be setting out on the caravan together.

I can hardly wait!

23

Lights Out on the Sahara

'NICHOLAS! ARE YOU FINE?'

Still a little weary from the desert, I clamber down at the riverside village of Tonka. Stretching towards me is my friend Abdramane. We met on the journey up river and he scribbled down his number before he disembarked. 'I want to greet you in my family home', he told me, 'and present you to my family.'

My *azalai* training is complete and I have a couple of weeks to spare. Abdramane helps me onto the wharf, and we fall into a hearty African hug. I feel like a stick embracing a tree. Warm, lambent eyes dip into his cheeks between two rows of tribal scars, markings of his Songhay ethnicity.

A pick-up truck is ready to leave for Goundam, so we hurry over to secure our berths. The bed is already crammed, some of the passengers swinging their legs over the cab. The usual triumvirate of driver, lubricator and mechanic are doing their rounds, checking the wheels and covering the luggage in netting, clipped to hooks on the gunwales. For the human cargo, however, there is no such precaution. It looks like a full-on way to ride, windy and dusty and exciting if you don't have to do it too often: a cross between a cattle truck and a roller-coaster. But Abdramane is insistent about where I should sit.

'Let us not take unnecessary risks, Nicholas. You must stay inside.'

An eerie world surrounds us: thorn bushes and colourless scrub, fuzzed by the odd stick-and-skin tent. I can understand why Abdramane is being cautious. The route could have been designed by a bandit chief: they could pounce on us while a herd of cattle trudges across the road, or conjure themselves out of the dust clouds raised by a passing jeep. When an army truck roars past, I feel a twinge of reassurance. At least there is state protection – nobody would dare to attack on a road used by the Malian army! I sit back in the comfort of the driver's cab, reminding myself why there is no reason to be worried. *Mali is safe these days. The Tuareg rebellions are in the past. No tourists have been kidnapped for a couple of years. What have you got to worry about? And anyway, you've survived a couple of weeks in the desert already. You've got* baraka!

Still, there is the odd disquieting detail. When we roll past a couple of guarded steel drums and grind to a standstill in a fly-blown market-place, I feel like an animal that knows it's being watched. Men in hoods and veils trench their hands in their pockets and scuttle between walls of broken mud. In a backwater like Goundam, I stand out like the Elephant Man. It isn't until we are safe inside that I can relax.

Abdramane's house is a two-storey fortress of mud brick, built by his late father 20 years earlier. Three slat-ribbed cows are tied to stakes pitched in the sand. Behind them, sitting under a roof of painted logs, is his mother, a warmly smiling woman in primary-coloured batik.

'Ça va bien?'

She pulls herself up and goes off to bring the tea things, gesturing for me to sit. Abdramane leans over a basin of water, splashing the dust off his face.

'Welcome to the family,' he says, his voice croaky from the journey.

Days pass in restful indolence: unfinishable bowls of rice, bottles of Fanta orange, ORTM news. We move between Abdramane's family house and his older sister's posher place, with a fake plum tree in the liv-ing room and a ceremonial cupboard loaded with 12 rows of cooking pots – presents from her wedding to a civil servant, which stand on permanent display and are never used. Her husband Baba works for the Department of Water and Forests, and admits they have their work cut out.

'The biggest problem', he says, 'is water. It's too far underground to dig and the river is too far away for irrigation, and the development money never reaches us. If we could find water, all our problems would be over.'

In Abdramane's bedless bedroom, which is built onto the rooftop, we sprawl across a mud floor, basking in pools of chocolatey shadow. Light gilds the roofs around us and creeps inside around siesta time to snaggle our feet. When the sun has sunk, a hurricane lamp illuminates the room, whose unpainted mud walls reflect nothing back.

These are idle, lotus-eating days. Abdramane talks about Songhay culture: the triple scars on most Songhays' faces, which are not only ritual but medicinal, keeping the dirt from the corners of your eyes.

He talks about the children he's teaching: the sparky ones, who gulp down their lessons like water after a drought; the mischievous ones, who pass secret notes and whisper behind his back. Most of his students are nomadic Fulani, and their mobile lifestyle can be a challenge when it comes to establishing a curriculum.

'Sometimes the children have to walk more than two hours to get to class,' he says. 'Or they stay with a host family in the village while their real family is with the herd. And they must work to pay for their board – preparing tea, doing the cleaning, looking after the animals. So they have no time for their homework.'

Many students disappear for several weeks if it is a busy time with the herd, and there is never enough time to bring them up to speed. But the boys, at least, do eventually return.

'If you have a class of 7- or 8-year-olds,' says Abdramane, 'there are as many girls as boys. But when they get to 12 or 13, the parents want them to marry so when you look at the top year, we have hardly any girls at all.'

Abdramane's is the settled perspective. He finds nomads hard to trust, because he comes from a culture in which they are seen as predators (his ancestors were enslaved by Tuareg herders) and sometimes this surfaces in proverbs and sayings. 'We say that trusting a Tuareg', one of his relatives tells me, 'is trusting a vagabond.' The way some of them talk about the Tuareg reminds me of the way many people in Britain talk about gypsies and Irish travellers. Except there is one key difference: it is modulated by awe. When the apocalypse comes, it is the Tuareg who are most likely to survive. What Abdramane and his family give me is a shoreline, tugging me back from the ocean of elegy, keeping me in sight of the other point of view.

∽

All this time I should be enjoying myself; I am certainly blessed in my host. But I can't help feeling anxious. Because, on my second night in Goundam, a man in uniform knocks on the door of the house. '*Venez*,' is the only word he says to me. Inside an office of flaking plaster, Inspector Maiga – official chief of the Goundam *gendarmerie* – glowers behind a broad metal desk.

'Are you from Goundam?' A bony finger shakes at Abdramane like a swagger stick.

My friend swallows and slowly explains.

'Yes, sir, certainly I come from Goundam. I have brought my friend here because I want to show him our hospitality.'

'You fool!' snarls the inspector. 'Do you not know the reality of Mali at the moment? Have you not watched the news?'

'What do you mean?' I ask. 'What's happened?'

He's too busy growling at Abdramane to hear me, leaning further across the desk, as if considering what to do with my friend's throat. So I ask the question again. He points to the television in the corner of the room: the blurred pictures of helicopters, soldiers with AK-47s, and the palm-spiked Djingereyber mosque.

'But that's... Timbuktu,' I say.

'Yes! They are evacuating all the white people.'

Slowly, the story unfolds. This morning, when most of the towns-folk were at Friday prayers, a truck swooped out of the desert and parked beside a guesthouse. Three tourists, from the Netherlands, South Africa and Sweden, were kidnapped, and a German man was shot dead for trying to resist. Four lives have been wrecked, one of them for good. I wish I could say my initial thoughts are for those poor travellers, mercilessly punished for their spirit of adventure. But my first impulse is selfishly precise: what about the *azalai*? It is due to leave – if the plan still holds – in just over a week.

Judging by the news report, all foreigners have been air-lifted out of town. It isn't an ideal time to be making tracks for Timbuktu. A phone call would be a more practical step. Yet I decide to leave it. I know if I call now, they will tell me not to come. They need time to recover; and I need time to get my head around the news.

I can't sleep for the lowing of the police motorbikes. I lie awake, thinking of the gentle noises round the campfire in the desert: the chomping camels, the soughing wind. But then I remind myself why the motorbikes are thrumming around us. Somebody has come out of the desert, somebody aggressive and cunning and cruel, infecting the town like a virus.[47] Like

---

47 The ringleader of the kidnappers, I later learn, is an Algerian called Belkacem Zaoudi, who fought in Bosnia and Afghanistan and lived in Britain during the 1990s.

the desert dwellers of the past, who filled the townsfolk with such terror, inspiring them to build their high-walled, fortified houses. *It's a one-off*, I tell myself, *it's not part of a pattern.* Then I remember the white tents in the desert, the uneasiness Jadullah and Lamina expressed about the 'strangers' pitching camp among them.

I hug myself tight, thinking of home, wondering if anyone has seen the news. I send a text message. Malitel beeps straight back: *le message n'a pas pu être envoyé.* I bash my phone on the mattress and close my eyes, trying to block out all the nastiness and complications of the world outside.

Three days later, several pounds fatter and bloated with indigestion, I mummify my face in an indigo cotton veil, button myself into an old shirt of Abdramane's and a pair of black gloves, and sit in the front passenger seat of a bush taxi. It is a strange experience, to be un-looked at. I haven't heard a cry of '*toubob*' for days. At last – this is what I've been trying to achieve for weeks. I'm like Claude Rains when he injects himself with monocaine in *The Invisible Man.*

Abdramane's advice is to return to the safety of the capital. He can accompany me to Tonka and wait there with me for the pinasse to Mopti. His mother agrees. His sister agrees. His brother-in-law agrees. The man in the local store agrees. It is the only sensible thing to do. Going back to Timbuktu would be crazy.

Even so... I have called my friend Mahmoud, and he says the situation in Timbuktu is calm again. If I can make it to Timbuktu, then I can find out if the *azalai* is feasible. A few times before, I've been warned against going to some dangerous place, only to find it quite secure. Maybe everything will turn out all right again.

'I'm sorry. But I *have* to go back to Timbuktu. I can't explain it really, I just need to find out.'

'In that case,' says Abdramane, 'I will take you to Diré. They have boats to Timbuktu. When we get there, we can find out the situation.'

I tip my head, too grateful to meet his eyes. 'Thank you,' I whisper. 'Thank you.'

A couple of boys bounce past on a beautiful *mehari*, a white camel. A herdsman with a spear for a goad is driving a couple of cows and a flock of sheep across the road, their yellow eyes slitted against the light. Impossible weights – sacks and trays of several tiers – glide down the roadside, raised on the heads of women in wind-tossed gowns. They are the only flashes of primary colour in the wasteland around us. Even the sky seems drained, listless and grey, as if the heavens are protecting themselves with a pane of frosted glass. Road-layer rollers paste the track with piles of heaped clay while guards twitch behind them, peering into the haze.

After a couple of hours, mud-brick walls nuzzle the sky and the ground splits into the rainbow colours of plastic rubbish, hardening the track for motorcycles and scurrying donkeys. At the back of the market of Diré, pinasses bob behind piled sacks of charcoal and millet. Be-gloved and be-turbanned, I follow Abdramane through the crowd, watching out for anyone who eyes me too long. I feel like an outlaw spirited into a forbidden city – Luke Skywalker driving into Mos Eisley with Obi-Wan Kenobi. My heart sounds in my ears like a drumbeat at a fantasia. *Well, isn't this what travelling is all about?*

We hide away the afternoon in a shop: me a silent heap of indigo cooling off beside the fridge, while Abdramane chats with the shopkeeper. I want to join in the talk – I can follow snatches of it when they meander from Songhay into French. But Malians rarely stick to a single language for long. Abdramane speaks Songhay, French, English, Bamanankan, a little Fulfulde, and during the course of the afternoon he uses all of them. Quite apart from the language, the veil keeps me out of the conversation. Watching my companions through the slit in my cowl, I feel like I'm occupying a different dimension. I wonder... is the notorious aloofness of the Tuareg simply a consequence of their turbanning?

Shortly before dusk, a wooden canoe peels away from Diré, curved like a melon rind, with karité roots straggling its tips. Abdramane is out for the count within minutes of bearing off, curled across sacks of millet and flour. But I can't find a comfortable position, so I sit against the side, looking up at the fat, creamy moon and the phantom boats of shadow it casts on the surface of the water.

I am glad the river is calm, because we are only a few inches above it. I have heard stories about the spirits dwelling among the whorls and eddies, as truculent as the *djinn* that haunt empty ruins and hill-sides. But the closeness of the water is a boon for anyone who needs to perform their ablutions. All around me, they kneel down to pray, prostrating themselves across planks of wood and charcoal sacks. Among them is a group of religious students surrounding their *mara-bout*, who carries a copy of the Quran in a painted calabash hanging from his neck.

It is impossible to sleep. Dirtwater and fuel mingle with the hot, milky air. The engine is grouchier than any camel, the sacks beneath me are too lumpy and I'm desperate for a pee. When we pull in near the village of Minnesengue, I roll up my trousers and splash through the shallows, wading to a bank of mud that gouts round my feet and curls between my toes, as oily as butter. I've been holding in for five hours, so it's a fantastic relief to empty my bladder, a flowering of ease right through my body. As if the political threats are no longer impor-tant and all that matters is the state of my organs.

Still, I'm unable to sleep; there are too many thoughts and feelings itching at my temples like fresh mosquito bites. I sit by the rim of the boat, looking over the sleek, serpent-like water, enjoying the burble of the current and the clarity of stars. It will be good to reach Timbuktu and find out what fate it holds for me.

The port of Koriumé appears before dawn and we moor in its har-bour, waiting until the light has drunk up most of the darkness before unloading the cargo. Squeezed into a pick-up, carefully arranging my veil, I peer out at stick-and-reed shacks and the gentle sway of bony-trunked eucalypti. We jolt onto tar, stopping at a checkpoint to show our documents.

A mulberry ribbon of dawn glimmers over the boards on the out-skirts of Timbuktu. USAid hovers near the Direction Regional des Eaux et Forêts and warnings against HIV. An upright sign promotes the Fond Libye, celebrating the planting of date palms under the aus-pices of 'le guide, Muammar el-Kadaffi'. It is a reminder of the close links between Libya and Mali; one of the reasons so many bandits are now at large around Timbuktu.

The streets are eerily empty, the last of the stars fading over the timber fingers of the mosques. I keep the turban tight around my face until I'm safe inside the limestone walls of the Hotel Colombe.

'You didn't sleep?' asks Abdramane.

'No, I couldn't.' I sit down on the bed, my aching buttocks sinking into the softness of the mattress.

'So you should get some rest. And be very careful, Nicholas.'

He helps me put down my bags, then leaves me to sleep. When I wake up a couple of hours later, he is already rolling back through the desert – the cheaper, more dangerous route to Goundam. It is hard to express how lucky I have been in Abdramane's friendship. He kept me free from prying questions and nudged me when my veil dropped. He advised me against returning to Timbuktu, but when he saw my mind was set, he did everything in his power to help me. Now I am on my own again, in a city that is just as sun hammered, but in every other sense has become far, far colder than when I was last here.

∽

I didn't notice before just how much the Quartier d'Abaradjou differs from the centre of Timbuktu. This is the northern district, abutting the desert, home to many of the town's semi-nomadic population. Glimpsed from low down, the lumpy mud brick tilts over you, jagged rows of bricks sticking out like fangs; the doors are crude flaps of rusty metal. I have wrapped myself in my veil, but I can sense people watching me. My disguise has lost its power, and when I hear a child call out 'toubob' I shiver – a strange sensation when it's 80 degrees.

My friend Mahmoud has found a car. He is a spiky black Tamashek who calls himself the 'future mayor' because he knows everyone in town. A few weeks earlier, we bumped into each other in the street, and for a decent price he ferried me around on his motorbike. But this trip calls for a more substantial mode of transport.

'Listen, Nicholas, I can get you a car,' he tells me, 'but there is one condition.'

'Anything!'

'You keep your head down.'

I do as I am told, until a blue metal gate hoves over the window. I dive into the courtyard of the Refuge de la Paix, introducing myself to a smiling, stocky man in a stripy blue gown. This is Bouge, the manager: the sort of guy who would normally be chatting up the female visitors and offering camel rides or his cousin's collection of Tuareg gewgaws. Now, he only has his smile. It is like a torch shining in the dark.

'I never thought this would happen.' He shakes his head, clutching the sides of his gown. 'That's why the gate was open – we never thought anyone would do this.'

We cross the dusty courtyard and climb up some steps to a small patio.

'The first I heard was shouting,' he says. 'I thought a dog had come in and was disturbing them. I looked out from my room and saw a man with a gun. That moment, I swear I died.'

He shudders and laughs. I think this is his way of dealing with the terror.

'The man kept the gun on me so I hid inside,' he continues, 'then after some moments I heard the gunshot and the sound of the truck and I ran outside and saw the German's body on the ground.'

I stand on the patio and try to imagine the terror those travellers suffered; the terror they are continuing to suffer. The awful realisation they had been picked out, chosen, by hard luck and fate and wrong-place-wrong-time, to undergo the nightmare that flickers in the mind of every traveller in the Sahara. I think of the German man, his life snuffed out in a moment, just because he was brave enough to stand up to those thugs. And I think of those three travellers, captured in the middle of a wonderful journey. Where are they now? How are they? What is going through their minds?

There but for the grace of God...

As we drive away from the Refuge, I look up at the towering Peace monument, where thousands of weapons were incinerated after the Tuareg uprising of the 1990s. That word 'peace' – shared by the monument, the garden in which it stands, the hotel, the road we are driving down, 'Rue de la Paix'. Sometimes words really do screw up.

I have been told to wait in the hotel this evening: Lamina will come to see me.

True to his word, he arrives soon after the dusk prayer, clutching the skirt of his robe over bare legs, glancing anxiously up the corridor. He takes hold of my shoulders, kissing the air on either side, letting out a series of grunts and loudly exhaled breaths. We nod silently to each other for several moments, recalibrating our relationship in terms of recent events. When Lamina finally breaks the silence, his words are serious and passionate, carrying with them the extremities of life in the desert. It is as if the sands themselves are speaking, through this wiry man who knows them so well.

'Yusuf, I tell you the truth. When you go to the wells, there is always somebody there. The desert is like a village, and everybody knows everybody else's business. I do not fear the desert. There is only one thing I fear: the people we do not know. Now there are too many of them, strangers with bad intentions, people who cannot be trusted. The desert is no longer the same place as before.'

We sit together for an hour or so. Lamina talks about the caravan – the lines of camels stretching across the dunes, the celebration of tam-tam drums when the caravan returns. It doesn't soften the blow to hear these details of an experience that remains tantalisingly out of reach. Yet I will cherish them, along with the only real consolation Lamina offers me.

'You must choose a sign,' he says. 'It will be your sign and nobody else's, and we will brand it on the necks of your camels. They are waiting for you, for Yusuf the British, and even if you do not come to collect them for a hundred years they will be there for you.'

I rack my brain for an idea. I outline a pattern, based on my initials, and draw it on a sheet of paper:

I ask Lamina what his brand is. He takes my pen and draws it on my notepad:

It reminds me of a camel saddle. I look at it, then at Lamina, and we smile at each other. It feels strangely intimate – as if, through these ciphers, we have signed a pact that can never be broken.

When they leave, I stand on the hotel steps, waving goodbye. Lamina isn't a natural motor passenger. His foot stumbles on the mud-guard of the 4x4 and he levers himself up, snagging his robe on the door, yanking it free with a wince of frustration. He presses his hands on the vinyl before lowering himself onto the seat, and looks down awkwardly at the folds across his lap. He is out of his element, like a capitaine fish flapping about in a pirogue. I hope that next time we meet, it will be in the desert he loves so much, and he will be riding a camel.

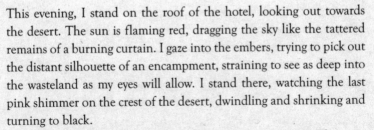

This evening, I stand on the roof of the hotel, looking out towards the desert. The sun is flaming red, dragging the sky like the tattered remains of a burning curtain. I gaze into the embers, trying to pick out the distant silhouette of an encampment, straining to see as deep into the wasteland as my eyes will allow. I stand there, watching the last pink shimmer on the crest of the desert, dwindling and shrinking and turning to black.

A month later, back in London, I turn on the television. The news pans to the familiar colours of the Malian desert: morning's apricot, noontime's cinnamon, afternoon's umber. Except that now, those colours are stained by the rusty metal tones of pick-up trucks and rocket launchers, machine guns shaking in the air and the cottony black of jihadist flags. The Tuareg separatist movement, the Mouvement National pour la Libération de l'Azawad, is charging through the Sahara, in league with shadowy, fundamentalist allies. It will be a long while before I can think about returning.

Lights out on the Sahara for now...

Part Nine

The Middle of Nowhere

(Revisited)

Welcome to the world's largest prison. A prison that has no boundaries, a prison that has no walls, no cells, no bars. A prison with a fear, where prison break is non-existent. This is the mujahideen's prison, the Sahara.

Belkacem Zaoudi, interrogator for Al-Qaeda in the Maghrib

24

Timbuktu the Broken

'NOTHING SO CRUEL HAD EVER HAPPENED TO THE PEOPLE OF TIMBUKTU. Never before had they known anything more bitter ... It is beyond our powers to tell the tale of all the violent and excessive acts that were committed within their walls.'

Ahmed Baba should know – he saw it for himself. It was the year 1591, and Sultan Al-Mansur of Morocco had sent a force of 5000 men, armed with blunderbusses, English cannons and 30,000 pounds of gunpowder, to conquer the lands of salt and gold. His commander, the Spanish-born Pasha Jawdar, sent a message to the Malian king, commanding him to surrender because his master, Sultan Al-Mansur, was 'a descendant of the Prophet, and to him legitimately belonged sovereignty'.

Then 421 years later, another Arabic-speaking army invaded Timbuktu from the north. This one also claimed religious authority (they called themselves Ansar ad-Dine, or 'Defenders of the Faith'), but instead of a Castilian eunuch they were led by a Tuareg ex-playboy called Iyad Ag Ghali.[48] Like the Moroccan army of 1591, they were armed with some of the most sophisticated weaponry in the region, but in outlook they were more like the eleventh-century Almoravids – burning down shops selling alcohol and destroying musical instruments. Comparing distant moments in history is like trying to talk to a Tuareg elder in a *tamelgoust*: you never know if you've made a true connection. Yet for the intellectuals of Timbuktu, recent events had certainly unwound a layer or two from their ancestors' ordeal.

'Everybody has suffered in these events.' The historian Salim Ould Elhadje sat, shaking his head, under the fretted windows of his

---

48 A mover and shaker since the 1990s, Ag Ghali had a reputation for making deals – whether between the Tuareg movement and the Malian government, or securing the release of Western tourists. Wildly inconsistent, he spun from an appointment in the Malian consulate in Saudi Arabia to establishing Ansar ad-Dine, forsaking his old whisky-drinking ways in favour of the austere lifestyle of a man pledging to bring *shariah* law to the people of Northern Mali.

limestone house near the market. 'You cannot find one person in Timbuktu who has not lost. But the people of Timbuktu are accustomed to tragedy. Nothing could be worse than the invasion of 1591.'

That it took place in the same century as Leo Africanus's visit is all the more disheartening. Leo paints a picture of a vibrant, welcoming city, not so much the back of beyond as utopia. He marvels at the 'stately temple', the king's 'magnificent and well-furnished court', the abundance of 'corn, cattle, milk and butter', the 'great store of doctors, judges, priests and other learned men', the wealth of the inhabitants, 'insomuch, that the king that now is, married both his daughters unto two rich merchants'. No wonder everyone is so 'gentle and cheerful'. Reading Leo's account today is heartbreaking.

Nevertheless, was Leo himself at fault? Did his *Description of Africa* help to bring down the curtain? It was published in Venice in 1550, so there was plenty of time for it to reach the ears of Sultan Al-Mansur. He would have had his own sources, but it is doubtful any were as detailed. As far as the scholar Christopher Wise is concerned, it was Leo's book that provided the inspiration, not only for the 1591 invasion, but also for the later incursions of the Europeans: 'His scouting trips to the ancient land of Songhay signalled the inauguration of both the Arab Muslim and European Christian conquest of West African civilisation.'

Is this fair? It flips Leo's journey back to front, like a gestalt painting, transforming a treasury of learning into an instruction manual for imperial conquest. But can such motives be laid at the door of a teenager travelling as his uncle's attendant? What is clear is that history has a cruel way of folding back on itself. Not so much circular as weblike, it weaves mischievous threads through time, gluing disparate moments like the 1591 invasion and the 2012 crisis. As I would discover on my return to the city, past and present have a habit of colliding in strange and unpredictable ways.

Winding through the heart of Timbuktu, Sarey Keyna is a labyrinth of mud brick and limestone. Walls are flush and tight, bellowing out the sun, like the neighbourhoods of Fez. But they aren't crutched by wooden scaffolds. Instead, there are rubble-toothed gaps where bricks have tumbled and tents have been pitched. Here, nomad architecture is often more durable.

Goats and sheep wander between these palm-reed hemispheres, which belong to recently sedentarised black Tamashek families (also known as 'Bella', indicating their status as former Tuareg slaves), who live cheek by jowl with the Songhay-speaking majority. It is a characteristic quarter of the old town, its narrow streets slick with dirt-water, its doorfronts spilling out children, its grown-ups benched on ledges, sipping tea and chatting to their neighbours. And, as my friend Mahmoud pointed out, 'it's impossible to find your way, so the jihad-ists will have a lot of trouble catching you'.

Mahmoud was waiting on his motorbike. He had missed out on the crisis: he was in Bamako when the jihadists arrived and stayed there until after their departure. Throughout the intervening period we had exchanged emails, and he was one of my main sources of information in that time.

'Things are starting to get back to normal,' he said, as his bike jud-dered into Sarey Keyna, 'but it's still not completely safe. We need to keep you somewhere the jihadists won't know to look.'

Although Mahmoud's family lived on a dune at the edge of town, he didn't recommend it as a lodging place for a *toubob*. So he had found a friend in the quarter: Sidi, a local gardener, who lived in a sprawl of limestone and mud off a narrow alley. Tall and loose limbed, welcoming but relaxed, Sidi was an ideal host.

'You are in your own home now,' he said, guiding us behind a gate of battered tin with a flashbulb smile.

Heaped rice sacks took the strain off our backs and a canopy of palm-reed matting kept out the sun. Planted in front of the white-limned wall around the drop loo was a satellite dish, transmitting foot-ball matches from the European leagues that Sidi's sons were watching with their friends inside.

'The Salafists[49] never left us alone,' said Sidi. 'They told us to wear our trousers short, they wouldn't let us pray for our ancestors in the

---

49 Salafist derives from '*as-salaf as-saliheen*', referring to 'the pious predecessors' of early Islam. The movement originated in nineteenth-century Egypt and spans a range of views, from

cemeteries, they beat people for smoking cigarettes. They wanted us to put our hands on our chests when we pray, but this is not our way. It was a foreign idea of Islam, it wasn't *our* Islam. It was hell.'

Sidi's work as a gardener had taken him to the Place d'Independence, where among his jobs before the crisis was responsibility for the vegetation around the city's symbol, the genie known as 'Al-Farook' (an icon so beloved his name was taken by Timbuktu's football club and its FM radio station). I remembered the monument – a turbaned figure in white, riding a winged horse on a slab of forked concrete, among feathery bushes and palm trees. At least, until the jihadists came and declared it blasphemous.

Sidi was working in the square that day. He saw the jihadists arrive with hammers and farming tools. The monument was too strong, so they requisitioned a road-laying tractor.

'They attached some cables,' said Sidi, 'and after a long time the monument fell to the ground. One of my friends, Harbey the tailor, tried to talk to them. He explained how it's our symbol. People in Timbuktu are proud of the fact we never worshipped pagan gods, because our city was established by Muslims. But the Salafists just said "it's pagan" and refused to listen.'

That first morning back in Timbuktu, I wandered over to the monument. It was still lying as the jihadists had left it: a fallen giant, bony with iron rods. Painted blocks and shards of rock were scattered around the carcase. It was one of the town's many wounds, gaping and unbandaged, waiting to be treated.

Nearby was the Cemetery of Three Saints, one of the city's most important places of contemplation. An old man in a turban was wandering between cairns of piled stone, offering prayers at amputated graves. In the heart of the cemetery was a hump of earth, a broken door lying on top, banked in heaps of rubble. Another saint was marked across the path; another pile of rubble. Although little known outside Timbuktu, the saints were locally revered. The desecration of the tombs had become one of the most widely broadcast events of Ansar ad-Dine's occupation.

---

non-violence and evangelism to terrorism. What is consistent is an emphasis on looking back to the early Muslim community and the aspiration for a unified Islamic state governed by *shariah* law. In Timbuktu during my visit, 'Salafist' was used as a general term for all the foreign jihadists.

You could walk all around the city with destruction as your guide: from the smashed-in prayer niches on the wall of the Djingereyber mosque in the centre, east to the mosque of Sidi Yahia (its grand door ripped down to disprove a tradition that it couldn't be destroyed until the End of Days), to the house of the vindictive *shariah* judge Hamid Moussa in the south, which had been torn down by his long-suffering neighbours after the jihadists fled.

Equally prevalent, swirling around Timbuktu like the wind-tossed dust, were stories of human suffering. Sometimes I didn't even have to leave Sidi's house to hear them. His wife, Assaytoun, told me about women she knew who had been attacked by the jihadists; his son Hamid recalled running from the jihadists when he was spotted talking to a girl on the street; his friend Harbey showed me the banner he'd made to welcome the French 'liberators', proclaiming President Hollande as an 'honorary citizen of the city of 333 saints'.

'The hardest thing was getting any work,' said Harbey. 'I'm a tailor and most of my work is for women's clothes. But most women were afraid to come out of their houses. And when they did, they usually got harassed. The Salafists said they were being provocative, just because they had big arses. They can't help that! Songhay women are big that way. I got a visit from one of my customers, and straight afterwards a soldier knocked on my door. "What are you doing with these women?" he said. I told him: "It's my livelihood. Don't you think you've made it hard enough for us?" But those Salafists never listened. "If I see any more women going into your house," he said, "I'll have you whipped for adultery."'

Well, at least there are the books. Nothing, surely, binds our period more pleasantly to Leo Africanus's. As he remarked, 'hither are brought diverse manuscripts or written books out of Barbary, which are sold for more money than any other merchandise'. The manuscript business was so lucrative that trade routes to Timbuktu were known as 'the Ink Road'.[50] And the centuries have only made the manuscripts

---

50 Timbuktu already boasted several libraries by the mid-sixteenth century, when Askiya Daoud established 'repositories of goods and even libraries' (according to the *Tarikh*

even more valuable. So what did the jihadists do about them? Surely they were keen to preserve this symbol of Timbuktu's past? Hmmm...

That's how screwed up Ansar ad-Dine's occupation was. They tore down shrines, brought back flagellation and mandatory *hijaab*, any throwback to the past they could think of – but they burned the manuscripts, most of which were written by Islamic scholars who understood their religion far better than any of the jihadists ever would.

One of Sidi's friends, Abdramane Moulaye, was a *marabout* who ran a small Islamic school and managed his family's collection of 20,000 manuscripts. Realising they were under threat, he hid them in metal boxes and distributed them among his neighbours until he could ferry them down the Niger. As an extra precaution, he used a technique that is all the more appealing because it would have infuriated the puritanical jihadists: a magic spell made from verses in the Quran, hung from the back of his door and buried in the sand.

'Because of this,' said Moulaye, 'the house was protected and the Salafists couldn't find it. They tried to look for it. They gave the children sweets to show them the way. But the house became invisible.'

For Abdel Kader Haidara, more worldly methods were required. As the manager of Timbuktu's most celebrated family-run library, he was in charge of an extraordinarily valuable collection, amounting to 370,000 manuscripts, ranging from works of philosophy, religion, poetry and astrology to medieval merchandise bills, biographical dictionaries and legal testimony.

'In the years before the crisis, we made a lot of progress,' said Haidara. I visited him in a scruffy apartment block in Bamako, shortly before my latest journey to Timbuktu. A thick-set man with round, penetrating eyes, he was sitting on a frayed rug, tearing a baguette and pouring tea from a samovar. 'The books were well treated and well guarded,' he explained, 'and we were improving our equipment for the cataloguing process.'

---

al-Fattash). 'He had calligraphers copying books for him, and would sometimes make gifts of these to scholars.' The size of these libraries is suggested by an anecdote about the scholar Ahmed Baba, who protested when he was deported to Morocco in 1591 that his library of 1600 books had been plundered – and he claimed that his was one of Timbuktu's smaller libraries.

However, with the arrival of the jihadists, it was clear something had to be done.

'They didn't threaten us directly. But they seized books from people in the street and destroyed them. So we made a plan: we brought up steel trunks from Mopti and filled them with the books. And gradually, one at a time, we transported them by cart to be stored in different houses around Timbuktu.'

Haidara had joined the trail of refugees to Bamako, and with the occupation showing no sign of ending, he was anxious to bring the books with him. So he sent a series of couriers, first to carry back hard drives, then to ferry boxes of manuscripts down to Mopti. Every available mode of transport was used – car, four-wheel drive, bush taxi, pirogue and pinasse.

'The boats were the easiest,' said Haidara, 'because you could carry dozens of boxes with just a couple of couriers. But we didn't want to risk too many at a time, in case the boats sank. Coming by road was harder, because of the checkpoints. If the jihadists or MNLA saw the books, they would try to destroy them, or steal them if they knew their value.'

There were many close calls. Once, in a village near the Niger, the couriers were held at gun point. They were only released after Haidara called up a friend who knew the local imam. Yet eventually, all the manuscripts were transported and dehumidifiers set up to preserve them, taking account of the more tropical conditions in Bamako. Still, I wondered if there was a feeling of dislocation; if Haidara felt the books were out of their proper place. He shook his head: he was too pragmatic to be troubled by such thoughts.

'These books are our identity.' He lifted a manuscript, running his fingers gently across the spine. 'They are our history, our pride, everything. But they aren't just for Timbuktu. They are for all humanity. The most important thing is to preserve them. It is not simply a question of having them in Timbuktu, it is a question of having them at all.'

Whippings, women forced into hiding, magic spells to fight the jihadists. At times, it felt as if Timbuktu had been trundling along some kind of reverse time track. Or, as Almehdi Dicko told me, 'the *shariah* brings back all the old things'. As an anti-slavery campaigner, he had seen plenty of this for himself.

'I have been to villages', he said, 'where masters took back their slaves and made them work: preparing the milk and food, cleaning their tents, looking after the animals. We are pursuing justice against these people, because slavery is illegal in Mali, but with this crisis it is hard to enforce the law. Many former slaves have moved back with their masters by their own choice, because they are scared in these times of uncertainty.'

While officially slavery was abolished across the French Soudan in 1908, it has never fully disappeared in Mali. The colonial officers exploited it themselves, using slave labour for construction, domestic service, haulage and military employment.[51] So deeply did slavery endure under French rule that Modibo Keita (later Mali's first post-independence president) argued there could only be full manumission when the yoke of colonialism was broken. But post-independence governments have failed to eradicate the phenomenon, largely because they have failed to create an economic system in which there is sufficient motivation for everybody to walk away from the security of bondage.

I met Almehdi in the office of Pastor Mohammed, a convert who was in charge of Timbuktu's small (and mostly ex-slave) Evangelical Christian community. Sitting in front of a *bogolan* mud cloth depicting Jesus the shepherd (an attractive image for people who've grown up in a pastoralist environment), the pastor called up Almehdi to give me a glimpse into life for Timbuktu's slaves.

'It's not like you think in the West,' he said.

His eyes fiery, he talked in punchy sentences, his own childhood in bondage simmering at the surface of every example. 'It still exists in Timbuktu in many forms, that's why it is so hard to eradicate. There

---

51 'Slavery is an age-old institution that forms the principal basis of the social organization of the peoples of the Soudan,' wrote the military governor of Timbuktu's colonial garrison in 1894, 'we must tolerate it unless we want to bring about a complete disruption of the economy of the country.'

are masters who use their slaves to work the fields in the harvest, but the rest of the year they leave them alone. There are people who are no longer slaves, but still the former master has influence over them. Let me tell you about my colleague. I work with him in the municipality, he has a very high position. But when he wanted to give his son a turban [a traditional coming-of-age ceremony], his former slave master found out. He was furious – he came out of the desert and criticised him for breaking the *wala* [the code of respect between manumitted slaves and their former masters]. He's a nobody, just a herder in the desert. But still, my colleague felt obliged to cancel the ceremony. Even in this neighbourhood, there is an Arab lady who still has many slaves and everybody knows about it.'

What a mess, when slavery is top of the links to Leo Africanus's time, while the wonders of his age, like the shrines of saints or the beautiful manuscripts, have been trashed. In Leo's era, the average price of a slave was less than the price of a book. His *Description* is chock-full of slaves. In Timbuktu, he tells us, 'they keep great store of men and women slaves'. But that's what makes the survival of slavery all the more unsettling: Leo was writing half a millennium ago. Listening to Almehdi, I thought of the slaves of Mauritania, and wondered how many others I had passed without being aware of it. That is one of the hazards of travel in faraway places. Life is so intricately coded you are constantly in danger of missing the signals. Throughout these journeys, I often felt like a blind man groping in the dark.

∽

The effect of Ansar ad-Dine's occupation hung over Timbuktu like a foul-smelling miasma. Mahmoud rode me around the quarters, introducing me to people who had stayed during the crisis: shopkeepers whose wares had been set on fire; *marabouts* whose students were too scared to attend their classes; even Bouge – manager of the ill-fated Refuge de la Paix, where the four Europeans had been abducted in 2011 – who unsurprisingly had been struggling for customers.

'Now it's better,' he told me. 'Some of the staff working for the foreign armies are here. So we have more guests now than any time since the disaster.'

If anybody's trade was going to cause him trouble, it was the man known locally as Baba Toubob, 'father of the whites'. His real name is Frederic Gordey, and he is the son of a French officer who left his Arab-Malian wife after independence. With his mixed identity, Frederic was always an outsider in Timbuktu society, and he established himself in that classic outsider's role, as manager of the only bar in town.

'You wanna meet someone interesting?' asked Mahmoud. Tumbling over precipitous sand hills, we rode like cowboys on a bucking bronco. By the time we arrived my nerves were milkshaked and I could really use a drink. Which was lucky, because here in the sand-clogged Sanfil district, Baba Toubob had established his post-occupation bar, discreetly tucked behind a metal gate. Pitchers and crates of empty Castel cluttered the yard. Behind them sat the barkeep, next to a stack of fresh Bavaria, smoking at the flies.

'Look at this place. Who comes now? *Mais autrefois...* if you came before the occupation, you would have nowhere to sit!' Baba Toubob had the sort of distinguished, clay-like head that looks like it has been glaze fired in a kiln. He shook it over a lopsided metal table, tapping ash into a rusty tray, occasionally mumbling instructions to his lackeys.

'Lots of people came to the bar, it was in the centre of town,' he continued. 'Local people, especially young people, used to come. They aren't concerned about Islam so much, that's for when you're older. They were Songhays mostly, but we did entertain some Arabs.'

'Didn't you think of leaving when the jihadists came?' I asked.

'Hmmm... I thought this is just something temporary, so I decided to stay. I kept the bar open, but in secret, just with people I knew. Then, a month after the occupation, someone called one of my customers and said "you need to get out of there", so we all left from a door at the back. The Islamists came in that evening and wrecked the bar. They broke the freezer, carried all the bottles out to the street and smashed them, and set the whole place on fire. I stood at the corner of the street and watched it burn.'

'I guess that was pretty hard,' I said, 'seeing your livelihood go up in smoke.'

He took a drag on his cigarette, pushing up his shoulders like some Parisian roué dismissing a bad run at the casino. 'I wasn't hurt, so I thought, it's not serious.'

'Did they give you any more trouble?' I asked.

'They tried to. One day, they took me in for an interrogation. But I had something on my side. You see, I'm related to some pretty important people. I'm from the Ould Aish, which is a famous tribe round here, and my family has produced a lot of jihadists. In fact, the head of Al-Qaeda in Timbuktu was one of my cousins.'

I could feel the flies taking advantage of my dropped-open jaw. How paradoxical! How ridiculous! And yet – how Timbuktu! Here was this French officer's son, sipping Castel beer at 11 in the morning, chain smoking, flapping his hands like any Parisian barfly – and he was related to some of the region's most prominent jihadists. It was a double-sided identity as stark as any I had come across.

'Do you feel a connection to your... cousins?' I asked.

'Well, we don't talk so much, as you can imagine. But I feel close to the Arab community as a whole. People say a lot of bad things about the Arabs. But you know what? Without them, this city is nothing. The Arabs are the masters of the economy here.'

I thought of the stories about Berabish Arabs from the nineteenth century, trading in salt and cloth and tobacco, outmanoeuvring the French on export taxes – people like Lamina and the caravaneers of the desert. They were the link between the town and the dunes. How much poorer Timbuktu would be without them.

As Baba Toubob pointed out, he wasn't hurt. In that respect he was lucky, because one of the most disturbing features of Ansar ad-Dine's occupation was the appetite for vicious corporal punishment. There's a fine line when you're visiting a place that has been through horrific trauma. You want to probe the dark heart of the matter, to look the thing square in the eye. Yet if you push too far, there is a risk you're sensationalising, foregrounding the most violent stories irrespective of context. I felt that I needed to hear some of these stories. I wanted to understand what Timbuktu had been through – and why it was proving so hard for the nomads to return. I think, I hope, I was trying to learn, and not just being a torture junkie.

Among the people I met through Mahmoud was a restaurant chef in the Abaradjou district, arrested for having a baby out of wedlock. He had been struck a hundred times with a cowskin camel whip and his wife (his girlfriend at the time) was so traumatised by the incident that she wouldn't speak about it. There was a boy whipped for chatting to his neighbour, who was so badly wounded he had to be phlebotomised to bring down the swelling. And there was a distant relative of Mahmoud's, a girl called Hady, who sat drawing patterns in the sand beside her mud-brick home. Of all the stories I was told, I found hers the saddest to hear.

'I was with my boyfriend,' she said, 'his name's Abdullai. We were just talking in the street. The jihadist soldiers saw us, so we ran. They fired in the air and another jihadist came round the corner and he grabbed Abdullai. I just carried on running.'

It took a while for the details to leak out. She drifted off sometimes, so we sat in spells of delicate silence, waiting for her to resume. It was as if the cord tying her to the world had been cut, and she wasn't sure if she wanted it reattached. Mahmoud, who knew her family, said she had been very different before the crisis.

'I went to a friend's house. I knew they'd look for me at home so I stayed there. But then my brother came. He told me they had taken my mother, they were saying they had given her the punishment in my place. So I put on my strictest Islamic clothes and went to the commissariat.'

There was a twig beside her in the sand. She picked it up and traced a line, her eyes fixed on the pattern she was drawing. Behind us was a palm-reed tent, which her family used in the hottest months. Its shadow had shifted a couple of inches by the time she resumed.

'I was in prison for four nights. I was so scared, I couldn't eat any of the food they brought me. I was on my own, in a big room, and all I could think about was what they were going to do to me.'

When she stood before the *qadi*, the *shariah* judge, she could barely stop herself shaking. She offered her excuse – she had been doing an errand for her parents and only greeted Abdullai out of courtesy. But it was given short shrift.

'The judge said I had made a big mistake, and it was his duty to make sure I didn't do it again. So he ordered me to be whipped a hundred times.'

She had to wait another night – 'the worst night of my life' – before the sentence was carried out. Flanked by jihadists, blinking at the fierce morning light, she could see hundreds of people gathering on the dusty square behind the Sankoré mosque – site of the university where so many of Timbuktu's intelligentsia had studied. The jihadists covered her face with a turban and stood behind her, taking turns to wield a stripped branch from an acacia tree. Every strike, said Hady, she thought she was going to buckle.

'I cried all the way through. I kept thinking, I'm not going to survive this.'

The whip tenderised her skin, breaking down its resistance; by the end it was tearing open at every lash, as if the whip had been spliced with razor blades.

'I had a lot of blood and there were scratches all over my back. My family took me home, massaged me and fed me meat to give me strength. I was sick for about a week and couldn't go out, but slowly I started to recover.'

It was hard to think of the right words after hearing a story like this. I asked Hady if she felt anger towards her persecutors. For many townsfolk, the jihadists were people from the desert, which was why many nomads were facing so much hostility when they tried to return. But Hady's answer showed the tensions were more complicated than a simple town–desert split: they sliced through the very heart of Timbuktu society.

'Sure, I hate those people. Sure, I want to shoot them with a big gun! But also... the people who watched. I don't understand why they could do that. Just stand there... and watch me getting beaten. I think I will always find that hard to understand.'

Everybody agreed: it was the 'perfect time' to visit. After the nightmare of the last couple of years, Timbuktu was sloughing off its trauma. One night after supper, we could hear the drumming of tam-tams and the pounding of feet, the double-time flowering of feast and song. Looking through the door with Mahmoud, I saw mobile phones and torches lighting people's way, painting the muddy alleys with trails of LED.

'Come on! You want to see?'

I followed Mahmoud down a zigzag of mud. We floated along vectors of light, lured like moths towards the glow in a cul-de-sac. A dozen women were dancing there, languidly turning their limbs around the bride.

'She's a beautiful one,' said Mahmoud, 'and she comes from a very popular family.'

The bride was luminous in her yellow headdress, strobed by the bright cottons and fluent limbs of her friends and relatives. Each woman rotated on her own turntable of dust, wreathed in an amber mist, ethereal in the glare of torches and phones.

'There haven't been any weddings since the crisis.' Mahmoud's smile was wider than I had ever seen it. 'When I was younger, we used to have weddings every day at this time of year. It's good to see this again!'

I thought of Leo Africanus, who writes so enthusiastically of the marriage festivities in Timbuktu. He describes how the inhabitants 'spend a great part of the night in singing and dancing through all the streets of the city'. Here was one of the loveliest moments in his *Description* brought to life: a reminder, after the miseries of *shariah* and slavery, that not all throwbacks to the past are rotten.

The next day, the Place d'Independence throbbed to the backfire of motorbikes and a crowd swelled in front of the mayor's office. The town had come out to greet the newlyweds emerging from the civil registration. Boys sat on car bonnets playing tam-tams, while military trucks swung around the square, drawing appreciative cheers from the crowd. At the moment, people wanted to feel they were protected.

Men in glossy-fronted *boubous*, heads smothered under turbans or squeezed into filigree caps, batted greetings and gossip about. The women glowed even brighter. Gold swung from their ears in fans and triangles, pins and squares, sparkled on Songhay headdresses, flashed in finger bands, traced glittery loops down goffered dresses. This was no superficial obsession with ornament. This was couture as culture:

a celebration of survival, a fist in the face of the jihadists. Their hair frizzy, braided, curled, straightened, triumphantly bared or caught up in crisply folded cloths, these women were brilliant in the literal as well as the conventional sense. They sparkled with a brightness that, in the light of Timbuktu's recent troubles, was magnificent.

As soon as the couples had emerged from the mayor's office to be swamped by well-wishers, the crowd bobbed on motorbikes, long speeding chains rattling under inkily lit limestone walls.

'Come on!' said Mahmoud, grinding his engine. 'Let's go and join the wedding party!'

'Do you know any of the grooms?' I asked.

'Of course, I'm the future mayor. I know everyone!'

Headlamps strobed the night, draining the colour from *boubous* and dresses, flashing on the folds of headscarves and lacquered wigs. The roar of engines drowned the beat of tam-tams; the odour of burned fuel smothered the hot scent of fritters in street-side pans. A boy leaped off his seat in the middle of the traffic, break-dancing with his motor, swinging it by the handles. Horns and klaxons beeped triumphantly. For a shining, breathtaking moment, it felt as if the whole of Timbuktu was united in celebration.

'We've been asleep for so long,' said Sidi that night. 'Now at last the city is waking up.'

25

Licking the Desert's Wounds

OFFICIALS CALL TIMBUKTU 'THE CITY OF PIROGUE AND CAMEL', WHERE the river and the desert meet. A rainbow city joining different ethnic groups together as one happy family. If you want more than sound-bites, you have to hang out in the dusty back rooms of shops and the fly-misted alleys. There, you pick up the tensions, and among the most articulate voices was Sidi's friend Harbey. We had met at a wedding party, sticking our fists in the same platter of greasy rice. He leaned in, one hand on my shoulder, and told me about a Songhay he knew whose hand was cut off for stealing some bags of rice and a few pieces of furniture.

'They brought him out in front of the Gaddafi Hotel', said Harbey, 'and cut off the hand with a sword. They threw it in a bowl and put the stump in a pot of hot butter to stop the bleeding. You should've heard him cry! Now, here's the thing. That boy was black, a Songhay, I know his family. But at the same time there was another thief, an Arab from the desert, who took a really big haul from the Gaddafi Hotel. And do you know what they did to him? They let him off with the whip. So tell me, what's the difference between those crimes? Why did they let off the Arab, but the Songhay lost his hand? I'll tell you why: because the Salafists were Arabs. They came from Algeria, from Libya, from Mauritania.'

One of the most disturbing developments of the twenty-first century is the rise of identity politics. Ideology took a beating in the Cold War, and tribalism has clambered on its grave. The conflict in Mali should have been ideological – *what form of society do you want?* – but it was ratcheted to ethnic lines. Hearing the stories of people like Harbey and poor Hady, it was clear the wounds were still raw. That wouldn't make them easier to probe: walls can rise very quickly when outsiders are stomping around. So I wasn't expecting to come across the kind of story that Emad told me. It was as heartbreaking as any I heard in Timbuktu, because it illustrated the terrible cost of the crisis to Mali's nomads.

Emad was a teacher who lived near the Sankoré mosque, sinewy
and high browed, with large eyes that bulged and blinked when he
talked. After meeting him at an evening 'peace concert', I was invited
to his house. There, in a plain tiled room, he opened up a box filled
with photographs: boys in handout T-shirts and dusty tunics, a few
headscarved girls, gathered in front of a sun-bleached limestone school-
house. Tapping a fingertip against the different faces in the picture, he
told me their fates.

'This one lost his father... this one's in the refugee camp in
Mauritania... this one's dead.'

The school was in a village called Agouni, 21 miles into the desert,
not far from where I had stayed with Lamina's family.

'We had around a hundred students,' said Emad. 'It was a good
school, and we were all proud of our work. The students' parents were
all herders, with camels and goats, and this was the first generation to
get an education. We were making a lot of progress with them, they're
really intelligent. Especially in maths, because they're used to counting
the herds and measuring out the grains of millet for the goats, so they
can work out the answer a lot faster than children in the town.'

To prove his point, he showed me test papers written on narrow
gridpaper, flashing green and red with ticks and high scores and bravos.

'Then,' said Emad, 'the jihadists came and they closed down the
school because they didn't approve of the modern education system,
they only wanted Quranic schools. So I came back here and stayed in
Timbuktu.'

'Have you seen any of the students since?' I asked.

'Actually, I did.' Emad tipped his head, his eyes flashing with the
memory. 'I passed the military barracks one day, here in Timbuktu.
And I saw them sitting there, three of my students, in the back of a
pick-up truck. They were wearing jihadist uniforms and carrying guns.
"What are you doing?" I asked. "Why did you enlist?" They said it was
necessity. There was no trade between the town and the desert, and
the jihadists were offering 150,000 CFA (about £165) every month to
anyone who became a soldier. These are poor people, and they were
suffering very badly. But I know they regret it very deeply. Those who
survived, at least.'

I asked if some of them had been killed, and the lines tightened on his brow.

'I saw a truck driven by the father of one of my students. Another had three of my students in it. They were going to Konna. I guess they weren't so precious to the jihadists, so they were chosen for the front line.'

Not all Emad's students had joined the jihadists. Many of them followed the long trail to the refugee camps; a few had come back to Timbuktu, although they were deeply traumatised by the conflict, he said.

These students were not unusual. It is a crushing irony that the violent movements who stripped security (and sometimes rustled herds) away from nomadic life were the same movements that lured so many herders' sons to their banners. When ideology is not enough, financial incentives will go a long way. Yet this irony bleeds into a paradox. For military occupation is alien to nomadism – historically, the martial spirit of the nomad was satisfied by raiding. There are nuances, of course, but it is telling that Yusuf Ibn Tafshin didn't hang around in Western Spain after his victory over Alfonso the Brave.

There are other aspects of modern warfare, however, that fit more snugly into the old nomadic paradigm: guerrilla tactics, kidnapping, lightning raids on vulnerable outposts. And as the people most likely to suffer from poverty and social exclusion (sitting on the margins of society not only in geographical terms), nomads have plenty of motivation to take the bait.

Former nomads like one-eyed Mokhtar Belmokhtar and Iyad Ag Ghali had been instrumental in presenting jihadism as an attractive proposition. *Marabouts* like Hamedou Kouffa, who led a string of Fulani youth into the decisive battle of Konna, had also played a part. As Emad's story underlined, nomads were entangled in the bloody mess of Mali's crisis along with everyone else.

Several of his students were working at the Arab market, on the northern side of Timbuktu, manning stores among boxes of Egyptian yeast and American Legend cigarettes. They wouldn't talk about the jihadists, although they were keen to tell me how their stores had been ransacked and some whispered of the 'disappearances' – a growing list of Arabs and Tuaregs, suspected victims of extra-judicial killings by the Malian army.[52] Still, another layer was added to Emad's story when I met a nurse called Niamoyu Touré. Wrapped in batik cloths, shuffling with the air of someone who has been worked too hard, she spoke in a gentle, measured voice.

'I've been a nurse in the camps and villages since 1994,' she said. 'I would go by motorbike, wherever there was a need. There were many problems: in the winter people suffered from the cold, in the summer from the heat. There was a lot of trouble with the animals, and the veterinarians don't visit very often, so we were often asked to help. We collaborate with the veterinarians, because we understand that if the animals are healthy, the people are healthy too.'

Niamoyu's experience pulled back the cover on nomadic isolation. Medicine in Africa tends to be hospital based and mobile outreach is expensive. The concrete separation between human and animal health is a sedentary one. It makes no sense for communities where diseases often pass between human and beast.

'What was it like going to the villages in the crisis?' I asked.

'It was really hard. Many bandits came to Agouni, the same with other camps and villages. Some of the people joined the jihadists; I would say about one in ten. They threatened us. Once, some men with guns came and told me to give them all my medicine or they'd beat me to death. Another time, some bandits took my motorbike and my luggage, which included my medical books. But you know, the jihadists weren't all like that. Some of them said the health centre is untouchable, and supported me. After they took my motorbike, I left the village and never went back. It became too hard.'

She was ambivalent about whether she would like to return.

'If I get paid, perhaps. But it's too hard. Riding through the sand is difficult, it's easy for the motorbike to break down and then you're

---

52 They had good reason to fear the army, for there is a growing stack of testimonies of army malpractice. In October 2012, eight Tuareg nomads were abducted by Malian soldiers from the military barracks at Diabali and executed. In another incident, soldiers invaded a nomad camp near Nara and took several men, who never returned. On 6 May 2013, nine men were taken from villages and nomadic camps near Léré and beaten, chained with ropes, tied to trees and slammed against pick-up trucks. These are a few among numerous examples of murder and abuse, many of them perpetrated against nomads, which have been recorded by Amnesty International and Human Rights Watch.

stuck. The camps are very far from each other. Many people don't accept our medicine, they say "God will decide" and go to the *marabouts* instead. But people are starting to appreciate what we're trying to do. Slowly, things are changing.'

Talking to Emad and Niamoyu, it was clear the people of the desert had been dealt a terrible blow by the crisis. I wanted to hear an official take on this, and there was none more rubber-stamped than Mohammed Taher Ould Elhadj. Officially titled the Mayor of Salam, he was chief of his 'fraction', a corridor of villages and encampments from Timbuktu all the way to the Algerian border – a population that he estimated at 40,000.

'The life of nomads here', he said, 'is nearly finished.'

Dressed in a crisp white *boubou*, his hair neatly combed, he sat at a metal desk in a small mud-brick office near the edge of the desert, speaking in soft, murmuring French.

'The nomads have been exhausted by this crisis. We had many problems even before – the lack of medicine, schools, markets, security. Life for nomads is hard, and it's expensive. For example, to buy a sack of rice in our area costs twice what you pay in Bamako.'

He was adamant about where the blame for the crisis lay: foreign jihadists from Algeria, Mauritania and Burkina Faso. The only Malian jihadists, he insisted, were Tuaregs.

'Our people weren't involved.' He beat out the emphasis with a sharp flap of hands. 'You cannot find one Arab chief in all our commune who was with the jihadists. Maybe there are some individuals who joined them, people who wanted to profit from the situation, but you cannot say they represent the community unless they are the chiefs.'

In its own way, this was an admission. But he wasn't going to let me push the subject any further. As he pointed out, for many of the region's nomads, jihadism is the least of their worries.

'If there is no intervention to help us, we will lose everything. We need development. We need better schools and hospitals, better administration and security. Our community didn't create this problem, but we are the ones who are suffering most from it. People are dying, from lack of medicine and many other problems, but also from the lack of hope.'[53]

I felt a shiver as I listened to him – because this wasn't only Mayor Ould Elhadj speaking. So many communities had spoken about these problems. The Berbers, hedged into inhospitable corners of the mountains. The Saharawis, denied their own identity. The Moors and Fulani, struggling to find pasture. The Bozo, at a loss for fish. Mayor Ould Elhadj was articulating the despair of the nomads I had met all across the region.

I needed to get out to the desert. Somehow. I had tried to find out about the *azalai* and heard only horror stories – camels incinerated by French gunships, caravaneers marooned in refugee camps. I sought out my old Tuareg friend Ousmane, and found him living in a concrete hut at the edge of town. His family had lost all their tents, along with their animals and smithy tools. Worse was the human cost.

'My cousin was killed by rocket fire when the French came,' said Ousmane. 'Him, his wife, his child, in their tent. We went to the camp in Mauritania. But there was so much sickness everywhere and the tents were so close together you couldn't even move between them. My uncle had lost all his food so when he got to the camp he hadn't eaten for a week, and he died a few days later.'

Ousmane was wearing his *tamelgoust* loose, his face exposed. I remembered how fastidious he had been in the past, proudly explaining there were more than a hundred ways to wear a turban. Had he lost faith in the old cultural cornerstones? There was no news of his brother, Haka, who had talked so wittily about the difficulties for Tuaregs. Ousmane said he hadn't seen him for months.

As for my old guru, the man who had shown me more of the desert than anyone else... well, what was I expecting? That Lamina would be waiting at the brink of a dune, ready to take me on the *azalai*? I had

---

53 Mayor Ould Elhadj's argument is echoed by the writers Majok and Schwabe in their important study, *Development among Africa's Migratory Pastoralists*: 'Not only their practices but their desires have not been known to many who propose "development" measures among them. Often pastoralists have not been even a part of the development equation.'

lost hope in good news, I just wanted *some* news. I wanted to know he was alive and hadn't been killed in the bombardment. I wanted to know that Jadullah was in good health, that their wives were well, that Abdul-Hakim had not been too badly scarred. That his old cousin Ismail was still chattering away, singing his songs of faith. But for days it was impossible to find out anything... until Mayor Ould Elhadj put me in touch with a contact in the Mauritanian refugee camp.

'*Alhamdulillah!* Praise to God! *Marhaba bek!* A thousand welcomes! A thousand welcomes! Praise to God!'

That reedy, magnificent voice was like a blast of fresh desert air. I wanted to hug that wonderful man. Hearing him speak, I felt as if he were there beside me, not trapped on the other side of a border. Nevertheless, a reunion would have to wait. He was stuck in the Mbera camp and having already travelled through Mauritania, I was unable to obtain short-term permission to visit the camp.

Sitting in the calm of Sidi's house later that evening, I spoke to Lamina again, my heart beating for my fantastic old teacher.

'Oh, Yusuf, life became very hard.'

'And Jadullah? And Abdul-Hakim?'

'They are with me, in the camp.'

'And the camels?'

'They are...'

A long, crackling pause. He didn't need to say any more.

We arranged to meet, a few days later, at the Malian–Mauritanian border. But Lamina got scared – the Malian soldiers had killed too many of his clan. He never showed up.

'The desert goes round in circles,' he told me the last time we spoke. 'One day you will come with us, Yusuf. One day, God willing, we will drink tea on the way to Taoudenni.'

It sounded less like a prophecy, or even a promise; more like a ritual phrase, its truth embedded in the emotion it conveyed. Like the branding symbols we had drawn together, hieroglyphics of a pact that could never be broken.

That was my last night in Timbuktu, and I sat clutching my phone long after Lamina's voice had receded, trying to visualise him on his camel, Abdul-Hakim bouncing on the perch, Jadullah galloping off like a gaucho.

I wouldn't see them in the desert, this time. But that didn't mean I couldn't see the desert itself. I wanted one last trip. It wasn't recommended, and Mahmoud took a little persuading to arrange it. Even so, I needed a final glimpse. A last dance with that world I had lingered in and loved. The world Lamina had introduced me to, like Mr Tumnus escorting Lucy Pevensie through the woods of Narnia.

It was time for a last trip into the desert.

Wrinkled metal barrels and wire-framed sand baskets barriered the back of town. Soldiers dozed in the shade while their colleagues twitched at the triggers of their rifles. Mahmoud had arranged a car, and I zipped myself into a second-hand cagoule, donned a pair of wraparound shades and knotted my turban in the back room of a tailor's shop, making sure to cover every inch of my skin. Everyone I met had told me, 'If you really have to go to Timbuktu, whatever you do, don't go out to the desert.' But nomads don't live in towns – not when they are still being nomadic. If I wanted to understand how their lives had been affected by the crisis, I needed to venture out to the dunes.

The red earth of the road decomposed into a rutted scrawl of tyre tracks. The sand around us, grey-cream and grainy, had the colour you would expect on a crater of the moon. Donkeys and goats scrambled under wild acacias, but they were rarely accompanied by people. We saw a woman carrying a sack on her head; a man bearing a mattock between the trees; no one else.

Five miles out of town stood a well. Its coping was unsealed and a rubber inner tube hung from its cross-pole. It looked like a siege engine waiting to be operated. This was where we'd been told to wait, so we stood beside the well, watching a pepper grain on the horizon, hurtling towards us with sandballing dimensions. A knobbled stick. A green *tamelgoust*. Grey eyes glowing through the turban, challenging and sharp.

'What did he say?' I scurried alongside Mahmoud, following our contact.

'He's going to take us to the chief.'

I felt like some captured earthman in a pulpy sci-fi movie. *Take me to your leader.*

A few minutes' trudge away, Sandy Ag Mostapha was standing in the middle of his herd, robed in loose blue cotton. A black turban framed his sombre face, pooling the light across a silver tuft of beard and the smooth planes above his cheeks. He tossed instructions at his son, who was drawing the water from a 50-metre-deep well, beating a donkey to draw the swollen sacks of water. The rope creaked on the pulley, the slosh of water echoed on the bore, and the stick cracked on the donkey's back. These sounds were echoes, reminding me of other watering holes on my travels. Sandy's son poured the water into a couple of troughs on either side of the well, while his daughter, wearing a Dallas Field Hockey anorak, filled up the *bidons*. She glanced round, eyes dark under her scarf, assessing us, then turned her head with a toss of indifference.

'You find us here at the source of nomadic life.'

Sandy smiled under his dusty turban. Tradition might dictate that Tuareg men cover their faces in the presence of strangers, but for him the practicalities of herding took priority.

'If I am in the town, or visiting another camp, I will do this,' he told me, 'but here I am at ease.'

While most of his neighbours had fled to the refugee camps, he was determined to hold his herd together. During the peak of the bombardment, he and his son had gone a few miles north, 'to a place where the animals wouldn't be frightened'.

'Was there a lot of shooting round here?' I asked.

'We are close to Timbuktu. The planes came overhead, many animals ran from the herd out of fear. And in this area, if an animal is lost it will die very soon. They need us to bring them water. Look over there. You see?' He pointed to a cluster of low-roofed banco buildings. 'It is our school building. One of the Islamists hid in there. The army came and shot at him. We still have the damage. By the time he came, most of the families had gone to the refugee camps. That was our biggest problem. We had no one to look after the buildings, so when the rains came, they were ruined.'

The disrepair was visible all over the building. Cobwebs frilled the edges of the piled desks; the windows were jagged and misshapen; the doors hung loose. In one of the huts, a collection of nomadic clobber – camel saddles, metal luggage trunks, a couple of food bowls – was scattered under a blackboard on which the last lesson remained, chalked up till the class came back.

'As soon as the jihadists took Timbuktu, people started leaving,' said Sandy. 'Some went by bush taxi, others by camel or donkey, whatever means were available. We were afraid of the jihadists, because there are many things in our culture they don't accept. Like the *grisgris*.' He rubbed the side of his arm. Bulging under the blue shift was a sheepskin armlet binding a prayer.

For Sandy, this crisis was another nail in a coffin that had been closing ever tighter for decades. He talked as if he'd been buried alive and was desperately looking for an airhole.

'Our camp used to be at the edge of Timbuktu. But when the government started selling the land, we had to move further out. When we first came here, the pasturage was better. We had date palms, jujubes, lots of fruit. Then the droughts killed everything. Now we only have the wild acacia. We get a lot of use from it, but we need so much more.'

As if to emphasise the difficulties he was talking about, cattle bones gleamed in the sand, among trails of donkey droppings and cow pats. They formed a grisly breadcrumb trail towards his tent. A couple of acacias provided shade, one of them bundled with dry grass for cattle feed. A solar panel – the only sign of technology apart from a longwave radio – was embedded in the sand. Sandy's wife, bare armed in a loose black shift, prepared tea while we crossed our legs on a reed mat.

I had a question to ask, and now felt like the right time. Many nomads had told me how hard their lives were. I had seen enough to know they weren't exaggerating. I often wondered why, in the face of such hardship, they chose to carry on.

'It is true,' said Sandy, 'many have left this life. But I will never leave it. To leave this life is to scorn the life of my parents, to say there is something superior to that life. Of course, we can do things to improve.

We should educate our children, so they can understand better how to treat the animals, how to work with people in the city. But that doesn't mean we should abandon this life. To be a Tuareg is to be a herder. We are free and independent. We walk differently from the people in the town. Our life is a good one, as long as there is pasture, water and security. It is the best life I know.'

I wondered at his words – the selflessness, but also the strictness of them. 'To leave this life is to scorn the life of my parents.' It had never occurred to me to follow my father's path. I came from a different culture. I had been nourished on a different way of thinking. I thought how hard it must be for those nomads who aren't cut out for this life, who lack the sanctuary of other options. One of the motivations for this journey, for all journeys I think, was to learn about other ways of interpreting the world; to stretch the muscles of empathy. Nomadic perceptions of space, reading the stars and desert tracks, Berber responses to nature, the Pulaaku code of the Fulani, attitudes to silence, the consolations of Islam...

Behind the camp, the plain spread to the horizon. There was little change in gradient. Apart from the odd wild acacia, it was flat and empty. Yet it wasn't featureless. I could see the dip of a blowout to the east, a flat-sided barchan dune to the west, a ripple of acacias and stalks of bunchgrass. Closer to my feet was the delicate embroidery of scarab tracks.

I sat down on my own for a moment. This was one of the best things about the desert. You were never more than a few steps away from solitude: the chance to sit by yourself, think about what you've been doing and where you want to go next.

A few inches below the horizon, I could see a man leading some animals. Some trick of the light convinced me they were camels (I think it was the heat waves, swelling their thoracic humps). They drew closer and I realised they were cattle, as emaciated as Sandy's. The herder looked like he was moving in the direction of the well. I had learned to draw water from Ismail, Lamina's garrulous cousin, and practised among the Fulani. If I found myself marooned here, there were a few tasks I could tackle, although there were other skills I'd learned for which there would be no call. The camp had no camels, so my lessons in riding and baggage loading would come to nothing. Hobbling the camels and guiding them to water would also be redundant, although some of my training might be transferable. Well, at least I could make the tea... except, as Lamina had pointed out, that wasn't really my forte.

Beyond practical training, I had learned other, abstract lessons. How to listen to your environment. How to interact with people when you don't share a language. Most importantly, I had learned a few lessons about the nature of companionship. There is no closing time around the campfire, no deadline, no pressing engagement. I doubted I would be able to appreciate this for long; I'd soon grow restless. Nevertheless, it was a peek into the social fabric of nomadic society, the fellowship nurtured by this hard, sometimes oppressive life.

Between Lamina and Abdul-Hakim, as between Boureima and his sons, I had seen father–son relationships that blew a hole through stereotypes of despotic parenthood in Muslim societies. The warmth among Aziza's family in the Atlas, or Iman and his friends on the Gondo plain, or the girls dancing under Mount Zarga, showed me that love and companionship thrive in places where they aren't compromised by endless distractions.

Observing relationships, and forging them, is the pith of travel writing. Like nomadism, the travel book is marginalised, and often misunderstood; maligned as a playpen for romance, inexpertise, egomania. (Hmmm... there may be something in that last one...) But what literary genre bears no scars? The travel book is the hunter-gatherer of literature, picking up whatever it can to sustain itself. And in this divided world of ours, is the attempt to connect, to explore a culture outside of our own, truly redundant?

Leo Africanus was the great travel writer of his age. It was he who lured me on this journey, although our paths had often diverged. I felt jealous of him sometimes: travelling in a large caravan, crossing the desert in places I didn't dare (or couldn't), dining with some of the Sahara's remotest tribes. No doubt if he knew about my malaria pills and ibuprofen, he'd have felt jealous right back! Still, jealousy was tempered by admiration. Leo really was a 'wily bird' who learned to thrive in different cultures. After Africa, he travelled extensively in Asia and lived a long while in Rome, hostage and house guest to the Pope. He wrote, he tells us, 'that I may promote the endeavours of such as are desirous to know the state of foreign countries'. Can any travel writer hope to achieve more?

Looking into the wilderness now, I felt a little deflated. I had tried to know the state of Saharan nomads, I had tried to connect. I had learned so much about the nomads of North Africa, but was it ever possible to learn *enough*? I could feel the grains running out on my journey – a homing call like the instinct that tows so much of the birdlife on the banks of the Niger back to Europe every year.

Behind me rumbled the steady chatter of the camp. Ahead, I couldn't see a single person, only the desert, broody and patient, waiting for the next stage of its story. I turned back, adjusting my feet to the slope of the dune, trenching my heels, tightening my turban as I moved towards the sun.

I knew where I wanted to go next. My friend Mansur had predicted it back in Fez: 'You will travel a long time perhaps, and see many things, but you will come back.' Now I knew where he meant. Nomads know it, because they're circling it all the time. Whenever they set off on a caravan, they know where home will be. Because they know it isn't bricks and mortar and roof tiles. It isn't a flat-screen television, a fantastic DVD collection, a first-rate cooker or a washing machine with a 10-year guarantee. It isn't even a fixed point on a map. It is simply the place where you make your fire.

I slid back down the dune to Sandy's camp. I couldn't wait to get back to town. A call to make... words to say... later, much later, lips to kiss.

I had worn my indigo-blue turban long enough, my slip-on sandals, my pantaloons. I had drunk tea with nomads, saddled camels and ridden with them, slept beside them, picked out cram-cram with them, drawn water with them, milked goats and camels with them, hobbled, tracked and herded with them, gazed at the stars with them, laughed and sung and shared stories with them. Now it was time to do the one thing I couldn't do with nomads. It was time to go home and make my fire.

Postscript

POSTINDUSTRIAL SOCIETIES ARE STORMS OF DISTORTION: EVERYTHING IS AN image for something else. Clouds are virtual, blue sky is cognitive, camel toes are waxed. As for 'nomad', in postmodern terminology this can be anyone who defines themselves by their mobility. Travel websites and tour companies claim it; so do backpackers, jetsetters and tax-evading non-doms. 'Nomad' has become a byword for cool, spontaneous, trendy. But there is nothing cool about the nomads of North Africa, nothing spontaneous, nothing trendy.

This is why the Arabic word '*bedawi*' is more revealing: 'the beginning people'. Nomads remind us how so many people used to live, back in the days before the fixed-harness plough scarred the earth and towed our ancestors into the urban rat race. That doesn't make them unsophisticated rustics, nor Luddites shaking their goads against the prevailing wind. What it does suggest is a more horizontal interpretation of progress. A successful nomad doesn't need to climb up a greasy corporate pole, drown in bonuses and drive a fancy car. He just needs to grow his herd.

'Don't romanticise' goes the warning – which is easy enough. What is really hard is holding the earthy realities in parallel with the romance that drove you here in the first place. Many of the travellers who have engaged most profoundly with nomadic life were drawn by the romance of their setting. Throughout my journey, I tried to juggle this contradiction as best I could. I tried not to perceive the people I met as folkloric museum exhibits, to be studied through a viewfinder, nor as the bloodless statistics of development reports, but as people I could try and make friends with. In some cases I think I succeeded, though not in all. 'If a log floats in the water for a hundred years,' as the Songhay proverb goes, 'it doesn't become a crocodile.'

I warmed to many of the nomads I met, and often found them easier to befriend than the government agencies or cultivators with whom they clash; and if my responses were often subjective... well, why not let the wind blow back against its normal path? 'Administrators regard pastoral populations as sources of trouble,' points out anthropologist

Dawn Chatty, 'backward entities that stand in the way of rational progress.' This is precisely why we need them. They are an antidote to homogeny and the increasingly narrow boxes we build around ourselves. Not so much 'bad boys needing firm hands to straighten them out', in Dan Aronson's satirical phrase, but teachers who can help us understand our world a little better. Representing a way of life that has endured at least 150 times as long as any postindustrial society, not only do nomads link us to our own distant ancestors, they offer possible answers to the environmental troubles we have sown. Would a world more practically influenced by nomadism – by flexible land use, less mechanistic handling of livestock, a holistic appreciation of the relationship between human, animal and landscape – really be such a bad place?

Nomads don't live in isolation. The names they call themselves are stereotyped as celebrations of freedom, but they are often more complex. Some celebrate freedom, others denote class, colour, language, ancestry. While it is hard to draw precise conclusions, their names tend to express a position of relativism. An Amazigh is 'free' or 'noble' in contrast to the enslaved; a *beidane* is 'white' in contrast to the 'black'. These are communities that have developed in complex matrices of inter-relatedness. They are enmeshed among their sedentary neighbours, and they will continue to have to search for ways to live between them.

'Life for nomads has always been hard,' said Sandy Ag Mostapha, the Tuareg chief I met on my last trip to the desert. 'There are so many problems: hunger, bad health, animals dying.' The number of people able to see it through – by some combination of fortitude, discipline, willpower, sheer luck or opportunity – is dwindling steadily (in relative more than absolute terms), just as the number aware of other choices, eager to tread a different path from their ancestors, is growing. Freedom, increasingly, is not the only value nomads covet. I met many nomads who wanted to give up the lifestyle. But I also met nomads like Moishin, the Saharawi camel herder, who couldn't imagine enjoying another lifestyle so much, or Sandy, who vowed he would 'never leave it'.

These are the people who can benefit from the enduring relevance of their way of life. 'The best of men', as the Prophet Mohammed reportedly said, 'is the one who is most useful to his fellow men.' Long after the last quant has left the last of the multinational i-hubs, there will still be herders plying the pasture trails – as long as there are still areas of low rainfall, and hungry cities hankering for animal products. Pure nomadism may diminish, but pastoralism will survive and evolve, interacting with other sources of income, powered by the energy that is waiting to be unleashed across the Sahara.

For this is not a poor region. Its untapped potential is enormous, offering the possibility of future wealth as magnificent as the era of Mansa Musa, when caravans bobbed between the dunes with ostrich plumes and gold (and, of course, slaves – let us hope the future will be very different). Morocco is leading the way, with $9 billion invested in its national Solar Plan, U-shaped mirrors and turbines in place to convert thermal energy to steam. Given the limitless potential of solar technology (the sun bombards the earth with enough energy in a single hour to power all our needs for a year), this represents a thrilling key to future prosperity. What a beautiful irony it would be if that prosperity could be driven by the same mighty inferno that has been afflicting the region's vegetation, dehydrating the herds, drying up the wells and scalding the people for millennia. If it could empower a new generation of pastoralists, facilitating the spread of transport, climate-related information, new models of export. If the people who live in the desert were to become guardians of the resource that powers us all through the next millennium.

Although whether the oil and uranium believed to exist under the Sahara's shifting sands will strengthen the people, or clad the current conflicts in more layers of deadliness, remains to be seen. The recent management history of the region – not to mention the resource curse, which has struck so many African states before – is not exactly encouraging. Yet these myriad possibilities do underline the growing relevance of the Sahara region. What happens here can no longer be dismissed as a sandstorm in the middle of nowhere. Whether through the spread of terrorist networks (all the more alarming with the tightening of links between African and Middle Eastern groups), narco-trafficking, the potential boon of solar power or mass migration, Europe and the wider world are embroiled in the desert's fate. And nothing will affect that future more than the health of the Sahara's nomadic communities. For only if they are empowered and supported can jihadism and smuggling be flushed out; only with their cooperation can an effective, fair infrastructure for energy exploitation be installed; and only if they prosper will the crowds diminish in the city slums of West Africa and the ports on the Mediterranean coastline.

Of all the nomads I met on my travels, none summed up this fragile future more succinctly than Khadija Jai. She was the 86-year-old mother of my Fulani friend Boureima, and she had lived through it all – colonialism, revolutions, coups d'état. She grew up when the bush was still canopied by trees, the baobabs were generous with fruit, and lion hunts were common. Listening to Khadija was listening to an epic saga of devastation and heartache. She had lost plenty during her lifetime – children, cattle, most of her teeth. Even so, she hadn't lost hope. She sat there, in the doorway of her millet-stalk hut, a wise, wizened woman who used to dance naked in fields of lush grass, wistful for the past but optimistic for a future over which so many analysts have already drawn a funeral shroud.

'Life is better now,' she told me. 'We have more varieties of food, transport is faster, and we can receive news more quickly. If we work hard, we will have a good future. But if we don't, then it will be very difficult for us.'

For Khadija, it wasn't about the governments or the multinationals, the aid agencies or the NGOs. It was about the people themselves. Is that a romantic notion? Perhaps it is, but I am going to stick with it all the same. Because the world keeps turning and the sun keeps rising, the stars keep whirling and the wind keeps blowing, the animals keep moving and so do the people. It would be nice to think some of them might have a say in how it all pans out.

Glossary

alhamdulillah   'thanks be to God' (Arabic).

Almohads   twelfth-century Berber dynasty, which replaced the Almoravids as the dominant force in the Maghrib and placed a strong emphasis on religion.

Almoravids   eleventh-century Arabic-speaking tribe of Berber heritage, which Yusuf Bin Tafshin led to glory in Spain. Their capital was Marrakesh.

Amazighen   the name by which Berbers call themselves, which can be interpreted as 'nobles' or 'free people'.

amesh-shaghab   nomadic baggage carrier, designed to be easily installed on a camel.

asabiyyah   the concept of solidarity or 'tribal glue', which the fourteeth-century historian Ibn Khaldun cited as the chief source of tribal/nomadic power.

azalai   the seasonal salt caravan, traditionally conducted between Timbuktu and Taoudenni.

babouche   a goatskin slipper.

baraka   a divine blessing (Arabic).

barchans   a crescent-shaped sand dune, produced by a mono-directional wind.

bedawi   a nomad (Arabic), anglicised as Bedouin.

bidon   a small, usually plastic, portable container.

boubou   a three-piece costume worn by men in Mauritania and Western Sahara, comprising tie-up trousers, a long-sleeved shirt and a sleeveless gown (similar to the Arabic *dara'a*).

caid   title given to local chiefs and governors in Morocco, traditionally dispensed by the Sultan.

dara'a   see *boubou*.

djellaba   traditional Arabic men's robe.

djinn   a spirit in Islamic culture, traditionally nurtured by fire and capable of both good and evil behaviour.

Eid   a collective name for the two major Islamic holy days, Eid al-Adha and Eid al-Fitr.

faqih   a religious teacher (Arabic).

fonio   a wild grass of the digitaria species, containing small but nutritious grains.

garabout   a student in a Malian Quranic school.

gigilé   *Boscia senegalensis*, also known as hanza, a perennial bush whose fruit contains a sweet jelly that can be made into syrup. The bitter taste is not for everyone, but it does protect the plant from insects.

griot   a storyteller or entertainer, usually a member of a hereditary caste, charged with maintaining the oral history of a village or tribe.

gris-gris	a religious talisman, usually in the form of a prayer written on paper and bound in animal hide.
guerba	a water container made from a folded-out goatskin, tied with a cord at the neck, which can carry up to 30 litres of water.
hajj	the Islamic pilgrimage to Mecca (one who completes the pilgrimage is entitled to the honorific *hajji*).
hammada	the hard crust where the sun has made the desert surface solid.
Hassaniya	Arabic dialect, widespread in Northwest Africa, which was propagated by the Bani Hassan, one of the Arabian tribes that migrated to the Maghreb in the eleventh century.
imbar	an armature tent, built around a frame.
inedan	Tuareg blacksmith or artisan caste (*enad* is the singular).
jamaa	a gathering of tribal elders.
kasbah	a high-walled, fortified building or citadel (Arabic).
kataif	Arabic pastry, made with honey and cashew nuts, shaped like pancakes.
keef	marijuana (Moroccan).
khayma	an easily collapsible tent, with a central pole and pegs around the sides.
kilim	a flat carpet with interwoven warp and weft strands.
kora	a 21-stringed Malian instrument, somewhere between a harp and a lute, usually made from a calabash cut in half and covered with cowskin.
koubba	Arabic word originally denoting a tent of hides, now refers to a tomb covered by a dome (and is the origin of the English word alcove).
marabout	a religious teacher or Islamic scholar in West Africa.
medina	Arabic for 'city', used for old towns such as Fez and Marrakesh, to distinguish them from their modern conurbations.
mehari	a breed of white camels known for their height and speed.
melhfa	a Saharawi woman's gown, consisting of a 4-metre-long cloth.
mithqal	a gold coin, or the equivalent of 4.25 grams of gold.
moussem	an Islamic holy day, in honour of a particular holy figure.
niqab	a woman's face veil, which leaves a horizontal band clear around the eyes.
ouguiya	the currency in Mauritania.
pinasse	a motorised longboat, usually with an open deck.
pirogue	a punt-operated narrow canoe, made from a single tree trunk.
qasida	an Arabic ode.
riad	a traditional Moroccan house with an interior courtyard.
sadriya	a knife used for smoothing animal hides in the tanning process.
Sahel	the transitional zone between the true desert (Sahara) to the north and the more vegetative Savannah and forests to the south.
sahib dukkan	shop master (Arabic).
shahada	Islamic declaration of faith – 'There is no God but God and Mohammed is his prophet.'

shariah	traditional Islamic law, gleaned from the Quran, the *hadith* (words and deeds of the Prophet, as established after his death by his followers and Islamic scholars) and centuries of debate.
sura	a chapter of the Quran (the individual verses are *ayat*).
tagine	traditional Berber dish, steam cooked in an earthenware pot.
Tamazight	the family of Berber languages.
tamelgoust	a Tuareg man's headscarf, traditionally 5 metres long and made of indigo-dyed cotton, although these days it is often made from cheaper rayon.
tidinit	a Moorish lute.
Tifinagh	the written script of Tamazight (the language of the Berbers, or Amazighen).
toguna	a meeting place for Dogon elders, traditionally built with a low roof so none of the elders can stand up in anger.
toh	a thick porridge made from pounded millet, which is a staple among the Fulani.
wadi	a valley or dry riverbed (Arabic).
yardang	a rocky protuberance, carved by wind abrasion and turbulence.
zawiya	an Islamic shrine. The word can also be used for a Sufi monastery.

Notes

Page x   'Africa, which country I have': Leo Africanus, *The Description of Africa and the Things Therein Contained*, Vol.3, p.971. (The translation was made by John Pory in 1600, but I have adapted the spelling to modern usage for the sake of clarity.)

'Before the coming of the red sun': Hawad, *Le coude grinçant de l'anarchie* (Anarchy's Delirious Trek), translated by George M Guyelberger & Christopher Wise, quoted in C Wise (ed.), *The Desert Shore: Literatures of the Sahel*, Vol.3, p.113.

Prologue

Page 2   'addicted to feasting': Leo Africanus, *The History and Description of Africa*, p.464.

'burn in lust': *ibid.*, p.458.

Page 4   'Pastoral peoples of Africa': Aggrey Ayuen Majok & Calvin W Schwabe, *Development among Africa's Migratory Pastoralists*, p.6.

Page 5   'progressive desiccation': discussed in James Webb, *Desert Frontier*; also Jeremy Keenan, *The Sahara: The Past, Present and Future*, and Bruce S Hall, *History of Race in Muslim West Africa*.

Page 6   'attached themselves to the country': Ibn Khaldun, *Muqaddimah*, Vol.1, p.305.

Page 7   'It is their nature to plunder': *ibid.*, Vol.1, p.303.

'closer to the first natural state': *ibid.*, Vol.1, p.254.

'death in life': TE Lawrence, *Seven Pillars of Wisdom*, p.29.

'the Tragedy of the Commons has underpinned': Katherine Homewood, *Ecology of African Pastoralist Societies*, pp.5–6.

Part One

Page 8   'Wide Afric, doth thy sun': Alfred Tennyson, *Major Works*, p.4.

Page 9   'Howbeit there is a most stately temple': Leo Africanus, *Description of Africa*, Vol.3, p.824.

Page 10   'a mythical city in a Never-Never land': Bruce Chatwin, *Anatomy of Restlessness*, p.27.

'the richest Mynes of Gold': Samuel Purchas, *Purchas His Pilgrimes*, p.75.

'until the discovery of America': Nehemiah Levtzion in JF Ade Ajayi & M Crowder (eds), *The History of West Africa*, p.141.

Page 11   Details of Mansa Musa's pilgrimage are from Hunwick, *Timbuktu and the Songhay Empire*, p.9.

'This negro lord is called Musa Malli, lord of the negroes of Guinea': quoted by E.W. Bovill, *The Golden Trade of the Moors*, p. 90.

Page 12   'a tyrant, a miscreant, an aggressor, a despot, and a butcher': As-Sadi, quoted in Hunwick, *Timbuktu and the Songhay Empire*, p.91.

Page 13   'such as drinking fermented liquors': As-Sadi, *ibid.*, p.194.

'Jawdar's troops broke the army of the askiya': As-Sadi, *ibid.*, p.190.

Page 16   'the true meaning of Touareg': Jacques Hureiki, *Essai sur les origins des Touaregs*, p.69.

'to raid' or 'plunder': Jeremy Keenan, *Lesser Gods of the Sahara*, p.63.

'a dry and barren tract': Leo Africanus, *Description of Africa*, Vol.1, pp.155–6.

Page 17   'many acts of gross injustice and tyranny': *ibid.*, p.33.

'most cruel depredations and exactions': René Caillié, *Travels through Central Africa to Timbuctoo*, p.65.

'one of those sinister pirates of the desert': Louis Frèrejean, *Objectif*, p.244, quoted in Hall, *History of Race in Muslim West Africa*, pp.136–7.

Page 18   'Considering that we will never succeed in making friends with these tribes': Aoudéoud, Commander of the French Soudan, to the Commander of Timbuktu, 13 September 1898, quoted in James McDougall & Judith Scheele, *Saharan Frontiers*, p.135.

'They are barbarians': Masqueray, quoted in Henry, *Touaregs des Français*, p.260, cited in Hall, *History of Race in Muslim West Africa*, pp.127–8.

'When I imagine their wandering life': Lieutenant de Vaisseau Hourst, *Mission Hourst*, pp.235–6, quoted in *History of Race in Muslim West Africa*, p.129.

Page 19   'cultures babylonienne': Hureiki, *Essai sur les origins des Touaregs*, p.671.

'nomads of the white race': Amouksou ag Azandeher, quoted in Baz Lecocq, 'That desert is our country', p.134.

Page 20   'Know that the Tuareg race was entirely self-reliant': letter from Muhammed 'Ali Ag Attaher to President Charles de Gaulle. Attached in a letter from the Cercle de Goundam to the Ministère de l'Interieur, 22 December 1959, quoted in Hall *History of Race in Muslim West Africa*, p.308.

Page 20   'nomad society, as it is left to us by the colonial regime': Bakary Diallo, quoted in Lecocq, 'That desert is our country', p.74.

Page 22   'Let us drive the nomads back into the sands': La Voix du Nord, reported by Hélène Claudot-Hawad in 'Touaregs au Mali: Negrafricanisme et racisme'.

Page 23   'rescue my name from oblivion': Alexander Gordon Laing, *Missions to the Niger* (ed. EW Bovill), p.286.

'the great emporium for all the country of the blacks': Shabeeny, in James Grey Jackson (ed.), *An Account of Timbuctoo and Housa*, p.20.

Page 24   'five sabre cuts on the crown of my head': Laing, *Missions to the Niger* p.302.

'situation in Tinbuctu': *ibid.*, p.312.

'ordered his negroes': *ibid.*, p.313.

'the houses whereof are covered only with gold': Jobson, quoted in Anthony Sattin, *The Gates of Africa*, p.9.

Page 26   'its wholesale value on arrival in Europe would exceed': Report by United Nations Overseas Development Commission (www.unodc.org/toc/en/reports/TOCTAWestAfrica.html).

Page 30   'I have a compulsion to wander': Chatwin, *Anatomy of Restlessness*, p.76.
Page 31   'apocalyptic sentiment': Anja Fischer & Ines Kohl, *Tuareg Society within a Globalized World*, p.13.
Page 34   'that I might present a proper silhouette': Lawrence, *Seven Pillars of Wisdom*, p.8.
Page 36   'This is a great island': al-Idrisi, quoted in Bernard Lewis, *The Muslim Discovery of Europe*, p.147.

Part Two
Page 38   'the goal of civilization': Ibn Khaldun, *Muqaddimah*, Vol.2, p.296.
Page 41   'enchanted labyrinth': Paul Bowles, *The Spider's House*, p.168.
Page 43   'a world it is to see': Leo Africanus, *Description of Africa*, Vol.2, p.419.
           'a wooden cage': *ibid.*, p.450.
           'in life he had been all undoubting impulse': WB Yeats, quoted in Margaret Harper Mills & Warwick Gould (eds), *Yeats' Mask*, p.302.
Page 44   'wily bird so indued by nature': Leo Africanus, *Description of Africa*, Vol.1, p.189.
           'From beyond the hils Atlas maior': George Abbot, *A Briefe Description of the Whole Worlde*, Folio F, 2 recto, quoted in Eldred Jones, *Othello's Countrymen*, p.20.
           'geographers and cartographers remained dependent': Bovill, *The Golden Trade of the Moors*, p.142.
Page 45   'frantic and distraught persons': Leo Africanus, *Description of Africa*, Vol.2, p.426.
           'nothing as fundamental or dramatic': Jones, *Othello's Countrymen*, p.26.
Page 47   'that make sword-scabbards': Leo Africanus, *Description of Africa*, Vol.2, p.431.
Page 51   'should sound like the bleating of a sheep': Peter Mayne, *A Year in Marrakesh*, p.33.
Page 54   'fall laughing': Leo Africanus, *Description of Africa*, Vol.3, p.722.
           'Sedentary people are much concerned': Ibn Khaldun, *Muqaddimah*, Vol.1, p.252.
Page 55   'commit unlawful veneries among themselves': Leo Africanus, *Description of Africa*, Vol. 1, p.148.
           'from the twentieth hour': *ibid.*, Vol.2, p.472.
           'to describe things so plainly': *ibid.*, Vol.1, p.188.
           'houses are very loathsome': *ibid.*, Vol.2, pp.323–4.
           'greater quantity of cloth': *ibid.*, Vol.1, p.158.
Page 58   'Their meat will not reach Allah': Quran, Surah 22, Verse 37.
Page 59   'is bound upon a rude altar': Saint Nilus, quoted in Robert Irwin, *Camel*, p.69.
           'pass through a cold hall': Leo Africanus, *Description of Africa*, Vol.2, pp.426–7.
Page 61   'keeping of doves': *ibid.*, p.454.
Page 65   'disobedient and ill-tempered': John Ruskin, *The Bible of Amiens*, Vol. 4, p.41.

'no animal is more stolid': Jonathan Raban, *Arabia through the Looking Glass*, p.160.

'They put me in mind of elderly English ladies taking tea together': Elias Canetti, *The Voices of Marrakesh*, p.11.

Page 65   'gentle and domesticall beasts': Leo Africanus, *Description of Africa*, Vol.3, p.939.

'What a masterpiece of nature's workmanship': Caillié, *Travels through Central Africa*, Vol.2, p.115.

Page 70   'Once the North African nomads became acquainted': Nehemiah Levtzion, in Ajayi & Crowder (eds), *The History of West Africa*, p.121.

'a habitable, controllable region': Labelle Prussin, *African Nomadic Architecture*, p.13.

Part Three

Page 69   'You shall find many among the Africans': Leo Africanus, *Description of Africa*, Vol.1, p.161.

Page 70   'the African tongue soundeth': Leo Africanus, *Description of Africa*, Vol.1, p.129.

Page 71   'The conquest of Africa is impossible': Abd al-Malik Ibn Marwan, writing to the Caliph, quoted in HT Norris, *The Berbers in Arabic Literature*, p.52.

'The Arabs search for towns': quoted in *ibid.*

'he has created and formulated a philosophy of history': Arnold Toynbee, *A Study of History*, Vol. 3, pp.321–2.

Page 72   'base and witless people': Leo Africanus, *Description of Africa*, Vol. 2, p.276.

Page 74   'The past resembles the future': Ibn Khaldun, *A History of the Berbers*, Vol.1, p.17.

'After the preaching of Islam': *ibid.*, Vol.1, p.28.

Page 75   'a Berber reserve': Jacques Berque, quoted in Jonathan Wyrtzen, in Driss Maghraoui (ed.), *Revisiting the Colonial Past in Morocco*.

'The result was financial ruin': John Shoup, in Dawn Chatty (ed.), *Nomadic Societies in the Middle East and North Africa Entering the 21st Century*, p.130.

Page 76   'became more and more integrated into a larger national entity': quoted in Jonathan Wyrtzen, *Making Morocco*.

Page 90   'Decision making power': Shoup, in Chatty, *Nomadic Societies in the Middle East and North Africa*, p.135.

Page 95   'The ground is all memoranda': Ralph Waldo Emerson, *The Complete Prose Works*, p.141.

'though without a compass': Caillié, *Travels through Central Africa*, Vol.2, p.91.

Page 96   'translucet, luminous, pure': Ibn Tufail, *Hayy Ibn Yaqdhan*, p.5.

Part Four

Page 97   'The lion slumbers in his lair': Felicia Hemans, *The Poetical Works of Mrs Felicia Hemans*, p.492.

Page 98   'I came not to this country': Yusuf Ibn Tafshin, quoted in Ronald A Messier *The Almoravids and the Meaning of Jihad*, p.84.

Page 99   'He girded himself': Qirtas, quoted in Charles André Julien, *History of North Africa*, p.82.

           'Indeed, we may say': Ibn Khaldun, *Muqaddimah*, Vol.2, p.296.

Page 101   'I have heard that in old time': Leo Africanus, *Description of Africa*, Vol. 2, p.268.

Page 103   'torrid zone... where the sun's orbit is': Pliny, *Natural History*, p.114.

Page 104   'a Moorman from Inner Marocco': *The Arabian Nights*, eds Malcolm C Lyons Ursula Lyons, p.281.

Page 105   'All I understood': Yusuf Ibn Tafshin, quoted in Messier, *The Almoravids and the Meanings of Jihad*, p.107.

           'Camels have again become': Mohamed Oudada, in McDougall & Scheele (eds), *Saharan Frontiers*, p.217.

           'they take great delight in poetry': Leo Africanus, *Description of Africa*, Vol.1, p.158.

           'and being as then but fifteen years': *ibid.*, Vol.1.

Page 110   'They have neither dominion nor yet any stipend': Leo Africanus, *Description of Africa*, Vol.1, p.146.

Page 111   'the court has not found legal ties of such nature': Summary Opinion of Advisory Court of International Court of Justice, 16 October 1975, www.icj-cij.org.

Page 116   'The Arab Spring': Noam Chomsky, speaking at Gaza's Almathaf Restaurant and Cultural House, reported by the Electronic Intifada, 22 October 2012, www.electronicintifada.net.

Page 118   'There is an immense desert': quoted in Tony Hodges, *Western Sahara*, p.28.

Page 125   'death in life': Lawrence, *Seven Pillars of Wisdom*, p.29.

Page 130   'water containing some pounded millet': Ibn Battuta, *Travels in Asia and Africa*, p.333.

Part Five

Page 132   'Wherein I spake': Shakespeare, *Othello*, Act 1, Scene 3.

Page 134   'the word Faraca': Leo Africanus, *Description of Africa*, Vol.1, p.122.

Page 136   'you get into those waggons called railway coaches': letter to Frank Budgen, July 1920, *Selected Letters of James Joyce*, p.267.

Page 140   'obnoxia Mauris': Calpurnius Siculus, *Eclogues*, 4.40–41.

           'honourable murderer': William Shakespeare, *Othello*, Act 5, Scene 2.

           'black in his look': George Peele, *The Battle of Alcazar*, Act 1, Prologue, l.16; *The Stukeley Plays*, p.64.

           'We have still': Lois Whitney, 'Did Shakespeare know Leo Africanus?', p.473.

Page 141   'by reason of jealousy': Leo Africanus, *Description of Africa*, Vol.1, p.154.

           'steadfast in friendship': *ibid.*

Page 144   'You know that the cause of enslavement': Ahmed Baba, quoted in Hall, *History of Race in Muslim West Africa*, p.53.

Page 145   'Exhausted by their sufferings': Caillié, *Travels through Central Africa*, Vol.2, p.114.

Page 149   'Though I had been accustomed': *ibid.*, Vol.2, p.26.

Page 154   'for supper they have certain dried flesh': Leo Africanus, *Description of Africa*, Vol.1, p.152.
           'the dues of hospitality': Lyons & Lyons (eds), *The Arabian Nights*, Night 281.

Page 158   'The African king landed': in HT Norris (ed.), *The Pilgrimage of Ahmad Son of the Little Bird of Paradise*, p.102.

Page 158   'There is nothing I love better than books': *ibid.*

Page 161   'Is there scholarship in your land?' *ibid.*, p.8.
           'We have taken the back of she-camels': Mohammed Wuld Buna, quoted in Graziani Krätli & Ghislaine Lydon (eds), *The Trans-Saharan Book Trade*, p.41.
           'It happens that the mimiya ode': *ibid.*, p.29.

Page 162   'Long, long ago, during the prehistoric ages': Lloyd Cabot Briggs, *Tribes of the Sahara*, p.34.

Page 164   'slumped to 6%': these statistics are supplied in the 2000 General Population and Housing Census in Mauritania: *Specific characteristics of the nomadic environment*, www.unstats.un.org.
           'a colony of barnacles': Norris, *The Pilgrimage of Ahmad*, p.xv.

Page 168   Elliot Fratkin, in Andy Catley, Jeremy Lind & Ian Scoones (eds), *Pastoralism and Development in Africa*, pp.203–5.
           'scientific speculation': Ibn Tufail, *Hayy Ibn Yaqdhan*, p.6.
           'are like irrational animals': *ibid.*, p.13.
           'previous sublime station': *ibid.*, p.13.
           'natural curiosity': *ibid.*, p.15.
           'It should be known': Ibn Khaldun, *Muqaddimah*, Vol.3, p.281.

Page 169   'There's more truth about a camp': Roger Deakin, *Wildwood*, p.15.

Part Six

Page 171   'The great affair is to move': Robert Louis Stevenson, *Travels with a Donkey in the Cévennes*, pp.68–9.

Page 180   'as broad as the Thames at Westminster': Mungo Park, *Travels in the Interior Districts of Africa*, pp.178–9.
           'said to be very comfortable and preservative': Leo Africanus, *Description of Africa*, Vol.3, p.971.

Page 188   5.08% rate of annual urbanization: this data covers 2010–15 and is cited in the *CIA World Factbook*, www.cia.gov.

Page 190   'They go to distant places': Caillié, *Travels through Central Africa*, Vol.1, p.349.

Page 191   'Jenne in her island has remained': Félix Dubois, *Timbuctoo the Mysterious*, p.148.

Page 192 'This place exceedingly aboundeth': Leo Africanus, *Description of Africa*, Vol. 3, p.822.

'the reason why caravans come to Timbuktu': As-Sadi, quoted in Hunwick, *Timbuktu and the Songhay Empire*, p.18.

'an hysterical mass': Félix Dubois, *Nôtre Beau Niger*, p.189.

Page 193 'dancers sauntered about': Dubois, *Timbuctoo the Mysterious*, p.159.

Page 197 'by the light of a great fire': Caillié, *Travels through Central Africa*, Vol 1, p.60.

Page 198 'a few charges of gunpowder': *ibid.*, Vol.1, p.259.

Page 200 'many are found lying dead': Leo Africanus, *Description of Africa*, Vol.3, p.798.

Part Seven

Page 202 'In the Maghreb': Gautier, *Le Passé de l'Afrique du Nord*, pp.279–80.

Page 204 'stripped me quite naked': Park, *Travels in the Interior Districts of Africa*, p.224.

'destroying the little commerce': Heinrich Barth, *Travels and Discoveries in North and Central Africa*, p.329.

Page 205 'The most dramatic political development': Hall, *History of Race in Muslim West Africa*, p.31.

'It subjected everybody': Victor Azarya, Anneke Breedveld, Mirjam de Bruijn & Han Van Dijk (eds), *Pastoralists under Pressure*, p.246.

Page 215 'The problem with the agricultural communities': AA Batran, in Ajayi & Crowder (eds), *The History of West Africa*.

'the creed of private property': Charles Grémont, in McDougall & Scheele (eds), *Saharan Frontiers*, p.138.

'State institutions clearly considered': *ibid.*, p.136.

Page 216 'constitute the chief wealth': Park, *Travels in the Interior Districts of Africa*, p.55.

Page 223 'If a woman's reproductive potential': Prussin, *African Nomadic Architecture*, p.205.

Page 225 'They display great skill': Park, *Travels in the Interior Districts of Africa*, p.54.

Page 229 'Therein is the tragedy': Garrett Hardin, *The Tragedy of the Commons*, quoted in Majok & Schwabe (eds), *Development among Africa's Migratory Pastoralists*, p.6.

Part Eight

Page 236 'The land of Negros': Leo Africanus, *Description of Africa*, Vol.1, p.174.

Page 238 'The Bozo fishing people': Homewood, *Ecology of African Pastoralist Societies*, p.22.

Page 247 'multitudes of ... water-birds': Caillié, *Travels through Central Africa*, Vol.2, p.15.

Page 250 'This land of Negros': Leo Africanus, *Description of Africa*, Vol.1, pp.124–5.

'a blunder of almost incredible magnitude': Bovill, *The Golden Trade of the Moors*, p.152.

Part Nine

Page 271 'Welcome to the world's largest prison': Belkacem Zaoudi, cited on www.361security.com.

Page 272 'Nothing so cruel had ever happened: Ahmed Baba quoted in Christopher Wise, 'Plundering Mali'.

'a descendant of the Prophet': from *The Account of the Anonymous Spaniard*, quoted in Hunwick, *Timbuktu and the Songhay Empire*, p.322.

Page 273 'stately temple' etc.: Leo Africanus, *Description of Africa*, Vol.3, p.824.

'His scouting trips to the ancient land of Songhay': Christopher Wise, 'Plundering Mali'.

Page 276 'repositories of goods and even libraries': Tarikh al-Fattash, in John O Hunwick & Alida Jay Boye, *Hidden Treasures of Timbuktu*, p.83.

Page 279 'Slavery is an age-old institution': Hall, *History of Race in Muslim West Africa*, p.211.

Page 280 'they keep great store of men and women slaves': Leo Africanus, *Description of Africa*, Vol. 3, p.825.

Page 285 'spend a great part of the night in singing': *ibid.*, p.825.

Page 290 On extra-judicial killings by the Malian army, see www.hrw.org/africa/mali and www.amnesty.org/en/region/mali.

Page 292 'Not only their practices but their desires': Majok & Schwabe, *Development among Africa's Migratory Pastoralists*, p.247.

Page 299 'that I may promote': Leo Africanus, *Description of Africa*, Vol.3, p.905.

Page 300 'Administrators regard pastoral populations': Chatty, in Philip Carl Salzman, *When Nomads Settle*, p.80.

Page 301 'bad boys needing firm hands': Dan Aronson, in *ibid.*, p.173.

'The best of men': quoted in Amin Maalouf, *Disordered World*, p.17.

Bibliography

Ade Ajayi, JF & Crowder, Michael (eds), *History of West Africa* (London: Longman, 1971).

Al-Koni, Ibrahim, *Gold Dust* (London: Arabia, 2008).

Arberry, AJ, *Moorish Poetry: A Translation of the Pennants: An Anthology compiled in 1243 by the Andalusian Ibn Sa'id* (Cambridge: Cambridge University Press, 1953).

Azarya, Victor, Breedveld, Anneke, de Bruijn, Mirjam & van Dijk, Han, *Pastoralists under Pressure? Fulbe Societies Confronting Change in West Africa* (Leiden: Brill, 1999).

Barfield, Thomas, *The Nomadic Alternative* (London: Prentice Hall, 1993).

Barth, Heinrich, *Travels and Discoveries in North and Central Africa* (London: Longman, 1857–58).

Benanav, Michael, *Men of Salt* (Guilford, CT: Lyons Press, 2006).

Besenyo, Janos, *Western Sahara* (Pécs: Publikon, 2009).

Bovill, EW, *The Golden Trade of the Moors* (London: Oxford University Press, 1968).

Bovill, EW (ed.), *Missions to the Niger* (Cambridge: Cambridge University Press, 1964).

Bowles, Paul, *Collected Stories* (Santa Barbara, CA: Black Sparrow Press, 1979).

Bowles, Paul, *The Spider's House* (London: Peter Owen, 1985).

Brett, Michael & Fentress, Elizabeth, *The Berbers* (Oxford: Blackwell, 1996).

Briggs, Lloyd Cabot, *Tribes of the Sahara* (Oxford: Oxford University Press, 1960).

Brown, Robert (ed.), *The History and Description of Africa and of the Notable Things Therein Contained by Leo Africanus* (New York: Cambridge University Press, 2010).

Bulliet, Richard W, *The Camel and the Wheel* (Cambridge, MA: Harvard University Press, 1975).

Caillié, Réné, *Travels through Central Africa to Timbuctoo; and Across the Great Desert, to Morocco, Performed in the Years 1824–1828* (London: Darf, 1992).

Calpurnius, Siculus, *Eclogues*, trans. EJL Scott (London: G. Bell, 1890).

Campbell, Dugald, *On the Trail of the Veiled Tuareg* (London: Seeley, Service, 1928).

Canetti, Elias, *The Voices of Marrakesh*, trans. JA Underwood (London: Penguin, 2012).

Catley, Andy, Lind, Jeremy & Scoones, Ian, *Pastoralism and Development in Africa* (London: Routledge, 2013).

Chatty, Dawn (ed.), *Nomadic Societies in the Middle East and North Africa Entering the 21st Century* (Leiden: Brill, 2006).

Chatwin, Bruce (ed. Jan Borm & Matthew Graves), *Anatomy of Restlessness: Uncollected Writings* (London: Cape, 1996).

Chatwin, Jonathan Michael, *'Anywhere out of the World': Restlessness in the Work of Bruce Chatwin* (Exeter: University of Exeter Press, 2008).

Claudot-Hawad, Hélène, 'Touaregs au Mali: Negrafricanisme et racisme', *Le Monde Diplomatique* (April 1995).

Dale, Stephen Frederic, *The Orange Trees of Marrakesh: Ibn Khaldun and the Science of Man* (Cambridge, MA: Harvard University Press, 2015).

Davidson, Robyn, *Tracks* (London: Picador, 1980).

Deakin, Roger, *Wildwood: A Journey through Trees* (London: Hamish Hamilton, 2007).

De Villiers, Marc & Hirtle, Sheila, *Timbuktu: The Sahara's Fabled City of Gold* (New York: Walker, 2007).

Diamond, Jared, *Guns, Germs and Steel: A Short History of Everybody for the Last 13,000 Years* (London: Vintage, 1997).

Diamond, Jared, *The World Until Yesterday: What Can We Learn from Traditional Societies?* (London: Allen Lane, 2012).

Dubois, Félix, *Timbuctoo the Mysterious*, trans. D White (London: W. Heinemann, 1897).

Dubois, Félix, *Notre Beau Niger* (Paris: E. Flammarion, 1911).

Emerson, Ralph Waldo, *The Complete Prose Works of Ralph Waldo Emerson* (Glasgow: Grand Colosseum Warehouse, 1895).

Fischer, Anja & Kohl, Ines, *Tuareg Society within a Globalized World* (London: Tauris Academic Studies, 2010).

Fukuyama, Francis, *The Origins of Political Order: From Prehuman Times to the French Revolution* (London: Profile, 2012).

Fukuyama, Francis, *Political Order and Political Decay: From the Industrial Revolution to the Globalization of Democracy* (London: Profile, 2014).

Gautier, EF, *Le Passé de l'Afrique du Nord* (Paris: Payot, 1942).

Gibbal, Jean-Marie, *Genii of the River Niger*, trans. Beth G Raps (Chicago, IL: University of Chicago Press, 1994).

Glantz, Michael H (ed.), *The Politics of Natural Disaster: The Case of the Sahel Drought* (London: Praeger, 1976).

Gordon, Murray, *Slavery in the Arab World* (New York: New Amsterdam, 1989).

Griffiths, Jay, *Wild: An Elemental Journey* (London: Penguin, 2006).

Hall, Bruce S, *History of Race in Muslim West Africa, 1600–1960* (Cambridge: Cambridge University Press, 2011).

Hare, John, *Shadows across the Sahara: Travels with Camels from Lake Chad to Tripoli* (London: Constable, 2003).

Harmon, Stephen A, *Terror and Insurgency in the Sahara-Sahel Region: Corruption, Contraband, Jihad and the Mali War of 2012–2013* (Ashgate, 2014).

Hemans, Felicia, *The Poetical Works of Mrs Felicia Hemans* (Philadelphia, PA: Grigg & Elliot, 1841).

Hennessy, Oliver, Talking with the dead: Leo Africanus, esoteric Yeats and early modern imperialism, *ELH: A Journal of English Literary History*, 71(4), 2004.

Hodges, Tony, *Western Sahara: Roots of a Desert War* (Westport, CT: Lawrence Hill, 1983).

Homewood, Katherine, *Ecology of African Pastoralist Societies* (Athens, OH: Ohio University Press, 2009).

Hudson, Peter, *Travels in Mauritania* (London: Flamingo, 1990).

Hunwick, John, *Timbuktu and the Songhay Empire* (Leiden: Brill, 1999).

Hunwick, John O & Boye, Alida Jay, *Hidden Treasures of Timbuktu: Historic City of Islamic Africa* (London: Thames and Hudson, 2008).

Hureiki, Jacques, *Essai sue les origines des Touaregs* (Paris: Karthala Editions, 2003).

Ibn Battuta, *Travels in Asia and Africa: 1325–1354*, trans. HAR Gibb (London: Routledge & Kegan Paul, 1929).

Ibn Khaldun, *Histoire des Berberes et des Dynasties Mussulmanes de l'Afrique Septentrionale*, translated by M. Le Baron de Slane (Alger, Imprimerie du Gouvernement, 1852).

Ibn Khaldun, *The Muqaddimah: An Introduction to History*, trans. Franz Rosenthal (London: Routledge & Kegan Paul, 1958).

Ibn Tufail, *Hayy Ibn Yaqdhan*, trans. George N Atiyeh (New York: Cornell University Press, 1963).

Ibn Warraq, *What the Koran Really Says: Language, Text and Commentary* (Amherst, NY: Prometheus, 2002).

Irwin, Robert, *For Lust of Knowing: The Orientalists and Their Enemies* (London: Allen Lane, 2006).

Irwin, Robert, *Camel* (London: Reaktion, 2010).

Jacobs, Michael, *In the Glow of the Phantom Palace: Travels from Granada to Timbuktu* (London: Pallas Athene, 2000).

Jackson, James Grey (ed.), *An Account of Timbuctoo and Housa* (London: Frank Cass, 1967).

Jayyusi, Salma Khadra (ed.), *Legacy of Muslim Spain* (Leiden: Brill, 1992).

Jones, Eldred, *Othello's Countrymen: The African in English Renaissance Drama* (London: Oxford University Press, 1965).

Julien, Charles André, *History of North Africa: Tunisia, Algeria, Morocco, from the Arab Conquest to 1830*, trans. John Petrie (London: Routledge & Kegan Paul, 1970).

Keenan, Jeremy, *Sahara Man: Travelling with the Tuareg* (London: John Murray, 2001).

Keenan, Jeremy, *Lesser Gods of the Sahara: Social Change and Contested Terrain amongst the Tuareg of Algeria* (London: Frank Cass, 2004).

Keenan, Jeremy, *The Sahara: The Past, Present and Future* (London: Routledge, 2007).

Kennan, Jeremy, *The Dark Sahara: America's War on Terror in Africa* (London: Pluto Press, 2009).

Keenan, Jeremy, *The Dying Sahara: US Imperialism and Terror in Africa* (London: Pluto Press, 2013).

Khazanov, Anatoly M & Wink, Andre (eds), *Nomads in the Sedentary World* (Richmond, VA: Curzon, 2001).

Krätli, Graziani & Lydon, Ghislaine (eds), *The Trans-Saharan Book Trade: Manuscript Culture, Arabic Literacy, and Intellectual History in Muslim Africa* (Leiden: Brill, 2011).

Kuper, Hilda (ed.), *Urbanization and Migration in West Africa* (Berkeley, CA: University of California Press, 1965).

Lacoste, Yves, *Ibn Khaldun: The Birth of History and the Past of the Third World* (London: Verso, 1984).

Lawrence, TE, *Seven Pillars of Wisdom* (London: Vintage, 2008).

Leante Chacon, Luis R, *See How Much I Love You* (London: Marion Boyars, 2009).

Lecocq, Baz, 'That desert is our country': Tuareg rebellions and competing nationalisms in contemporary Mali (1946–1996), PhD thesis (University of Ghent, 2002).

Lecocq, Baz, *Disputed Desert Decolonization, Competing Nationalisms and Tuareg Rebellions in Northern Mali* (Leiden: Brill, 2010).

Lewis, Bernard, *The Muslim Discovery of Europe* (London: Phoenix, 2000).

Lopez, Barry, *Desert Notes: Reflections in the Eye of Raven* (Kansas, MO: Sheed, Andrews & McMeel, 1976).

Lyons, Malcolm C. & Lyons, Ursula (trans.), *The Arabian Nights: Tales of 1001 Nights* (London: Penguin, 2010).

Maalouf, Amin, *Leo the African*, trans. Peter Sluglett (London: Quarter, 1988).

Maalouf, Amin, *Disordered World*, trans. George Miller (London: Bloomsbury, 2011).

Mackintosh-Smith, Tim, *Travels with a Tangerine: A Journey in the Footnotes of Ibn Battuta* (London: John Murray, 2001).

Maghraoui, Driss (ed.), *Revisiting the Colonial Past in Morocco* (London: Routledge, 2003).

Majok, Aggrey Ayuen & Schwabe, Calvin W, *Development among Africa's Migratory Pastoralists* (Westport, CT: Bergin & Garvey, 1996).

Malick Ndiaye, Tafsir, Illegal, unreported and unregulated fishing: Responses in general and in West Africa, *Chinese Journal of International Law*, 10(2), 2011.

Massonen, Pekka, *The Negroland Revisited: Discovery and Invention of the Sudanese Middle Ages* (Helsinki: Finnish Academy of Science and Letters, 2000).

Maxwell, Gavin, *Lords of the Atlas: The Rise and Fall of the House of Glaoua* (London: Century, 1966).

Mayne, Peter, *A Year in Marrakesh* (London: Eland, 1953).

McDougall, James & Scheele, Judith, *Saharan Frontiers: Space and Mobility in Northwest Africa* (Bloomington, IN: Indiana University Press, 2012).

Meakin, James Edward Budgett, *The Land of the Moors: A Comprehensive Description* (London: Swann Sonnenschein, 1901).

Messier, Ronald A., *The Almoravids and the Meaning of Jihad* (Santa Barbara, CA: Praeger, 2010).

Mills Harper, Margaret & Gould, Warwick (eds), *Yeats' Mask: Yeats Annual No. 19* (Cambridge: Open Book Publishers, 2013).

Monod, Theodor, *Les Déserts* (Paris: Horizons de France, 1973).

Moorhouse, Geoffrey, *The Fearful Void* (London: Hodder and Stoughton, 1974).

Morgan, Andy, *Music and Culture in Mali* (Copenhagen: Freemuse, 2013).

Napoleoni, Loretta, *Rogue Economics* (New York: Seven Stories, 2009).

Nicolaisen, Johannes & Nicolaisen, Ida, *The Pastoral Tuareg: Ecology, Culture and Society* (London: Thames and Hudson, 1997).

Norris, HT (ed. and trans.), *The Pilgrimage of Ahmad Son of the Little Bird of Paradise* (Warminster: Aris and Phillips, 1977).

Norris, HT, *The Berbers in Arabic Literature* (London: Longman, 1982).

Olson, James S, *The Peoples of Africa: An Ethnohistorican Dictionary* (London: Greenwood Press, 1996).

Ould Elhajje, Salim, *Tombouctou & Tombouctou II: Connaissance* (Louvain-la-Neuve: Éditions Panubula, 2010, 2011).

Park, Mungo, *Travels in the Interior Districts of Africa* (Ware: Wordsworth, 2002).

Porch, Douglas, *The Conquest of the Sahara* (Oxford: Oxford University Press, 1984).

Potts, Deborah, *Whatever Happened to Africa's Rapid Urbanisation?* (London: Africa Research Institute, 2012).

Prussin, Labelle, *African Nomadic Architecture: Space, Place and Gender* (Washington, DC: Smithsonian Institution Press and National Museum of African Art, 1995).

Purchas, Samuel, *Purchas His Pilgrimes* (Cambridge: Cambridge University Press, 2014).

Raban, Jonathan, *Arabia through the Looking Glass* (London: William Collins, 1979).

Raine, Craig, *A Martian Sends a Postcard Home* (Oxford: Oxford University Press, 1979).

Rogerson, Barnaby, *A Travellers' History of North Africa* (London: Duckworth Overlook, 2008).

Ruskin, John, *The Bible of Amiens* (Orpington: George Allen, 1884).

Salzman, Philip Carl, *When Nomads Settle: Processes of Sedentarization as Adaptation and Response* (New York: Praeger, 1980).

Sattin, Anthony, *The Gates of Africa: Death, Discovery and the Search for Timbuktu* (London: HarperCollins, 2003).

Schama, Simon, *Landscape and Memory* (London: HarperCollins, 1995).

Scheele, Judith, *Smugglers and Saints of the Sahara: Regional Connectivity in the Twentieth Century* (Cambridge: Cambridge University Press, 2012).

Selby, Bettina, *Frail Dream of Timbuktu* (London: John Murray, 1991).

Seligman, Thomas & Loughran, Christine, *The Art of Being Tuareg: Sahara Nomads in a Modern World* (Los Angeles, CA: UCLA Fowler Museum of Cultural History, 2006).

Shah, Tahir, *The Caliph's House: A Year in Casablanca* (London: Doubleday, 2006).

Shakespeare, William, *The Complete Works*, ed. John Jowett, William Montgomery, Stanley Wells & Gary Taylor (Oxford: Oxford University Press, 2005).

Sheils, Barry, *W.B. Yeats and World Literature: The Subject of Poetry* (Farnham: Ashgate, 2015).

Smith, David C, *The Transcendental Saunterer: Thoreau and the Search for Self* (Savannah, GA: FC Beil, 1992).

Stevenson, Robert Louis, *Travels with a Donkey in the Cévennes* (London: Kegan Paul, 1879).

Stewart, Kathlyn Moore, *Fishing Sites of North and East Africa in the Late Pleistocene and Holocene: Environmental Change and Human Adaptation* (Oxford: BAR, 1989).

Swift, Jeremy, *The Sahara* (Amsterdam: Time-Life International, 1975).

Tennyson, Alfred Lord, *Alfred Tennyson: A Critical Edition of the Major Works*, ed. Adam Roberts (Oxford: Oxford University Press, 2000).

Thesiger, Wilfred, *Arabian Sands* (London: Penguin, 2007).

Toynbee, Arnold, *A Study of History, Vol. 3: The Growths of Civilizations* (Oxford: Oxford University Press, 1962).

Webb, James LA, *Desert Frontier: Ecological and Economic Change along the Western Sahel, 1600–1850* (Madison, WI: University of Wisconsin Press, 1995).

Weissleder, Wolfgang (ed.), *The Nomadic Alternative* (The Hague: Mouton, 1978).

Whitney, Lois, Did Shakespeare know Leo Africanus?, *PMLA*, 37 (1922).

Williams, Joseph John, *Hebrewisms of West Africa: From Nile to Niger with the Jews* (New York: Lincoln Mac Veagh/Dial Press, 1930).

Wise, Christopher, *The Desert Shore: Literatures of the Sahel* (London: Lynne Rienner, 2001).

Wise, Christopher, Plundering Mali (*Arena Magazine*, 123, April/May 2013).

Wyrtzen, Jonathan, *Making Morocco: Colonial Intervention and the Politics of Identity* (Ithaca, NY: Cornell University Press, 2015).

Zemon Davis, Natalie, *Trickster Travels: A Sixteenth Century Muslim between Worlds* (London: Faber, 2007).

Zunes, Stephen & Mundy, Jacob, *Western Sahara: War, Nationalism and Conflict Irresolution* (Syracuse, NY: Syracuse University Press, 2010).

Index

Acknowledgements

THIS LIST MUST OF NECESSITY BE QUITE SHORT, AS I AM UNABLE TO NAME many of the people who helped me in the course of my travels. I have changed several names in the narrative, in the hope that nothing I have written will cause anyone any trouble.

To the following I would like to express my gratitude: Sandy Ag Mostapha, Mohammed Ag Ossade of Tumast, the staff of the ALIF course in Fez, Amee, Assaytoun and family, David A. Andelman and Yaffa Fredrick at *World Policy Journal*, Boucoum in Bamako, Shindouk Ould Najim and Miranda Dodd, Salim Ould Elhadje, Bert Flint, Dr Habibulleye Hamda and the staff of the Ahmed Baba Institute in Timbuktu, Abdel Kader Haidara, Dr Jeremy Keenan, Andy Morgan, Omar in Timbuktu, Danielle Smith at Sandblast, Dr Jeremy Swift, Seydou and his friends in Sevaré.

On the writing and publishing side, I am especially grateful to Sophie Lambert for her suggestions and advice. Thank you to Nick Brealey for taking on the book, and for all his editorial suggestions; and thanks to Nick, Louise Richardson, Sally Lansdell and everyone at Nicholas Brealey Publishing and John Murray for their work in producing the book.

I am hugely indebted to Mahmoud Dicko for all his help in and around Timbuktu. And I cannot express enough my thanks to my friend Abdramane Sabane (along with his family), who showed me so much generosity and kindness from our first encounter on the Niger river. Finally, I am grateful to my family for their support and patience, Milo and Rafe for inspiration, and Poppy for a thousand and one impossible things.